A PLACE IN HISTORY

TWENTY YEARS OF ACQUIRING
PAINTINGS, DRAWINGS AND PRINTS
AT THE
NATIONAL ARCHIVES OF CANADA

Introduction by Jim Burant

Texts contributed by

Jim Burant
Jennifer Devine
Lucie Dorais
Lydia Foy
Eva Major-Marothy
Martha Marleau
Terresa McIntosh
Susan North
Douglas E. Schoenherr
Allison Thompson

National Archives of Canada
Archives nationales du Canada

Canadian Cataloguing in Publication Data

National Archives of Canada.
A place in history.

Issued also in French under title: Un moment dans l'histoire.
DSS cat. no. SA2-213/1990E
ISBN 0-660-13740-2

1. Art — Canada — History — Archival resources — Ontario — Ottawa — Exhibitions.
2. National Archives of Canada — Exhibitions.
 I. Burant, Jim II. Title.

N910.072N37 1991 708.11'384 C90-099204-2

An exhibition presented at the National Archives of Canada, Ottawa, 30 October 1990-31 March 1991.

National Archives of Canada
395 Wellington Street
Ottawa, Ontario
K1A 0N3
(613) 995-5138

Cat. No.: SA 2-213/1990E
ISBN: 0-660-13740-2

This publication is printed on alkaline paper.

Cover: W.G.R. Hind
Harvesting Hay, Sussex, N.B., ca. 1880
C-103003

CONTENTS

LETTER TO THE PUBLIC

Dear friends,

To know history, one must "relive" the past, not just grasp intellectual bits and pieces of it by reading thousands, millions of words and numbers. Human beings are complex wholes; they are not just abstract minds, but persons with feelings, sensations, understanding, passions and sometimes awe for experiences that transcend normal day-to-day life. History is not the dead ashes of people and events gone by, the simple scratch of reasoned acts on the map of time. It is a living tissue, an evolving adventure that has led us to where we are now and is still driving us further. We are the result of the past and cannot easily jump out of its main current. Thus, studying it means more than peering at one aspect or another. It means trying to encompass in one understanding vision the forces at play, the people in interaction, as well as the sense of time and place, the permeating surroundings, personalities and other intangible "breaths" that drive life beyond the mechanical. This total sense, an ideal of course, cannot be attained unless records of all types, particularly documentary art, add to the dry knowledge of words and numbers.

When I first accepted the duties as Canada's national archivist, I anticipated many of the joys of exploration in this country's treasure-house of historical records. I was not disappointed; everything from fifteenth-century maps to electronic records produced in this generation became part of my responsibility. But one of the unanticipated joys, too little known by the general public, was to be found in the fabulous vaults of the documentary art collection. For over one hundred years, the Archives has been collecting Canadian art with an eye to recording our national history and society in pictures of unique documentary value. In this publication, and the exhibition it accompanies, you are about to see the human face of history in paintings, drawings and prints acquired over the past twenty years.

An archives is about the past; indeed, our staff, together with myself, feel privileged in our unparalleled access to our favourite pursuit: the study, acquisition and preservation of records from the past.

But an archives is also about the future; where else will our children turn to answer their questions about our history? How can we preserve those events of today, which, to them, will be their past? We must predict the past for them now. This responsibility to the future is the greatest of the challenges faced by an archivist.

An essential part in responding to that responsibility is the need to preserve a visual record for each age, a record that makes the "whole" more tangible, more concrete. What did our forefathers see when they looked upon their world? Of the world we see around us today, what will be important for our children also to see?

I am pleased and proud to present this selection of our efforts to preserve Canada's visual heritage. I believe that the documentary talents of artists in Canada will find an appreciative response not only among historians, but also in the heart of every Canadian. A fascinating world welcomes here all those who, like me, wonder "what was it really like when...?"

Jean-Pierre Wallot
National Archivist of Canada

FOREWORD

What is archival art? The term suggests a limited and obscure scope. What artist intended his work for an archives? The answer is, of course, none. Most creators of records about our civilisation did not have an archives in mind as they wrote that fateful letter or drew that exploratory map. Likewise, the artists whose work is now represented in the collections of archives across Canada thought only of their immediate needs as they produced their work. Those needs could have been to illustrate, to describe, to inspire, to educate, to propose, to symbolise, to opine, to praise or to condemn. However, it is the gift of the descendants to their forefathers to see in that work more than the first intent, to see the reflection of a nation, and to preserve these precious records to become the historical memory of our own descendants and every succeeding generation.

What makes a work of art valuable to an archives? The answer here, so apparently simple, is that the work must be revealing. It may reveal things, people or events in a straightforward manner, trying to represent the reality perceived by the eye with as little distortion and as much completeness as talent allowed to the hand of the creator. Or it may reveal the mind and intent of the creator and the society from which the work derives through symbolic or metaphorical means. The former gives us still lifes, portraits, landscapes and scenes of activity; the latter adds caricatures, commercial and ephemeral art, heraldry and commemorative art. However, the finest historical interpretations of all archival art occur when these two directions are seen to work together in one image: Realistically produced art is seen to have an underlying value touching the opinions and desires of its generation, thereby revealing the heart as well as the body of another age.

The National Archives of Canada is proud of its long tradition of recognizing and collecting this crucial and complex documentation of our past. This catalogue, and the exhibition that it accompanies, is an opportunity to invite Canadians to reflect on a selection of some of the most treasured records acquired over the last twenty years and now held by the Documentary Art and Photography Division. It is an affirmation of the power and value of the picture in communicating our history to our children. The selections from the twentieth century all emphasize the continuing presence of this power, particularly in communicating our values through visual symbols. Like our children, we look forward to many years of looking at, considering and collecting these records of delight for future knowledge and past remembrance.

Lilly Koltun
Director
Documentary Art and Photography Division

ACKNOWLEDGEMENTS

Many people have provided invaluable assistance to the staff of the National Archives involved in the preparation of this exhibition catalogue. The research and expertise shared by colleagues in other institutions, and the help of individuals and specialists have enabled a wealth of information to be shared. While specific contributions are noted in the catalogue entries, we take this opportunity to acknowledge the special contributions made by those mentioned below.

In Canada, Harold Averill, University of Toronto Archives; Claude Boudreau, Archives nationales de Québec; Dr. T.J. Brasser, Dr. M.K. Foster, Dr. Andrea Laforet, Renée Landry and Dr. J. Garth Taylor, Canadian Museum of Civilization; Carol Brice-Bennett, Memorial University; Benoit Cameron, Royal Military College of Canada; Margaret Campbell, Public Archives of Nova Scotia; Douglas E. Cass and Pat Lee, Glenbow Museum; Nathalie Clerk and Ron Macdonald, Canadian Parks Service; William H. Cooper, Archives of Ontario; Helen Kilgour, Royal Ontario Museum; Glen Lucas, the United Church of Canada Archives; Geoffrey Morrow and Elaine Phillips, National Gallery of Canada; Raymond Peringer, Arts and Letters Club, Toronto; Rhonda Richardson, the Anglican Church of Canada General Synod Archives; Scott Robson, Nova Scotia Museum; Karen Smith, Royal Ontario Museum; Jane Sproull Thomson, Newfoundland Museum; and Keith Stotyn, Provincial Archives of Alberta.

In the United States, Laura Bowler and Anna Jean Caffey, Stark Museum of Art, Orange, Texas; Phyllis DeMuth, Alaska State Library; Clyde Eller, Buffalo and Erie County Historical Society; Christine Hennessey, National Museum of American Art; Alexander Mackay-Smith, National Sporting Library, Middleburg, Virginia; Annette Masling and John Sanford, Albright-Knox Art Gallery; Ellen G. Miles, National Portrait Gallery, Washington; George Miles, Yale University Library; Vernon H. Nelson, the Moravian Church Archives, Bethlehem, Pennsylvania; Amy Ryan, Minneapolis Public Library and Information Center; Carol Simon, Beloit College, Wisconsin; Ida M. Johnson, Brown & Bigelow, St. Paul, Minnesota; Rose D. Vitzthum, New York State Historical Association; Dr. Peter Walch, University Art Museum, the University of New Mexico; Lucille Wehner, the Newbury Library, Chicago; Kennedy Galleries, New York; the Missouri Historical Society; and the Munson-Williams-Proctor Institute.

In Europe, I. Baldauf, Archives of the United Brethren, Herrnhut, Germany; J.S. Birrell, Lloyd's Register of Shipping, Glasgow; Paul Brough, Suffolk Record Office, Ipswich; Noelle Brown, Ashmolean Museum; Mary Clapinson, Bodleian Library, Oxford; Lt.-Col. Angus Fairrie, Queen's Own Highlanders (Seaforth and Camerons), Inverness; Paul Goldman, Mark Jones and Lindsay Stainton, British Museum; Janet Halton, Moravian Church House, London; Jean Kennedy, Central Library, Norfolk; Jane Munro, Fitzwilliam Museum, Cambridge; Jacob Simon, the Iveagh Bequest, Kenwood; Lt.-Col. David Ward, King's Own Scottish Borderers, Berwick-Upon-Tweed; Mrs. S. Wernberg-Moller, St. Edmund Hall, Oxford; the Bernisches Historisches Museum, Berne; and the Scott Polar Research Institute, Cambridge.

The following individuals have also provided valuable information due to their professional expertise in or their personal connection with specific areas of our research: Henry Benjamin; the Reverend Robert M. Black; Louise Comfort; Helen Dupuy; the late Elzire Dionne; Pauline Dionne; James Dixon; Bernadette Driscoll; Stan and Hazel Guignard; Charles Henry; Rev. Siegfried P. Hettasch; Betty Issenman; Prof. J. Peter Johnson, Jr.; Rose Killam; Judy McGrath, *Them Days* magazine; Prof. Lorraine McMullen; Dr. Eileen Marcil; Mr. and Mrs. Marmor; the Duke of Northumberland; Doris Peacock; Dr. Ruth Phillips; Cliff Sinclair; Marian Scott; Wilfred A. Seaby; Colin Shrimpton, Northumberland Estates; Frances K. Smith; Bruno Spinner; and Mrs. P. Whitmore.

A final thank-you to colleagues in various areas of the National Archives who have assisted in this project in innumerable ways: from Historical Resources Branch: Tim Dubé, Anne Goddard, Patricia Kennedy and Marianne McLean; from Conservation Branch: Maria Bedynski, Jim Bordeaux, John Grace, Greg Hill, Barbara Klempan, Gaston Tremblay and others too numerous to mention; from Public Programs Branch for the production of both the catalogue and the exhibition; and from Documentary Art and Photography Division Gilbert Gignac and former student assistants, in particular Lis Stainforth and Jennifer Trant. Special thanks are due to Lucie Dorais, Lydia Foy and Eva Major-Marothy who coordinated the catalogue and exhibition production for the Documentary Art and Photography Division. A thank-you also to Georges Delisle, former director of the Picture Division, under whose tenure many of the items featured in the exhibition were acquired. Special acknowledgement is due Douglas E. Schoenherr, formerly of the National Archives, now at the National Gallery of Canada, who as head of art acquisitions initiated this project and inspired a commitment to produce this major exhibition and catalogue exploring the richness of the National Archives' documentary art collection.

INTRODUCTION

The National Archives of Canada maintains the nation's largest collection of works of art relating to Canadian history, encompassing some 200,000 paintings, drawings, prints, posters, cartoons, medals and other related visual documents. The holdings date from the sixteenth century, and the majority are still in almost pristine condition. This exhibition is intended to acquaint the public with a treasured part of this national heritage, a selection of the paintings, drawings and prints acquired over the last twenty years.

To inform, to record, to educate, to persuade, and to remember – these works satisfy aims different from those of pure artistic expression. Although these works often demonstrate a high quality of execution, it is primarily the circumstances surrounding their creation that explain their permanent and unique historical value as documentary records. Whether sketching first-hand impressions or sitting comfortably in a studio indulging romanticized Victorian visions, these artists have succeeded in showing Canadians what no words can say: how art can transcend purely aesthetic boundaries to find a place in history.

The National Archives has been acquiring these works for documentary purposes, for their value both as representations of places, persons and things, and also as interpretations of how we have seen ourselves over three centuries of nation-building. This exhibition concentrates on the paintings and drawings in the collection, which were acquired both because they are some of the finest surviving records of the past, and because they exemplify the continual attempt of artists in Canada to address the changing realities of their society and geography. Rigourous selection criteria based on our acquisition policy have resulted in a wide-ranging documentary art collection whose scope will be invaluable for the study of Canadian history and society for generations to come. It is our belief that they will always embody a sense of Canada's unique place in the world.

Among the variety of subjects included in the holdings are portraits in a variety of forms, including silhouettes, miniatures, individual and group portraits, informal sketches and full-length formal poses; landscape, cityscape and architectural views in both anecdotal and commissioned formats; historical events; views of social life, sports and recreation; and costume and commercial design. A broad definition of "documentary" has been essential in order to respond to the requirements of changing historical trends; its application to places, people and events has resulted in a collection that encompasses art work created in Canada by Canadians and others, as well as work done abroad that relates to Canada.

The definition of what constitutes "art" is equally broad; it includes original works of art on paper, canvas and other supports, and in all media, including oil, acrylic and tempera paintings, watercolours, drawings and collages; original and reproductive prints, including engraving, lithography, serigraphy, wood engraving and a host of other processes; metallic, stone, wooden and plastic objects not normally acquired by other institutions, such as medals, political buttons, seals, heraldic devices and coats-of-arms; and related printed material, including illustrated books, broadsides with pictorial inserts, and publicity material.

The first recorded acquisition of documentary art by the then Public Archives of Canada occurred in 1888. Its systematic acquisition dates only from 1906, however, when the dominion archivist, Arthur Doughty, was authorized to expend money on acquiring paintings, drawings, prints and other visual documents of historical interest; thus a Picture Division was established. The early focus of its collecting policy was to acquire original and copied documentary art items of places, people and events for the period up to 1900, while the twentieth century was to be documented by means of photography. Documentary art was pursued through an active network of collectors, dealers and auction houses in Canada, the United States, Great Britain and France. Living artists were also commissioned to execute historical reconstructions for scenes and events for which no contemporary visual documentation existed. By 1925, a collection of some 25,000 original works of art and reproductions of works in other collections had been acquired.

In the 1930s, the Depression severely affected acquisition activity. Regional efforts were abandoned in the Maritimes as provincial institutions began collecting the same material. The acquisition budget was first reduced and then eliminated. Donations continued to be received on a regular basis, but the retirement in 1935 of Arthur Doughty, whose personal efforts to solicit donations had been a major factor in acquisition strategy, caused a decline even in this aspect of collecting. Acquisition activity in the 1940s and 1950s remained largely unsystematic and passive, the significant exceptions being the acquisition of copies of most war posters produced by the Wartime Information Board, and the transfer of a large number of printed portraits and views from the Parliamentary Library. Most acquisitions continued to be small-scale private-sector donations.

By the 1960s, however, there was a growing interest in Canadiana and Canadian studies as well as an expanding Canadian art market. A more active Paintings, Drawings and Prints Section gave new vigour to acquisition activity in visual documentation. A staff of professional archivists and support persons was built up, and larger budgets for the purchase of collections permitted the acquisition of major corporate and private collections, while other gaps in the visual record were filled through auction purchases. At the same time, systematic contacts with major auction houses and art dealers in Great Britain, the United States and Canada resulted in acquisitions that augmented already-existing holdings. The present exhibition includes fifty items (of the total of seventy-eight) acquired from auction houses and private dealers in the past twenty years. Donations from private individuals have also continued to be a major source of collections. These have ranged from the extensive accumulations of collectors such as Andrew Merrilees to single items documenting the activities of Canadians in many walks of life. In this exhibition, such generosity is exemplified by fourteen items (Cat. nos. 42, 43, 47, 50, 55, 56, 59, 61, 62, 64, 73, 74, 76 and 78), which represent donations from private individuals, from the artists themselves or their surviving spouses, from private foundations, and, in one case, from a political organization.

In 1968, a significant event occurred in relation to what the National Archives has endeavored to do with its documentary art collection. In this year, an agreement between the dominion archivist and the director of the National Gallery of Canada confirmed the Archives as the domain of the National Portrait Collection. Since that time, the Division has striven to acquire portraits – not just of politicians, military men and clergy (Cat. nos. 42, 45, 47 and 58); fur traders and commercial leaders (Cat. nos. 51, 52 and 54); and the extraordinary personalities of both our past and present (Cat. nos. 44 and 78) – but also portraits that represent different classes of society, from the French-Canadian middle-class (Cat. nos. 55 and 56) to one of the last surviving members of the Indians of the Beothuk tribe, a poignant reminder of a shameful aspect of Canada's past (Cat. no. 49). The exhibition contains only a small proportion of the many portraits acquired since 1968; future plans include a major exhibition devoted exclusively to the portrait.

The second significant influence on acquisitions was the proclamation in 1977 of the *Cultural Property Export and Import Act*. This Act prevented the exportation of cultural property from Canada without prior review by a board of experts in the heritage field, and it provided financial support to institutions wishing to repatriate cultural property from abroad. As a result of this Act, the National Archives has, since 1977, been able to acquire a large number of items that otherwise would not have been within reach for lack of funds. In this exhibition alone, twenty-six of the objects on display (Cat. nos. 1, 2, 6-11, 12-17, 19, 20, 21, 23, 24, 25, 28, 29, 31, 32, 38 and 39) have been acquired with the assistance of the Canadian Cultural Property Export Review Board and the minister of Communications.

In 1984, plans were begun for this exhibition to celebrate twenty years of acquisition of paintings, drawings and prints at the National Archives of Canada. It was designed to bring to public attention the magnificent holdings of documentary art acquired by the National Archives of Canada, with a focus on more traditional media. It should be pointed out that the National Archives also has vast holdings of posters, costume design, heraldry and medals, which space alone did not permit us to represent at this time. The immense amount of material reviewed in making the selection shown here includes some of our newest acquisitions, such as Cat. no. 20, the Rodolphe von Steiger watercolour of *Deputation of Indians from the Mississippi Tribes*, dating to 1814. We are especially proud of this acquisition because it is such a rare representation of native-white relations in this period.

The intent was to show the best of what had been acquired among paintings, drawings and prints, and, at the same time, to present an exhibition reflecting the mandate of the National Archives to acquire items of national significance in terms of Canada's historical development. The seventy-eight items that were finally chosen have been placed into the framework of four major themes. The first, *"As long as the sun shall shine": The first peoples*, presents a visual record of the original inhabitants of Canada from the brush of military and settler artists such as Rodolphe von Steiger and Paul Kane. In the second, *Artists in a new land*, depictions of the cities, landscapes, scenery, social life and natural phenomena of the country, ranging from the Atlantic coast to the far north to the Pacific Ocean, have been grouped together to present an impression of how this vast territory looked to the European eye. *Timeless mementos*, the third section, brings together portraits of the famous and the obscure in sizes ranging from a tiny miniature to life-size paintings, and includes one of the greatest treasures of the National Archives of Canada, the portrait of Mary March, already mentioned as one of the last survivors of the now-extinct Beothuk Indian tribe of Newfoundland. Finally, the section *Our times: Art as record in the 20th century*, demonstrates the relevance of acquiring documentary art in the present day, and its continued ability to bear unique witness to our history and attitudes.

The research for this exhibition has been prodigious and fruitful. Thousands of hours were spent in learning about the context of the creation of the works, and about their makers. The distillation of that research, presented in this catalogue, should be useful for future generations of researchers and scholars. Furthermore, the investigations of the archivists involved in this exhibition have solved several mysteries about the identities of artists of other works in the holdings of the National Archives and elsewhere. To take one example, Cat. no. 37, *Harvesting Hay, Sussex, New Brunswick*, was originally identified as the work of an artist named "R. J. Best." Through a combination of research on the subject of the painting and on the name of the artist, and a comparative examination with works already held in the National Archives, this work was re-attributed to the renowned Canadian artist William G. R. Hind. Such a re-attribution has repercussions not only for the holdings of the National Archives, but also for those of other institutions, such as the Art Gallery of Ontario and the National Gallery of Canada, which also own works previously attributed to "R.J. Best." The research conducted on Cat. no. 31, George St. Vincent Whitmore's *Aurora Borealis, Quebec*, not only led to a donation of fourteen watercolours to the National Archives of Canada, but also solved the mystery of the identity of the artist of some twenty-five watercolours that have been in the holdings for almost twenty years. As such information accumulates, the importance of the work or works in question becomes greater, not just to the archivists who work with the collections on a daily basis and to the scholars in art history and other academic disciplines who make use of the collections, but also to the communities whose past is forever captured in these works.

Since the National Archives is primarily a research rather than an exhibiting institution, the documentary art collection is normally stored in secure, environmentally controlled vaults. Access is provided in many ways, through finding aids, copy photographs and transparencies; by access to the originals; and by making loans to other institutions. On average, several hundred works are loaned out to approximately thirty exhibitions annually. The National Archives of Canada also prepares unique exhibitions of the works for display in its headquarters building in Ottawa. Some of these exhibitions also travel to other venues across Canada, and to other countries.

The exhibition *A Place In History: Twenty Years of Acquiring Paintings, Drawings and Prints at the National Archives of Canada* demonstrates the Archives' continuing commitment to documenting the Canadian experience in all its aspects, both past and present, regardless of medium. The title reflects our belief that each of these works has a unique place in history and can put the past into a visual as well as an intellectual context; finally, the title also reflects the fact that documentary art plays a role in both explaining and illustrating our history. While important in themselves, the items presented here are only representative of the mass of visual documentation that has not found room in the exhibition. We hope that this exhibition and its accompanying catalogue, the product of twenty years of collecting and five years of researching and sifting, will be viewed with pleasure and pride. We are only its trustees: This collection belongs to the people of Canada.

Jim Burant
Chief, Art Acquisition and Research

Notes for Use

The catalogue is divided into four distinct topic areas: native peoples (Cat. nos. 1-23), topographical views (Cat. nos. 24-41), portraits (Cat. nos. 42-59) and twentieth-century documentary art (Cat. nos. 60-78). Catalogue entries have been written for each item; sometimes two or more are discussed in the same entry when they are related. The entries explore the documentary content of the items, as well as the context of their creation, including new information about the artists. Extensive research has been carried out both in the National Archives' own holdings and at many other institutions, as well as with several private individuals.

The titles of the works are based on inscriptions when possible, or are otherwise descriptive of the subject matter based on research. Misspellings and archaic usage in inscribed titles have usually been retained in instances where the artist has given the title prominence. Since few of the works are dated by the artists, most of the dates given are based on an analysis of the artist's career and of the subject matter.

Measurements are given in centimetres, height followed by width. Inscriptions on the works or on associated mounts or attachments have been transcribed in italics when they are contemporary with the work or have information pertinent to provenance. The method and year of acquisition are given, followed by the accession number and negative number.

Endnotes include references to publications and manuscripts, as well as to contacts with individual specialists. Manuscript citations state the institution holding the original material, and in the case of privately held manuscripts no location is given. In instances where the National Archives has copies of the originals, the National Archives citation is also given.

The supplementary illustrations that accompany several of the entries are identified by artist, title (sometimes shortened), date, general medium and collection.

Every effort has been made to obtain copyright permission when reproducing or citing material to which copyright restrictions may apply.

Abbreviations, Terminology and Symbols

The following list pertains largely to the transcription of the inscriptions appearing on the works. Other abbreviations used in this catalogue are those in common usage.

NA National Archives of Canada

b. bottom
c. centre
c.l. centre left
c.r. centre right
l.c. lower centre
l.l. lower left
l.r. lower right
t. top
u.c. upper centre
u.l. upper left
u.r. upper right

recto front
verso back

[ ] the transcription of illegible or cropped inscriptions are noted in [ ], as is other information pertinent to the inscription

/ a slash used in the transcription of an inscription indicates a line change

A PLACE IN HISTORY

"As long as the sun shall shine": The First Peoples

The National Archives has recently added a number of important paintings and drawings to its already extensive holdings of works depicting our native peoples and their way of life in the eighteenth and nineteenth centuries. Among the recent acquisitions are several important ethnographic and anthropological records that depict native dwellings, clothing and artifacts, as well as ritual and hunting activities. By contrast, other works give a more romantic notion of the native peoples' culture and of the encounters with white society as interpreted by European artists. Most poignant, perhaps, are the revealing portraits that bring us face-to-face with the first people to embrace this land for "as long as the sun shall shine."

ANGELICA KAUFFMANN (1741-1807)

1. *Woman in Eskimo Clothing from Labrador*, ca. 1768-1772

Oil on canvas

76.5 x 63.5 cm

Inscribed in brushpoint and black paint, recto, l.l.: *Angelica Kauffm*

Purchased in 1978 with the assistance of a grant from the minister of Communications under the terms of the *Cultural Property Export and Import Act*

Accession no.: 1978-23-1

Negative no.: C-95201

2. *Man in Eskimo Clothing*, ca. 1768-1772

Oil on canvas

76.5 x 63.5 cm

Purchased in 1978 with the assistance of a grant from the minister of Communications under the terms of the *Cultural Property Export and Import Act*

Accession no.: 1978-23-2

Negative no.: C-95202

These unusual paintings by Angelica Kauffmann, depicting a man and a woman dressed in clothing from the Arctic, are examples of eighteenth-century documentary art. The subject itself is not unusual, as the inhabitants of newly discovered regions of the world had frequently been portrayed from the outset of such explorations. The size and the medium of the works are noteworthy, however, because such subjects were usually depicted in smaller drawings or engravings, more suited for intimate study and for book illustrations.

Angelica Kauffmann was born in Switzerland in 1741. A child prodigy, she had been carefully trained by her artist father Johann Joseph Kauffmann (1707-1782). After travelling and studying in Italy, and especially in Rome, the artistic metropolis of the eighteenth century, Kauffmann moved to London, and lived there from 1766 until 1781. She later returned to Italy, where she spent the rest of her life. She was a very popular portrait painter in England and also received commissions to decorate several aristocratic houses. She was one of two women founding members of the Royal Academy in 1768, and exhibited portraits and historical subjects in its annual exhibitions until 1797. The paintings under discussion, one of which is inscribed with an apparently authentic signature, are not dated, but circumstantial evidence points to their having been painted while the artist lived in England.[1] First, they do not appear in the memorandum that Kauffmann kept, after her departure from England, of her paintings and new patrons, which suggests that they were executed prior to her departure.[2] Moreover, the subject was very topical during her first years in London, when, in order to establish herself with new patrons, she may have been ready to paint subjects that were unusual for her. As will be pointed out later, other artists of her standing and calibre also painted such subjects.

Explorers of new regions of the world often brought back inhabitants of newly discovered lands to authenticate their discoveries. During the late eighteenth century, when Kauffmann was living in London, several such visits occurred, and such native visitors were portrayed by contemporary artists in various ways. Nathaniel Dance's drawing of *Omai* from 1774 (Fig. 1.1) is such a record. The drawing illustrates the eighteenth-century penchant for idealization. It shows Omai, a native of a Tahitian island, who came to London on one of Captain Cook's ships in 1774, as a noble savage, wearing classical robes he wore neither in London nor in his own country.[3] There were other similar visits to London. In 1768, Governor Hugh Palliser of Newfoundland brought back three Inuit visitors from Labrador, a woman named Mikak, her son Tutauk and another boy, Karpik.[4] Mikak was very popular during her stay in London, visiting with royalty and with members of the aristocracy. Royal Academician John Russell painted *Portrait of Micoc and her son Tootac, Esquimaux Indians, brought over by Commodore Palliser,* which was included in the first Royal Academy exhibition in 1769.[5] Another visit took place in late 1772, when George Cartwright brought a group of five Inuit from Labrador.[6] They were also very popular, receiving many invitations from and being visited by both the members of the aristocracy and of the scientific community, including the naturalist Joseph Banks, the botanist Daniel Solander and the noted anatomist, John Hunter.[7] The latter commissioned a portrait of Ickongogue, one of the women in the group, entitled *A Labrador Woman* (Fig. 1.2), to include in his collection of paintings depicting racial types.[8] Joseph Banks was also interested enough to commission Nathaniel Dance to make drawings of two of the members of the group, Attuiock and his wife Caubvick.[9] These he added to a copy of the John Russell Micoc portrait, which he also had in his collection.[10] Banks's interest in the clothing of the Inuit is revealed by the note on the back of the drawing of Attuiock:

> Esquimaux man who was brought over from Cape Charles on the Coast of Labrador by Captain Cartwright in the year 1773. He was a Priest in his country which is denoted by the thong of leather hanging down from his girdle.[11]

The portraits commissioned by Banks and Hunter differ from the idealized portrait of Omai. They are the result of a scientific interest in other races and civilizations prompted by the beginnings of anthropology in the eighteenth century. In the sixteenth century, little effort had been made to distinguish among the inhabitants of the newly explored regions of the world.[12] They were all regarded as curiosities. By the eighteenth century, however, scientists began to focus on the different manners and ways of life of the various native societies, regarding them in a more benevolent manner and wishing to contribute to their welfare.[13] Kauffmann's paintings belong in this latter category. They are not studies of racial types, however, such as those commissioned by Hunter. Indeed a closer examination of them reveals that neither model is Inuit. This is clearly visible in the case of the man. The woman's face is hidden behind snow-goggles, but her slender build indicates European origin.[14] What places these works in a scientific category is the attention with which some of the clothing has been depicted. It is so accurate that it is possible to identify the material from which the clothing was made and, in the case of the woman, its geographical origin. The depiction of the woman, from both front and back, as in a fashion plate, to allow a better view of her garment, confirms this interest.

The man's upper garment – a *qulituk* –is made of birdskin, an important and widely used material for clothing all over the Arctic.[15] It has been suggested that the bird species used was puffin.[16] A similar jacket was depicted by Capt. G.F. Lyon when he was in Igloolik in 1822[17] (Fig. 1.3). There are some birdskin jackets in ethnographic collections that closely resemble the one in our painting (Fig. 1.4). In addition, the pattern of assembling the birdskins – three rows of four skins horizontally, one row over the shoulder, and two or three for the sleeves, edged with the skin of some other animal such as bear or fox – conforms to the recorded specimen of such clothing.[18] The striking headdress worn by the man, which consists of a whole bird, has also been documented in both Greenland and North America.[19]

The woman's garment has also been carefully observed. The cut and decoration of her *amautik*, or "mother's parka," identifies the garment as originating from Labrador or Baffin Island.[20] The following is a description of an Eastern Arctic (Labrador/ Baffin Island) *amautik*. It describes the garment in our painting very well:

> ...the *amaut* and hood are formed from a single piece of skin. The *amaut* is a roomy pouch [for carrying the baby], the shape of which is formed by a leather belt worn around the waist. The tail, which has a curvilinear cut, is joined to the *amaut* by a seam at waist-level [visible in the back-view].... The sleeves, which extend in a continuous line from the hood, are marked with... dark strips of sealskin around the lower arm.[21]

The skin of the garment has been so carefully painted that it is possible to identify the pelt as ringed seal.[22] A comparison with a photograph of a traditional sealskin parka reinforces its authenticity[23] (Fig. 1.5).

No specimen of the large boot in which children were carried has been preserved.[24] Several explorers of the eighteenth century mention such a custom, but by the nineteenth century it seems to have gone out of usage. Engravings exist of the large boot, but this painting may be the only large-scale representation of the custom[25] (Fig. 1.6).

Since the winter-harpoon and the snow-goggles are also genuine, it is impossible that Kauffmann could have arrived at all these recognizable details without having actual specimens in front of her. But there are details in the paintings that are inconsistent and inaccurate. The background in *Man in Eskimo Clothing* does not convey the Arctic; it is an ideal Italianate landscape. The method of fastening the woman's hood under the chin is completely inaccurate.[26] The mixture of close observation and artistic licence, added to the fact that European models are wearing the clothing, may help to establish the origin of these paintings.

The provenance of the works is problematic. They were sold at Christie's, London, in 1962 from the collection of J.C.P. Langton of Spilsby, Lincolnshire.[27] Their provenance was given as "Sir Joseph Bunker." However, after much research, the identity of Bunker has remained a mystery. One can only speculate whether Bunker is an error for Banks, the same Sir Joseph Banks already mentioned in connection with the Inuit visits to London. Reinforcing this speculation is the fact that the Banks and Langton families were related through marriage at the time of Sir Joseph's grandfather, Joseph Banks (1695-1741); also, their two country homes, Revesby and Spilsby, were about fifteen kilometres apart.[28]

Sir Joseph Banks (1743-1820) was an important patron of the sciences in the eighteenth century. His interests were wide-ranging, the chief of them being botany; his large and important collection now forms part of the British Museum. He accompanied Capt. James Cook on his first famous voyage on the *Endeavour* from 1768 to 1771. He was also interested in zoology, agriculture and horticulture, and in the native customs and languages of the inhabitants of the places he had visited.[29] He was president of the Royal Society from 1778 until his death in 1820.

Joseph Banks' interest in the Inuit was reinforced by the fact that he had spent several months in Newfoundland and Labrador in 1766, gathering plants and animals for his collection.[30] He did not have the opportunity to meet with Inuit during this visit.[31] To satisfy his collecting instinct and his curiosity about the Inuit, he asked one of his friends to gather specimens of Inuit clothing and other objects for him, much as he asked people to gather botanical and zoological specimens. The following letter was sent to Banks in 1767 by Andrew Wilkinson, captain of the *Niger*, the ship that had originally taken Banks to Newfoundland:

> As my meeting with the Indians was very uncertain, the Cask of things you left on board of the Niger for Truck with'em Mr. Palliser took on board the Guernsey to Chatteaux, & I believe he has procured you some of their dresses etc I'd got a Canoe for you which I sent home in the Grenville....[32]

It seems, therefore, that Banks had a collection of Inuit clothing, and, in the same way that he commissioned artists to paint his natural history specimens, he may have commissioned an artist to record his clothing collection. This would explain the fact of European models wearing Inuit dress, as well as their air of having been posed in a studio. Moreover, Joseph Banks was acquainted with Angelica Kauffmann, since she had painted a portrait of his sister, Sarah Sophie Banks, who lived with him all her life.[33]

To date, none of Banks' papers relating to the Inuit visits have been found.[34] Nor are there records of his ethnographic collections from the Arctic. However, fur clothing is very fragile and would have quickly deteriorated. By the time Banks gave his collection to the British Museum in 1792, the fur garments would likely have already disintegrated.

E.M.-M.

1.1 Nathaniel Dance
Omai, 1774
Red and black chalk
NA C-2446

1.2 Unknown artist
A Labrador Woman, ca. 1772-1773
Oil on canvas
Hunterian Museum, London. Reproduced by permission of the president and council of the Royal College of Surgeons of England.

1.3 E. Finden, after G.F. Lyon
An Esquimaux of Igloolik, In a bird-skin jacket Carrying his canoe down to the water, 1822
Engraving
NA C-127970

1.4
Birdskin Jacket, ca. 1900
Birdskin and red fox fur
Deutsches Ledermuseum, Offenbach am Main, Germany
Photograph by Christel Knetsch

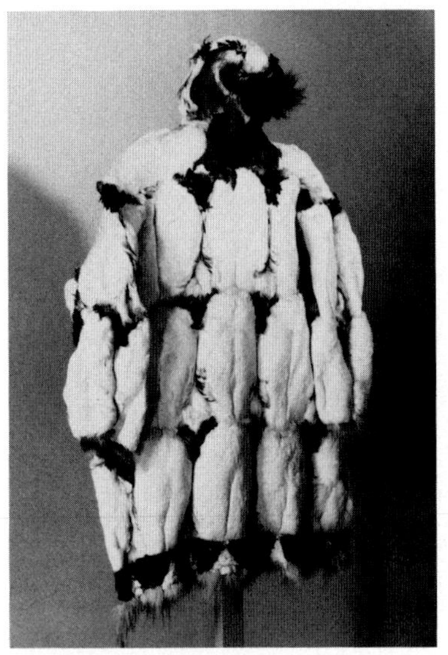

1.5
An Eskimo Nursemaid, ca. 1908-1912
Photograph
Reproduced from S.K. Hutton. See note 23.

1.6 H. Ellis
Esquimaux making Fire and Striking Seals, 1748, detail
Engraving
NA C-100071

1. Letter to the author from Peter Walch, director, University Art Museum, University of New Mexico, Albuquerque, 7 March 1986.

2. Lady Victoria Manners and G.C. Williamson, *Angelica Kauffmann R.A.: her life and her works* (New York: Hacker Art Books, 1976), 141-174.

3. H.C.C. Cameron, *Sir Joseph Banks* (London: The Batchwork Press, 1952): 104n. Even Sir Joshua Reynolds, the president of the Royal Academy, painted Omai's portrait.

4. J. Garth Taylor, "The Two Worlds of Mikak," *The Beaver*, Winter 1983, 4-13; and Spring 1984, 18-25.

5. Algernon Graves, *The Royal Academy of Arts* (Wakefield: S.R. Publishers Ltd.; Bath: Kingsmead Reprints, 1970), vol. 3. Mikak was a very popular subject in 1769, and there were portraits of her by Catherine Read in both the Society of Artists and the Free Society exhibitions of that year. Society of Artists No. 146: *Portrait of the Esquimaux princess (Miscoe)* and Free Society No. 174: *The Esquimeaux woman and child*. A. Graves, *The Society of Artists of Great Britain (1760-1791); The Free Society of Artists (1761-1783)* (London: Bell & Sons, 1907), 209. Many thanks to Douglas Schoenherr for bringing this to my attention.

6. C.W. Townsend, ed., *Captain Cartwright and His Labrador Journal* (Boston: Dana Estes & Co., 1911), 115-140.

7. A. Lysaght, *Joseph Banks in Newfoundland and Labrador, 1766* (Berkeley: University of California Press, 1971), 86-87.

8. Anthony A. Pearson, "John Hunter and the woman from Labrador," *Annals of the Royal College of Surgeons of England* 60 (January 1978): 7-13.

9. Hugh Honour, *The European Vision of America*, (Cleveland: Cleveland Museum of Art, 1975), 109.

10. The Russell portrait may have been the one hanging in his library. W.R. Dawson, *The Banks Letters* (London: Trustees of British Museum, 1958), 114.

11. Honour, 109.

12. Honour, 28-29.

13. H. Plischke, "Insulaner aus der Sudsee in Europa am Ende des 18. Jahrhunderts," *Ethnologica N.F.* (1960:2), 95.

14. I would like to thank Bernadette Driscoll, Ph.D. Candidate, Johns Hopkins University, for pointing this out to me.

15. Gudmund Hatt, "Arctic Skin Clothing in Eurasia and America: An Ethnographic Study," *Arctic Anthropology* 5 (1969): 9.

16. Letter to the NA from J. Garth Taylor, Arctic ethnologist, Canadian Museum of Civilization, 23 February 1978.

17. Capt. William Edward Parry, *Journal of a second voyage for the discovery of a Northwest Passage from the Atlantic to the Pacific* (London: John Murray, 1824), plate facing 274.

18. Letter to the author from Betty Issenman, guest curator, McCord Museum, Montreal, 10 April 1986.

19. John Granlund, "Birdskin Caps: A Cultural Element of the Arctic and Northern Countries," *Ethnos* 18 (1953): 130. I would like to thank C. Feest, Museum für Völkerkunde, Vienna, Austria, for bringing this article to my attention.

20. Bernadette Driscoll, "The Amautik in Inuit History and Culture" in *The Inuit Amautik* (Winnipeg: Winnipeg Art Gallery, 1980), 14, and Franz Boas, *The Central Eskimo* (Toronto: Cole Publishing Co., 1974), Figs. 70 a and b.

21. Driscoll, 16.

22. Conversation with Bernadette Driscoll, 8 January 1986.

23. S.K. Hutton, *Among the Eskimos of Labrador* (Toronto: The Musson Book Co., 1912), facing 82. I would like to thank J. Garth Taylor for bringing this photograph to my attention.

24. J. Garth Taylor, "Eskimo Answers to an Eighteenth Century Questionnaire," *Ethnohistory* 19 (Spring 1972): 141.

25. H. Ellis, *A Voyage to Hudson's Bay by the Dobbs Galley and California in the Years 1746 and 1747* (London: H. Whitridge, 1748), facing 132.

26. Conversation with J. Garth Taylor, 8 January 1986.

27. Christie's (London). *English Pictures, Drawings and Bronzes*, 22 June 1962, lot 72.

28. J.W.F. Hill, ed., *The Letters and Papers of the Banks Family of Revesby Abbey, 1704-1760* (The Lincoln Record Society, 1952), vii and 168.

29. C.C. Gillespie, ed., *Dictionary of Scientific Biography* (New York: Charles Scribners' Sons, 1970), 1:433-437.

30. Lysaght, 111-174.

31. Lysaght, 84.

32. Quoted in Lysaght, 245. The terms "Eskimo" and "Indian" were used quite indiscriminately at this time, and Banks himself, in his Newfoundland diary, called the Inuit "Esquimaux indians," 128.

33. Lysaght, illustration no. 8.

34. Lysaght, 49.

AUGUSTUS ROCKWELL (1822-1882)

3. *Grove Point, Coast of Labrador*, 1867

Oil on panel

17.4 x 25.2 cm

Inscribed in pencil, verso, u.r.: *Grove Point/ Cost* [?] *of Labrador/Rockwell/Pt/1867*...

Purchased in 1985

Accession no.: 1985-78-2

Negative no.: C-124474

4. *Grove Point, Coast of Labrador, Esquimaux Huts*, 1867

Oil on panel

17.4 x 25.5 cm

Inscribed in pencil, verso, u.r.: *Grove Point/ Cost* [?] *of Labrador/Esquimaux Huts/ A Rockwell/P* [?] *t* [?] */1867*...

Purchased in 1985

Accession no.: 1985-78-1

Negative no.: C-124170

These two charming paintings of Labrador, although relatively small in size, are delightful examples of the landscapes that were produced by skilful artists in mid-nineteenth century North America. The vibrant colour and painterly technique are visually pleasing, yet the paintings still convey with a direct realism the details of aboriginal life; the renditions of the costumes, artifacts and dwellings of the Indian and Inuit aboriginal peoples of Labrador are examples of good documentary art. When these two works were first offered to the National Archives, they were considered highly desirable acquisitions. Documentary depictions of Labrador are rare yet vital to the understanding of the historical and ethnological past of this area of Canada.

The paintings are signed on the verso *Rockwell* and *A Rockwell*, respectively, and both are dated 1867. Since there are no known Canadian artists by this name who painted at this time, it was thought that Rockwell might be an American painter. The hypothesis that these scenes were the work of Augustus Rockwell (1822-1882), a landscape and portrait painter who worked in Buffalo, New York, proved to be correct. On his death in 1882, numerous obituaries appeared in the local press;[1] these contained significant details about the artist's life and work that were important in linking him to the two paintings.

Born in Manlius, New York, on 7 April 1822, Rockwell early developed a love of art and the wish to become an artist. He went to Troy, New York, and studied under Abel Buel Moore (1806-1879), a portraitist and instructor of apparently mediocre reputation who had studied under John Quidor. Moore also worked in New York City and Albany, and exhibited at the National Academy in 1835-1836.[2] He is described in Rockwell's obituary as being "well known."

Augustus Rockwell moved to Buffalo by at least 1850, when he married a Miss Meritt. He became a member of the Buffalo Academy of Fine Arts, an honorary member of the Buffalo Historical Society, and an honorary member of the Bisby Club. He was known for his landscapes, especially those of the Adirondack region, which he frequented, and also for his seascapes and portraits, which were highly saleable in the surrounding area.

Portraiture was one of his specialties and an area for which he gained considerable reputation. In fact, he painted portraits of United States President Millard Fillmore and his wife; according to an obituary, they were both important patrons and also personal friends of the artist. In 1885, the Buffalo Historical Society received a large collection of his paintings bequeathed by Mrs. Fillmore.

The author of one Rockwell obituary had some quite positive opinions about Rockwell's character and about his artistic skills:

> His drawing was excellent; his coloring was always pleasing and strong; and he never failed to get good effects. He had fewer eccentricities than most artists, and there was an evenness about his life and work that was rare. He labored in his studio from morning till night, and always seemed to find enjoyment in his work. Indeed he applied himself too closely to his business and his summer vacations scarcely afforded him the recreation he needed. He was a most exemplary citizen, a devoted husband and father; a true friend and an ardent lover of nature....[3]

Although described as having "few eccentricities," the Labrador paintings prove that his work was far from bland and unimaginative. They are solid compositions with good colouration, and although conforming to acceptable traditional standards, the painterly effects used, for example as seen in the highlights of the water, make them visually appealing as well as documentary.

Finding the Canadian link to this American artist who worked within such a limited geographical area in the United States, and who also knew of the more isolated and rugged region of Labrador, was accomplished when a simple statement was found in an obituary:

> He was an enthusiastic Adirondack traveler, and many of his most beautiful pictures represented the romantic scenery of that region. He had also made a sketching trip to Labrador.[4]

Although the only manuscript evidence known to date, this statement, when linked to the more abundant pictorial evidence, is conclusive proof of his visit to Labrador.

After establishing that the author of these paintings must indeed be the Augustus Rockwell from Buffalo, it was decided to check with American galleries and museums thought to have either biographical information or knowledge of his work. *The Inventory of American Paintings*, prepared by the National Museum of American Art in Washington,[5] lists three works by "A. Rockwell," one of which, dated 1874, is another Labrador scene, and fifteen works by "Augustus Rockwell," two of which are landscapes of areas in upstate New York, while the remainder are portraits.

Beloit College, in Wisconsin, which has three paintings by him, provided some biographical information and details of his American subjects. As one of the owners repeatedly listed in *The Inventory*, the Buffalo and Erie County Historical Society, which owns a collection of fourteen portraits, was most helpful in providing physical details about signatures and inscriptions. He evidently signed some of the portraits "A. Rockwell," in the same way as those presented here.[6]

The Albright-Knox Art Gallery, formerly known as the Buffalo Fine Arts Academy, provided some details, as in the following excerpt from a letter of 16 January 1985:

> The artist Augustus Rockwell is mentioned in Lars Sellstedt's history of *Art in Buffalo* as having been a respectable painter of portraits and "acceptable" landscapes active in Buffalo between 1851 and 1880. His most admired work according to Sellstedt was his portrait of U.S. president, Millard Fillmore. Sellstedt gives no mention of his origins or where he studied.... Besides portraits, Rockwell painted from studies made on fishing excursions to the Adirondacks, and evidently Labrador's coastline. Lars Sellstedt was a member of the National Academy who lived in Buffalo, was active on the Board of the Buffalo Fine Arts Academy, and wrote the above work in 1910 while in his 90's.[7]

Paintings by Rockwell frequently appeared in exhibitions of the Buffalo Fine Arts Academy. The *Catalogue of Works of Art* lists three pictures by A. Rockwell that were lent to the exhibition by owner E.P. Dorr in 1865: 34. *North West River, Coast of Labrador*; 35. *Esquimaux Bay, Coast of Labrador*; 36. *North West River, Coast of Labrador*. A fourth was lent by the artist himself and was offered for sale: 38. *Caribond* [*sic*, Caribou?] *Island, Coast of Labrador*.[8] This of course suggests that by 1865 Rockwell had already made a sketching trip to Labrador.

Records of the Albright-Knox Art Gallery indicate that in 1873 A. Rockwell loaned to them a painting entitled *Wolf Cove, Coast of Labrador*. Further, in 1875, owner J.F. Forsyth loaned another painting of a Canadian subject, *Esquimaux Bay, Coast of Labrador*, which may have been either the Dorr picture exhibited earlier or a second painting of the same subject. The Fillmore collection was then bequeathed in 1885, and among the twenty-five Rockwells, which included portraits, there were also more Labrador subjects, as listed in the *Catalogue of Works of Art* exhibited in 1887: 100. *Ane* [*sic*, Anse ?] *du Loup, Coast of Labrador*; 127. *Coast of Labrador*; 165. *Salmon Station, Coast of Labrador*; 180. *Coast of Labrador*.[9] As part of a major de-accessioning in 1920, it seems that some of the Labrador pictures owned by the Gallery were given to the Buffalo Science Museum; other Rockwells had been given to the Buffalo and Erie County Historical Society in 1861.[10] The artist's ties with the Buffalo Fine Arts Academy seem to have continued throughout his life, as he was elected to a one-year term on the Board of Directors in 1882, the year of his death.

It is known that another Labrador subject, entitled *Nascopic Indians, Coast of Labrador*, was painted in 1874, as it was reproduced in the *Old Print Shop Portfolio*.[11] Therefore, it is known that Rockwell painted at least eleven scenes of Labrador in addition to the two owned by the National Archives. Some were undoubtedly produced from sketches taken during an initial trip in 1865 or earlier, although it is possible that he made more than one trip north.

The two paintings in the National Archives collection are inscribed as scenes of Grove Point, Coast of Labrador. In the *Gazetteer of Canada*, Groves Point is described as being east of Goose Airport, Labrador, latitude 53° 21′ by longitude 60° 22′. Access is gained to this area of Labrador by Hamilton Inlet, southwest through Lake Melville and Goose Bay.

Henry Youle Hind, brother of the artist William Hind, records in a contemporary account of his trip through Labrador in 1861 this description of Hamilton Inlet:

> As we proceed in a north-westerly direction along a very rugged line of coast, with deep bays and indents, the Great Inlet, called Esquimaux Bay, Invertoke Bay, or Hamilton Inlet, opens to view. It is situated 250 miles beyond the Straits of Belle Isle.... It is by far the largest of many inlets which indent that part of the coast. At its entrance it is upwards of thirty miles in breadth.... At the western extremity of the lake, it again contracts to a narrow width for a short distance, above which it forms another lake about seven miles wide and twenty long, when the head of the inlet is reached.... On ascending the bay the landscape is improved by trees.... Above the Port of Rigolette, and on the shores of the Salt-water Lake mentioned above, the scenery becomes very grand....[12]

It is important to note that in addition to commercial fishing in Newfoundland and Labrador, which was well established by this time, sport fishing was also becoming internationally known and publicized. Since we know Rockwell went on a fishing trip to Labrador, it is not inconceivable that he had either read about fishing in Labrador or heard of it from his friends in the Adirondacks, an area also known to fishermen. One book published in 1860, *Salmon-Fishing in Canada*, outlines where to go on Canadian rivers, and although the author's advice is directed to travellers from England, it is still indicative of the type of guide being published at the time:

> I have already mentioned that from Quebec [City] the fisherman must set sail in his yacht for the fishing ground. But it is just possible that the gentleman may not have a yacht of his own or his friend's to embark in. What then is he to do? He must hire a schooner. And this he will best be able to do with the assistance of some one of the many respectable merchants or brokers of the city. There are many schooners employed in the coasting trade and in traffic with Newfoundland, New Brunswick, Nova Scotia, Gaspé and the Magdalen Islands....[13]

He also later mentions the good salmon fishing on the Moisie River, explored by the Hind brothers in 1861.

By the early twentieth century, there were more books about sport fishing in Canada, some anecdotal and others written as guides to good fishing areas. One such guide published in 1909, *Where the Fishers Go*, describes the native people occupying Labrador. The author speaks of isolated Eskimo families being found along the Atlantic coast, although the majority were located at the Moravian mission settlements. The dwellings these families used for spring fishing were called *tepik*, and are described as skin or canvas tents, like those depicted in the Rockwell painting (Cat. no. 4).[14]

The Indians encountered on the Labrador coast, to the south of Lake Michikaman and to the east of the George River, were most likely Montagnais rather than Naskapis. Apparently they paid regular visits to the Hudson's Bay posts and other settlements along Labrador's southern coast, and although primarily hunters, they would catch salmon and trout for barter in early summer. Their dwellings when migrating have been described as wigwams or cotton tents.[15] Depictions of these dwellings by the artist William Hind (see Cat. nos. 5 and 37), *Montagnais and Nasquapee Lodges at Seven Islands*, and *Montagnais Lodge at Mingan* (Figs. 3.1 and 3.2) correspond to the Rockwell painting. Photographic evidence supports the accuracy of these depictions.

Both of the Rockwell scenes depict native people likely engaged in the coastal fishing activities of the spring and summer months around Hamilton Inlet. The first depicts wigwams, a canoe and the costume likely of the Montagnais tribe (Cat. no. 3). The second illustrates a temporary dwelling of the Inuit, set up on the rocky shore, where an Inuit in his native dress stands poised in front of his kayak, preparing to fish (Cat. no. 4). Both paintings are invaluable documentary records of the Montagnais and Inuit peoples and their ways of life that have all but vanished from Labrador. Augustus Rockwell's attraction to the Canadian wilderness has meant the fortunate preservation of a record of this aspect of Canada's heritage.

M.M.

3.1 W.G.R. Hind
Montagnais and Nasquapee Lodges at Seven Islands, 1861
Watercolour
NA C-33682

3.2 W.G.R. Hind
Montagnais Lodge at Mingan, 1861
Watercolour
NA C-33685

1. Obituaries from the Buffalo and Erie County Historical Society, Buffalo, New York. *Buffalo Commercial Advertiser*, 15 May 1882, p. 2; *Buffalo Daily Courier*, 15 May 1882, p. 2; *Buffalo Morning Express*, 15 May 1882, p. 3.
2. George C. Groce and David H. Wallace, *The New York Historical Society's Dictionary of Artists in America 1564-1880* (Boston: Yale University Press, 1957), 451.
3. *Buffalo Daily Courier*, 15 May 1882, p. 2.
4. *Buffalo Daily Courier*, 15 May 1882, p. 2.
5. This is a computerized inventory.
6. Letter to the author from Clyde H. Eller, director of resources, Buffalo and Erie County Historical Society, 16 January 1985.
7. Letter to the author from John Sanford, archivist, Albright-Knox Art Gallery, Buffalo, 16 January 1985.
8. *Catalogue of Works of Art on Exhibition at the Gallery of the Buffalo Fine Arts Academy* (Buffalo, New York: Franklin Printing House, 1865), 8 and 11.
9. *Catalogue of Works of Art on Exhibition at the Gallery of the Buffalo Fine Arts Academy* (Buffalo, New York: The Courier Company, Printers, 1887), 13-15.
10. Letter to the author from John Sanford, 16 January 1985.
11. Harry Shaw Newman, ed., *The Old Print Shop Portfolio* 21 (February 1962): 141.
12. Henry Youle Hind, *Explorations in the Interior of the Labrador Peninsula* (London: Longman, Green, Longman, Roberts & Green, 1863), 2:186-187.
13. Colonel Sir James Edward Alexander, ed., *Salmon-Fishing in Canada* (London: Longman, Green, Longman and Roberts; Montreal: B. Dawson and Son, 1860), 66.
14. Rev. P.W. Browne, *Where the Fishers Go* (New York: Cochrane Publishing Co., 1909), 26.
15. Browne, 15.

Nasquapees
Otelne, the Tongue
Arkaskhe, the Arrow

WILLIAM GEORGE RICHARDSON HIND (1833-1889)

5. *Nasquapees*, 1861

Watercolour over pencil with opaque white on paper

25.4 x 32.4 cm

Inscribed in pen and brown ink, recto, u.r.: *78*; l.c.: *Nasquapees/Otelne, the Tongue Arkaskhe, the Arrow;* inscribed in pencil, verso, l.l., with pencil drawing of landscape with boats: *ron* [?] *Moisey R./g up the River)* / *2*

Purchased in 1984

Accession no.: 1984-100-1

Negative no.: C-121927

This watercolour of two Naskapi Indians was prepared by William Hind to serve as an illustration for his brother Henry Youle Hind's account of an expedition up the Moisie River during June and July of 1861.[1] The purpose of the expedition was to explore this area, which had never been mapped by Europeans; to survey it for the possible exploitation of its timber, fishery and mineral resources; and to study its Indian inhabitants.[2] The party consisted of Henry Youle Hind, two government-appointed surveyors, six French-Canadian voyageurs and three Indian guides. William was invited "for the purpose of making sketches and watercolour drawings of scenery, Indians, and any novelty in the vegetable or mineral world which it might be desirable to transfer to his portfolio."[3] He joined the party in Quebec City, having just returned from abroad.[4]

The fact that this area of Canada was *terra incognita* had great attraction for Henry Hind.[5] He noted in his introduction that the Moisie River was not listed in the survey of the Canadas published in 1832 by the surveyor-general, Joseph Bouchette, who had described the interior as being "the undisputed haunt of the prowling wolf and savage bear."[6] Edward Cayley, one of the surveyors, noted: "There is a certain charm in exploring a country, entirely unknown, that none but the Indian has traversed...."[7]

"Charming" is not the best word for describing the voyage up the rugged Moisie River, which is navigable for only a short distance at its mouth, after which it is filled with rapids that have to be portaged. Although the "gentlemen" on the journey found the landscape inspiring and Henry was constantly in search of sublime views, the hired men found it exhausting work. The illustration done after William's drawing, entitled *Resting on the Portage Path* (Fig. 5.1), demonstrates William's attitude, which was to leave the description of the overwhelming grandeur of the wilderness to his brother and to concentrate instead on the exact details of the journey.[8] The image captures both the wild, inhospitable landscape and the weariness of the men, drained by the arduous work.

Born in Nottingham, England, William Hind had followed his older brother Henry (1823-1908) to Toronto in 1851.[9] William became drawing master in the normal school where Henry had taught before his appointment as professor of chemistry and geology at University of Trinity College. Little is known about William's youth, his artistic training or his activities in Canada before the Labrador expedition. He had exhibited two paintings at the Upper Canada Provincial Exhibition of 1852. In addition, although he seems not to have been a member of the two Northwest expeditions Henry led in 1857 and 1858, William made twenty watercolour drawings from the on-the-spot sketches of the assistant surveyor, J. Fleming. These watercolours were attached to the report of the expedition published in 1859.[10]

Judging from the over one hundred drawings, watercolours and oils William produced during and after the Labrador journey, he also found the expedition stimulating. There are several descriptions in Henry's narrative of William sketching. While the hired men carried the canoes and baggage, William was invariably busy with his pencil.[11] He persevered despite the mosquitoes and blackflies that tormented the party and found the seams and openings in his kid gloves, so that his hands were marked with spots of blood.[12] The others could cover their faces, but for him "a veil was out of question, as that would destroy distinctness of vision" and so his face was also inflamed.[13] The on-the-spot pencil drawings, which he usually inscribed and dated, reveal a desolate rugged country, an arduous voyage and a lack of homely comforts. In one drawing Hind focuses on the box of tea, the only luxury item they carried.[14]

Back in Toronto after the expedition, William enlarged some of his sketches in watercolour to be chromolithographed for illustrations in the narrative of the journey.[15] Some sketches were reproduced through wood engravings; others he worked up into meticulously detailed oils.

The images depicting Indians can be divided into two types. One type consists of reconstructions of scenes that neither William nor Henry witnessed but that are based on verbal descriptions by the Indians they encountered during the journey. Henry spent a lot of time eliciting information from the Indians about their life, traditions and beliefs. A major portion of his publications consists of the retelling of these accounts. William provided drawings to illustrate them. *Conjuror in his Vapour Bath* is an example of such a reconstruction.[16]

The second type consists of images depicting actual events during the expedition. The watercolour in the exhibition (Cat. no. 5) belongs to this category. Otelne and Arkashke were Naskapi Indians whom the explorers met in Seven Islands upon their return from the Moisie expedition.[17] They were among a small number of Naskapi who had come down from the interior, their usual home, to be near the Roman Catholic Mission. We know from the narrative that they had promised to come to Hind's tent to have their portraits taken.[18] Subsequently, the Hind brothers were invited to Otelne's lodge, and the description of this visit provides another glimpse of William's tenacity for exact detail. Henry was unable to tolerate the crowd, the heat and the unpleasant cooking odours in the tent, "which the aroma of the best Virginia inhaled without intermission... was incapable of concealing."[19] William, however, more committed and tolerant, "remained for an hour in the lodge, making a water-colour sketch of the interior, taking advantage of an opportunity which might not occur again."[20] The two Indians were important sources for Hind's description of Naskapi traditions.

Many of the watercolours for the illustrations are highly finished and dense in colouring, such as *Second Gorge*, (Fig. 5.2). In contrast, the drawing of the Naskapi Indians is quite sketchy and unfinished, suggesting it may have been done on the spot. However, there is evidence that it is a composite. A pencil drawing of an unidentified Indian, inscribed *Naskarpe Indian*, is the preliminary study for Arkashke, the figure on the right (Fig. 5.3). A comparison of the drawing and the watercolour reveals minor changes such as the addition of tattoos on the cheeks, which Henry had described in detail.[21] Hind has also simplified the clothing in the watercolour by turning the Indian away from us, so that the details of the collar could be eliminated. The pipe Otelne is holding appears in a careful ethnographic study (Fig. 5.4). Henry had acquired it in exchange for tobacco, tea and flour.[22] The emphasis in the watercolour is on the faces of the Indians, which are boldly depicted, and on the hand holding the pipe. The landscape background is rather sketchy, especially on the left side where part of the image has been cut away, leaving the viewer wondering what was edited. The clothing is indicated with only a few strokes of wash. It is an anthropological study in keeping with Henry's detailed description of the Naskapi. In particular, Henry had singled out Otelne as "a very handsome Indian, with delicately chiselled features, a deep copper-coloured skin, long and intensely black hair, small and delicately formed hands and feet, handsome and expressive eyes, and a thoroughly Indian manner in everything he does."[23] In the chromolithographed illustration, equal attention has been paid to faces, clothing and background, eliminating the focus of the watercolour and resulting in a much less striking image[24] (Fig. 5.5).

The National Archives' extensive holdings of works by Hind covers most periods of his life. It includes several drawings and watercolours from the Labrador journey, a sketchbook and some oil paintings of his trek with the Overlanders in 1862, and a self-portrait. Finally, there are images dating from his later life in New Brunswick, such as Cat. no. 37. His depictions of native life are especially important, since the National Archives' holdings include only a few other images relating to the Naskapi.

E.M.-M.

5.1 After W.G.R. Hind
Resting on the Portage Path, 1863
Colour lithograph
NA C-13980

5.2 W.G.R. Hind
Second Gorge, 1861
Watercolour
NA C-121966

5.3 W.G.R. Hind
Naskarpe Indian, 1861
Pencil
Metropolitan Toronto Library

5.4 W.G.R. Hind
Montagnais Pipe, 1861
Watercolour
NA C-33689

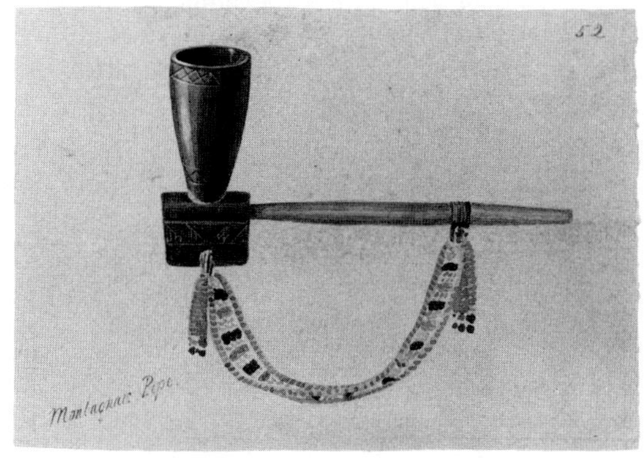

5.5 After W.G.R. Hind
Nasquapees, 1863
Colour lithograph
NA C-128914

---

1. Henry Youle Hind, *Explorations in the Interior of the Labrador Peninsula, the Country of the Montagnais and Nasquapee Indians*, 2 vols. (London: Longman, Green, Longman, Roberts & Green, 1863). It was reproduced in vol. 2 opposite p. 96 in the chapter describing the Naskapi Indians.

2. Hind, *Explorations* 1:v and 11.

3. Hind, *Explorations* 1:2.

4. George F.G. Stanley and Laurie C.C. Stanley, "The Brothers Hind," *Collections of the Nova Scotia Historical Society* 40 (1980):111.

5. Edward Cayley, "Up the River Moisie," *Literary and Historical Society of Quebec*, new series, 1 (1863): 76.

6. Joseph Bouchette, *The British Dominions in North America*, 2 vols. (London: Longmans, Rees, Orme, Brown, Green & Longman, 1832), 1:293.

7. Cayley, 76.

8. Hind, *Explorations* 1, facing 43.

9. J. Russell Harper, *William G.R. Hind 1833-1889*, Canadian Artists Series, (Ottawa: The National Gallery of Canada, 1976), 9.

10. Henry Youle Hind, *Reports of Progress; together with a Preliminary and General Report on the Assiniboine and Saskatchewan Exploring Expedition, made under the instructions from the Provincial Secretary of Canada*. Printed by order of the Legislative Assembly. (Toronto: John Lovell, 1859) Appendix V, 193-194, A List of Water-Colour Drawings, and Photographs accompanying this Report. The whereabouts of these watercolours is not known.

11. Hind, *Explorations* 1:144, 146, 182.

12. Hind, *Explorations* 1:151.

13. Hind, *Explorations* 1:151.

14. In the collection of the Metropolitan Toronto Library, Accession no.: 941-3-3.

15. Harper, *Hind*, 16.

16. Hind, *Explorations* 2:14, wood engraving.

17. Hind, *Explorations* 1:320.

18. Hind, *Explorations* 1:323.

19. Hind, *Explorations* 1:325.

20. Hind, *Explorations* 1:325.

21. Hind, *Explorations* 2:97.

22. Hind, *Explorations* 2:323.

23. Hind, *Explorations* 1:322.

24. Hind, *Explorations* 2, facing 96.

Indians Returning from War

Inside of an Indian Tent

PETER RINDISBACHER (1806-1834)

Bushnell Collection of Canadiana

Cat. nos. 6-11 were purchased in 1981 with the assistance of a grant from the minister of Communications under the terms of the *Cultural Property Export and Import Act*.

6. *Indians returning from War*, 1825

Watercolour with pen and black ink on paper

25.8 x 21.3 cm

Inscribed in pen and brown ink, recto, b.: *Indians returning from War*; l.r: *P. Rindisbacher. 1825*

Accession no.: 1981-55-72

Negative no.: C-114471

7. *Inside of an Indian Tent*, 1824

Watercolour with pen and black ink on paper

25.8 x 21.3 cm

Inscribed in pen and brown ink, recto, b.: *Inside of an Indian Tent*; l.r.: *Peter Rindisbasser* [?] *1824*

Accession no.: 1981-55-73

Negative no.: C-114484

Peter Rindisbacher was a fifteen-year-old boy when he travelled to the Red River Territory (present-day Manitoba) in 1821. His family was one of fifty-seven Swiss families recruited to settle in the colony founded by Thomas Douglas, the Earl of Selkirk. Rindisbacher was born in Eggiwill, in the Canton of Bern, Switzerland, in 1806, and apparently showed a strong interest in drawing at an early age.[1] He had very little formal artistic training, having studied only briefly, when he was twelve years old, with Swiss artist Jakob Samuel Weibel (1771-1846), a landscape painter and engraver. The young artist's keen interest in the adventures of the Swiss colonists made up for his lack of artistic training. He created many drawings and watercolours, most of which are in the collection of the National Archives of Canada, which depict the settlers' journey across the ocean and overland to the colony. The Rindisbacher family stayed at Red River for five difficult years, during which time Peter became quite well known as an artist in the area. He received commissions for pictures from several employees of the Hudson's Bay Company and from the successive governors of the Red River Colony, for whom he depicted the local Indians and Métis, the wildlife and scenes of the settlement. Four of his paintings, depicting the activities of the governor, were sent to London in 1825 to be lithographed and published as a set entitled *Views in Hudson's Bay*.[2] In 1826, following heavy spring flooding, the family moved to the lead-mining area around Gratiot, Wisconsin. Rindisbacher continued painting, and in 1829 he moved to St. Louis, Missouri, at that time the headquarters for the United States Indian Affairs Department and the starting point for all expeditions heading west. George Catlin, the important American painter of Indians, began his trip to the West from St. Louis in 1830, as did the Prussian explorer, Maximilian, Prince of Wied Neuwied, during his 1833-1834 journey to study Indian tribes. Rindisbacher seems to have become quite well established as an artist in St. Louis. The *American Turf Register and Sporting Magazine* began to publish his drawings fairly regularly, and when Maximilian arrived in St. Louis, it was Rindisbacher he commissioned to paint two Indian scenes.[3] Unfortunately, Rindisbacher died in 1834 at the age of twenty-eight.

Rindisbacher was, of course, not the first artist to depict the American Indian, but his situation differed somewhat from that of other artists in the West. He was not connected with any expedition, as was, for example, the German Carl Bodmer, who was Maximilian's artist. Nor was he motivated, as George Catlin had been, to record every aspect of the vanishing culture of the Indian. Rindisbacher came to North America as a young immigrant, and, following his artistic bent, he proceeded to make a visual record of many aspects of life in the colony, which, of course, included scenes of Indian life. His method of working, which was to repeat, seemingly upon demand, various scenes from an established repertoire, reveals that his choice of subjects was likely suggested by his patrons, who would order specific scenes, such as buffalo hunts.[4] He did not share Catlin's profound interest in the Indian as an individual, and thus painted few portraits of them. He concentrated instead on an accurate depiction of their clothing and artifacts, superimposed on a portrayal of the Indian as a classical hero, with stances and compositions taken from the antique.[5] As he matured, some of his subjects became more dramatic, such as the murder of a settler family by Indians or an Indian scalping an enemy.

Rindisbacher worked almost exclusively in watercolour, reinforcing his outlines and adding details with pen and ink. He circumscribed his scenes with a dark border, which suggests the format of book illustrations. This layout lends itself to inscriptions, which appear on much of his work. The handwriting of titles and of the artist's signature varies widely, suggesting that collectors did some of their own labelling.

A comparison of *Indians returning from War* (Cat. no. 6) with *Scene in an Indian tent* (Fig. 6.1), a later work, will illustrate his working method and the maturing of his style. The arrangement of the figures is reminiscent of groupings in a classical pediment, with the reclining man on the right and the seated girl on the left bracketing a triangular composition. In addition, the prone figure, instead of being involved in the main action in the tent, looks towards the viewer, or the artist, completing a compositional circle. The model for both pictures remains the same, but details have been changed in the clothing so that two different Indian tribes are portrayed in the two works. The later work (Fig. 6.1) has been embellished by the addition of more feathers, baskets, ducks and even fish, resulting in a more composed studio piece than the earlier, simpler watercolour. The treatment of the figures is different: The heads are larger, the modelling of the muscles less angular in the later work, showing more assurance on the part of the artist. In addition, the format of the painting has been subtly changed so that the later work is horizontal instead of vertical. This reduces the amount of space above the figures and makes them all seem larger, although they retain their proportions in relation to the size of the picture. All the

8. *The Dogs discover a Herd of Buffaloes*, before 1824

Watercolour with pen and black ink on paper

24.1 x 43.7 cm

Inscribed in pen and brown ink, on strip of paper accompanying the work, b.: *The Dogs discover a herd of Buffalo's and immediately run from the Indians and cause great confusion*; l.r.: *Peter Rindisbacher.*

Accession no.: 1981-55-71

Negative no.: C-114462

9. *The Method of Crawling up to a Herd of Buffaloes*, before 1824

Watercolour with pen and black ink on paper

24.1 x 43.5 cm

Inscribed in pen and brown ink, on a strip of paper accompanying the work, b.: *The method of crawling up to a herd of Buffalo's in the Winter killing several without disturbing the rest*; l.r.: *Peter Rindisbacher.*

Accession no.: 1981-55-70

Negative no.: C-114464

pictorial elements in both works, as in all of Rindisbacher's pictures – including the linear technique, the sparkling, well-defined colours, the careful arrangement of figures and objects – are orchestrated to yield maximum detail and information.

These six watercolours (Cat. nos. 6-11) have the added interest of having been in the collection of David I. Bushnell Jr., an American anthropologist who owned an extensive collection of pictures of North American Indians by artists such as Paul Kane and Seth Eastman.[6] Bushnell was one of the first anthropologists to study these works of art for their ethnographic content, realizing their inestimable value for the period prior to photography.[7] At the time of his death in 1941, he was working on a comprehensive publication about "artistic representation of Indians and Indian life," a subject that now concerns many anthropologists.[8] An in-depth analysis of these watercolours reveals that Rindisbacher was an ideal painter for the anthropologist, because he did not deviate from accuracy for the sake of making pleasing pictures.

Rindisbacher's pictures of the Red River area are the earliest depictions from the Canadian mid-west. The native inhabitants consisted of a mixture of Indian tribes, such as the Cree, the Western Ojibwa, the Saulteaux – who were Woodlands people – and the Assiniboines, who were Plains Indians. Added to them were the Red River Métis, who were the descendants of French-Canadian workers in the fur trade and their Indian wives.

In addition to being rare scenes of tipi interiors, *Indians returning from War* and *Inside of an Indian Tent* (Cat. nos. 6 and 7) demonstrate the ethnographic mixture peculiar to the Red River area. In *Indians returning from War*, the warrior with his back to us is wearing a Plains Indian painted buffalo robe, decorated with a typical sunburst design (Fig. 6.2). The rest of the clothing and artifacts, however, are of Woodlands Indian origin, including the hood worn by the person on the far right and the woman's strap dress.[9] The cradleboard is typical Western Ojibwa of the very earliest kind; the later ones would have a hoop to protect the head of the child.[10]

In *Inside of an Indian Tent*, the man seated with his back to us wears a breech-clout and leggings typical of the Saulteaux Indians. The knife sheath in his belt, with the long fringe (also seen secured to the wall of the tipi in *Indians returning from War*), is of the southern Manitoba type (Fig. 6.3). The two distinct types of pipes in this picture are another illustration of the mingling of cultures. The ones on the right, smoked by the Indians, are Woodlands type, carved from black stone, sometimes decorated with lead inlay (shown white in the painting). The European is smoking a Plains Indian-type pipe, made from catlinite (after artist George Catlin), a red clay from the upper Missouri region long used by Indians for making pipes.

Rindisbacher may very well be depicting himself in *Inside of an Indian Tent*, in which case he could have witnessed the presentation of a scalp, depicted in *Indians returning from War*. The principal enemies of the Ojibwa were the Sioux and the Iroquois, and warfare among them was fairly constant. Whoever slew an enemy would bring the scalp home and could then wear an eagle feather in his hair.[11] The warrior bearing the scalp has obviously slain several enemies already, judging by the number of feathers he wears. The old man sitting on the ground wears a bear-claw necklace as a hunting trophy. Both the warrior carrying the scalp and the young European in *Inside of an Indian Tent* (Cat. no. 7) carry powder horns. The European also has a Métis-type quilled shot-pouch, the same type as the hunter on horseback carries in *Buffalo Hunting in the Summer* (Cat. no. 10). The flintlock rifles of the early nineteenth century, carefully depicted in several of these paintings, needed both gun powder and shot, which were loaded by the muzzle.

Interaction with the Europeans is signified not only by the presence of rifles but also by the silver jewellery, such as ear-pendants and a brooch (worn in the hair), of the Indians in both interior scenes. These are items of trade silver made by the Europeans in the eighteenth and nineteenth centuries especially for commerce with the Indians.[12]

While the interior scenes are rich in details of Indian artifacts and clothing, the other four watercolours (Cat. nos. 8-11), are exciting portrayals of that quintessentially western occupation, the buffalo hunt. Rindisbacher would have had ample opportunity to observe and even participate in buffalo hunting during his years of residence in Red River, especially since the settlers were often short of food. Judging by the four scenes, he had made drawings of all the salient features of the hunt and had depicted both "modern" hunting on horseback and the more ancient forms of pursuit (Cat. nos. 9 and 11).

Buffalo Hunting in the Summer (Cat. no. 10), shows Red River Métis on horseback, clearly identifiable by some of their clothing and horsegear. These people were well known for using floral patterns in decorating clothing and other objects.[13] The crupper

10. ***Buffalo Hunting in the Summer***, before 1824

Watercolour with pen and black ink on paper

24.0 x 44.0 cm

Inscribed in pen and brown ink, on a strip of paper accompanying the work, b.: *Buffalo hunting in the Summer*; l.r.: *Peter Rindisbacher*

Accession no.: 1981-55-69

Negative no.: C-114472

11. ***Indian Hunters pursuing the Buffalo in Spring***, before 1824

Watercolour with pen and black ink on paper

23.5 x 40.4 cm

Inscribed in pen and brown ink, on a strip of paper accompanying the work, b.: *Indian Hunters pursuing the Buffalo early in the spring when the Snow is sufficiently frozen to bear the men but the)/Animal breaks through and cannot run*; l.r.: *Peter Rindisbacher*

Accession no.: 1981-55-68

Negative no.: C-114467

worn by the horse on the left has such decoration and can be likened to a similar article collected in 1841 in the Lower Red River area (Fig. 6.4).[14] In addition, the hunter on the right is wearing knee-length skin leggings over trousers, a typically Métis adaptation.

Red River Métis were famous for their expertise in buffalo running and in shooting the animals from the saddle.[15] Contemporary written accounts of the buffalo hunt dwell on points similar to those Rindisbacher has depicted, such as the horse, of its own accord, carrying the rider alongside the marked animal, allowing him the use of both arms for shooting.[16]

The winter scenes are of special interest, because no other early artist had the opportunity to observe the hunt during that season. Catlin's painting of a winter buffalo hunt shows the Indians in summer clothing. *The Method of Crawling up to a Herd of Buffaloes* (Cat. no. 9) shows perhaps one of the most ancient ways of hunting.[17] Several early travellers mention this painstaking and slow method, among them Sir John Franklin, the Arctic explorer, who added that the thirty or forty degrees below zero temperature would have made this form of hunting extremely uncomfortable.[18]

In *Indian Hunters pursuing the Buffalo in Spring* (Cat. no. 11), the hunters can be identified as belonging to the Assiniboines, a Plains tribe of the Red River area. The skin shirt worn by the hunter in the centre foreground, fringed over the shoulders and decorated with circles woven of quills, is quite typical of the clothing from the Northern Plains (Fig. 6.5). The fact that the hunters are not using guns is also important. Robert Simpson, who was in the same area in the 1830s, mentioned that among the Assiniboine "the bow is still more used than the gun."[19] In addition, Rindisbacher has also observed how the seasoned hunter will shoot the buffalo to dispatch it quickly and without wasting arrows.

> The fatal spot is from 12" to 18" in circumference, and lies immediately back of the foreleg, with its lowest point on line with the elbow.[20]

The Dogs discover a Herd of Buffaloes (Cat. no. 8) does not depict a methodical part of the hunt, but an incident that seems to have been familiar to Western residents. The description of the scene, cited below, was written specifically to describe Rindisbacher's painting and was published in the *American Turf Register* in 1830. The writer's aim was to emphasize Rindisbacher's accuracy in his depiction of various scenes:

> They [the dogs]... are obedient under all circumstances but one: Should their repast the night previous have been less liberal than usual, and that great delicacy, a buffalo cross their path, it is impossible to restrain them:...
>
> In utter disregard of the proprieties of the situation, and the resistance of the driver, away they dash, and succeed, generally, in killing the animal, with the cooperation of the master, who is no indifferent spectator of the struggle; for now and then, the buffalo tosses a dog upon his horns, and entangling his enemies in their harness, bears them off, with the blankets, provisions, and other indispensables, of the now destitute voyageur....[21]

If Rinsdisbacher is not considered a major artist, it must be remembered that he is being judged by works executed at an age when most artists are just beginning their careers. The ethnohistorical content of his works, however, makes them the most valuable documents of Red River history.[22]

E. M.-M.

6.1 P. Rindisbacher
Scene in an Indian Tent, after 1825
Watercolour
West Point Museum Collections, United States Military Academy

6.2
Painted robe, Sioux type, 1843
Canadian Museum of Civilization 74-7928

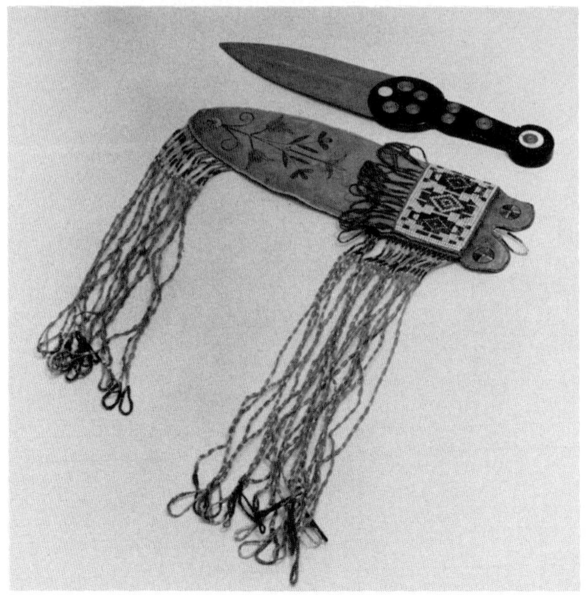

6.3
Knife sheath and knife, Métis type, ca. 1840
Canadian Museum of Civilization 74-895

6.4
Crupper, Métis type, ca. 1840
Canadian Museum of Civilization 72-16128

6.5
Shirt decorated with quill rosettes, Northern Plains type, ca. 1860
Canadian Museum of Civilization 74-7399

---

1. For a complete account of Rindisbacher's life, see Alvin M. Josephy Jr., *The Artist was a Young Man* (Fort Worth: Amon Carter Museum, 1970). A *catalogue raisonné* of works by Rindisbacher is available in E.H. Bovay, *Le Canada et les Suisses, 1604-1974* (Fribourg: Editions Universitaires, 1974), 211-237.

2. The full title of the set was as follows: *Views in Hudson's Bay. Taken by a Gentleman on the Spot in the Years, 1823 and 1824. Illustrative of the Customs, Manners and Costumes of those Tribes of North American Indians Amongst whom Capt'n. Franklin had passed in his present and former arduous undertaking.*

3. M.V. Gallagher and D.C. Hunt, "Travels in the Interior of North America," in J.C. Ewers, *Views of a Vanishing Frontier* (Omaha, Nebraska: Center for Western Studies, Joslyn Art Museum, 1984), 28.

4. In 1824, George Barnston, an employee of the Hudson's Bay Co., ordered some paintings from Rindisbacher, via the accountant in Fort Garry, and cited specific titles: "Do not forget if you please my commission about the Drawings. The ones I should like to have in particular are. . . the death of the buffalo and two or three Buffaloes Pieces in which I think the lad excells. Of all these I have seen several different copies, so that I conclude he keeps one copy to take another from as occasion may require." Quoted in M.A. MacLeod, G.L. Nute, and C. Wilson, "Peter Rindisbacher: Red River Artist," *The Beaver* (December 1945), 32. The previous owner, David I. Bushnell, purchased the four Buffalo Hunt pictures (Cat. nos. 8-11), as a set in 1909, according to Bushnell's notes in the Peabody Museum, Harvard University. Their similar size and the identical manner in which they are mounted and labelled suggest that they may have been similarly ordered as a set.

5. Rena Neumann Coen, "The Indian as the Noble Savage in 19th-Century American Art." PhD thesis (University of Minnesota, 1969), 65.

6. The collection was given to the Peabody Museum, Harvard University, upon the death of David Bushnell in 1941. Through deaccessioning procedures in 1981, the NA was able to acquire several pieces including Cat. nos. 6-11, 12-17, 19 and 25.

7. Letter to the author from T.J. Brasser, Plains ethnologist, Canadian Museum of Civilization, 6 June 1986. I would like to thank Dr. Brasser for most of the ethnological identification in these paintings.

8. John R. Swanton, "David I. Bushnell, Jr.," *American Anthropologist* 44 (1942):105-106.

9. Woodlands strap-dresses are only known from paintings and descriptions, as no specimen has survived. Conversation with T.J. Brasser.

10. E.S. Rogers and J.G. Taylor, "Northern Ojibwa" in Wm. Sturtevant, ed., *Handbook of North American Indians*, vol. 6, *Subartic* (Washington: Smithsonian Institution, 1981), 235.

11. Diamond Jenness, *Indians of Canada*, 7th ed. (Toronto: University of Toronto Press, 1977), 278-279.

12. N. Jaye Fredrickson and Sandra Gibb, *The Covenant Chain: Indian Ceremonial and Trade Silver* (Ottawa: National Museums of Canada, 1980), 21.

13. T.J. Brasser, "Métis Artisans," *The Beaver* (Autumn 1975), 52-57.

14. The crupper is a looped strap that goes under the tail of the horse and keeps the saddle from slipping forward.

15. W.L. Morton, *Manitoba: a History* (Toronto: University of Toronto Press, 1957), 40.

16. Thomas Simpson, *Narrative of the Discoveries on the North Coast of America* (London: Richard Bentley, 1843), 402-403.

17. George W. Arthur, *An Introduction to the Ecology of Early Historic Communal Bison Hunting among the Northern Plains Indians*, Archaeological Survey of Canada, Paper no. 37 (Ottawa: National Museums of Canada, 1975), 62.

18. Capt. John Franklin, *Narrative of a Journey to the Shores of the Polar Sea in the years 1819-20-21-22* (London: John Murray, 1824), 1:177-178.

19. Simpson, 405.

20. Arthur, 69.

21. Quoted in J.F. McDermott, "Peter Rindisbacher: Frontier Reporter," *Art Quarterly* 12 (Spring 1949): 139-140.

22. Morton, 65.

91

Kee-akee-ka-saa-ka-woo
Head Chief of the Crees

PAUL KANE (1810-1871)

Bushnell Collection of Canadiana

Cat. nos. 12-17 were purchased in 1981 with the assistance of a grant from the minister of Communications under the terms of the *Cultural Property Export and Import Act.*

12. *Rocky Mountain Indian,* August 1847

Watercolour over pencil on paper

13.5 x 11.9 cm

Inscribed in pencil, recto, u.l.: *91* [over erased *96*]; verso, c.l.: *65* [encircled and partially erased]; in erased pencil, t.: *White Buffalo Calf/Blackfoot*

Accession no.: 1981-55-43

Negative no.: C-114389

13. *Kee-akee-ka-saa-ka-wow, "The Man that Gives the War Whoop," Cree Indian, Fort Pitt,* January 1848

Watercolour over pencil on paper

13.5 x 11.0 cm

Inscribed in pencil, recto, u.l.: *94 on* [?]; in pen and brown ink, l.l.: *Kee-akee-ka-saa ka* [added above the line with a caret]*-wow/ Head Chief of the Crees*; in pencil, verso, c.: *84/19* [latter number encircled and upside down]; l.r.: *The man that gives/the war whoop*; l.l.: [remainder of inscription from verso of Cat. no. 15]

Accession no.: 1981-55-44

Negative no.: C-114386

> Mr. Paul Kane a native Canadian artist of great talent who has devoted much of his attention to Indian subjects... is very desirous of going over untrodden ground (artistically speaking) of the interior and from what I had the opportunity of seeing of himself and his works for some months past in Toronto will I am sure produce not only vivid but faithful sketches of all its novelties. . . .[1]

This letter, written in 1846, was Paul Kane's introduction to George Simpson, governor of the Hudson's Bay Company. It secured Simpson's help, and Kane's journey to the West, from which the watercolours in this exhibition originate, began on 9 May 1846 and lasted until 13 October 1848.[2] During these two and a half years, the artist travelled all the way to the Pacific coast, braving rough weather and hostile Indians; enduring lack of food, water and all homely comforts; and nearly losing his life several times. The result was hundreds of sketches, landscape and portrait logs that would serve to identify the images; a journal that would form the basis of Kane's book *Wanderings of an Artist among the Indians of North America from Canada to Vancouver's Island and Oregon through the Hudson's Bay Territory and Back Again*; and a wealth of ethnographic knowledge about various Indian tribes that the local scientific community would draw upon for the rest of the artist's life.[3]

The inspiration for this undertaking had come to Kane in London. Born in Ireland in 1810, he emigrated to Toronto with his parents in 1819. As there were no institutions in Toronto for formal art training, the aspiring young artist did sign painting, furniture decorating and some portraits to gain practice and earn a living. Such preparation, however, was quite inadequate for someone intending to become a professional artist, and by the mid-1830s Kane was determined to go to Europe – to Italy especially, the early nineteenth-century artistic metropolis, where a student could receive the most complete overview of the source of Western art: classical art. Kane left Toronto in 1836 and travelled in the United States as far as Mobile, Alabama, painting portraits. From 1841 to 1843 he was in Europe, visiting museums and doing what all dutiful nineteenth-century art students did – copying well-known works of art.[4]

The most important part of his European journey, however, seems not to have been the acquaintance with the art masterpieces of Italy, France and England. It was, instead, the meeting in 1843 with another North American, the painter George Catlin. The latter was not in London to study art but to exhibit his "Indian Gallery." He had spent the years from 1830 to 1836 travelling among and painting numerous Indian tribes on the American plains and in the Rocky Mountains. Catlin had become a crusader on behalf of the North American Indians, having witnessed the upheavals they were subjected to in losing their lands and in having to radically alter their way of life. At the same time, Catlin was making a record, in his paintings and his collection of artifacts, of the culture and existence of these people, who he believed would very soon be extinct. He had exhibited his paintings in America and then brought them to England for display. His book, *Letters and Notes on the Manners, Customs and Conditions of the North American Indians*, was published in 1841, and served to complete the exhibition by providing a narrative description of his travels. It would become the model for Kane's own book, *Wanderings*. Kane, in search of suitable subject matter for his own career, was deeply impressed by Catlin's work. Although Indians were to be seen in the environs of Toronto when Kane was growing up, these were not ones to inspire an artist. As Daniel Wilson, anthropologist and Kane's contemporary, wrote:

> The Indian, as seen in his worst debasement, haunting the centres of civilization, is little calculated to attract the eye of the artist or ethnical observer.[5]

Seeing them out of their normal context helped to direct Kane's attention to the possibility of making Indians the subject matter of his art, and he resolved to execute his own record of them. He returned to Toronto in 1845, and almost immediately set out on his first journey into Indian territory.

Lasting for only the summer of 1845, and taking him around the Great Lakes, this journey served as an introduction for his later, more extensive voyage from 1846 to 1848. He established a method of working: Carrying compact and light sketching materials, consisting of pencil, watercolours and some oils, small-format sketchbooks and oiled paper, he travelled to areas where Indians congregated, and sketched notable chiefs and personages, houses, villages, everyday objects, ceremonial artifacts and unusual landscape formations. Moreover, he must have realized during this short expedition that an extensive journey to the West would require more than determination. He therefore approached several Hudson's Bay Company officials, showed them his sketches and shared with them his plans for going west. Thus the letter of introduction and recommendation to Simpson, who gave Kane a letter of introduction to company employees, asking

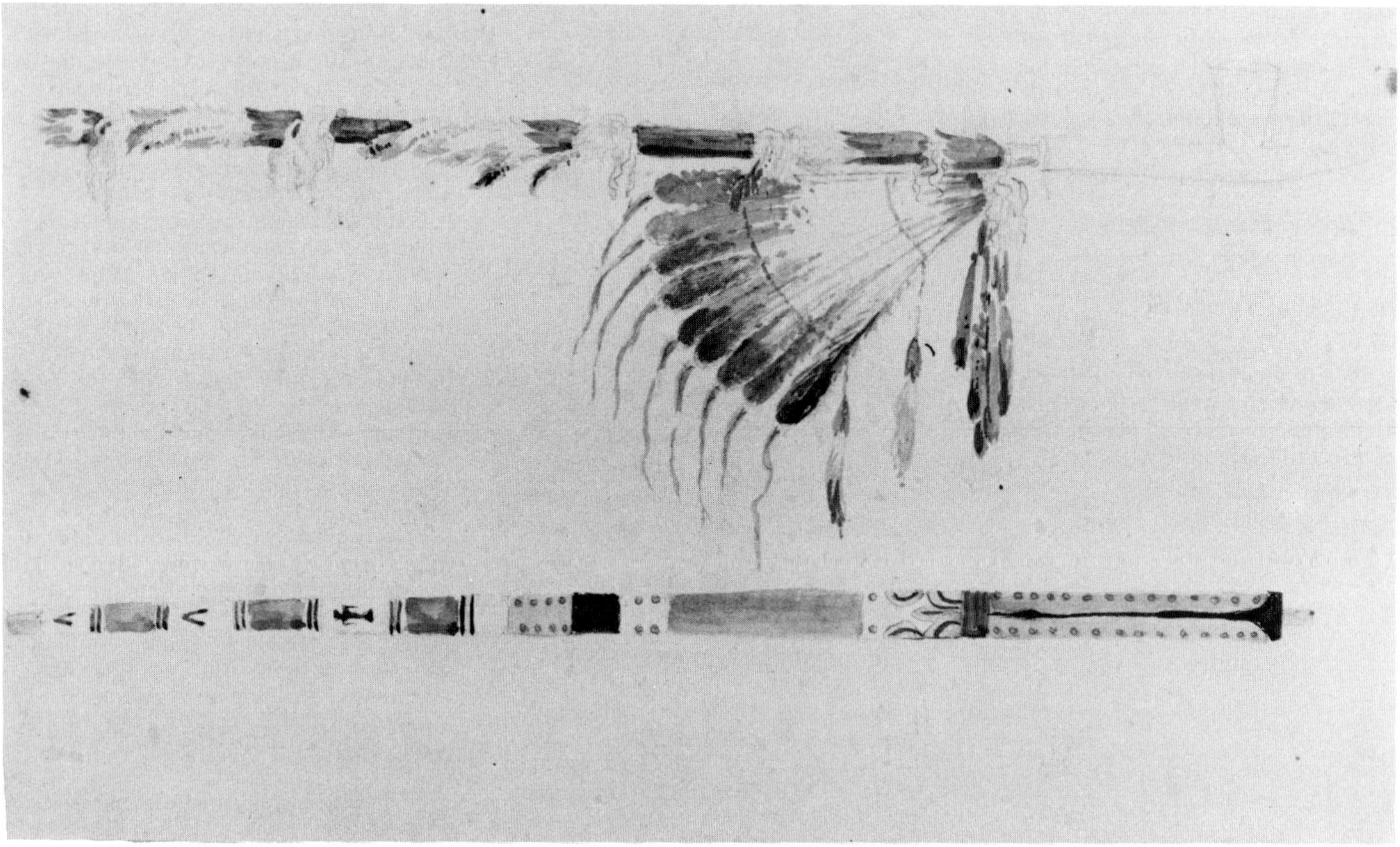

Cree Indian

14. *Pipe Stems Carried by Kee-akee-ka-saa-ka-wow, Cree Indian, Fort Pitt*, January 1848

Watercolour over pencil on paper

13.7 x 23.4 cm

Inscribed in pencil, verso, c.: *91* [encircled and partially erased]

Accession no.: 1981-55-45

Negative no.: C-114385

15. *Pea-a-pus-qua-hum, "One that Passes through the Sky," Cree Indian, Rocky Mountain House*, April 1848

Watercolour over pencil on paper

13.5 x 11.8 cm

Inscribed in pencil, recto, u.r.: *96* [?]; in pen and brown ink, l.c.: *Cree Indian*; in pencil, verso, c.: *85/62* [latter number encircled]; b.: *Pea a pus qua hum (one that/passes through the sky) a Cree Indi* [an] */living among the Assinaboines Rock* [y] *Mountain House* [the letters in [ ] appear on the verso of Cat. no. 13]

Accession no.: 1981-55-47

Negative no.: C-114388

them to show "your kind attentions and hospitalities of such of the Company's posts as he may visit; and you will be pleased to afford Mr. Kane passages from post to post in the Company's craft – free of charge."[6]

Less than a month after his return to Toronto from his longer expedition of 1846-1848 to the Canadian West, an exhibition of 240 of Kane's sketches and an assortment of Indian artifacts was arranged at city hall. At least three of the portrait sketches in this exhibition (Cat. nos. 13, 15 and 17) were on display, along with the sketch of the Indian lodges (Cat. no. 16).[7] This event reveals the high regard that Kane's accomplishment was given by the community. In the first half of the nineteenth century, the preparatory sketches of an artist were almost never exhibited because they were not considered finished enough for public scrutiny. Moreover, when such "one man" shows were held, they were done privately in the artists' studios.[8] Lastly, the few art exhibitions held in Toronto up to 1848 had drawn poor attendance and even poorer sales.[9] In contrast, Kane's exhibition was a huge success, was well attended, and was praised by all the newspapers for the truthfulness and accuracy of the drawings. Ironically, those very qualities would suffer extensively when the artist turned his portrait sketches into the finished paintings that fulfilled his own requirements of a work of art. In addition to the public success, Kane met his second important patron, G.W. Allan, during the exhibition.

With Catlin as a model, Kane decided to execute, from his sketches, a cycle of one hundred oil paintings depicting the Indians and the western landscape he had encountered. By purchasing the projected cycle of paintings in 1852, along with Kane's collection of Indian artifacts, for $20,000, Allan enabled Kane to devote his time entirely to painting. In addition, Kane also gave Allan many of the watercolour sketches, including the ones in this exhibition, which served as models for the oil paintings. In 1932, the American anthropologist David Bushnell Jr. managed to convince Allan's daughter, Mrs. E. Cassels, to part with eleven Kane drawings and one oil sketch.[10] Some of these are now in the collection of the National Archives of Canada.[11]

All the drawings in the exhibition (Cat. nos. 12-17) were done on the return leg of Kane's journey, which began on 1 July 1847. Chronologically, the first is the *Rocky Mountain Indian* (Cat. no. 12), identified as a native of that area by his striking facepaint.[12] It was sketched during August, when Kane had left the Hudson's Bay brigade in the company of a Métis guide, in order to explore more of the awesome wilderness of the Columbia River area and to sketch both the magnificent landscape and the Indians inhabiting it.[13]

A detailed examination of this drawing reveals the problems inherent in researching Kane's art. The most important sources for identifying his sketches are his landscape and portrait logs and his journal. These consist of numbered entries, which match in numbering many, but not all, of the drawings.

The previous title for this drawing, *Nez Perce Indian*, was given by David Bushnell, who had no access to Kane's logs and journal.[14] However, during his trip to Toronto to visit Mrs. Cassels, Bushnell had carefully examined all the Kane oil paintings on exhibit in the Royal Ontario Museum. Because the details of the facepaint in the oil *Nezperee Indian* (Fig. 12.1) have been modelled on this sketch, Bushnell proposed that the sketch was identical to the one Kane recorded in *Wanderings*, a secondary account of his journey, as having been executed on 29 July 1847.[15]

> During the day we passed a large encampment of Nezperees, [*sic*]... I took a sketch of a man....[16]

The log lists two portraits of Nez Percé Indians:

> 75. I-e-ash-an (leash) the foolish, a Cham-nass-am (Chamnapam), at the mouth of the Nezperce River. A small tribe, a branch of the Nezperces.
> 77. Nach-a-wish, a Nezperce Indian. This tribe is large and live on the Nezperce River.[17]

Sketch 75 has not been located, but the sketch of Nach-a-wish, inscribed with the number 77, in Kane's handwriting, is in the Stark collection, in Texas (Fig. 12.2). A comparison of *Rocky Mountain Indian* and *Nach-a-wish* shows that the latter has none of the detailed face paint that is so striking in the former. The lack of detail and hurried execution of *Nach-a-wish*, moreover, is in keeping with the rather rough conditions of Kane's travel at this time, which did not allow for making detailed drawings.

Rocky Mountain Indian (Cat. no. 12) is inscribed with the number 91 in the top left corner.[18] The corresponding journal entry reads:

> 91. a spocan on the river of the same name[19]

Spokan indians are a Rocky Mountain group who were known for wearing red face

16. *Cree or Assiniboin Lodges in front of Rocky Mountain Fort*, April 1848

Watercolour over pencil on paper

13.9 x 23.5 cm

Inscribed in pen and brown ink, recto, l.r.: *Cree Lodges*; in pencil, verso, along right margin: *Rocky Mountain Fort;* c.: *27* [encircled and partially erased]

Accession no.: 1981-55-46

Negative no.: C-114374

17. *Maydoc-game-kinungee, "I hear the Noise of the Deer," Ojibway Chief, Michipicoten Island*, September 1848

Watercolour over pencil on paper

13.4 x 11.4 cm

Inscribed in pen and brown ink, recto, u.r.: *Head Chief Ojibwah*; in pencil, verso, c.: *69* [encircled]

Accession no.: 1981-55-51

Negative no.: C-114382

paint.[20] Moreover, this entry immediately follows a number of drawings Kane made at Fort Colville, where he spent almost a week and had plenty of time to make detailed drawings.[21] A comparison with sketches of Chualpay women dancers from Fort Colville (Fig. 12.3) reveals elaborate and beautiful face paint somewhat like that of *Rocky Mountain Indian*.

A close comparison of *Nach-a-wish* (Fig. 12.2) and *Rocky Mountain Indian* (Cat. no. 12) with the oil portrait of *Nezperee Indian* (Fig. 12.1) reveals that Kane used both drawings for the oil. The posture, facing towards the right, the hair length, the facial features (especially the mouth) and the neckline of the shirt have been taken from *Nach-a-wish*, while the model for the facepaint and for the fringe of hair over the forehead was the sketch in the exhibition (Cat. no. 12). The curious nose-piece seen in the oil appears in neither sketch. Obviously Kane added the decoration to correspond with the name of the tribe, although he made no mention of such a custom in his writings. The Nez Percé, moreover, despite their appelation, did not wear such ornamentation.[22] Other discrepancies between the sketches and the oil are the powerful upper body, barely contained by the canvas, the altered facial features resulting in an oval head and a more carefully proportioned face, and the tidier hair. The addition of a neck in the oil approximates European sitting posture, in contrast with the sketches, which suggest being seated on the ground.

The use of two sketches to make one painting and the additional transformations illustrate Kane's traditional artistic practice. He was following established rules in altering a sketch to conform to an ideal and to improve upon nature. Kane was using what he had learned in Europe to produce a portrait of a noble savage.

The remaining sketches, except that of the pipes, have been identified through their having been exhibited in the 1848 Toronto exhibition and through their inscriptions. They will be discussed in chronological order.

Kane arrived at Fort Pitt, on the North Saskatchewan River, in January 1848. During his month-long stay he made a point of studying Cree customs, including the gathering of a vengeance party by the Cree chief, Kee-akee-ka-sa-wow, to attack Blackfoot Indians[23] (Cat. no. 13). The custom consisted of gathering pipestem bundles from different families as a pledge that they would join in the attack. Kane convinced the chief that making sketches of the pipes would improve their power and was thus allowed to sketch them[24] (Cat. no. 14). Kee-a-kee conducted a special ceremony for opening the pipe bundles, during which he wore a wolf-skin on his shoulders, visible in the sketch. The portrait sketch served as a model for an elaborate oil (Fig. 12.4) used to illustrate the original edition of *Wanderings*. It is another dramatic example of Kane's method of elaborating his portrait sketches to produce the image of the noble savage.

In April of the same year, Kane arrived at Rocky Mountain Fort, where he sketched *Pea-a-pus-qua-hum* (Cat. no. 15) and the landscape *Cree or Assiniboin Lodges in front of Rocky Mountain Fort* (Cat. no. 16). Both works are carefully finished, in keeping with the fact that he stayed at the fort for two weeks and thus had plenty of time for careful recording. Kane sketched many of the Hudson's Bay Company forts at which he stayed, likely out of a feeling of duty to the Company but also as landmarks of security during an otherwise hazardous voyage. The landscape sketch was the model for the oil *Rocky Mountain Fort* (Fig. 12.5). Contrary to the changes he made in his portraits from model to final work, there are very few alterations in this landscape, because the sketch, with its elevated prospect and central division balancing the fort and the Indian camp on the two sides, had already been carefully composed according to the current practice of picturesque landscape painting.[25]

The fourth portrait, *Maydoc-game-kinungee* (Cat. no. 17), may well be the last sketch that Kane made on his journey. It was executed just a few days before he reached Sault Ste. Marie, where he considered his Indian travels finished. Kane wrote:

> The head chief of the Ojibbeways, who resides near the post, [Michipicoton] sat for me in his red coat trimmed with gold lace. These coats are given by the company to such Indian chiefs as have been friendly and serviceable to them, and are very highly prized by their possessors.[26]

The changes between the sketch and the final painting (Fig. 12.6) are not as striking as in other works; cliffs and sky have been added as a dramatic background. This is not an idealized Indian but an older man, whose dependence on the European is shown by his ill-fitting red jacket, white shirt and medal. The medal he holds in the sketch is a personal gift, struck in 1840 for the marriage of Queen Victoria and Prince Albert, and was not officially given to Indian chiefs[27] (Fig. 12.7). A comparison with the oil painting shows that Kane substituted the official George III medal, given to Indian chiefs following the War of 1812.

The change is once again towards generalizing the portrait.

The two major repositories of Kane drawings are the Royal Ontario Museum, which received the drawings owned by the Allan family in 1942, and the Stark foundation in Texas, which purchased the collection owned by Kane's grandson in 1957. With the acquisition of nine drawings and one oil sketch from the Bushnell collection, the National Archives collection has become an important one as well.

E. M.-M.

12.1 P. Kane
Nezperee Indian, 1848-1856
Oil on canvas
Royal Ontario Museum 912.1.72

12.2 P. Kane
Nach-a-wish, a Nez Perce Indian, July 1847
Watercolour
Stark Museum of Art, Orange, Texas
31.78/36 WWC 36

12.3 P. Kane
Painted faces of Chualpays women dancers, Fort Colville, August 1847
Watercolour
Stark Museum of Art, Orange, Texas
31.78/72 WWC 72

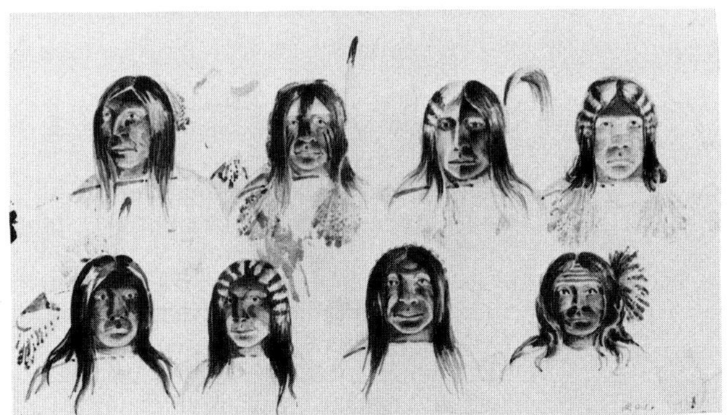

12.4 P. Kane
Kee-a-kee-ka-sa-coo-way, 1848-1856
Oil on canvas
Royal Ontario Museum 912.1.42

12.5 P. Kane
Rocky Mountain Fort, 1848-1856
Oil on canvas
Royal Ontario Museum 912.1.57

12.6 P. Kane
Maydoc-gan-kinungee, 1848-1856
Oil on canvas
Royal Ontario Museum 912.1.16

12.7 J. Davis
Victoria and Albert Marriage Medal,
1840
British Museum

---

1. Hudson's Bay Company Archives (Winnipeg), Governors' papers, D5/16; NA, MG 20, microfilm, reel HBC 3M 73, John Henry Lefroy to George Simpson, 30 March 1846. I would like to thank Lis Stainforth, Carleton University practicum student at the NA, for her help in researching this entry.

2. J. Russell Harper, *Paul Kane's Frontier* (Toronto: University of Toronto Press, 1971). This publication contains the most detailed account of Kane's life, and includes a catalogue raisonné of his paintings and drawings and a reprint of *Wanderings of an Artist among the Indians of North America from Canada to Vancouver's Island and Oregon through the Hudson's Bay Territory and Back Again*, published in 1859. All references to Kane's book will be to the reprint in this publication.

3. Kane's journal and logs are in the Stark Museum of Art, Orange, Texas, 11.85/5 and 11.85/4.

4. The NA owns a European sketchbook by Kane, Accession no. 1984-79.

5. Daniel Wilson, "Paul Kane, the Canadian Artist," *The Canadian Journal* (new series) 13 (1873):66.

6. Kane family papers, George Simpson to Hudson's Bay Company Posts, 31 May 1846, as quoted in Harper, *Frontier*, Appendix 10, p. 327.

7. This identification was made by Harper, by matching the numbers in the published list of works in the Toronto exhibition, *Catalogue of Sketches of Indians, and Indian Chiefs, Landscapes, Dances, Costumes, &c. &c. by Paul Kane* (November 1848), with either pencilled numbers that appear on the verso of certain drawings or with the inscriptions on others. Harper, *Frontier* Appendix 3, pp. 317-320. Thus Cat. no. 13 was no. 84, entitled *Ka-ah-ke-ka-sahk-a-wa-ow – The man that gives the war whoop – The head chief of the Cree tribe*; Cat. no. 15 was no. 85, entitled *Pe-a-pus-qua-hum – One that passes through the sky – a Cree Indian living among the Asseneboines, Rocky Mountain House*; Cat. no. 16 was no. 211, entitled *Rocky Mountain House*, and Cat. no. 17 was no. 81, entitled *May-dwi-ga-mi-ki-nun-ge – I hear the noise of the deer – The head chief of the Ojibwah tribe, on the Kaministaquoiah River.*

8. Nancy L. Kirkpatrick, "The Promotion of Art in Toronto: 1830-1870," Master of Museology thesis (University of Toronto, 1979), pp. 59-60.

9. Kirkpatrick, 5ff.

10. Earl Greg Swem Library, College of William and Mary (Williamsburg, Virginia), David Ives Bushnell papers, Dora Hood to Bushnell, 8 and 18 April 1931. These letters indicate that Bushnell purchased the oil sketch in 1931 with the help of Dora Hood, a Toronto antiquarian book dealer. Bushnell then contacted Mrs. Cassels directly for other items, according to correspondence from Cassels to Bushnell also in the Bushnell papers.

11. Upon Bushnell's death, his art collection was deposited in the Peabody Museum, Harvard University. In 1981, some of the items that had Canadian content were deaccessioned, and the NA was fortunate to be able to acquire them. Several other items in this exhibition, such as *Two Ottawa Chiefs* (Cat. no. 19), the Rindisbacher watercolours (Cat. nos. 6-11) and the Arctic scene by Louis Choris (Cat. no. 25), were part of Bushnell's collection.

12. Letter to the author from T.J. Brasser, Plains ethnologist, Canadian Museum of Civilization, 3 April 1987.

13. Kane, *Wanderings*, 118ff.

14. They were in the collection of Paul Kane Jr., the artist's grandson, who lived in Winnipeg.

15. David I. Bushnell Jr., "Sketches by Paul Kane in the Indian Country, 1845-1848," *Smithsonian Miscellaneous Collections* 99 (1940):9.

16. Kane, *Wanderings*, 118-119.

17. Paul Kane's Portrait Log, Stark Museum of Art, Orange, Texas, as quoted in Harper, *Frontier*, Appendix 2, p. 317.

18. This is not in Kane's handwriting. However, Kane's drawings are full of notations by others, such as perhaps Allan, Kane's wife and his son. This is another area requiring research.

19. Stark Museum of Art (Orange, Texas), Paul Kane collection, "Landscape and Portrait Journal, 1846-1848," 11.85/4, [99].

20. Frederick Webb Hodge, *Handbook of American Indians North of Mexico*, Part 2 (New York: Pageant Books Inc., 1959), 625.

21. Kane, *Wanderings*, 122-125.

22. B.A. Leitch, *A Concise Dictionary of Indian Tribes of North America* (Algonac, Michigan: Reference Publications, Inc., 1979), 308.

23. Kane, *Wanderings*, 144-145.

24. Stark Museum of Art, Paul Kane collection, "Landscape and Portrait Journal, 1846-1848," 11.85/4, [101].

25. Ian MacLaren, "Notes Towards a Reconsideration of Paul Kane's Art and Prose," *Canadian Literature* 113-114 (Summer 1987):179-205.

26. Kane, *Wanderings*, 157.

27. I would like to thank Norman Willis, medal collection, NA, for help in the identification of this medal.

Mid.(?) HALL, after Maria Spilsbury (1777-1820)

18. *A Moravian Missionary Conversing with the Eskimos at Nain, Labrador,* 1807–ca. 1830

Watercolour on paper

51.0 x 66.0 cm

Inscribed on mount in pen and brown ink, recto, l.l.: *...s* [?] *Spilsbury inv.* [?]; l.r.: *Mid* [?] *H.* [?] *Hall delin.... Labr* [?] *...d* [?]

Purchased in 1985

Accession no.: 1986-35-1

Negative no.: C-124432

This watercolour presented many mysteries when it first arrived at the National Archives. It was tentatively called *A Moravian Mission in Labrador*, and was dated from the first half of the nineteenth century.[1] Research indicates that the settlement depicted is probably Nain, on the coast of Labrador, where the first Moravian mission was established. The missionary in the watercolour, identified by his skyward gesture,[2] may be Jens Haven (1724-1796), the Danish Moravian who founded Nain. Accompanied by his son, he preaches to six Inuit, who have been given European features. The group is gathered outside a tent. In the background the settlement can be seen, with its simple wooden buildings and mission house. The watercolour is the work of an artist "Hall," who apparently copied a painting (or a print after it) by Maria Spilsbury. Little is known about the copyist, although the designation of "Mid" in the inscription may be an abbreviation of "midshipman."

The United Brethren (Unitas Fratrum) were also known as the Moravian Brethren, the Moravian Church and Church of the Brethren. This Christian group had their origins in fifteenth-century Bohemia. The Bible was their standard of faith, and they developed a strict system of discipline that emphasized conduct over doctrine. When new headquarters were established in Herrnhut, Germany, in the early eighteenth century, the renewed Moravian Church took on new vigour. After missions were successfully established in Greenland and the southern colonies of North America, their efforts were directed towards Canada – first in Labrador, and then, at the close of the eighteenth century – in Upper Canada.[3]

Jens Haven was determined to establish a mission in Labrador after the first attempt had failed following the murder of the mission's leader, John Christian Ehrhardt, in 1752. With the assistance of the Brethren and the help of Hugh Palliser, the governor of Newfoundland and Labrador, Haven first set sail for Labrador in 1764. "Little Jens," so-called because of his small stature,[4] had learned the Inuit language and wore native dress; he was welcomed by the Inuit, who proclaimed: "Our friend is come."[5] The declaration of friendship pleased Palliser, who was anxious to make peace with them and to ensure the security of trade and fishing in the area. Haven acted as a translator during the governor's peace treaty negotiations with the Inuit, and chose prospective sites for a new mission before going back to England. In 1770, after petitioning the British government, Haven was given permission to establish a mission at "Esquimaux Bay."

In 1771, Haven returned to Labrador to begin the construction of the settlement. He obtained the help of Mikak, an influential Inuit woman who had been brought to England in 1768.[6] With the aid of her husband, she guided the missionaries to the mouth of Nain Bay, where they would locate the settlement of Nain. By August 1771, an eight-foot-high palisade had already been built, and by the late fall the three married couples (among them Jens Haven and his wife) and eight single brethren were ready to spend their first Labrador winter in their newly finished house. The settlement was described in a 1773 official report:

> They have chosen for their residence a place called by the Indians Nonynoke, but to which they have given the name of Unity Bay.... Their house is called Nain. It is a good situation and well contrived. They have a few swivels mounted, although they have no occasion for them, as the Indians (Eskimoes) are awed more by their amiable conduct than by arms. There is a sawmill, which is worked by a small stream conducted thither by their industry from the mountains.... They have already one store-house, and they are building another, which will be pretty large.... They have a small sandy garden and they raise salads in tolerable perfection.[7]

The mission station was now a reality, and all that remained was to bring the Inuit into their flock. The first of the converts were baptized at Nain, and although Mikak was to continue to visit this settlement often before her death in 1795, ironically she was never among those baptized.

It is tempting to imagine that the watercolour depicts Jens Haven preaching to Mikak, since their destinies were so intermingled, but analysis of the work suggests that, rather than representing a precise historical event, the scene is fanciful. Although there are no known portraits extant of Haven, the details of the missionary figure conform to what is known of the founder of the Labrador missions. The small boy at his side might be his son John-Benjamin, of whom the Inuit were "exceedingly fond," and who was born in 1772.[8] Since the boy appears to be about six years of age, the scene would represent Nain in about the year 1778. Although at this time Haven was not actually stationed at Nain but at the second mission, Okak, founded in 1776, it is known that he travelled between stations. By 1778, Mikak would have been about thirty-five years old, and her son Tutauk eighteen. Since she had no more children, the presence of the small child who holds the hand of the woman in this painting, and of the baby, is problematic. It is therefore difficult to imagine that the Inuit woman is meant to be Mikak.

The absence of snow, the green washes of the landscape, and the sealskin clothing and bare heads indicate it is spring or summer. In the warm seasons when kayaks could easily navigate the ice-free waters of "Unity Harbour," the Inuit were more likely to travel to the missions such as Nain to hear the gospel. They would then camp near the main buildings in tents, like the one to the left of the picture, that were so spacious that they could contain a family of six, eight, ten and sometimes more. The missionaries would go to these tents to preach to them.[9]

The straight cut of the male garments without side vents, the pointed hoods, and the trousers cut close to the leg are consistent with Labrador Inuit clothing of the time. The female's *amauti atigi* (woman's upper garment, fur to the inside), with the long back tail and the shorter front flap, decorated with beads and carved bone pendants, is a costume that was found in Labrador. The fact that the hood does not seem large enough to hold a baby's body demonstrates a misunderstanding of the female attire, since in actual fact the *amaut* is more than a simple hood, but rather it is an enlargement of the back and shoulders of the *amauti*, which allows the mother to carry her child on her back, and even move it from back to front.[10]

The tiny village planted in the dreamlike setting is typically Moravian, with its wooden red-roofed buildings and its large fenced-in gardens. The general lay-out of the village compares favourably with known drawings and prints of other Moravian settlements in Labrador and Greenland (Figs. 18.1 and 18.2). There exist several drawings of Moravian missions by Jens Haven. One, entitled *Okkak in Labrador from the Island of Kiwalek* (Fig. 18.3), appears to have resulted from at least two preparatory sketches. Another is of *Nain in Labrador*, (Fig. 18.4).[11] Below the image in the Nain sketch there is a key written in German that identifies landmarks and buildings such as the public (mission) house, the sawmill and the salt house. After comparison with this drawing, the village in the watercolour is undisputably Nain, as it must have first looked. The topography is similar, the village being on an upwardly sloping bank at the foot of hills, and the configuration of the buildings is generally accurate. Even architectural details are the same in both, for example the mission house has a belfry, four windows and a central doorway on the side facing the bay. In the missionary's sketch, small trees are present, and a fascinating group of three figures stand in the foreground. The costumes they wear suggest a male and female Inuit, perhaps engaged in conversation with a missionary.

It is possible that the Hall watercolour represents the successful establishment of the first Moravian mission in Labrador at Nain. One of the more appealing theories is that the missionary (presumably Jens Haven) is preaching the gospel to the "First Fruits," or first Christian Inuit of Labrador, a concept that played a very important role in the eighteenth-century doctrine of the Moravians. Several known paintings by J.V. Haidt dating from the mid-eighteenth century deal with this theme.[12] The supply ship in the centre of the composition beside the missionary was the link with the homeland; it was crucial to the survival of the Labrador missions of the desolate coast. It is a symbol used in other Moravian illustrations.

The inscriptions on the mount of the watercolour were at first difficult to decipher, since they are partly cut off and damaged. Still, there appears a partially intelligible pen-and-ink inscription at the lower left, a surname followed by the abbreviation *inv.* (invenit, Latin for "designed it") and at the lower right, the name Hall, followed by *delin.*, (delineavit, Latin for "drew it"). Because of the manner in which the information appears in the inscription, it was initially thought that likely the watercolour was a copy from a print, although the print has not been found.

The suggestion that the surname in the inscription at the lower left, and thus the name of the artist of the original sketch, might be "Spilsbury"[13] led to the discovery of the oil painting, now lost, which must be the ultimate source of this watercolour copy. In 1807, Maria Spilsbury (1777-1820) exhibited *A Missionary of the United Brethren conversing with the Esquimeaux. Scene in the Terra Labrador, month of June; with a distant view of Nain* at the Royal Academy of Arts in London.[14] The missionary subject and the Labrador setting were quite different from the usual portrait, genre and religious subjects she had been showing since 1792.

Maria's father, Jonathan Spilsbury, was her link with the United Brethren. He married in 1775, and two years later Rebecca Maria Ann was born, surviving her twin brother who died at birth.[15] Jonathan was received as a member of the Moravian Church in 1781, and was admitted to Holy Communion the following year, although hopes of ordination as a minister were never realized. Although biographies state that Maria was a member of the Church of England, there is some evidence that she may have also joined the Moravian Church.[16] It seems that neither of them ever visited Labrador, although Jonathan must have had frequent contact with the Society for the Furtherance of the Gospel (composed of Moravian members, and ultimately responsible for the successes in Labrador), and may even have had the opportunity to meet Jens Haven.

Both Jonathan and Maria were members of the talented Spilsbury family of painters and engravers, active in England in the mid-eighteenth century. Jonathan (1737-1812) was a portrait painter, mezzotint engraver and miniaturist,[17] who settled on engraving as a career, once he realized his daughter was the more talented painter.[18] He produced mezzotint portraits of many Moravian clergymen, several of whom worked in North America, including Benjamin La Trobe, John Gambold and Samson Occam.[19]

The Spilsburys were not well off, but fortunately Maria's artistic endeavours were recognized at an early age, with one of her first pictures being exhibited at the Royal Academy in 1792 when she was just fifteen years old. A second picture from this early period is a striking self-portrait of the artist at the age of sixteen.[20] She became a fashionable and sought-after artist as her career developed, and she eventually executed many commissions for the Prince Regent, her chief patron. The words of James Northcote, as recounted by Joseph Farington (both artists were contemporaries of Maria Spilsbury), perhaps best describe her work:

> I prefer pictures painted by Miss Spilsbury afterwards Mrs. Taylor, a clever painter now forgotten; Her thoughts are *her own*, and are often very natural & beautiful.[21]

Could Maria Spilsbury have seen the Jens Haven sketch of Nain and based her painting on it? The sweet, fine-boned faces of her English children are very much like those of the Inuit depicted. The addition of the large ungainly-looking evergreen trees in the right foreground is an earmark of a European artist, such imaginary foliage often being used to enhance North American scenes (see Fig. 18.5). The flaps of the doorway of the tent that stand magically without supports and the misinterpretation of the female Inuit costume are errors that might be explained by the artist's unfamiliarity with the subject, since she had never been to Labrador, although such discrepancies can often be blamed on the copyist. An obvious weakness of the unknown amateur Hall would seem to be a lack of sophistication, seen in the awkward application of pigment, and the crude execution of detail, very unlike Spilsbury's own personal technique.

Whatever the inspiration for the composition, the result documents an intriguing part of Labrador's early coastal settlement, opened up by the zealous efforts of the Moravians in the early eighteenth century. Although these missions have for the most part died out, their effect on the Inuit has been long-term. This watercolour copy is the only known record of the unusual painting of Labrador created by a fashionable English painter. It must have caused quite a stir when it was exhibited in London in 1807.

M.M.

18.1 L. Kraatz, after L.T. Reichel
Nain in Labrador, ca. 1860-1870
Lithograph
Location unknown
Photograph courtesy of private collection

18.2 W.F. Neuhasen
Okkak in Labrador, ca. 1850-1860
Lithograph (?)
Location unknown
Photograph courtesy of private collection

18.3 J. Haven
Okkak in Labrador from the Island of Kiwalek, ca. 1781
Grey wash (?)
Location unknown
Photograph courtesy of private collection

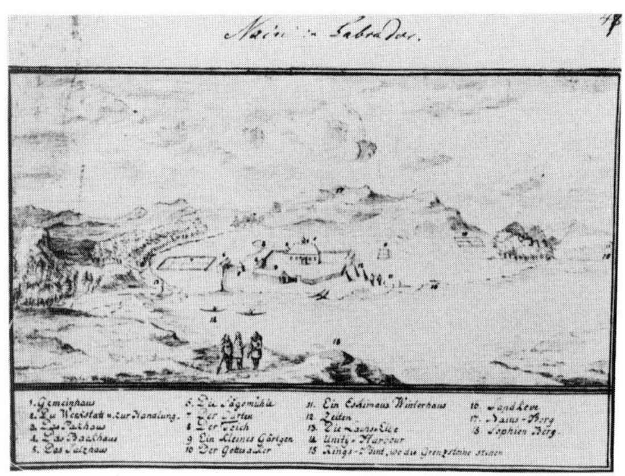

18.4 J. Haven
Nain in Labrador, ca. 1781
Pen and ink (?)
Location unknown
Photograph courtesy of private collection

18.5 Kronhiem and Co., for the Church Missionary Society

The Missionary Arriving at an Indian Camp, North-West America, ca. 1870

Colour lithograph

NA C-125031

---

1. Analysis of the paper by NA staff sets the date of the paper as ca. 1800-1830. Observations about the subject were made by Conrad Graham, registrar, and Betty Issenman, guest curator, McCord Museum, Montreal.

2. Letter to the author from Janet Halton, librarian at the Moravian Church House, London, 1 May 1985.

3. *Encyclopedia Canadiana* (Ottawa: The Canadiana Co. Ltd., 1958), 7:158-159.

4. Benjamin La Trobe, *A Brief Account of the Mission Established Among the Esquimaux Indians, on the Coast of Labrador by the Church of the Brethren or the Unitas Fratrum* (London: Brethren's Society for the Furtherance of the Gospel, 1774), 8 and letter to the author from Janet Halton, 1 May 1985.

5. Rev. B. La Trobe, *The Moravian Missions A Glance at 164 Years of Unbroken Missionary Labours* (London: The Moravian Church and Mission Agency, 1896), 20.

6. J. Garth Taylor, "The Two Worlds of Mikak," *The Beaver*, Winter 1983, pp. 4-13, and Spring 1984, pp. 18-25.

7. Rev. J.W. Davey, *The Fall of Torngak* (London: S.W. Partridge & Co. and Moravian Mission Agency, 1905), 142-143. Taken from the official report of the Mission "by Lieutenant Curtis, who had been deputed to investigate the work."

8. La Trobe, *A Brief Account*, 16.

9. La Trobe, *A Brief Account*, 11, 20.

10. Letter to the author from Betty Issenman, 25 July 1985.

11. Letters to the author from Doris Peacock, St. John's, Newfoundland, 24 June 1986; Carole Brice-Bennett, Memorial University of Newfoundland, 7 July 1986; I. Baldauf, chief archivist, Archives of the United Brethren, Herrnhut, Oberlausitz, German Democratic Republic, 16 May 1986. There are other related drawings at the Moravian Archives in Bethlehem, Pennsylvania. Source information provided by the Rev. Siegfried Hettasch, Perkins, Quebec, who recently was in charge of the Nain mission, has been invaluable.

12. Letter to the author from I. Baldauf, 16 May 1986.

13. Letter to the author from Janet Halton, 1 May 1985.

14. Algernon Graves, *The Royal Academy of Arts* (Wakefield: S.R. Publishers Ltd., and Bath: Kingsmead Reprints, 1970), 4:222.

15. Letter to the author from Janet Halton, 5 March 1986. Information in the London records seems contradictory, since it states that Jonathan "was an Elder, married to [?] Rebecca [?], delivered a son, Jonathan, June 24, 1779," although neither the German records nor the biographies mention this child. In Ruth Young, "Maria Spilsbury, 1777-1820. A Woman Artist of the Regency," *Country Life* (May 1938), xliv, it is stated that Maria "adored children, possibly because she was an only child, her twin brother dying at birth."

16. Letter to the author from I. Baldauf, 16 May 1986. The German records of the Moravian Church at Herrnhut contain biographical information about both Jonathan Spilsbury (the painter) and a Mary Spilsbury, who seems to have joined the Moravian Church. However, the information within the records is contradictory and does not correspond with that found in Ruth Young, *Father and Daughter Jonathan and Maria Spilbury* (London: The Epworth Press, 1952).

17. Young, *Father and Daughter*, 5. Some biographies confuse details of the lives of the artist's father Jonathan, and her uncle John. Young states that John, a younger brother, was also an engraver and publisher, who died before reaching the age of thirty.

18. Young, *Father and Daughter*, 20-21. Many thanks to Anita Burdett, formerly of the London Office of the National Archives, for research she conducted on this matter.

19. Freeman O'Donoghue, *Catalogue of Engraved British Portraits Preserved in the Department of Prints and Drawings in the British Museum* (London: British Museum, 1912), 3:19; 2:270; 4:317.

20. Young, "Maria Spilsbury," xliv.

21. Joseph Farington, *The Farington Diary* (New York: George H. Doran Company, 1924), 3:219.

SIR JOS JEBB.

Deputation of Indians from the Mississipi Tribes
to the Governor General of British North America - Sir George Prevost Bar. Lieut. General &c. in 1814.

UNKNOWN ARTIST and RODOLPHE VON STEIGER (1791-ca. 1835)

UNKNOWN ARTIST

19. *Two Ottawa Chiefs who with others lately came down from Michilimackinac Lake Huron to have a talk with their Great Father the King or his representative*, ca. 1813

Watercolour over pencil on paper

29.5 x 24.4 cm.

Inscribed in pen and brown ink, verso, u.l.: [Ta]*ken from Nature – /* [T]*wo Ottawa Chiefs who with / others lately came down from /* [Michi]*llimackinac Lake Huron to /* [ha]*ve a talk with their great Father / the King or his representative;* stamped in black ink, recto, l.c.: *SIR*JOS*JEBB.*

Bushnell Collection of Canadiana

Purchased in 1981 with the assistance of a grant from the minister of Communications under the terms of the *Cultural Property Export and Import Act*

Accession no.: 1981-55-41

Negative no.: C-114384

RODOLPHE VON STEIGER
(1791 - ca. 1835)

20. *Deputation of Indians from the Mississippi Tribes to the Governor General of British North America, Sir George Prevost, Bart. Lieut. General &c in 1814*, 1814

Watercolour with gouache and gum arabic on paper

30.4 x 36.9 cm

Inscribed in pen and brown ink, recto, l.l.: *R v Steiger del.*; b.: *Deputation of Indians from the Mississipi Tribes/to the Governor General of Brittish North America – Sir George Prevost, Bart. Lieut. General & c. in 1814.*

Purchased in 1989 with the assistance of a grant from the minister of Communications under the terms of the *Cultural Property Export and Import Act*

Accession no.: 1989-264-1

Negative no.: C-134461

Two of the most intriguing recent watercolours acquired depict Indian tribal deputations in Upper Canada during the War of 1812. The first, entitled *Two Ottawa Chiefs*, was acquired in 1981 and had been attributed to Sir Joshua Jebb because his name appears stamped on the work. In 1989, the National Archives acquired a second work at auction, entitled *Deputation of Indians from the Mississippi Tribes to the Governor General of British North America, Sir George Prevost, Bart. Lieut. General &c in 1814.* This work was sold at the same time as a companion piece entitled *Deputation of Indians from the Chippawa Tribes to the President of Upper Canada, Sir Frederic Ph. Robinson, K.C.B. Major-General &c in 1815*, which was acquired by the National Gallery of Canada (Fig. 19.1). The latter two watercolours are signed by "R v Steiger," stated in the sale catalogue to be Rudolph von Steiger, a Swiss-born officer who served in the De Watteville Regiment in Canada during the War of 1812.

All three watercolours relate to an important period in the history of British North America, when the active support of Indian tribes was required to maintain the British presence in Canada against American territorial ambitions. Their importance, as well as their interest, stems from their documentary content. The *Two Ottawa Chiefs* has been reproduced widely because of its rich and accurate documentation of Ottawa tribe artifacts and culture of the time,[1] the clothing and the trade cloth worn by the Indians,[2] and the trade silver they proudly display.[3] They also stand as portraits commemorating specific individuals.[4] There is little doubt about the purpose of this work. Based on the fort depicted in the distance and the geography of the area, the location has been identified as Amherstburg. Probably taken at Bois Blanc, the view shows Fort Malden across the narrow expanse of the Detroit River between the island and Amherstburg.[5]

The threat of war with the United States forced the British as early as 1808 to recognize the need to revitalize their relations with the native tribes. As a result, thousands of Indians visited Fort Malden in the years 1808-1814. Considered the key Indian centre in Upper Canada,[6] it was here that Matthew Elliot, "the King's representative," i.e., the superintendent of Indian Affairs at Fort Malden,[7] distributed supplies and presents to secure native loyalty to the King. At the same time, he was instructed to dissuade the Indians from premature attacks upon American settlers encroaching upon their lands in the Ohio and Mississippi River valleys. In July 1808, more than one thousand warriors and chiefs, including the influential leader Tecumseh, came to Amherstburg to receive gifts, and by the autumn of that year, more than five thousand Indians had visited Fort Malden,[8] all of them increasingly restless about developments in the American Mid-West.

The problems of Indian unrest reached a peak in November 1810 when two hundred Potawatami, Ottawa, Winnebago, Sauk and Shawnee assembled at Amherstburg for a council. Tecumseh acted as spokesman for the tribes, stating that they were on the eve of an Indian war to protect and regain their own land.[9] Up until the summer of 1811, British Indian Department officials strove, in councils with influential Indian chiefs, to prevent war with the Americans, but to no avail; at Tippecanoe on 7 November 1811, an American army defeated the Indians in a pitched battle. The Americans surmised, rightly or wrongly, that the Indians had been to some extent goaded by the British, yet another reason for them to declare war on Britain, which occurred in June 1812.

The *Two Ottawa Chiefs* may represent an early meeting between the Indians and the British Indian Department's representative, but the specific reference to Michilimackinac suggests a date later than July 1812. Michilimackinac, an American fort considered the key to the Indian country of the upper Mississippi valley,[10] had been captured by Captain Charles Roberts and a mixed command of 45 British soldiers, 180 loyal fur traders and 300 Ottawa and Ojibwa Indians on 27 July 1812. This early victory resulted in a swelling of Indian support for the British cause, with hundreds of Indians moving south from Michilimackinac to Amherstburg to join Maj.-Gen. Sir Isaac Brock. Brock, with 300 British regulars, 400 Canadian militia and 600 Indians under Tecumseh, then forced the surrender of Detroit on 16 August 1812.[11]

During the next year, Robert Dickson, agent and superintendent to the Western Indians, was responsible for sending fifteen hundred Indians to Amherstburg; in July 1813 Dickson arrived with a force of Ottawa as well as Ojibwa, Menomee, Winnebago and Sioux.[12] It is probable that the Ottawa Indians who came to Fort Malden in the summer of 1813 to meet with "the King's Representative" are the very ones depicted in the *Two Ottawa Chiefs*. By September 1813, the Americans had recaptured Detroit and taken Fort Malden, meaning that the journey referred to must have occurred before this date, which is before Jebb, the presumed artist, arrived in Canada.

The subject of the *Two Ottawa Chiefs* makes its similarity to the watercolour acquired in 1989 all the more notable. This work, *Deputation of Indians from the*

Mississippi Tribes, is also a "group portrait" of Indians who have made a special journey to meet with a British official during the War of 1812, in this case Sir George Prevost (1767-1816), the highest-ranking British officer in North America. In 1814, Prevost had requested a meeting with the sister and son of Tecumseh, who had been killed the previous autumn.[13] At the same time, Prevost indicated his willingness to meet any chiefs from the Western Indians, "as a deputation from their tribes," who might accompany Tecumseh's relatives.[14] This watercolour probably depicts several of these chiefs.

Stylistically there are many similarities with the *Two Ottawa Chiefs*, both subjects being depicted in a simple, naive yet direct manner, although the *Deputation* is less translucent, exhibiting a heavier use of watercolour, as if the composition had been reworked. The colours are similar, namely strong blues, reds and yellows, and some details in the two watercolours are almost identical, particularly the standing figure in the blue cloak with his right arm placed awkwardly behind his back. Although these two works are clearly related to one another, they are not by the same hand. Other copies of the *Deputation of Indians from the Mississippi Tribes* indicate some relationship between these two works, but its exact nature remains unclear.[15]

The *Treaty of Ghent*, ending the War of 1812, was signed on Christmas Eve, 1814. By its terms all posts and land captured during the war was to be returned to its original owners; the British regained possession of Amherstburg on 1 July 1815, and Michilimackinac was formally restored to the Americans on 18 July. At the same time, the United States undertook to end hostilities with the Indian tribes and to restore to them the rights and privileges they had possessed in 1811. The Indian chiefs, however, did not trust the Americans, and continued to maintain their alliances with the British Indian Department's officers at Fort Malden, accepting presents and seeking advice from their former allies. It was probably in this spirit that a group of Indian chiefs requested a meeting with Sir Frederick Robinson (1763-1852), the provisional lieutenant-governor of Upper Canada, in July 1815.[16] *Deputation of Indians from the Chippawa Tribes* (Fig. 19.1), probably depicts this visit.

The two watercolours of the deputations belonging to the National Archives and the National Gallery of Canada, respectively, are very similar. The compositions are related, with figures arranged in a frieze-like variety of poses. In each of the works there is a figure in a blue cloak with his right arm behind his back, a central seated figure distinguished by trade silver, and a figure on the far right seen from behind with a fur cloak pulled around his body. The colouring is also very close, and details of costume and trade silver are treated identically. Again, there are existing copies of this composition, which makes one consider more closely the relationships among the various compositions.[17]

Although the *Two Ottawa Chiefs* depicts a smaller group, it has at some point been cropped on one side, and one speculates as to whether there were once other figures in the picture, in addition to the two seated near the canoe in the background. Based on its similarities in style and subject to the von Steiger watercolours, one must also speculate about the existence of other variants, its relation to von Steiger's works, and whether its artist was also Swiss.[18]

Because of the importance and strength of *Two Ottawa Chiefs*, it is remarkable that there would be few other known works by the same artist or other works bearing the same stamp mark of "Sir Jos. Jebb." Joshua Jebb (1793-1863) was born at Chesterfield, Derby, was educated at the Royal Military Academy at Woolwich, and was posted to Canada as a first lieutenant in the Royal Engineers in October 1813. He served under the command of General de Rottenburg on the frontier of Lower Canada until the summer of 1814, and following that under Sir George Prevost. Remaining in Canada after the war, he performed duties for the military, including a survey of a canal route between Kingston and the Chaudière Falls in 1816. Jebb returned to England in 1820 and was stationed at Woolwich, then spent a short time in the West Indies in the late 1820s before being appointed adjutant to the Royal Sappers and Miners at Chatham in 1831. As the surveyor general of prisons, he designed several county and borough prisons, his most important contribution being to the construction of the Model Prison at Pentonville.

Is the *Two Ottawa Chiefs* really executed by Sir Joshua Jebb? The peculiar stamp on the watercolour is more like a collector's stamp than an artist's signature, and the few watercolours and other works of art known to be by Jebb do not have the same stylistic qualities.[19] It is more likely that the name stamped on the work indicates that Jebb owned it. Furthermore, he was not posted to Canada before October 1813, and the work was probably executed in July of that year.

Having questioned Jebb's relationship to *Two Ottawa Chiefs*, we should turn to the presumed artist of the other watercolours, Rodolphe von Steiger of the De Watteville Regiment. When the works were sold,[20] it was stated that von Steiger had been born in Switzerland in 1791, served as an officer of the De Watteville Regiment in Canada from 1813 to 1816, received serious head injuries in a battle before Lake Erie in September 1814, returned to Switzerland in 1816, and died in Berne in 1824 ostensibly as a result of his injuries. In fact, further research indicates that Rodolphe von Steiguer (later corrected in the *Army Lists* to von Steiger) joined the De Watteville Regiment as a lieutenant on 27 March 1811,[21] and came to Canada with the regiment in spring 1813, being stationed in Kingston by June.[22] In May 1814, the regiment participated in the raid on Oswego, and later in the summer was sent to the Niagara frontier, where it participated in the August 1814 attack on Fort Erie.[23] On 17 September 1814, during an American sortie from Fort Erie to attack the British besiegers, Lieutenant von Steiger was slightly wounded.[24] A second officer, a captain also named Rodolphe von Steiger, was captured. This Captain von Steiger was later exchanged by the Americans, and under the terms of the exchange, was sent to Portugal in October 1814.[25] Captain von Steiger later returned to Canada, and after he was placed on half-pay in October 1816, settled in Three Rivers. Here he became a justice of the peace in 1817, a commissioner of oaths in 1818 and a captain in the 7th Battalion of the Eastern Townships in 1821.[26] In 1825, he applied for a medical license,[27] and in the same year he resigned from the Army.[28] He died in Sorel in May 1847.

Lt. Rodolphe von Steiger may have remained behind on the Niagara Frontier as a result of his wounds when Louis De Watteville and Lt.-Gen. Sir Frederick Philipse Robinson exchanged commands in October 1814, De Watteville going to Kingston and Robinson taking over on the Niagara Frontier.[29] It may be that von Steiger was attached to Robinson's command in some capacity over the next year or so, which may account for his watercolour of the *Deputation of Indians from the Chippawa Tribes*. As Robinson was the provisional lieutenant-governor of Upper Canada only from July to September 1815, the watercolour probably dates from this time. In April 1816, Lieutenant von Steiger was stationed at Kingston with the rest of the De Watteville Regiment.[30] The 1825 *Army List* notes that Lt. Rodolphe von Steiger had been placed on half-pay on 24 October 1816,[31] and he continued to be listed on foreign half-pay in the British *Army Lists* until 1835, when his name no longer appears. He is not listed in the death or retirement lists, but it may be presumed that he died in either 1834 or

1835. It is probable, therefore, that the Lieutenant von Steiger who joined De Watteville's regiment in 1811 is the artist who signed the two watercolours sold at Sotheby's in May 1989, one of which is now in the National Archives collection. Rudolphe von Steiger was certainly in a position to execute the two watercolours dated 1814 and 1815, but his connection with the earlier one of *Two Ottawa Chiefs* is tenuous. What is clear about the three watercolours is that they are fascinating and important works, two of which add significantly to the Documentary Art and Photography Division's holdings relating to the conduct of the War of 1812, and to our knowledge of an important period in European-native relations.

A.T. and J.B.

19.1 R. von Steiger

Deputation of Indians from the Chippawa Tribes to the President of Upper Canada, Sir Frederic Ph. Robinson, K.C.B. Major-General & c in 1815, 1815

Watercolour

National Gallery of Canada 30273

1. Ted J. Brasser, *Bo'jou Neejee – Profiles of Canadian Indian Art* (Ottawa: National Museum of Man, 1976), 193.

2. William C. Sturtevant, ed., *Handbook of North American Indians* (Washington: Smithsonian Institution, 1978), 15:783.

3. N. Jaye Fredrickson and Sandra Gibb, *The Covenant Chain: Indian Ceremonial and Trade Silver* (Ottawa: National Museums of Canada, 1980), 111.

4. *The Painter and the New World* (Montreal: The Montreal Museum of Fine Arts, 1967), no. 64.

5. We would like to acknowledge the assistance of Tim Dubé of the Manuscript Division, NA, who confirmed that the view depicted was Fort Malden and suggested that it was taken from the southern end of Bois Blanc looking north towards the fort.

6. Robert S. Allen, "The British Indian Department and the Frontier in North America 1755-1830," *Canadian Historic Sites: Occasional Papers in Archaeology and History* (Ottawa: Indian and Northern Affairs, 1975), 14:5-125.

7. Matthew Elliot was reinstated as superintendent in 1808 to replace the incapacitated Thomas McKee who had replaced Elliot in 1797. See *Dictionary of Canadian Biography* (Toronto: University of Toronto Press, 1983), 5:301-303.

8. Allen, 70.

9. Allen, 70.

10. Allen, 82.

11. Allen, 74.

12. Allen, 76.

13. NA, British Military and Naval Records, RG 81A, Correspondence of the Military Secretary of the Commander of the Forces, vol. 1222, p. 27, Noah Freer (military secretary to Prevost) to Lt.-Col. Gordon Drummond, 29 January 1814. The letter mistakenly refers to Tecumseh's "daughter" and son.

14. NA, RG 8 IA, vol. 1222, p. 27, Freer to Drummond, 29 January 1814, and NA, Sir Gordon Drummond papers, MG 24 A41, letterbook, p. 52, Drummond to Prevost, 16 February 1814. This last letter lists:

Chippewa	Kishkawabask
Ottawa	Naiwash
Sarcee [?]	Mitah
Sauk	Walassika
	Kenailonnak
Kickapoos	Waikitchai
Delawares	Pammanac
Munceys	John Gray
	Wabackwiba or White Horn
Six Nations	Oanagechtai
	Twalva or PaacOetus
Winebago	Vapapkum

and Tecumseh's sister and son of the Shawnees.

Drummond indicated, "I have afforded them every accommodation & supplies," and stated that they travelled via Kingston.

15. In the Missouri Historical Society (MHS) collection there is another watercolour titled and inscribed *Deputation of Indians from the Mississippi Tribes to the Governor General of British North America Sir George Prevost, Bart: Lieut: General &c in 1814*, which is attributed to Peter Rindisbacher. See Alvin Josephy Jr., *The Artist Was a Young Man: The Life Story of Peter Rindisbacher* (Fort Worth: Amon Carter Museum, 1970), plate XIX. Its style and date, however, make this clearly erroneous. In some details this work is very close to the *Two Ottawa Chiefs*, particularly in terms of the use of colours, the same standing Indian figure with his arm awkwardly behind his back, and the long bow leaning to the right. The artist had to be familiar with both of the NA's watercolours in order to execute the MHS work, but at the same time a comparison of the NA's version and the Missouri version demonstrates that the latter is very likely only a copy of the NA work. The absence of some compositional elements, differences in colouring, the cavalier treatment of details in the faces and trade silver all indicate that the NA's version preceded the MHS one.

16. NA, RG 8 IA, vol. 258, p.172, Lt.-Col. Reginald James, commanding officer at Amherstburg, to Lt.-Col. Cadwell, Indian Department official, 18 July 1815; regarding arrangements for the deputation of Indian chiefs at Fort Erie.

17. A second version of *Deputation of Indians from the Chippawa Tribes* is in a private collection, but it was examined in the NA in 1968, at which time it was attributed to the same artist who did the *Two Ottawa Chiefs*. However, in comparing it to the Missouri Historical Society (MHS) version of the *Deputation of Indians from the Mississippi Tribes*, it is evident that they are intended to be a set; not only is the wording in the inscription similar, but it is also written in the same hand. The inscription on the MHS *Deputation...from the Mississippi Tribes* is written below the image on the mount on which the watercolour is laid down; the inscription on the private collection *Deputation...from the Chippawa Tribes* is written below the image but on the same piece of paper. A comparison of the work in the private collection with the von Steiger in the National Gallery shows a crude handling of details and the absence of some design elements that would lead one to believe the von Steiger work was probably the original version. In Switzerland, there is a third set of deputations in the Bernisches Historisches Museum in Berne, executed by Kaspar Anton Menteler (1783-1837), which are said to be copies of the set by von Steiger, but this has not been pursued.

18. The links with Switzerland are intriguing. The von Steigers were formerly held in a private collection in Switzerland, and the private collection *Deputation of Indians from the Chippawa Tribes* had been purchased in Switzerland. Sir George Prevost, referred to in one of the inscriptions, was of Swiss ancestry, as was Peter Rindisbacher, to whom one of the copies was attributed.

19. Jebb was the author of numerous technical works written after his return to England, many of which contain lithographed illustrations bearing his signature. In such compositions, Jebb's military artistic training is shown by compositions that, while competently executed, lack the naive, anecdotal qualities of the *Two Ottawa Chiefs* While a few works attributed to Jebb have surfaced at auctions over the past decade, none bear the distinctive stamp. Lot 223 of the Montreal Book Auction of 31 October 1974 listed "2 different sketches, pen and ink, and one copy of a sketch" of the Quebec Driving Club by Sir Joshua Jebb. Erroneously listed as pen and inks, these small informal lithographs were printed at the Royal Engineers Office in Quebec and were probably executed and used by members of the club as letterheads or to decorate club menus and announcements. Another Quebec Driving Club lithograph, a variant of *Patron His Excellency Matthew Lord Aylmer K.C.B. &c.*, in a private collection, bears the inscribed name of Sir Joshua Jebb on the verso. According to Mary Allodi, curator, Royal Ontario Museum, the names written on these prints may indicate the original owners, members of the club, or the inventors of the sketches. Watermarks indicate that the works in the Montreal Book Auction and others listed in Allodi's *Printmaking in Canada* were executed in the 1830s, long after Joshua Jebb had left Canada. Since they were printed in Quebec, it seems likely that Jebb's name was appended to them to indicate that they be sent to him, or were delivered to him and marked once they were in his collection. Lot 224 from the Montreal Book Auction, *Ice Cutting on the St. Lawrence*, by Sir Joshua Jebb, is described as "Ice Cutters and military officers in foreground, city of Quebec in background." Although listed as a pen and ink sketch, it may also be a lithograph, and it is dated 183?. Finally, a pencil and watercolour drawing entitled *Iroquois Half-breed, Hudsons Bay Company Service*, offered in the Reford collection sale, Sotheby's (Toronto), 27-29 May 1968, lot 238, is inscribed *Sir Joseph Jebb, Royal Engineers, circa 1839.* There is little doubt that the name should be that of Sir Joshua Jebb (the stamp on the *Two Ottawa Chiefs* uses only the abbreviation "Jos"). The present location of this work is unknown, and the black and white illustration in the catalogue does not permit a rigid comparison with the *Two Ottawa Chiefs*; the two works, however, do not appear to be by the same hand. This may be another work in the collection, rather than one by Sir Joshua Jebb.

20. Sotheby's (Toronto), *Important Canadian Art*, 17 May 1989, lots 228 and 229.

21. *Army List*, 1814, p. 475.

22. *Dictionary of Canadian Biography* (Toronto: University of Toronto Press), 7:897.

23. Charles H. Stewart, comp., *The Service of British Regiments in Canada and North America: A Resume*, 2nd. edition (Ottawa: Department of National Defence, 1964), 407.

24. *Select British Documents of the War of 1812*, (Toronto: The Champlain Society, 1926), vol. 3, Part I, 199.

25. *Army List*, 1815, p. 667.

26. Entries in the *Quebec Gazette*, 16 October 1817, 31 December 1818, and 9 April 1821.

27. NA, Quebec, Lower Canada, Canada East: Applications for Licences, Bonds and Certificates, RG 4 B28, Medical Licences, vol. 50, pp. 1041-1044.

28. *Army List*, 1827.

29. *Select Documents*, vol. 3, Part I, 229, letter from Lieutenant-General Gordon Drummond to Sir George Prevost, 23 October 1814.

30. NA, RG 8 IA, vol. 1, pp. 59-60, financial accounts for von Steiger at Kinsgston, April 1816.

31. *Army List*, 1825, p. 669.

FRANCES ANNE HOPKINS (1838-1919)

21. *Left to Die*, 1872

Oil on canvas

86.1 x 151.7 cm

Inscribed in brushpoint and brown paint, recto, l.l.: *FAH* [in monogram] / *1872*

Purchased in 1985 with the assistance of a grant from the minister of Communications under the terms of the *Cultural Property Export and Import Act*

Accession no.: 1986-28-1

Negative no.: C-136573

Frances Anne Hopkins did justice to both the artistic and the explorer traditions that ran in her family. She was the granddaughter of Sir William Beechey, R.A., the British portrait painter, and of Lady Anne Phyllis Beechey (née Jessop), the miniaturist.[1] Her father was Admiral Frederick William Beechey, geographer and explorer, who had sailed to the Canadian Arctic several times.[2] Apparently Mrs. Hopkins had no formal artistic training, but since, in addition to her grandparents, three of her uncles on her father's side were artists, two of them professional, she was likely given excellent instruction in painting and drawing at home.

In 1858, when she was twenty years old, she married Edward Martin Hopkins, chief factor for the Hudson's Bay Company. Since 1841, Hopkins had been the private secretary and friend of the governor of the Company, Sir George Simpson.[3] The Hopkins first lived in Lachine, and from ca. 1861 in Montreal, on a lovely property on Côte-des-Neiges. They occupied an important position in Montreal society and frequently entertained visiting dignitaries. In addition to a busy social life, Mrs. Hopkins had a family to look after. Her husband had three children from his first marriage, and together they had three more by 1863. She managed, however, to make time for art, and her sketchbooks contain homely drawings of her family, their house and the surrounding countryside, and scenes from various excursions. Beginning in 1860, she began showing her work in various exhibitions in London, England, culminating in the inclusion of her paintings in the Royal Academy's annual exhibitions intermittently from 1869 until 1918.[4] She was deeply impressed by her stay in Canada and continued to draw on her experiences here for the subject matter of her paintings long after her return to England.[5] Nor did she neglect the opportunity to exhibit in Canada. In the Montreal Art Association exhibition in 1870, she showed sixteen watercolours.[6] Canadians were not unaware of her artistic accomplishments. Prompted perhaps by the comment in the review of the Royal Academy annual of 1871, in which the painting was exhibited, Sandford Fleming used *Running a Rapid on the Mattawa River* as one of the illustrations in *Ocean to Ocean*, published in 1873.[7]

Her explorer spirit is demonstrated by the fact that she accompanied her husband on at least one major journey as far as the Port Arthur (now Thunder Bay) area, and on several short excursions when he was inspecting company posts. The sketches from these outings formed the basis for her large-scale oil paintings of Canadian landscape and canoeing scenes. The canoeing pictures are stunning portrayals of this uniquely North American mode of travel, romantic in their evocation of the era of the explorer, and yet very accurate in detail, because she had had direct experience of such travel.[8] In 1870, Hopkins resigned from the Hudson's Bay Company and the family returned to England.

A painting entitled *Left to Die* was exhibited by Mrs. Hopkins in the Royal Academy annual exhibition in 1872.[9] Although we cannot be certain, the large size of the painting, its corresponding date of 1872, and the elaborate frame that had accompanied it all suggest that it is the very one shown in London. Because the subject matter was not familiar to the British audience, the following note was attached for explanation:

> The Indians of the prairies when passing through an enemy's country on the 'war path' are obliged to desert and leave to his fate any one of the party who, disabled by wounds or sickness, cannot travel on horseback at the pace necessary for safety.[10]

There are only two known oil paintings of Indian subjects by Mrs. Hopkins, *Minnehaha feeding the Birds* (Fig. 21.1) and *Left to Die* (Cat. no. 21). They both belong to the then popular narrative style of painting, wherein some anecdote is partially depicted, leaving the viewer to puzzle over the details and to guess at the outcome of the story. It is possible that she was inspired to paint Indian subject matter because she had an opportunity to study Sir George Simpson's collection of paintings by Paul Kane depicting Indians. Her sources, however, are not direct contact with the Indian, but literature. Minnehaha was the wife of the noble Indian hero in the popular poem *The Song of Hiawatha* by Henry Wadsworth Longfellow, published in 1855. Although Mrs. Hopkins is not describing a specific scene from the poem, she portrays the young Indian woman in the same romantic spirit as had Longfellow: natural man in harmony with nature. *Left to Die* is much more dramatic and ominous. It depicts a Plains Indian sitting by a campfire in a vast prairie landscape, staring after a group of riders and a horse, presumably his own, about to disappear over the horizon. The posture of the Indian is reminiscent of classical sculpture, specifically the *The Dying Gaul*, which was well known through both casts and engravings. The biblical overtones of self-sacrifice and the classical posture reiterate the popular nineteenth-century view of the Indian as the noble savage. It is unlikely that Mrs. Hopkins witnessed such a scene of abandonment, but she may have heard of it in conversation or read about it in one of the many available travel accounts. A children's book, entitled *Savage Habits and Customs*, published in London in 1865, and which one of her older sons could have been reading, mentions the custom in connection with the Chippewa Indians of the Northwest:

> The Chippewas, who were *en route* for a scalping foray upon the Sioux villages... fell into an ambuscade. Four of their number fell dead in their tracks. Another, named the War Cloud, a leading brave, had a leg broken by a bullet. His comrades were loth to leave him.... But he commanded them to leave him, telling them that he would show his enemies how a Chippewa could die.
>
> At his request they seated him on a log, with his back leaning against a tree. He then commenced painting his face and singing his death song.[11]

Available research shows that Mrs. Hopkins did not travel further west than Port Arthur, and therefore did not visit Plains Indian territory. She may, however, have seen Plains Indians through her husband's close connections with the Hudson's Bay Company. Chance encounter, however, would not have resulted in the exactitude with which she has depicted Plains Indian clothing. Edward Hopkins had assembled a collection of Plains Indian clothing during his trips to the northwest, which he gave to the Oxford Museum in 1893.[12] Two items collected by Hopkins stand out in particular in their resemblance to what is being worn in the painting: a fringed deerskin shirt with quill epaulettes (Fig. 21.2) and a pair of deerskin leggings decorated with beads (Fig. 21.3). A close comparison reveals that Mrs. Hopkins made use of these very items in her husband's collection to add a measure of accuracy to an otherwise imagined subject.

Although we do not have contemporary commentary on the painting, there is a contemporary photograph of it in an album assembled by Capt. Thomas J. Grant, who was district inspector of musketry for North America from 1865 until 1870 (Fig. 21.4).[13] Since Grant was posted to Montreal, he may well have been acquainted with the Hopkins, since their time of residence in Montreal coincided. The album is a record of his stay in Canada and consists of photographs of events, people and picturesque views. Grant obviously considered Mrs. Hopkins' painting important, because he placed it on the first page of the album. The photograph bears the blind stamp of Arthur Lucas, a London art publisher.[14] Because the corners of the Grant photograph have been rounded for decorative purposes, the signature and date of the painting are not visible. Moreover, a comparison of the photograph with the painting reveals several differences between the two. The horizon line in the painting is much higher than in the photograph, and the number of riders in the distance has been increased from two (in the photograph), to four (in the painting). Close inspection of the painting reveals this lower horizon-line, and X-rays confirm it. In addition the *pentimenti*, or ghostly images, of the original riders are also discernible to the naked eye. This evidence suggests that the photograph records the first version of the painting, which was then altered to result in the composition as we see it. Mrs. Hopkins' reasons for reworking the canvas are not known, but the higher horizon-line evokes the vast prairie space better than the lower one did.[15]

Left to Die is a fascinating addition to the already rich collection of paintings by Frances Anne Hopkins owned by the National Archives.

E.M.-M.

21.1 F.A. Hopkins
Minnehaha Feeding the Birds, ca.1880
Oil on canvas
Minnesota Historical Society, St. Paul

21.2
Blackfoot or Piegan deerskin shirt fringed and trimmed with scalp locks
Pitt Rivers Museum, University of Oxford
1893.67.4

21.3

Blackfoot or Piegan men's deerskin leggings, with beads and scalp locks

Pitt Rivers Museum, University of Oxford
1893.67.8

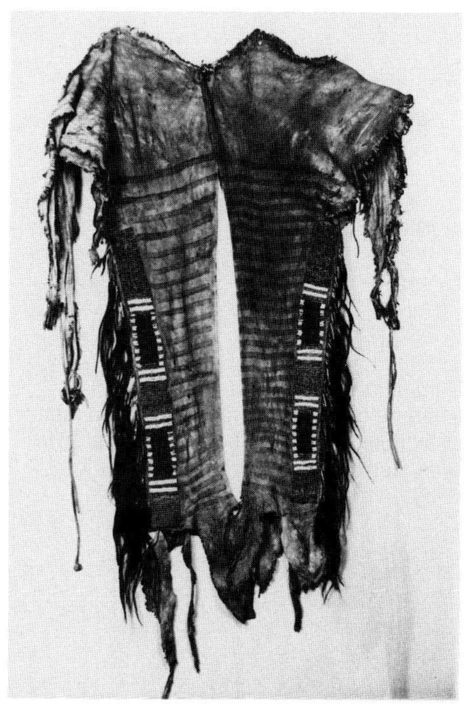

21.4

Left to Die, a painting by F.A. Hopkins, shown before reworking by the artist,
ca. 1880s

Photograph

NA PA-143696

1. Miss Jessop was Sir William's second wife. W. Roberts, *Sir William Beechey, R.A.* (London: Duckworth, 1907), 8. Most of the research for this entry was done by Douglas Shoenherr, curator, National Gallery of Canada, and Jennifer Trant, Canadian Centre for Architecture, Montreal, both formerly NA staff. In addition, Phillip Shackleton, who is currently writing a biography of the artist, provided some new information.

2. William R. O'Byrne, *A Naval Biographical Dictionary* (London: John Murray, 1849), 66-67.

3. For a detailed account of the life of both Edward and Frances Hopkins, see Alice M. Johnson, "Edward and Frances Hopkins of Montreal," *The Beaver* (Autumn 1971), 4-19.

4. Algernon Graves, *A Dictionary of Artists* (Bath: Kingsmead Reprints, 1970), 143; Algernon Graves, *The Royal Academy of Arts* (Wakefield: S.R. Publishers Ltd.; Bath: Kingsmead Reprints, 1970), vol. 2; *Royal Academy Exhibitors 1905-1970* (Wakefield: EP Publishing Ltd., 1979), 4:150.

5. Of the thirteen paintings she exhibited in the Royal Academy, nine had Canadian subject matter.

6. *Art Association of Montreal Sixth Exhibition, 1870* (Montreal: John Lovell, 1870), 9.

7. The reviewer had written: "The picture would make a capital illustration to a book of travels." In "The Royal Academy," *The Art Journal* 10 (1871): 178. George M. Grant, *Ocean to Ocean: Sanford Fleming's Expedition through Canada in 1872* (Toronto: James Campell & Son, 1873), plate 12.

8. K.G. Roberts and P. Shackleton, *The Canoe* (Toronto: Macmillan of Canada, 1983), 216.

9. Graves, *The Royal Academy*, vol. 2.

10. Graves, *The Royal Academy*, vol. 2.

11. James Greenwood, *Savage Habits and Customs* (London: S.O. Beeton, 1865), 114-115.

12. Letter to the author from B.A.L. Cranstone, curator, Pitt Rivers Museum, University of Oxford, 8 March 1985.

13. Captain Thomas J. Grant Album, NA, Accession no. 1960-51. There are two photographs of paintings by Mrs. Hopkins in the Grant album. The other one is *Running a Rapid on the Mattawa River.*

14. Rodney K. Engen, *Dictionary of Victorian Engravers, Print Publishers and Their Works* (Cambridge: Chadwyck-Healey, 1979), 241.

15. Recent X-rays of other paintings by the artist in the collection of the NA reveal that she invariably reworked her compositions.

J Richardson.

THEODORE J. RICHARDSON (1855-1914)

22. *Totem Poles and Houses of the Kaigani Haidas at Old Kasaan, Prince of Wales Island, Alaska*, after 1902

Watercolour and gouache with scraping out over pencil on grey paper

41.5 x 56.1 cm

Inscribed in brushpoint and brown watercolour, recto, l.l.: *T.J. Richardson* [TJR in monogram]

Purchased in 1982

Accession no.: 1982-80-1

Negative no.: C-102057

Theodore J. Richardson's artistic career occurred in the time-frame when American landscape artists were fulfilling a painterly manifest destiny.[1] As the North American continent was opened up by explorers and settlers, artists followed closely behind to record the new scenery. Richardson was one of the first to explore the new American territory of Alaska, purchased from Russia in 1867. Between the time of Johann Webber's visit with Captain Cook's last expedition in 1778 and the arrival of Richardson, only a handful of artists, for example Louis Choris in 1817 (Cat. no. 25) and more notably Frederick Whymper, in the 1860s, had painted on the Northwest Coast. Canadian artists, such as John A. Fraser and Lucius O'Brien, also travelled to the West Coast after 1885, when the Canadian Pacific Railway was complete, and joined Western artists, such as Edward Roper, in depicting the sublime aspects of the British Columbia landscape and the achievement of the CPR.

Richardson was born in Readfield, Maine, in 1855, and his family moved to Red Wing, Minnesota, when he was still a child.[2] Because he showed an aptitude for drawing, he was sent to an art college in Boston, and upon his return to Minnesota he became an instructor in art, penmanship and geometry at the State Normal College. His career was varied. He was involved in making artistic activities an established part of his community: He developed the art curriculum in the Minneapolis Public Schools and was a charter member, in 1883, of the Minneapolis Society of Fine Arts, from which both the Walker Art Center and the Minnesota Institute of Arts would later emerge. His discovery of Alaska was the result of a trip to California in 1884 to do illustrations for a Minneapolis newspaper. After being persuaded to take the steamer up to Alaska, the twenty-nine-year-old artist discovered the subjects that he would make his own for the rest of his life. Except for a period of six years spent in Europe (1896-1902), Richardson visited Sitka, then the capital of Alaska, annually until his death in 1914. Essentially a landscape painter in watercolour, he specialized in the painting of glaciers, the unique feature of the Alaskan landscape, and by 1891 had added views of West Coast Indian villages to his repertoire.[3] In a small rowboat fitted up as a floating studio, he travelled to remote Indian villages accompanied by Indian guides, recording what he, and most of his contemporaries, felt was a dying culture. In addition to his artistic preoccupations, he was also under commission to the Smithsonian Institution for several years to make observations of glaciers and of the Indian villages he visited.[4]

The village depicted in this watercolour, *Old Kasaan* (Cat. no. 22), which was located on Prince of Wales Island in Alaska, had been founded by a migrating group of Kaigani Haidas who had split off from the Haidas living on the Queen Charlotte Islands.[5] It was frequently visited because it lay along the route of the mail and freight steamers that brought wealthy tourists to visit the coastal Indian villages during the 1880s and 1890s.[6] The village seems to have been a favourite with Richardson also. Appearing in a photograph of the interior of Richardson's studio, likely taken after 1902 by E.W. Merrill of Sitka, are nine exterior views of Indian villages (Fig. 22.1).[7] A comparison of these paintings with photographs of the village reveals that at least seven are of Kasaan.[8] The village was abandoned by 1904, when New Kasaan was built close to a copper mine where Haida men could find employment.[9] In 1904 also, at least five totem poles were removed from the village to be shown at the St. Louis Exposition, and afterwards some were installed at the Sitka National Monument.[10]

Richardson's working method was to make small on-the-spot sketches that he would enlarge and finish in greater detail in his studio. *Totem Poles* (Fig. 22.2) seems to be the preliminary sketch for this painting, smaller both in size and in the segment of landscape it portrays. It shows the village in mid-day sunlight, an ideal time for sketching, with soft browns, greens and yellows predominating. In contrast, the larger watercolour is dramatically portrayed at dusk, when the house and poles are greyish-purple in the twilight. In the smaller sketch the carving on the poles has been completely left out, and only the location and relative height of each has been indicated. In the final sketch, however, the figures on the totem poles are rendered with an exactitude which, in its linear quality and accurate detail, is surely derived from photographs. Because Old Kasaan is one of the Northwest coast villages that have been extensively documented in photographs dating from the time when Richardson was painting in Alaska, it would have been easy for the painter to obtain such photographs. A comparison of some of these photographs with the watercolour also reveals that Richardson selected the most popular vantage point from which to portray the village – from the water looking east to west (Fig. 22.3). This angle shows the most complete vista of the village and the manner in which the inhabitants meant their homes to be seen.[11] From this vantage point the most prominent poles, the so-called Twins, grouped on either side of the small steps on the right of the painting, are clearly visible.

The fact that the village was dismantled in 1904 does not help in the dating of this watercolour because of Richardson's working method. He made several copies of the same scene, perhaps at different times.[12] However, because of photographic evidence, it is possible to establish that the preliminary sketch was done after Richardson returned from Europe in 1902. This is based on the presence and absence of certain structures in the village. The house on the extreme right was built after 1893, and a 1902 photograph shows it in the dilapidated condition depicted in the painting (Fig. 22.3).[13] In addition, a house in the centre of the village, with an attached totem pole, appears in a photograph from ca. 1900 (Fig. 22.4), but it does not figure in either the 1902 photo nor in the sketch (Fig. 22.2).[14] The sketch, therefore, could not have been done before 1900.

Richardson's views of Northwest coast villages played an important role in the development of Canadian art history. When Emily Carr and her sister Alice took a three-week Alaskan cruise in the summer of 1907, they met Richardson and visited his Sitka studio.[15] Carr described his paintings in her usual deprecating manner:

> ... drab little scenes which might have been painted in any place in the world. He did occasionally stick in a totem pole, but only ornamentally as a cook sticks a cherry on top of a cake.[16]

A comparison, however, of Carr's watercolours of that time with those of Richardson show that his are far more accomplished.[17] In addition, Carr's assessment of Richardson's arbitrary depictions of totem poles was quite wrong, as the foregoing discussion has revealed. He may not have been a daring painter, but he was accurate in both his topography and his depiction of the totem poles.

In contrast, Richardson's opinion of Carr's work was high and, upon seeing her sketching, he apparently said: "I wish I had painted that. It has the true Indian flavour."[18] It was his example and his praise that led Carr to make the decision "to picture totem poles in their own village setting, as complete a collection of them as I could."[19] This work, therefore, is highly important in documenting an early influence on the career of one of Canada's best-known artists, as well as being a work of documentary art in its own right.

E. M.-M.

22.1 E.W. Merrill
Theodore J. Richardson's Studio, Sitka, after 1902
Photograph
Minneapolis Public Library and Information Center M1758

22.2 T.J. Richardson
Totem Poles, 1902-1904
Watercolour
Burlington Northern Inc.

22.3 C.F. Newcombe
Kaigani village of Kasaan, 1902
Photograph
British Columbia Provincial Museum PN301

22.4 F. La Roche
Kasaan #1117, ca. 1900
Photograph
British Columbia Provincial Museum
PN9459

---

1. Some of the research for this entry was done by Douglas Schoenherr, curator, National Gallery of Canada, formerly NA staff.

2. Michael S. Kennedy, "Alaska artist: Theodore J. Richardson," *The Alaska Journal* 3 (Winter 1973): 31-40.

3. *The Alaskan*, 14 March 1891, quoted in Kennedy, 39.

4. *Minneapolis Journal*, 8 December 1912, p. 8.

5. Margaret B. Blackman, *Window on the Past: The Photographic Ethnohistory of the Northern and Kaigani Haida*, National Museum of Man, Mercury Series, Paper 74 (Ottawa: National Museums of Canada, 1981), 75.

6. Blackman, 79.

7. This photograph was dated 1890s in the article by Kennedy. However, Merrill only established himself in Sitka in 1899, at which time Richardson was in Europe. Another photograph taken during the same session includes the artist. The photographs therefore were likely taken after Richardson's return from Europe in 1902. "E.W. Merrill, Sitka's Father of Pictures," typescript manuscript from the Sheldon Jackson College Library, Sitka.

8. The photographs are published in Blackman, 98-112.

9. Blackman, 80.

10. Letters to the author from Margaret Blackman, anthropologist, State University of New York at Brockport, 15 September 1986, and from A. Laforet, West Coast anthropologist, Canadian Museum of Civilization, 8 September 1986.

11. Blackman, 71.

12. In the Merrill photo of Richardson's studio (Fig. 22.1), the large uppermost landscape in the second row from the right is an almost identical view of Kasaan as our painting. Close scrutiny reveals some differences in the reflections.

13. Blackman, 86.

14. This is the third house from the right in the ca. 1900 photograph, with a pole attached to its facade. In the 1902 photo there is a space, with some scaffolding, but no house. The scaffolding is visible in the watercolour. The totem pole remains.

15. Maria Tippett, *Emily Carr: A Biography* (Toronto: Oxford University Press, 1979), 74.

16. Emily Carr, *Growing Pains* (Toronto: Oxford University Press, 1946), 281-282.

17. Tippett, 74.

18. Carr, 282.

19. Carr, 283.

SIR HENRY WENTWORTH ACLAND (1815-1900)

23. *Oronhyatekha, Chief Mohawk*, 8-11 September 1860

Watercolour over pencil with opaque white on paper

54.6 x 36.6 cm

Inscribed in pencil, recto l.r.: *Burning Cloud / Oronhyatekha / Cainsville / Brant Co. / C.W. / Chief Mohawk*

In "Miscellaneous Sketches," vol. 6 of the Acland collection

Purchased in 1985 with the assistance of a grant from the minister of Communications under the terms of the *Cultural Property Export and Import Act*

Accession no.: 1986-7-255

Negative no.: C-122434

This portrait of Oronhyatekha is the work of the eminent Victorian doctor, Sir Henry Wentworth Acland, and was drawn during the tour of Albert Edward, the Prince of Wales, through North America from 15 July to 15 November 1860. It was the first official British royal tour of Canada and was made ostensibly in response to an invitation to open the Victoria Bridge at Montreal, and to lay the cornerstone for the Parliament Buildings in Ottawa. Queen Victoria sent the Prince in her stead. Acland was asked to join the party as his personal medical attendant, and travelled with the royal entourage through the Maritimes, Quebec, Ontario and the United States, participating in official functions and visiting various medical and scientific institutions along the way. In all, Acland made some 287 drawings during the trip, which he later mounted into six albums and gave to his wife Sarah at Christmas in 1860. The National Archives of Canada was fortunate to acquire the albums, along with a letterbook and a scrapbook of souvenirs, through the Acland family. On the first page of the letterbook, Acland described the collection thus: "About 250 sketches illustrate the several points & subjects alluded to in the letters – they are bound up for preservation, (some scarce worth their paper) in six volumes."[1]

Together the albums chronicle the sights, events and people encountered en route. Acland was obviously fascinated by Canada and, in his own words, "her advanced state of development," as well as her natural beauty, and he set out to describe "just what I see and do and know and what the whole race of 'our owns' [reporters] neither see nor know nor care to describe."[2] From the landing at St. John's, Newfoundland, where he visited a cod-liver oil establishment, to the wharves at Sarnia, Acland expressed his interest in many spheres of Canadian life through his sketches and watercolours. Attracted by natural phenomena, he recorded the tides of the Bay of Fundy (Fig. 23.1), the geological formations of the Saguenay River, the Rideau Falls, the Lachine Rapids and the Thousand Islands. Like many tourists past and present, Acland was captivated by Niagara Falls and produced a number of freely drawn views from above and below the thundering waters. He also demonstrated his able sense of humour by depicting the Prince completely draped in a water-proof cape, taking the requisite ride on the *Maid of the Mist* (Fig. 23.2).

His sketches also record the approaches to several waterfront towns and cities, with the welcoming flotillas and the accompanying hoopla (Fig. 23.3). More intimate moments are also recorded; there are several informal and candid portraits of members of the Prince's suite taken between tour stops and while pursuing private activities, such as canoeing on the Saint John River, or fishing on the St. Marguerite River in Quebec. Protocol prevented Acland from drawing a portrait of the Prince.

Acland's drawings are greatly enlivened by the informative and often humorous inscriptions he added to the album pages. One drawing of a riverside estate takes on a whole new dimension when his inscription reveals that it depicts the Quebec patriote, Louis-Joseph Papineau, saluting the Prince's boat as it passed his seigneury on the Ottawa River. The irony of this situation was not lost on Acland. Another drawing, which Acland humorously titled *Orange Bitters*, shows a view from the Prince's steamboat in the harbour at Kingston, Ontario. The local Loyal Orange Lodge, an Irish Protestant association, had gathered to welcome the Prince. To avoid the controversy such an acknowledgement on the part of the Prince would have invoked, the entourage stayed on board the ship, while well-wishers lined the harbour hoping for a glimpse of His Royal Highness.

Of particular interest to Acland were the Indians who were often part of the festivities and formal presentations arranged for the Prince (Fig. 23.4). He made some forty-five drawings of Indians, one of which is this portrait of Oronhyatekha, a young Mohawk from the Six Nations settlement near Brantford (Cainsville), Ontario, whom Acland met while in Toronto between 8 and 11 September. Acland recounted in a letter that upon seeing Oronhyatekha in a passageway, he asked if he could make a drawing of him.[3] The Indian agreed, and during the course of the sitting Acland found out about the young man's struggle to obtain an education.

Oronhyatekha, then nineteen years old, had already attended the Wesleyan Academy at Wilbraham, Massachusetts, and Kenyon College in Ohio, where he studied for three years. Impressed by his obvious intelligence and accomplishments, Acland offered to help him. The two were to meet at least twice more during the tour – on 14 September at Brantford, where Oronhyatekha presented an address to the Prince on behalf of the Six Nations, and between 15 and 17 September at Niagara Falls, when the two spent an evening discussing the plight of the Indian. Both agreed that education was the cornerstone of the Indian's future; Oronhyatekha insisted, however, that the customs of the Indian must be preserved if his identity was to be retained.[4] With this in mind, Oronhyatekha was encouraged by the Prince and the doctor to attend Oxford, where Acland was regius professor of medicine. Acland raised the necessary funds, and the young Mohawk entered St. Edmund Hall, Oxford, on 6 May 1862.[5]

Owing to some contentious circumstances, Oronhyatekha soon left Oxford[6] and returned to Canada, where he taught school and married Ellen Hill, great grand-daughter of Joseph Brant, in 1863. In 1864, he continued his studies at the Toronto School of Medicine, which was affiliated with the University of Toronto.[7] He obtained his medical degree in 1867 and practised for the next fourteen years in Frankford, Stratford and London, Ontario. In 1881, he abandoned this profession to become the international head of the Independent Order of Foresters, then a fraternal society primarily involved in life insurance and health care schemes. He remained active in this and other organizations and businesses, where his great capacity for management and leadership brought him much recognition. It is ironic that he should achieve such prominence in organizations some of whose very constitutions prohibited all but "whites" from becoming members. Oronhyatekha was always very proud of his Indian heritage and used his Mohawk name (which he translated as Burning Cloud) rather than Peter Martin, his anglicized name. During the course of his busy life, he maintained a correspondence with his mentor Dr. Acland and visited him in England on several occasions (Fig. 23.5). As a tribute to this friendship, he named his two sons Henry and Acland. Oronhyatekha died in 1907, at the age of sixty-five, as the result of a heart condition, and was laid in state at Massey Hall, Toronto, where he was mourned by thousands.[8]

Although Acland's portrait of Oronhyatekha does not possess great artistic merit, it is a striking record of the first encounter between the distinguished English doctor and the ambitious and intelligent Mohawk. Acland felt that he had "spoiled" the drawing and made Oronhyatekha "ill-looking."[9] His attempts to improve the face are evident by the correcting and heavy shading. His self-appraisal may have been harsh, but Acland had very high standards against which to measure his artistic endeavours.

Apart from his medical and scientific interests, he made a pastime of sketching and counted among his acquaintances several well-known English artists of the day, including Samuel Palmer, George Frederick Watts, Holman Hunt, John Everett Millais, Frederick Leighton and, in particular, John Varley and George Richmond, both of whom gave the doctor instruction. Probably the most interesting friendship was that with John Ruskin, the controversial art critic and advocate of the Pre-Raphealite artists, some of whom Acland came to know intimately. It is difficult to make any claim for the influence of these associations on Acland's artistic ability or style, but certainly his committed interest in art and architecture, combined with his pioneering work in medical education and public health, made him a keen observer of the Canadian scene at mid-century.

His portrait of Oronhyatekha, apart from being an interesting likeness, also shows the Indian costume in some detail. It is typical of that worn in the nineteenth century on ceremonial occasions by the Iroquois tribes, of which the Mohawks are one.[10] The costume combines traditional Iroquois dress with that of other tribes, as well as displaying elements of European influence. For instance, the head-dress, although similar to the bonnet-type worn by the Cayugas or Senecas, also among the Iroquois tribes, has more in common with the type worn by the Plains Indians, which has longer showy feathers. Such borrowings were not unusual in the nineteenth century, and were especially common in the costumes worn for official meetings with "whites," when elaborate, exotic costumes were expected. More unusual than the head-dress is the large gold nose ring. It is not considered characteristic of Iroquois adornment, and the only explanation for its presence comes from Oronhyatekha himself. While drawing his portrait, Acland asked the Indian why he wore the ring. He answered, "I take delight in all that concerns my people, this ring is part of the old Indian dress.... It is the custom, this is enough."[11]

Dr. Acland's drawings document in a most intimate way the course and tenor of the first official British royal tour of Canada. The exhaustive pace of the trip made it impossible for Acland to record every event, so he left it to the reporters to record the details of the parades, balls and receptions, while he concentrated on what he described as the more "personal" aspects of the trip.[12] One such personal experience was a visit to the village of St. Martin on Île-Jésus near Montreal. While visiting an observatory there, Acland took the opportunity to call on a few of the local residents, as was his habit. A resulting drawing (Cat. no. 38) is also part of this exhibition and demonstrates his concern with the living conditions of ordinary people.

Until the Acland collection came to light, visual documentation for the Prince of Wales' tour of 1860 was primarily made up of pictures in the illustrated newspapers and published accounts by various authors, including Gardner D. Engleheart, who, like Acland, was an official member of the royal party. A number of drawings related to the tour are in the royal collection at Windsor Castle. They are by George H. Andrews (1816-1898), who worked as special artist for the *Illustrated London News* during the Prince's Canadian tour. Photographs of the tour consist of some rather formally posed group portraits. By contrast to all of these, Dr. Acland's sketches afford a unique and private view of an important social event in Canadian history.

L.F.

23.1 H.W. Acland

The Suspension Bridge over the Saint John River, New Brunswick, 7 August 1860

Watercolour

NA C-96916

23.2 H.W. Acland
H.R.H. on the deck of the* Maid of the Mist, *Niagara Falls, 15 September 1860
Pen and ink
NA C-96941

23.3 H.W. Acland
The people in a state of wild enthusiasm... escort the Prince out of Saint John Harbour, New Brunswick, 7 August 1860
Watercolour
NA C-96914

23.4 H.W. Acland
Mrs. Thomas Thomas, Micmac Indian, Prince Edward Island, 11 August 1860
Watercolour
NA C-124443

23.5 S.A. Acland
Professor Acland and Dr. Oronhyatekha, ca. 1894
Photograph
Bodleian Library, University of Oxford, Minn collection 201/10

1. NA, Sir Henry Wentworth Acland papers, MG 40 Q40, "Letters from North America," p. 1. This is a book of transcriptions of letters and notes written by Acland in 1860 during the North American royal tour.

2. NA, MG 40 Q40, "Letters," p. 47.

3. NA, MG 40 Q40, "Letters," p. 113.

4. NA, MG 40 Q40, "Letters," p.116.

5. Joseph Foster, *Alumni Oxonienses: The Members of the University of Oxford, 1715-1886* (Oxford and London: Parker and Co., 1888), 1045. This information was further confirmed through the archivist of St. Edmund Hall, the Rev. H.E.J. Cowdrey, and the college librarian, S. Wernber-Møler, who consulted the Battel Books, Caution Book and Manciples Account Book for 1862.

6. Bodleian Library, University of Oxford, Department of Western Manuscripts, Acland manuscripts, d. 101, fol. 106; d. 91, letters concerning Oronhyatekha, 1860-1894. Thanks to Mary Clapinson, senior assistant librarian, for securing this information.

7. University of Toronto Archives, Department of Graduate Records, A73-0026. Thanks to assistant archivist Harold Averill, who provided this information and helped me to interpret it.

8. Selected biographies of Oronhyatekha: Oronhyatekha, *History of the Independent Order of Foresters* (Toronto: Hunter, Rose & Co., 1895), 61-69; Ethel Brant Montrue, *Canadian Portraits, Brant, Crowfoot, Oronhyatekha, Famous Indians* (Toronto and Vancouver: Clarke, Irwin & Co., Ltd., 1960), 131-158; Mary Temple Bayard, "Dr. Oronhyatekha," *Canadian Magazine*, vol. 7, no. 2 (June 1896), 135-142. These biographies contain much the same information and should be studied in conjunction with the original documentation referred to in notes 4, 5 and 6. There are discrepancies between the published biographies and this documentation regarding Oronhyatekha's Oxford education.

9. NA, MG 40 Q40, "Letters," pp. 115-116.

10. I am indebted to Michael Foster, Iroquois ethnologist, Canadian Museum of Civilization, for his comments on the costume worn by Oronhyatekha in Acland's drawing. In addition, the following sources were consulted: Lewis H. Morgan, *League of the Ho-dé-sau-nee or Iroquois.* (New York: Dodd, Mead and Company, 1901); Bob Gabor, *Costume of the Iroquois* (Ohsweken, Ontario: Iroqrafts, 1983); Gertrude Prokosch Kurath, *Dance and Song Rituals of Six Nation Reserve, Ontario*. Bulletin No. 220, Folklore Series No. 4 (Ottawa, National Museums of Canada, 1968), 170-175.

11. NA, MG 40 Q40, "Letters," p. 114.

12. NA, MG 40 Q40, "Letters," p. 47.

A PLACE IN HISTORY

Artists in a New Land

Few subjects eluded the artists' scrutiny as they recorded the changing face of Canada during the critical years of exploration and development in the eighteenth and nineteenth centuries. Among the highlights of our recent acquisitions are depictions that carry us from a bustling city to an isolated northern coastline, and from a picturesque farm in New Brunswick to the front lines of the North-West Rebellion. Most of the artists represented were gifted amateurs whose skill and keen observations have also left us with pictures of everyday events such as an ice-skating party and maple sugar making, as well as natural wonders like the aurora borealis and Niagara Falls. As artists in a new land, they have provided us with valuable records that chronicle the aspirations and endeavours of Canadians during this formative period of our history.

H.M.S "Resolute".
Abandoned 15th May. 1854.

WILLIAM THOMAS MUMFORD (1830-1908)

24. *HMS "Resolute" Abandoned 15th May, 1854*, 1854

Brown wash with red and blue watercolour over pencil on paper

12.1 x 20.4 cm

Inscribed in pen and brown ink, recto, b.: *H M.S "Resolute". | Abandoned 15th May. 1854.*

From "Private Journal Of an Expedition to the Arctic Regions to ascertain the fate of Sir John Franklin, and his Crews, under the Command of Captain Sir, Edward Belcher Kt., C.B. ...in the years 1852.3.4. By W.T. Mumford, late of H.M.S. Resolute," ca. 1854-1855

Purchased in 1985 with the assistance of a grant from the minister of Communications under the terms of the *Cultural Property Export and Import Act*

Accession no.: 1986-18-26

Negative no.: C-126055

In 1845, Sir John Franklin and his crew of 129 men left England aboard HMS *Erebus* and HMS *Terror*, on what was to be a fatal attempt to discover the North West Passage between the Atlantic and Pacific oceans. When Franklin was not heard from after three years, a critically lengthy period for his survival in the Arctic, an unparalleled series of maritime relief expeditions were begun, funded by the British government and by private individuals, most notably Lady Franklin.

After their previous attempts were criticized, the British Admiralty launched a final search expedition in the spring of 1852. Five vessels, under the command of Canadian-born Sir Edward Belcher, sailed north under orders to determine the fate of Franklin's lost expedition. They were also to provide assistance to Commander McClure and Captain Collinson and their long overdue vessels, HMS *Investigator* and HMS *Enterprise*. Their search for Franklin had been sent out in 1850, and had taken them from the Pacific Ocean to the Arctic through the Bering Strait.

Among the ninety men on board the *Resolute*, there was a young member of the carpenter's crew named William Thomas Mumford, who had previously attempted to join the search parties of Ross, Collinson and Austin.[1] The twenty-two-year-old seaman kept a personal journal recording daily activities of the trip, as did many of the ordinary seamen and officers. Some, like Mumford, also produced drawings, adding visual documentation of the journey to the written accounts. Mumford's included topographical scenes, depictions of the ships and the hazards they encountered, and renderings of events of the voyage.[2]

The Mumford journal is approximately 250 pages long and is dated ca. 1854-1855. In addition to the manuscript entries, it is interleaved with sixteen largely brown wash drawings, four pencil drawings, two maps, a list of animals hunted, and seven printed playbills. Letters of a later date, written to Mumford from his captain, Henry Kellett, and from Capt. F.L. McClintock, as well as poems, a prayer and newspaper clippings, are also found within the journal. This volume is an autograph copy of the original, which was damaged on the sea voyage home. When his ship was abandoned, the original was among the allowable five pounds of personal belongings he packed on the sledge. Heavy gales encountered by his rescue ship HMS *Phoenix* caused her to take on water, damaging the journal. An unsuccessful attempt was made to dry it in a hot oven for ten hours, leaving it in a "sad plight." The volume was rewritten in England, and the good condition of the sketches suggests that the majority were re-worked at this time.[3]

The journal begins with a decorated title page (Fig. 24.1), an introductory sheet of calligraphy embellished with scrolls and floral motifs that may have been executed by a professional calligrapher at Mumford's request upon his return to England. The general awkwardness and simplicity characterizing the drawings that follow suggest that Mumford had no professional art training. The drawings record the path of the *Resolute* as it passed from the Orkney Islands in Scotland to the first glimpse of Greenland and as it sailed on through Barrow Strait to Beechey Island, approaching Melville Island. The first winter, 1852-1853, was spent here, near the smaller Dealy Island. Four detached pencil sketches on green paper, dated 1852, are likely some of Mumford's original Arctic sketches that have survived. Two of these relate to the finished wash drawings, *The First View of the Coast of Greenland, Cape Desolation*, 21 May 1852 (Fig. 24.2), and *Winter Quarters in Melville Island 1852-3. Taken from the East*, winter 1852-1853.

The sketches record the most exciting moments of the voyage, such as a scene of the *Resolute* almost keeled over in the crushing pack ice at Melville Bay, with her companion ship lying helplessly by. Mumford sketched Beechey Island, where the *North Star* was left as a rendezvous depot ship. There he visited and described the graves of three of Franklin's men, W. Braine, John Hartnell and John Torrington. Their bodies were exhumed and examined by Canadian scientists in 1984, and again in 1986.[4] The tests conducted on tissue samples suggest that lead poisoning was a major cause of the failure of the Franklin expedition. Mumford was witness to the discovery of the missing vessel HMS *Investigator*, found frozen in at Bank's Land, when, as part of Lieutenant Pim's exploratory sledging party of April 1853, their meeting with Captain McClure and discovery of his ship effectively joined the known east and west segments of the North West Passage. The watercolour *"Resolute" & "Intrepid" in Winter Quarters 1853-54. Taken from the "Long Walk" looking Northeast* (Fig. 24.3) records the second winter spent north of Prince of Wales Land. The top-decks of the vessels were covered over with wagon-cloth so that the crew could exercise in all weather, and ramps and stairways of ice led off the ships, which sat high upon winter ice. Visible are telegraph wires that were strung between the two ships, providing diversion for the crew and aiding in communication.[5]

The rare playbills (Fig. 24.4) relate to the Theatre Royal, Melville Island. They were actually printed in the Arctic by the Melville Island Press to announce coming dramatic events. The amateur theatricals boosted the morale of the men during the long periods of winter isolation. Mumford, as the carpenter's mate, was involved in the construction of the sets and the printing of the playbills, and he was also a performer.[6]

Commander Belcher underwent a court-martial upon his return to England for the abandonment of four of his vessels, a loss many of his officers and superiors felt unjustifiable. His officers, reluctant to leave the Arctic, had advised that the favourable weather conditions and the good health of the crews warranted attempting a further search in the winter of 1854-1855, especially since Franklin's disappearance remained a mystery. Mumford's depiction of *HMS "Resolute" Abandoned 15th May, 1854*, would not have helped in Belcher's defence. The handful of seemingly robust men, pulling a heavily laden sledge, who were just beginning their trek to Beechey Island, left behind a very sound-looking vessel, proudly flying the British ensign. Mumford left the following description of this controversial event:

> ...in the evening took a solitary walk round the ship which had been a home to us upwards of two years, and though it had been the Stage of Dangers. – Hardships. and discomfort, it still caused us much regret to leave the only spot we could call our home till we could reach the shores of old England. ...at 6 PM the Captain went the rounds... at 6.45, all hands being up from below... secured & caulked the Main Hatch. Hoisted the red Ensign at the Mizen the Pendant at the main and, Letter D (signal for Pilot) at the Fore, shipped the Gangway port and manned the sledges Captain Kellett giving the ship a parting salute by kissing the side, started, giving the ships three cheers... the sledges were 4 in number....[7]

The *Resolute* became free from the pack ice and, after drifting more than 1,200 miles, was picked up by an American whaler and was eventually returned to England to haunt Belcher.

Aside from the journal, little is known of Mumford's artistic talents.[8] The voyage may have helped to improve his station in life, as he later became a surveyor at Lloyd's Register of Shipping, first in London in 1857, moving on to Sunderland, to Liverpool and finally, in 1876, to Glasgow, one of the world's most important ports, as principal surveyor.[9]

Views by other seamen were taken during Belcher's expedition. The account of George F. McDougall, the sailing master of the *Resolute*, was published in 1857, and is illustrated by lithographs after his drawings, some of which deal with subjects similar to the Mumford material. Both Lt. Walter W. May of HMS *Assistance*, who also painted drop scenes for the theatre, and Belcher himself produced sketches of the trip. Collinson's expedition and the travels of HMS *Investigator* and *Enterprise*, an endeavour closely intertwined with Belcher's search, was recorded in a print set by Lt. Samuel Gurney Cresswell.

The Mumford sketches, which are characterized by the freshness of the amateur hand, enhance the existing Arctic material at the National Archives, providing new insights and information about the Franklin searches. While it was not unusual for officers to leave iconographic documentation of their Arctic voyages, it is very rare to encounter sketches like those of Mumford's made from below deck.

M.M.

24.1 W.T. Mumford

Decorated title page, "Private Journal Of an Expedition to the Arctic Regions,"
ca. 1855
Gouache
NA C-126053

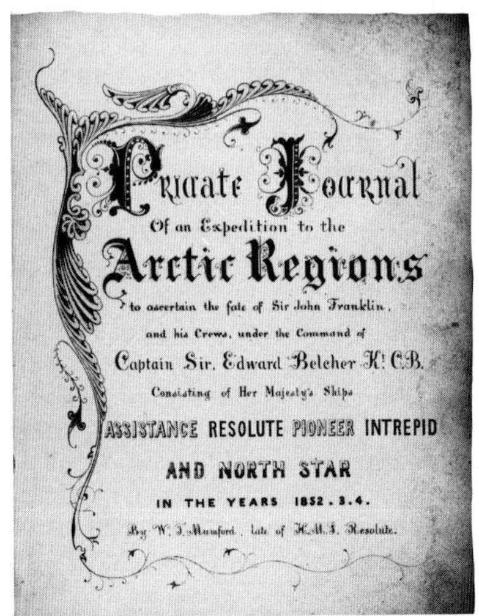

24.2 W.T. Mumford

The First View of the Coast of Greenland, Cape Desolation, 1852-1855
Brown wash
NA C-126051

24.3 W.T. Mumford
"Resolute" & "Intrepid" in Winter Quarters, 1853-1854
Brown wash
NA C-126056

24.4 W.T. Mumford
Playbill, Raising the Wind, 1852-1854 (detail)
Letterpress
NA C-96565

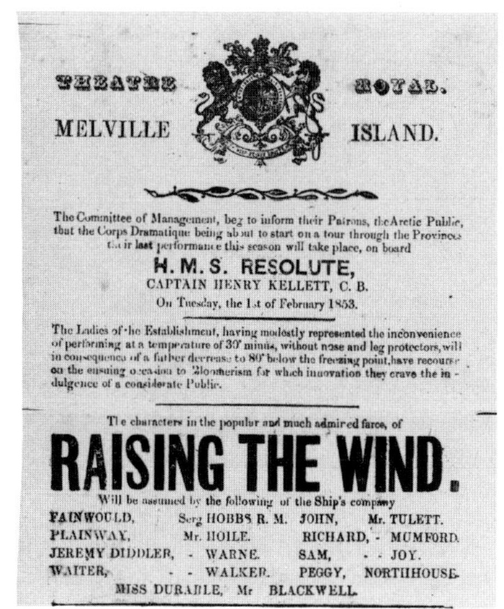

THEATRE ROYAL.
MELVILLE ISLAND.

The Committee of Management, beg to inform their Patrons, the Arctic Public, that the Corps Dramatique being about to start on a tour through the Provinces their last performance this season will take place, on board

H. M. S. RESOLUTE,
CAPTAIN HENRY KELLETT, C. B.
On Tuesday, the 1st of February 1853.

The Ladies of the Establishment, having modestly represented the inconvenience of performing at a temperature of 30° minus, without nose and leg protectors, will in consequence of a futher decrease to 80° below the freezing point, have recourse on the ensuing occasion to Bloomerism for which innovation they crave the indulgence of a considerate Public.

The characters in the popular and much admired farce, of

RAISING THE WIND.

Will be assumed by the following of the Ship's company

FAINWOULD,	Serg HOBBS R. M.	JOHN,	Mr. TULETT.
PLAINWAY,	Mr. HOILE.	RICHARD,	- MUMFORD.
JEREMY DIDDLER,	- WARNE.	SAM,	- - JOY.
WAITER,	- - WALKER.	PEGGY,	NORTHHOUSE.

MISS DURABLE, Mr BLACKWELL.

1. NA, W.T. Mumford papers, MG 24 H80, Journal, introductory pages.

2. The scene of the lower deck transformed for Christmas dinner is described as follows: "...shelves, & c, were hidden by flags, against which were placed every available picture in the ship, besides several original cartoons, some emanating from the officers, others from the men themselves. As the pictures were not only numerous but good, the whole formed a highly respectable gallery." From George F. McDougall, *The Eventful Voyage of H.M. Discovery Ship "Resolute" to the Arctic Regions In Search of Sir John Franklin and the Missing Crews of H.M. Discovery Ships "Erebus" and "Terror" 1852, 1853, 1854* (London: Longmans, Brown, Green, Longmans & Roberts, 1857), 353-354.

3. NA, MG 24 H80, Journal, introductory pages, "The last week in the Resolute," Saturday 13 May 1854 and Monday 15 May 1854; "The original Journal – ," Monday 18 September 1854.

4. Owen Beattie and John Geiger. *Frozen in Time* (Saskatoon: Western Producer Prairie Book, 1988), 160-161. Hair samples taken from the bodies of the three crew members contained twenty to forty times the normal contemporary levels of lead. According to the American scientist Owen Beattie, an assistant professor of anthropology at the University of Alberta who headed the project, lead poisoning likely contributed to the demise of the Franklin expedition. Solder evident in the remains of cans found near the gravesite suggest the source of contamination was the sailors' consumption of canned food, the lead causing disturbances in the nervous system, resulting in disorientation and illness.

5. NA, MG 24 H80, Journal, "Songs all around," Wednesday 28 December 1853; "The Electric Telegraph," Friday 30 December 1853 and Saturday 31 December 1853.

6. Mumford is announced as a performer on three of the playbills found in the journal. He played the role of Smart in the comedy "Who Speaks First," staged on 23 November 1852; Richard in "Raising the Wind," 1 February 1853; and Baptista in "Taming the Shrew," 20 November 1853. See NA, MG 24 H80, Journal, "Preparing Theatricals," Saturday 13 November 1852 and Tuesday 23 November 1852.

7. NA, MG 24 H80, Journal, "The Farewell," Monday 15 May 1854; see also "Orders to abandon the Ships," Friday 28 April 1854; "The last week in the Resolute," Sunday 14 May 1854.

8. Letter to NA from Eileen Mumford, whose great great great uncle was William Thomas Mumford, 4 July 1985. She states that Mumford made a footstool from the timber of the *Resolute*, and also carved a model of the vessel, which he presented to Lloyd's Register of Shipping.

9. Many thanks to Marianne McLean, Manuscript Division, NA, for her assistance.

Die Eisberge im Kotzebue-Sund

LOUIS CHORIS (1795-1828)

25. *The Icebergs in Kotzebue Sound*, after 1818

Watercolour on paper

28.0 x 43.3 cm

Inscribed in pencil, recto, u.l.: *12*; in pen and brown ink, recto, b.: *Die Eisberge in Kotzebue-Sund*; in brushpoint and grey wash, recto, b.: [cropped]; in pencil, verso, u.l.: *800*

Bushnell Collection of Canadiana

Purchased in 1981 with the assistance of a grant from the minister of Communications under the terms of the *Cultural Property Export and Import Act*

Accession no.: 1981-55-17

Negative no.: C-114512

This watercolour of the southern shore of Kotzebue Sound in Alaska is yet another example of the rich collection of material held by the National Archives documenting the search for the North-West Passage. Among other recent acquisitions recording this quest is a coastal view of the Island of Unalaska by William Ellis, the surgeon's second mate on the HMS *Discovery* during Captain Cook's expedition from 1776 to 1780, and a sketchbook by Midshipman A.M. Skene, who accompanied both Capt. John Ross in 1818 and Captain Parry in 1819-1820 in search of the same passage.[1]

This watercolour was painted by a young Russian, Louis Choris, in his capacity as official artist to the round-the-world expedition of the ship *Riurik*, commanded by the Russian naval officer, Otto von Kotzebue (1787-1846).[2] The voyage, which took place between 1815 and 1818, was the first Arctic expedition after the Napoleonic wars, but not the first by the Russians to the northwest coast of America. They had fur trade interests in the area by the early eighteenth century, in addition to later expeditions claiming land and conducting scientific studies.[3] The voyage led by Lieutenant Kotzebue was part of the upsurge of maritime activity that followed the restoration of peace in Europe after the Napoleonic Wars. Although part of the impetus for the voyage was a desire to bring glory to the state, the expedition was not financed by the Russian government.[4] The former chancellor of the Russian Empire, Count Nikolai Petrovitch Rumiantsev, who had a long-standing interest in Arctic exploration and in promoting science and scholarship, paid for the construction and equipment of the expedition.[5] Its purpose was to find a passage between the Pacific and the Atlantic in the Arctic regions. They were to achieve this by attempting to sail farther North than Captain Cook had in his last voyage to the same area (1776-1780), and by sailing closer to the shore than Cook had been able to, hindered as he was by shallow water.[6] To this end the *Riurik* was equipped with the latest navigational equipment from England, including a camera lucida, presumably to assist the artist in making more accurate sketches of the landscape.[7] Unfortunately, there is no mention in the account of the voyage of this instrument being used. In addition to the artist, there were two naturalists on board to study and collect items of natural history, a subject in which the ship's surgeon also took an interest.

The expedition left Kronstadt on the Baltic coast in July 1815, sailed around Cape Horn and arrived in Kamchatka in July 1816. They spent the next two months exploring the Northwest coast of America, which included the discovery and mapping of Kotzebue Sound and, within it, Choris Peninsula, named after the commander and the artist. The expedition wintered in California and Hawaii and returned to the Aleutians the next spring with plans to penetrate further north than the previous year. Because Lieutenant Kotzebue fell ill, however, they turned back in July 1817, reaching European Russia one year later. Although they had explored the land more intimately, they did not penetrate any farther North than had Cook.

Upon their return, Kotzebue published a three-volume account of the voyage, which included extensive sections by the scientists and several illustrations engraved after Choris' drawings. To meet the enormous popular demand for travel literature, the book was immediately translated into Dutch, English and German.

Louis Choris was born in 1795 to German parents in the Ukranian government city of Yekaterinoslav (now Dnepropetrovsk).[8] As a student in the Kharkov gymnasium, he showed such an aptitude for drawing that he attracted the attention of the botanist F.A. Marschall von Bieberstein, who engaged him to make drawings of a selection of his botanical specimens and also to accompany him as botanical draughtsman on one of his expeditions to the Caucasus Mountains in 1813.[9] His drawings for these undertakings were so successful that the young artist earned the recommendation of the president of the St. Petersbourg Academy, when he offered his services to the Kotzebue expedition. One year after his return, in 1819, Choris went to Paris, where he continued his studies in the studios of artists J.B. Regnault and Baron Gerard.[10] He had of course made a large number of drawings during the three-year expedition, of which only a few were used to illustrate the official account of the voyage. Choris showed these to several important scholars in Paris and was encouraged to publish them, resulting in a folio of 104 lithographs entitled *Voyage pittoresque autour du monde*, published in Paris in 1820-1822, followed by a second volume of twenty-four lithographs, *Vues et paysages des régions équinoxiales*, in 1826.[11] Like many of his contemporaries, the artist was obsessed with the need to travel, and he left France in 1827 for Mexico, where he was murdered by bandits on the road between Vera Cruz and the capital on 22 March (his birthday) 1828. He was buried at Xalappa. He had planned to publish another illustrated book entitled *Recueil de têtes et de costumes des habitants de la Russie...*, but this work apparently never appeared.

The watercolour depicts what is now called Elephant Point in Kotzebue Sound, so named because of the mammoth fossils found there. The expedition had used some ivory to fuel their campfires during the night.[12] It is perhaps the first depiction of permafrost landscape in America. The sight aroused some excitement among the members of the expedition, and was described in detail by Kotzebue, by the naturalist Chamisso and by the artist. However, given the strange nature of the terrain and lack of precise vocabulary for its description, the verbal accounts, especially that of the naturalist, are quite unclear without the aid of Choris' illustration.

On 8 August 1816, a small party from the ship, which included Choris, was exploring the shore in Kotzebue Sound. A storm prevented them from returning to the *Riurik*. The following is an excerpt from Kotzebue's account of what they discovered:

> It seemed as if fortune had sent this storm, to enable us to make a very remarkable discovery .... We had climbed much about during our stay without discovering that we were on real ice-bergs. The doctor, who had extended his excursions, found part of the bank broken down, and saw, to his astonishment, that the interior of the mountain, consisted of pure ice. At this news, we all went, provided with shovels and crows, to examine this phenomenon more closely, and soon arrived at a place where the back rises almost perpendicularly out of the sea, to the height of a hundred feet; and then runs off, rising still higher. We saw masses of the purest ice, of the height of an hundred feet, which are under a cover of moss and grass.... The place which, by some accident, had fallen in, and is now exposed to the sun and air, melts away, and a good deal of water flows into the sea. An indisputable proof that what we saw was real ice, is the quantity of mammoths' teeth and bones, which were exposed to view by the melting....[13]

The broken-down bank of ice described by Kotzebue is clearly visible in the watercolour. The stream resulting from the melting ice can be seen in the middle ground of the picture, lined with clumps of small trees that Choris, putting his botanical knowledge to use, described as alders.[14] The black areas in the drawing represent a muddy sediment washed down by the melting ice, which usually forms around these exposed areas.[15] The profusion of grasses, the full-foliage trees and the flowering meadow seem too luxuriant for the Arctic. However, the depiction is in keeping with the verbal descriptions of the land. Some days earlier they had taken tea on one of the islands and had remarked that "the shore was clothed in luxuriant verdure."[16]

There are several indications, however, that the drawing in the exhibition was made after the voyage was over. It seems that Choris was very thrifty with his drawing paper while he was on the journey, and he frequently crowded several sketches on the same page.[17] This drawing, however, is rather large, and, moreover, it is squared for transfer, indicating that it was prepared for some type of reproduction.[18] In addition, there is no sign of hurry in its execution, because the artist dwelt at length on the colouring of the meadow, the lush pinwheel foliage on the right and the grasses on the left. *The Icebergs in Kotzebue Sound Beyond Bering Strait* (Fig. 25.1) is more likely to be the sketch done on the spot. It is a somewhat smaller drawing and a pure landscape, in keeping with the verbal descriptions, which emphasized the fact that they met no Inuit at this place. Nor is there mention of what looks like a collapsed pingo to the left of centre in the drawing. In preparing the sketch for reproduction, Choris has created a composite depiction, in which he has altered the vegetation, increased the contrast of colour in the landforms and added details, such as the pingo, for interest. The inclusion of the figure not only continues the seventeenth-century tradition of "staffage," an artistic technique used to provide a sense of scale and to enliven landscape painting, but it also reveals Choris' main interest during the voyage — the inhabitants, their customs and their artifacts. Because the expedition had numerous encounters with the inhabitants of this part of Alaska, Choris was able to make many detailed sketches of them and to acquire examples of clothing and weapons.[19] He also observed their lip ornament made of bone, decorated in the centre with a blue glass bead, which the figure on the left is wearing.[20]

A comparison of the preparatory drawing with one of the illustrations in Kotzebue's account of the voyage is illuminating, because it reveals the inaccuracies that crept into the copy, revealing a constant problem in book illustration until the invention of photography. The coloured aquatint *Die Eisberge des Kotzebue-Sundes* (Fig. 25.2) is from the 1821 Weimar publication.[21] The landscape and vegetation remain more or less the same. The figure, however, has been Europeanized. His head shape and hair style, typically Asiatic in the drawing, have been altered, and his lip ornament, likely because the illustrator did not comprehend it, has been replaced by a beard. In another illustration, his jacket, reddish-brown to approximate animal skin, has become a deep, military red, and the handle of the lance he carries has been extended to the ground.[22]

Choris' move to Paris coincided with the first appearance of the very popular publications entitled *Voyages pittoresques*, which were collections of views, with commentaries, of various parts of France and of the world.[23] His *Voyage pittoresque* was thus one of several such publications, but it was the first to depict a journey around the world.[24] These publications were closely connected with the newly discovered reproductive process of lithography.[25] Most artists who drew illustrations for these publications handed their drawings over to professional lithographers.[26] Choris, however, learned the process, so that he himself drew the illustrations on the lithographic stone, and the Parisien lithographic printer Langlume printed them[27] (Fig. 25.3). The Arctic vegetation in the print has become even more luxuriant. Moreover, the artist has replaced the native figure on the left with a self-portrait, complete with top hat and portfolio of sketches.[28] The figures on top of the bluff are no longer Inuit, but are, instead, members of the expedition.

An extremely interesting addition to the Documentary Art and Photography Division's holdings of Arctic exploration landscapes from the nineteenth century, this watercolour was acquired from the David I. Bushnell collection.[29] Bushnell was an American anthropologist whose interest in art revolved around images depicting North American Indians and Inuit. *Two Ottawa Chiefs* (Cat. no. 19), and the watercolours by Peter Rindisbacher (Cat. nos. 6-11) and Paul Kane (Cat. nos. 12-17) in this exhibition all share the same provenance.

E.M.-M.

25.1 L. Choris
The Icebergs in Kotzebue Sound Beyond Bering Strait, 1816
Watercolour
Yale University, Beinecke Rare Book and Manuscript Collection

25.2 L. Choris
Die Eisberge des Kotzebue-Sundes, 1821
Handcoloured aquatint
Metropolitan Toronto Library

25.3 L. Choris
Vue des Glaces dans le Golfe de Kotzebue, 1822
Handcoloured lithograph
Metropolitan Toronto Library

1. William Ellis, *The Harbour of Sangoonoodha, in the Island of Unalaschka, N.W. Coast of America*, 1778, Accession no. 1984-102; Andrew Motz Skene, Sketchbook, ca. 1815-1820, Accession no. 1988-43.
2. Some of the research for this entry was done by Douglas Schoenherr, curator, National Gallery of Canada, formerly NA staff. Choris is sometimes called Ludwig, Ludovick or Loggin Andrevitch.
3. Alix O'Grady, "Russians on the West Coast," *The Beaver* 68 (December 1988-January 1989): 23-29.
4. Glynn Barratt, *Russia in Pacific Waters, 1715-1825* (Vancouver: UBC Press, 1981), 176.
5. Otto von Kotzebue, *A Voyage of Discovery into the South Sea and Beering's Straits* (New York: Da Capo Press, 1967 reprint of 1821 London edition), 1:8.
6. Kotzebue, *Voyage* 1:10.
7. Kotzebue, *Voyage* 1:12-21.
8. Michaud, *Biographie universelle ancienne et moderne*, 2nd. ed. (Paris: Louis Vives, 1880), 8:201-202.

9. Marschall von Bieberstein, *Centuria Plantarum Rariorum Rossiae Meridionalis Praesertim Tauriae et Caucasi Iconibus Descriptionibusque Illustrata* (Charkov, 1910).

10. Choris apparently assisted Gérard in the painting of *Le Sacre de Charles X*, which is now in Versailles. P. Larousse, ed., *Grand dictionnaire universel du XIXe siècle* (Paris: Administration du grand dictionnaire universel, 1869), 4:191.

11. The full titles are as follows: *Voyage pittoresque autour du monde, avec des portraits de sauvages d'Amérique, d'Asie, d'Afrique, et des îles du grand Océan; des paysages, des vues maritimes, et plusieurs objets d'histoire naturelle; accompagné de descriptions par M. le baron Cuvier et M.A. de Chamisso, et d'observations sur les crânes humains par M. le docteur Gall* (Paris: Firmin Didot, 1822); *Vues et paysages des régions équinoxiales, recueillis dans un voyage autour du monde* (Paris: Paul Renouard, 1826).

12. Kotzebue, *Voyage* 3:299.

13. Kotzebue, *Voyage* 1:219-220.

14. Choris, "Kamchatka, le golfe de Kotzebue et la terre des Tchouktchis," *Voyage pittoresque*, 9-10.

15. Letter to the author from Prof. J. P. Johnson, Jr. Department of Geography, Carleton University, Ottawa, 28 October 1986.

16. Kotzebue, *Voyage* 1:214.

17. Jean Charlot, *Choris and Kamehameha* (Honolulu: Bishop Museum Press, 1958), 17.

18. Prints based on this drawing appear in all but two (the Russian and one German) editions of Kotzebue's account of the voyage. Otto von Kotzebue, *Entdeckungsreise in die Süd-See und nach der Berings-Strasse zur Erforschung einer nordostlichen Durchfahrt*, 3 vols. (Weimar: Gebruder Hoffmann, 1821), colour aquatint, vol. 1, following 146; *Entdeckungsreise in die Süd-See und nach der Berings-Strasse zur Erforschung einer nordostlichen Durchfahrt*, 3 vols. (Wien: Kaulfluss & Krammer, 1825), engraving, vol. 1, plate [2], following 243; *Ontdekkingsreis in de Zuid-zee en naar de Berings-Strasse, in de jaren 1815, 1816, 1817 en 1818...*, 3 vols. (Amsterdam: Johannes van der Hey, 1822), vol. 1, title page engraving; *Voyage of discovery in the South Sea, and to Behring's Straits, in search of a north-east passage* (London: R. Phillips, 1821), engraving, plate [2], following 110; *A Voyage of Discovery into the South Sea and Beering's Straits...*, 3 vols. (London: Longman Hurst, Rees, Orme and Brown, 1821), colour aquatint, vol. 1, facing 219.

19. The Beinecke Rare Book and Manuscript Library at Yale University owns 44 drawings by Choris from this expedition. Over half of the these depict the inhabitants of the northwest coast of North America.

20. Choris, "Kamchatka," 4-5.

21. Kotzebue, *Entdeckungsreise* (1821), vol. 1, following 146.

22. Kotzebue, *Voyage*, vol. 1; colour aquatint, facing 219.

23. Jean Adhémar, "Les lithographies de paysages en France à l'époque romantique," *Archives de l'art français*, nouvelle période 19 (1935-1937), 189-350.

24. Adhémar, 284-289.

25. Adhémar, 284-289.

26. Adhémar, 284-289.

27. Choris, "Kamchatka," plate ix.

28. A similar self-portrait is included in *Entrevue de l'expédition de M. Kotzebue avec le Roi Tammeamea, dans l'île d'Ovayhi*, plate 18 of Choris's *Vues et Paysages*.

29. Parts of the Bushnell collection were deaccessioned by the Peabody Museum, Harvard University, in 1981, and the NA was able to acquire several items relating to Canada.

GEORGE ALEXANDER FRAZER (act. 1817-1863)

26. *Sir John Franklin and Party Stopping for Breakfast on the North Shore of Lake Huron*, 1825(?)

Watercolour over pencil with scraping out on paper

21.0 x 29.5 cm

Inscribed on mount, in pen and brown ink, verso, c.: *Reminiscences of Early life / Sir John Franklin & party – stopping for / breakfast on the North shore of Lake Huron / in 1825 – Sketch'd by G: A: F-* [in monogram]

Purchased in 1975

Accession no.: 1975-19-1

Negative no.: C-11433

One of the great treasures of the Documentary Art and Photography Division is George Back's sketchbook of 1825-1826, containing sixty-four superb watercolours that document the passage in 1825 of John Franklin's second overland expedition from New York State to its winter base at Fort Franklin on Great Bear Lake.[1] In the spring of 1826, the expedition divided into two groups to undertake the main purpose of the journey: the charting of the Arctic coast to the east and west of the mouth of the Mackenzie River. A second sketchbook by Back, also in the National Archives' collection, records in mostly pencil sketches this difficult and only partly successful venture.[2] We were therefore very intrigued when the present watercolour appeared in a sale at Sotheby's, since it provided another look at the expedition by a hitherto unknown artist identified then only by the initials "G.A.F."[3]

It was logical to think that G.A.F. must have been one of the members of the Franklin expedition, but no such person was recorded. The artist's identity remained unknown until a reading of Back's diary revealed that George Alexander Frazer, master's mate and draughtsman of the Royal Navy, travelled with the expedition for only a few weeks.

Frazer first appears in a letter of Capt. Robert Barrie, acting commissioner of the Kingston Dockyard, dated 24 March 1825, in which he instructs Frazer to join Captain Franklin's expedition at Penetanguishene and to continue with it to "St. Marys" (i.e., Sault Ste. Marie) or Fort William, where he would join the Surveying Service on the Lakes of Canada under Lt. Henry Wolsey Bayfield. In a postscript, Barrie added: "Should you join Captain Franklin at York or any of his party from Kingston to Penetanguishene, you are to proceed in company."[4]

According to Back's diary for 5-6 April, Franklin and the officers had gone on ahead to Penetanguishene, leaving Back in York to conduct the rest of the men when they arrived.[5] On 9 April, Back records:

> In the afternoon a schooner from Kingston arrived with 24 men for the expedition... and a Mr. Fraser [*sic*] (a Midshipman) had been sent by Commissioner Barry [*sic*], who requested us to give him a passage to Lake Superior, to enable him to join a Surveying Party under the direction of Lieut. Bayfield.[6]

Four days later, Back embarked from York in a canoe that had Frazer as a passenger.[7] On 16 April, Frazer was sent ahead in a half-loaded canoe to join Franklin at Penetanguishene, which Back reached six days later, on 22 April.[8] The following day, the reunited party set out on Lake Huron in "the two *maitre* or larger canoes that had been sent from Montreal for us," which one sees in Frazer's watercolour. Back enumerated the total party as follows: "Our whole number was therefore 35 persons, viz. the officers, Messers. Fraser and Shaw, 4 Marines and 24 Canadians."[9] Since the expedition entered Lake Superior on 2 May, the breakfast on the north shore of Lake Huron depicted in the watercolour took place sometime between 23 April and 2 May, while the party was crossing Lake Huron from Penetanguishene to Sault Ste. Marie. It is noteworthy that only ten of the thirty-four members are depicted at their picnic. Unfortunately we cannot tell if Frazer intended two of his small figures to represent Franklin and Back.

By 5 May, the waves of Lake Superior had become too heavy for the canoes, so the party entered a bay "and waited a few hours until it moderated; this little respite from motion allowed Mr. Fraser, who had been taken seriously ill, a quiet repose."[10] Back took advantage of the stop to make a sketch showing the men repairing the two canoes in front of a large white tent where the unfortunate Frazer was probably trying to recover from *mal de mer* (Fig. 26.1). Back inscribed his sketch: "A Bay in Lake Superior. where we were detained by a high Wind. May 5th."[11] Shortly thereafter they arrived at the Michipicoten River "near whose entrance stands the Hudson [*sic*] Bay Company post, where we more particularly called on account of Mr. Fraser, whose increasing illness now required more comfort than was attainable in our mode of travelling."[12] Finally on 10 May, the expedition reached Fort William, where "we had the pleasure also of meeting Lieutenant Bayfield's party, which had nearly completed the survey of the lake."[13] Here Frazer left Franklin's party and joined Bayfield's survey of Lake Superior.

By November 4, Bayfield was back in England, where he wrote to the Admiralty:

> I have the honour to report to you for the information of my Lords Commissioners of the Admiralty my arrival from the Lakes of Canada with my assistant Mr. P.E. Collins Midshipman and Draughtsman Mr. Frazer Master's Mate in the Merchant Brig Alexander Henry according to the orders of acting Commissioner Robt. Barrie C.B., having... finished the surveys of Lakes Superior, Huron & Erie which I have brought with me, but which will require some time to prepare for their Lordships inspection, Lake Huron being as yet in pencil & Lake Superior not yet plotted.[14]

As Bayfield's draughtsman, Frazer continued to work on the survey charts, as the following letter from Bayfield to the Admiralty on 8 December reveals:

> I have the honor to inform you that I and my assistant, Mr. Collins, and Draughtsman Mr. Frazer were paid our salaries by Mr. Glover, the Naval storekeeper at Kingston, U.C., up to the 3rd of September last inclusive.... And as since that time, and during the passage home, we have been continually working at the surveys of Lakes Huron & Superior, I beg you will be pleased to give the necessary order to the Navy Board that we may be paid our salaries....[15]

Frazer was still in Bayfield's service, now as his assistant, on 17 July 1826, when both men applied for leave:

> Having been advised by Dr. Guthrie (under whose care I have been the last five months) to take an excursion to the sea coast for the benefit of bathing – Mr. Frazer (my assistant) having been in delicate health for sometime and wishing to visit his friends in Ireland, I request you will be pleased to grant us three weeks leave of absence, from Tuesday, the 25 Inst.[16]

An original pen and ink chart of Lake Superior in the Cartographic and Architectural Archives Division, National Archives of Canada (Fig. 26.2), is inscribed as follows:

> [Stamp of the Hydrographical Office] / SURVEY / of / LAKE SUPERIOR / BY / LIEUT. HENRY. WY. BAYFIELD, RN. / assisted by MR. PHILIP. ED. COLLINS. MID. / Between the Years / 1823 & 25. / DRAWN BY MR. GEORGE ALEXR. FRAZER MATE. / All the Soundings are in Feet / H.W.B.[17]

Two other charts in the same collection may also have been drawn by Frazer.[18]

In later life Frazer continued his naval career with surveying vessels on the coast of Ireland, publishing a book on the subject in 1842.[19] He attained the rank of captain in 1851 and retired in 1861, being placed on an out-pension list of Greenwich Hospital on 21 March 1863.

Only three watercolours from Frazer's brief Canadian sojourn are currently known: the present *Breakfast on the North Shore* and two almost identical versions of a view of Niagara Falls (Fig. 26.3).[20] All three are laid down on old mounts whose versos bear inscriptions beginning "Reminiscences of Early Life" and containing references to Sir John Franklin. It seems quite clear that Frazer inscribed the works many years after his contact with Franklin in Canada, which he proudly wished to commemorate in his pictures. It is hard to say whether the watercolours date from his Canadian posting or whether they were made at a later date, perhaps based on on-the-spot sketches that are no longer known. The fact that the Niagara Falls view exists in two almost identical versions might support the idea that the watercolours were worked up in England at a later date.

We are nonetheless very grateful that George Alexander Frazer took the time and effort to record the Franklin expedition encamped for a delightful picnic breakfast on the north shore of Lake Huron. The party may have been en route towards a difficult and dangerous task in the frozen wastes of the Arctic, but they were clearly travelling in style, as the neat blanket and lunch provisions indicate. The centrepiece of the breakfast spread is a large bottle which was no doubt a continuing comfort to the intrepid explorer and his men as they upheld the English niceties of existence even in the remote Canadian wilderness.

D. E. S.

26.1 G. Back
A Bay in the Lake Superior, 1825
Watercolour
NA C-93002

26.2 H. W. Bayfield
Survey of Lake Superior, ca. 1825
Pen and ink
NA NMC 17418(D)

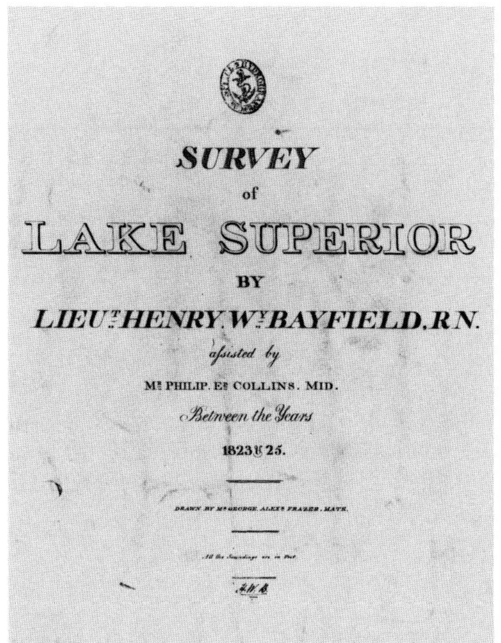

26.3 G.A. Frazer
Niagara Falls, 1825 or after
Watercolour
Art Gallery of Hamilton, Stitt collection

---

1. See *Archives Canada Microfiches*, microfiches 11-12 (Ottawa: Public Archives Canada, 1980).

2. *Archives Canada Microfiches*, microfiches 12-14.

3. Sotheby's (Belgravia, London), *Topographical Paintings, Drawings, Watercolours and Prints*, 28 April 1975, lot 85 (illustrated).

4. NA, Robert Barrie papers, MG 24 F66, vol. 3, Letterbook, 1819-1839, pp. 247-248, Barrie to Frazer, 24 March 1825.

5. Scott Polar Research Institute, Cambridge, England, "A Journal of the proceedings of the Land Arctic Expedition under the command of John Franklin Esquire Captain RN., F.R.S. &c. by Lieut[t] G Back RN., January 1825," MS 395/6, NA, MG 24 H62, microfilm, reel A-821, entry for 5-6 April 1825. Permission to quote from this diary has kindly been given by its owner and the Scott Polar Research Institute, where it is on deposit.

6. Scott Polar, MS 395/6, 9 April 1825.

7. Scott Polar, MS 395/6, 13 April 1825.

8. Scott Polar, MS 395/6, 16 and 22 April 1825.

9. Scott Polar, MS 395/6, 23 April 1825.

10. Scott Polar, MS 395/6, 5 May 1825.

11. *Archives Canada Microfiches*, microfiche 11, no. B3.

12. Scott Polar, MS 395/6, 5 May 1825.

13. Scott Polar, MS 395/6, 10 May 1825.

14. Public Record Office, London, Admiralty Records, Adm. 1, vol. 2792, Letters B218, NA, H.W. Bayfield papers, MG 24 F28, vol. 1, p. 3, transcripts, Bayfield to John Barrow, 4 November 1825.

15. Public Record Office, Adm. 1, vol. 2792, Letters B245, NA, MG 24 F28, vol. 1, p. 6, transcripts, Bayfield to John Barrow, 8 December 1825.

16. Public Record Office, Adm. 1, vol. 2792, Letters B104, NA, MG 24 F28, vol. 1, p. 7, transcripts, Bayfield to I.W. Croker, 17 July 1826.

17. NA, NMC 17418.

18. William R. O'Byrne, *A Naval Biographical Dictionary* (London: John Murray, 1849), 379; W. Mudge and G.A. Frazer, *Sailing Directions for the North-East, North, and North-West Coasts of Ireland* (London, 1842).

19. *Navy List*, 1866, p. 416.

20. Andrew J. Oko, *Canada in the Nineteenth Century: The Bert and Barbara Stitt Family Collection* (Hamilton: Art Gallery of Hamilton, 1984), Cat. no. 26, p. 38 (20.6 x 29.4 cm), and Sotheby's (Belgravia, London), *Topographical Paintings, Drawings, Watercolours and Prints*, 28 April 1975, lot 86, (illustrated, 21 x 29.5 cm). The two works are very similar, but may be distinguished by the placement of the oars on the boat in the foreground, those in the Stitt version being wider apart than those in the Sotheby's sale, where they are almost touching.

HENRI DELATTRE (1801-1876)

27. *A View of the Quarantine Station at Grosse Isle*, 1850

Oil on canvas

20.2 x 25.2 cm

Inscribed in brushpoint and black paint, recto, l.l.: *H. Delattre, / 1850*

Purchased in 1983

Accession no.: 1983-121-1

Negative no.: C-120285

Grosse Isle is a small island lying north-east of Quebec City between Île d'Orleans and Île aux Oies in the St. Lawrence River. During the nineteenth century, it was used as a quarantine station for immigrants entering Upper and Lower Canada (Ontario and Quebec, respectively). The station was established in 1832 in preparation for an outbreak of Asiatic cholera that was spreading through Europe from India. For the first seven years, the station at Grosse Isle was administered and paid for by the British Army in Lower Canada. After 1840, the civil government took over the administration and expenditures, although, apart from the years 1844 to 1847, detachments of British troops were present on the island until 1857.

The station initially consisted of sheds for the immigrants and a signal station at the south-west end of the island. In the centre of the island on the south shore were the barracks for the soldiers, officers and civilian medical personnel. In 1847, new sheds were built at the east end of the island to accommodate the sick emigrants and separate them from the healthy, who remained at the western end. The view in our painting is of the officers' quarters on the south shore. One of the two cannons on the island is visible, as is the sentry. The cannons were to be used to prevent a ship from passing Grosse Isle without stopping. This part of the island did not change much in the years between 1832 and 1857, and the view in Delattre's painting is similar to several other views in the National Archives' collections painted by army officers stationed at Quebec in the 1830s and 1840s, including Henry Ainslie and James Alderson.

The role of the military on Grosse Isle was to ensure that the quarantine regulations were enforced and to afford any assistance required to the health officer or medical superintendant on the island. The commandant was responsible for ensuring that every vessel carrying steerage passengers or originating from an infected port stopped; that all passengers disembarked, that the vessel, its crew and its passengers were inspected; that vessels, passengers and luggage were disinfected; and that the vessel was given a clean bill of health before continuing on to Quebec City or Montreal.[1] The troops were also to maintain order amongst the healthy immigrants landed on the island, who, after several weeks of confinement below decks, celebrated their disembarkation most exuberantly.[2] Distributing food and bedding and putting up tents were other duties carried out by the military. Great care was taken to prevent contact between the soldiers and the sick immigrants — other than that required by their duties — in order to prevent their exposure to disease.

The quarantine station opened every spring, usually in May, and the Proclamation of Quarantine was published in *The Canada Gazette*. The civil secretary of the governor of Lower Canada would request from the military secretary of the commander of the forces in Canada that a detachment of troops be sent to Grosse Isle for the season. A captain, a subaltern, a varying number of sergeants and rank and file, with sufficient artillery men to take charge of the cannons, made up the troops sent for the summer. Wives and children sometimes accompanied the detachment. With the closing of the station each October, the troops were reduced to a small party of a sergeant and several men to stay the winter.

Col. E.W. Cumming, of the 79th Highland Regiment (Queen's Own Cameron Highlanders), recorded this description of Grosse Isle in 1849 when he served there as a lieutenant:

> In the beginning of May I started in a small tug with 80 men, all selected as the greatest drunkards in the Regiment; Grosse Island was a strictly temperance station, no liquor being permitted on the island, and the Colonel considered that six months enforced sobriety would effect their reformation — the result was not encouraging. The St. Lawrence is about 20 miles in breadth, and on a summer's morning I have never beheld anything more beautiful than the surrounding scenery. The only residents on the island were the commandant, Capt. Scott, 71st Regiment; the medical officer, Dr. Douglas and his hospital staff....
>
> I used often to board the ships with Dr. Douglas in his official visits, and saw many Gaelic-speaking emigrants from the Highlands of Scotland. It did not strike me that emigration, as then carried out, was at all a matter for sympathy. They seemed to go in entire families of two or three generations; they would be like the patriarchs of old, or the ancient Trojans, taking their 'household gods' with them.
>
> The quantities of wild duck, teal and geese were fabulous, but they were very wary, and it was difficult to get within shot as we had only an ordinary fowling piece.
>
> Early in September we returned to Quebec, when the 80 reformed drunkards at once relapsed.[3]

The years 1832 and 1847 were the worst for disease on Grosse Isle. The latter year saw an out-break of typhus on board the ships that brought thousands of Irish immigrants to Canada. Weakened and malnourished as a result of the potato crop failures of 1845 and 1846, the majority of passengers succumbed to the crowded and unsanitary conditions that prevailed on board the vessels bringing them to the Canadas. There were also cases of smallpox on ships from Edinburgh that year.[4] It is estimated that more that 3,000 people died at Grosse Isle in 1847.[5]

The horror of death and suffering at the quarantine station contrasted with the natural beauty of the island, a phenomenon commented on by many even during the worst outbreaks. The years between epidemics were often uneventful, and the island was a popular spot for a day's picnic, especially for members of the Citadel garrison.[6] The year of our painting, 1850, was one of the more tranquil, with only 359 cases of illness recorded.[7] At least one pleasure trip to Grosse Isle was advertised in the *Morning Chronicle* that summer.[8]

The author of this painting, Henri Delattre, was born in St. Omer, France, in 1801 and earned a reputation as an animal and landscape painter. He exhibited frequently at the Paris Salon in the years between 1824 and 1876. Delattre made two extended trips to North America – first in the 1830s when he established himself in Virginia painting portraits of race horses, and then sometime in 1848 or 1849, when he took up residence in Philadelphia.[9]

In 1850, after exhibiting at the Pennsylvania Academy of Fine Arts in May, he visited Quebec City to escape the heat of the Philadelphia summer.[10] In that year, the Cameron Highlanders and the 19th Regiment of Foot were doing garrison duty, with detachhments of soldiers on Grosse Isle. One of the Camerons' senior officers, Major E.J. Elliot, was a keen sportsman[11] and had Delattre paint a portrait of his horse. The *Morning Chronicle* noted:

> A gentleman is at present in this city who has given to animal painting much attention – Mr. Hy. Delattre from Paris. In the bookstore of Mr. Sinclair, Fabrique Street, we noticed the portrait of a horse, excellently well done, belonging to Major Elliot of the 79th Highlanders, and on enquiry, found that it had been executed by Mr. Delattre.[12]

It was probably through his association with Major Elliot that Delattre visited the quarantine station and recorded this view of the military quarters with the sentry in the kilted uniform of the 79th Regiment.

Contemporary newspapers note that Delattre was working for several citizens of Quebec City, although to date only Major Elliot has been identified. On 9 October, Delattre exhibited a portrait of a horse at the Quebec Industrial Exhibition, a local show of industrial, agricultural and artistic accomplishments.[13] There is a *Portrait of a Brood Mare* in a private collection in the United States, dated 7 September 1850, by Henri Delattre, showing a horse with Grosse Isle in the background (Fig. 27.1). Executed too late to be the portrait for Major Elliot recorded on 20 August in the *Morning Chronicle*, it is possible that Delattre painted it for another officer of the 79th, or perhaps an officer of one of the other regiments at Quebec. Or, it could be that Delattre executed the portrait for a local patron and added the shoreline of Grosse Isle for a backdrop. There is no record of the army using horses on Grosse Isle other than to transport supplies; the island was too small.

Delattre's work outside of the United States and France is relatively unknown. Because of its specific subject matter (animal and sporting scenes), that which is known appeals to a limited audience. It is very likely that the results of his summer in Quebec City in 1850 are still hanging in the homes of the descendants of his Canadian and British patrons.

S.N.

27.1 H. Delattre
The Brood Mare, 1850
Oil on canvas
Private collection
Photograph courtesy of Kennedy Galleries, New York.

1. "Quarantine," *The Canada Gazette* (Montreal), 6 April 1850, pp. 8298-8301.

2. Susanna Moodie recorded her impressions of Grosse Isle in *Roughing It in the Bush* (London: Richard Bentley, 1852), 1:13.

> I was deeply disappointed, but my husband laughingly told me that I had seen enough of the island, and, turning to the good-natured soldier, remarked that "it could be no easy task to keep such wild savages in order."
>
> You may well say that, sir – but our night scenes far exceed those of the day. You would think they were incarnate devils, singing, drinking, dancing, shouting and cutting antics that would surprise the leader of a circus.

3. "A Short History of the Regiment by Colonel Cumming, from 1846-1881. Part II, 1848-1854," *79th News*, no. 210 (April 1935), 195-196. Col. Cumming says that he kept a thick journal for the years he was stationed at Quebec, but that he destroyed it before leaving for the Crimea. Since life at the Citadel was dull by his own description, it is tempting to think that Delattre's visit would have been reported in detail.

4. Edwin C. Guillet, *The Great Migration* (Toronto: T. Nelson and Sons, 1937), 149.

5. Alain Rainville,"The Grosse Isle Quarantine Station 1832-1937," *The Archivist*, vol. 12, no. 5 (September-October 1985), 8.

6. Such a military social outing is described in the *Quebec Mercury*, 15 August 1835, p. 2.

> Yesterday His Excellency the Commander of the forces, with his personal Staff and the Heads of Departments embarked, shortly after noon on board the steamer at Grosse Isle. The day was cool and pleasant, and a numerous company availed themselves of the opportunity to enjoy the river breezes, doubly refreshing after the sultry heat of the three preceding days. The excellent Band of the 66th Regiment was on board, and added to the zest of the excursion by their excellent music. The steamer returned to the wharf about 9 o'clock, after a delightful, though short, voyage on our noble river, whose picturesque banks never appeared in more luxuriant beauty. The pleasures of the day were greatly enhanced by the grateful recollection that the country is this year, hitherto happily exempt from the dreadful visitation, which occasioned the formation of the Sanitary Establishment that was the immediate object of His Excellency's visit.

The sister-in-law of Dr. G.M. Douglas, medical superintendent of the Quarantine Station from 1832 to 1853, records in her memoirs a much lengthier account of a summer picnic on Grosse Isle in 1847 as told to her by Capt. Bradford. Margery Durham Noble, *A Long Life* (Newcastle-upon-Tyne: Andrew Reid & Co., 1925), 33-44.

7. Helen I. Cowan, *British Emigration to British North America* (Toronto: University of Toronto Press, 1961), 295.

8. *Morning Chronicle* (Quebec), 13 July 1850, p. 3.

9. Delattre's career as a painter of race-horses in the United States is described in Alexander Mackay-Smith, *The Race Horses of America 1832-1872* (Saratoga Springs, New York: National Museum of Racing, 1981).

10. The *Journal de Québec*, 20 August 1850, p. 2, reported:

> Mr. de Lattre is busy working for several citizens of this town; but he only passes through, staying as far north as possible so as to avoid the suffocating heat of his place of residence, Philadelphia, which weighs heavily on his European shoulders.

There is no evidence of friends or family in the city, which might explain why Delattre chose to visit Quebec.

11. Major Elliott was a steward for the Queen's Plate in 1850, held by the Quebec Turf Club (*Morning Chronicle*, 13 June 1850, p. 3). He was also a keen fisherman. A journal of a fishing expedition entitled "Rough Notes Taken during an Expedition to the Salmon Rivers on the North Shores of the St. Lawrence in the Summer of 1849" (NA, James McGill Strachan papers, MG 24 H72), attributed to Capt. James Strachan, mentions the arrival on 29 June of Major Elliott and Captain Hunt of the 79th, to join the fishing party.

12. *Morning Chronicle*, 19 August 1850, p. 2.

13. *Journal de Québec*, 12 October 1850, p. 2:

"Also noteworthy is a horse painted by Mr. Delattre, of whom we have spoken...."

JOHN ELLIOTT WOOLFORD (1778-1866)

28. *Quebec from the Harbour*, ca. 1819

Brown wash over pencil on paper

21.4 x 63.7 cm (two sheets)

Inscribed on left sheet in pencil, recto, u.c.: *C Diamond*; on mount of left sheet in pen and black ink, verso, b.: *Quebeck* [from] *the* [?] *h*[arbour] [inscription largely cropped]; on right sheet in pencil, recto, l.c.: *wall*; on mount of right sheet in pen and black ink, recto, l.r.: *Continuation of the preceed-ing sketch*

In "Sketches in the Canada's 3," ca. 1819

Purchased in 1978, in cooperation with the Nova Scotia Museum, with the assistance of a grant from the minister of Communications under the terms of the *Cultural Property Export and Import Act*

Accession nos.: 1979-9-1.1 and 1.2

Negative nos.: C-99521 and C-99522

When George Ramsay, the ninth Earl of Dalhousie (1770-1838), was appointed lieutenant-governor of Nova Scotia in 1816, he brought with him as his official draughtsman a talented artist named John Elliott Woolford (1778-1866). Although Lord Dalhousie commissioned works of art from many of his staff and acquaintances in Canada, like Capt. John Crawford Young, Lt. Henry Pooley, Col. William Denny and Col. Charles Ramus Forrest (Cat. no. 29), to name only some, Woolford in his official position produced the most significant number of commissioned works for Dalhousie.

The longstanding military contact between the two men was the basis for their later association. In 1797, Woolford began his military career when he joined the 2nd Queen's Regiment of Foot. Ramsay, later the ninth Earl of Dalhousie and one of Woolford's commanding officers, recognized his talent and encouraged him to sketch in his leisure time. By the Egyptian campaign of 1801, Dalhousie had convinced Woolford to record the whole operation resulting in a portfolio of sixty-four watercolours, comprising scenes of Malta and the Bay of Mamorice, the surrender of the French at Alexandria and the return via Gibraltar. This portfolio is now in the collection of the National Gallery of Canada. Following the campaign, Woolford returned with Lord Ramsay to Dalhousie Castle, near Edinburgh, Scotland, to complete these sketches.

In a letter written to the 10th Earl of Dalhousie in 1857, Woolford described his activity in Scotland:

> His Lordship after a time assumed the command of the Edinburgh district and I performed the duties of Clerk. In 1803 I was anxious to leave the service and by the kind recommendation of His Lordship I was permitted by the then Commander in chief the late Duke of York to do so...I then took up my residence in Edinburgh, married & followed the profession of a Landscape Painter with some success during which period I was frequently employed and much patronized by His Lordship and his Brothers....[1]

When Woolford arrived in Nova Scotia he was thirty-eight, and he remained in Canada until his death in Fredericton in 1866. Although it is uncertain what his artistic training actually was, he lived during the age of the military artists, when recording the landscape in watercolour was a required course at the Royal Military Academy of Woolwich. It is speculated that he may have studied as an apprentice in the Drawing Room of the Board of Ordnance in the Tower of London, and then have been instructed by Paul Sandby, professor of drawing at Woolwich, from whom he may have learned the process of aquatint.[2]

Although in 1817 Woolford had filled a vacant position as a clerk in the Barrack Department, as official draughtsman to the lieutenant-governor, he travelled extensively, accompanying Dalhousie on tours of the Maritime region in 1817-1818. In 1819, Woolford drew, etched, printed and published four highly accomplished views of Halifax, including two views of the Province Building and two of Government House. This series is thought to be the most unique example of single-sheet prints issued in Halifax, and the set was one of the first of its kind to be issued in Canada.[3] In 1819, the lieutenant-governor also made the traditional pilgrimage to Niagara Falls. The trip to Niagara that began at Halifax on 22 June was accomplished in less than one month. The party returned by virtually the identical route, reaching Nova Scotia by 13 August. Woolford accompanied his patron to take sketches of the places they visited, a labour Dalhousie felt was the only way to truly document the magnificence of the Canadian landscape. The journals Dalhousie kept during his stay in Canada provide details of the itineraries and sometimes quite candid observations about places he had visited and their inhabitants, giving us some insight into his personality. The comments reveal the overwhelming excitement he felt, like other visitors who for the first time were confronted with the splendour of Niagara Falls.

Ramsay became governor general of Canada in 1820 after the sudden death of the Duke of Richmond. In 1821, Woolford joined another excursion that led to Niagara, where the route of the North West Company voyageurs was followed by canoe through the Great Lakes as far as Lake Superior, and back by the Ottawa River. The resulting sketches from this last trip appear closely related to a group of sketches by Charles Ramus Forrest, although the exact relationship of their work warrants further investigation (Cat. no. 29).

The album of sketches in the National Archives collection documents the Niagara trip of 1819. The volume came to the Archives in 1978 as part of the repatriation, in cooperation with the Nova Scotia Museum and with the aid of a Cultural Property grant, of Woolford material from the Dalhousie collection. It is half-bound in morocco leather, and stamped in gold on the spine is the title "Sketches in the Canada's 3." There is also a small label inscribed *American Sketches* on the first of its marbled cardboard covers, which is likely a later addition. It is a fairly large – 25.6 x 38.7 cm. There are forty-four individual drawings (the first two being two parts of a panorama of Quebec City, Cat. no. 28), and the whole is presented in a sequence that fairly accurately follows the itinerary of the early Niagara trip. The dates of the watermarks to be found on various pages of the sketch paper itself are 1811, 1818 and 1819.

Inside the front cover, Lord Dalhousie's coat-of-arms appears on the bookplate, which was engraved by James Smillie Jr.[4] The drawings themselves, executed on paper of different colours, have been cropped to the image and mounted on the folios of blue-grey paper. The drawings are largely pencil with grey and brown wash. It appears that there may originally have been forty-six sketches, since two stubs with torn edges are found in the album, suggesting that two folios have been removed. The sketches that have been removed are a view of Montmorency Falls and one of Niagara Falls.[5]

The first two sketches in the album form a panorama of Quebec City from the harbour, the left portion or first sketch showing the steep precipice and fortifications of the Citadel, and the right depicting the prominent churches of Quebec and the details of the buildings and harbour-front in lower town (Cat. no. 28). This panorama was likely executed at the beginning of July, when the party had reached this point in their journey from Halifax. Dalhousie makes a particularly emotional reference in his journal to the subject of the next drawing, *Wolfe's Cove from the Heights of Abraham.* Following this are three views taken from Pointe Lévis, the first southwest or upriver, entitled *View on Point Levi* (Fig. 28.1), the second and third looking northeast back toward Montmorency. The simplicity of the scene of Lévis hardly compares to the commercial activity depicted at a later date in the panorama of the harbour by George Seton (Cat. no. 30).

The spell cast on the travellers by the scenery of the St. Lawrence route is evident throughout the Dalhousie journal. The waterfalls the party encountered made a profound impression on the author, and likely on the artist, judging from the number of times he recorded a particular setting. Five sketches of Montmorency follow — two of the falls, one of the Montmorency looking upriver, one view from the bridge above the falls, and lastly a distant view of Quebec from Montmorency. Following this are a series of four similar views of the Chaudière Falls, taken from slightly different vantage points. Dalhousie's account of this visit testifies to his feelings at this moment, as well as to his faith in Woolford's talent.

> We went up the river...& landed in a cove nearly opposite to Sillery, & a mile above the entrance to the Chaudiere river... [then overland to the Falls]...Here indeed it was tremendously grand....We sat down to rest ourselves & to enjoy at leisure this awful & yet delightful scene. It is impossible to describe it otherwise than by pencil, and I am glad I have brought my draftsman Woolford with me. He shall be kept hard at work during my rambles in Canada, so that hereafter I may refer to his sketches for the beauties of the Country.[6]

Late on the evening of 5 July, the party arrived at Montreal. The following morning Lord Dalhousie's first order of business was to walk out to the parade of the 37th Regiment, which he described in his journal:

> The parade is a handsome public walk immediately behind the New Court House & Jail — both of them fine buildings, ornamental & creditable to the city. In front of them is a column, in honour of Lord Nelson bearing a statue of him on top, but it is very poor altogether — ill proportionate & unpleasing.[7]

Woolford took three sketches at Montreal, the first, *On the Parade at Montreal* (Fig. 28.2), is a handsome drawing with crisp clean lines and distinct light and shaded areas to define space. Colour notations on the roofs of the buildings suggest that the drawing was perhaps intended for publication as a print. The treatment of Lord Nelson's monument seems to bear out Dalhousie's unflattering description of it.

From Montreal the travellers went on to Ste. Anne via the shore road to Lachine, crossed at the ferry and went on to Coteau-du-Lac. Woolford took a sketch of the ferry at Ste. Anne, one of the Lachine rapids, and two of the Coteau Fort. In the first view of the fort, Woolford has used very precise lines, yet the second is a more distant and fluid view, bringing to mind a later sketch by John Arthur Roebuck from the Roebuck album (Cat. no. 35), taken from the opposite side. At this point Dalhousie made a rather revealing comment when speaking of Woolford's attempt to record the scene at the river at Coteau-du-Lac.

> Here the river is tumultuous & broken and is divided by several islands richly wooded into the very stream. At Sunset I made Woolford try to sketch it, but I much fear he is not equal to it....[8]

On 9 July the group reached the Long Sault rapids. This is represented at about the mid-way point in the album. There are two sketches of this spot. The second, *Long Sault from the Bottom* (Fig. 28.3), depicts men pulling tow ropes to help boats moving upstream, as the journal describes.

> Under the bank where we stood is a road or towing path to assist the boats poling upwards. A little way down is a building or Mill on piles in the river, which appears to be in ruins, but adds to the picturesque scenery.[9]

On 10 July, they passed through the Thousand Islands, which are documented by two sketches. The party reached Kingston by evening. Woolford again produced two sketches at Kingston; one, the *Perspective View of the Barracks, Fort Henry, Kingston* (Fig. 28.4), shows a meticulous and rather cold architectural rendering of the barracks, uncluttered by traces of human life save one wooden soldier marching on the roof of the arch in dead centre. This work is treated very much like *On the Parade at Montreal,* being defined in tonalities, and also bearing inscribed colour notations above the buildings. It was also possibly intended for future publication. These drawings are reminiscent of one of the Halifax prints by Woolford earlier mentioned, *Architectural Elevation of the Province Building,* demonstrating the translation of this type of architectural drawing into the print medium.[10]

Following these sketches are one of Fort York and a charming depiction of the *Mills Three Miles from York* (Fig. 28.5) that reveals the artist's versatility of style in his use of delightful curved lines.

On 14 July, the party visited Fort George, where Woolford once more drew two sketches. Comments from the journal compare well with the drawing *Fort Niagara from Fort George* (Fig. 28.6).

> At the mouth [of the Niagara] stands on the one side the American Fort Niagara, bold & bullying; clean whitewashed, & displaying the "Star-spangled banner" as large as the British standard. On the other side, a small English jack not bigger than a pocket hand kerchief, worn & blown to rags, shews [*sic*] an earth fort crumbled down on all sides, utterly defenceless....[11]

On the 14th they reached their ultimate destination, Niagara Falls, and made several visits over the next two days. On the 15th, Dalhousie stated that Woolford had "taken a collection of sketches & these small pieces on the whole are very good."[12] In fact there are six in the album, consisting of scenes of the American Falls, *The Canadian Falls from Goat Island, Niagara Falls* (Fig. 28.7), a view from the bridge to Goat Island, and a rather surrealistic sketch of *The Whirlpool, Niagara Falls.* Dalhousie boasted in his journal that they had accomplished their goal "not only without difficulty, but with the utmost ease & comfort, not yet a month from Halifax."[13]

The next two sketches are of *The Steam Boat "Frontinack"* (Fig. 28.8) in which the party travelled for a portion of the trip. Woolford left the main group at Kingston to proceed back to Halifax alone, and perhaps the last four sketches relate to his return, although they were likely places he had encountered on the way to Niagara. There is one of Brockville, one of the Cedar Rapids, and one entitled *Passing Down the Long Sault*, once again reminiscent of another drawing in the National Archives collection attributed to William Roebuck.[14] The final sketch of the album is a view of the Cascades.

In 1820, Woolford returned to Halifax and soon after designed Dalhousie College. After accompanying the governor general on a canoe trip in 1821, he was appointed assistant barrack-master at St. John, New Brunswick, in 1823. Following that he became barrack-master general at Fredericton, retiring from this post in 1859. After Dalhousie left Canada in 1828, Woolford continued to produce architectural designs, including those for Government House in Fredericton, and King's College of the University of New Brunswick. He also created drawings used to illustrate the book *New Brunswick, with notes for emigrants*, by Abraham Gesner. He remained in Fredericton until his death in 1866.

The Woolford album is a good example of early art patronage in Canada that created an environment where a talented artist could capture with pencil the vigour of Canadian scenery. As a complement to the Dalhousie journals, it is valuable evidence of the activities of a colonial official in the early nineteenth century. When understood within the context of the other material from the Dalhousie collection that has returned to Canada, it is noteworthy as an exciting piece of a larger treasure. The album itself is a testament to the skill and versatility of an artist who came to Canada and decided to make it his home.

M.M.

28.1 J.E. Woolford
View on Point Levi, ca. 1819
Brown wash
NA C-99524

28.2 J.E. Woolford
On the Parade at Montreal, ca. 1819
Brown wash
NA C-99543

28.3 J.E. Woolford
Long Sault from the Bottom,
ca. 1819
Brown wash
NA C-99553

28.4 J.E. Woolford
Perspective View of the Barracks, Fort Henry, Kingston, ca. 1819
Grey wash
NA C-99557

28.5 J.E. Woolford
Mills Three Miles from York, ca. 1819
Brown wash
NA C-99560

28.6 J.E. Woolford
Fort Niagara from Fort George, ca. 1819
Brown wash
NA C-99561

28.7 J.E. Woolford
The Canadian Falls from Goat Island, Niagara Falls, ca. 1819
Brown wash
NA C-99570

28.8 J.E. Woolford
The Steam Boat "Frontinack," ca. 1819
Brown wash
NA C-99574

1. University of New Brunswick Archives, Saunders family papers, John E. Woolford's account of his services in the army, 1797 to 1860.

2. *Dictionary of Canadian Biography* (Toronto: University of Toronto Press, 1976), 9:849-850.

3. Mary Allodi, *Printmaking in Canada* (Toronto: Royal Ontario Museum, 1980), xiii, 34.

4. Marie Elwood, "The Discovery and Repatriation of the Lord Dalhousie Papers," *Archivaria* 24 (Summer 1987): 110.

5. Inscriptions remaining on adjacent stubs identify the sketches as *Fall of Montmorency from the bottom*, and *From the Bottom of Canadian Fall of Niagara*.

6. Marjory Whitelaw, ed., *The Dalhousie Journals* (Ottawa: Oberon Press, 1978), 119-120.

7. Whitelaw, 123.

8. Whitelaw, 125.

9. Whitelaw, 126.

10. Allodi, 39. "John Woolford's experience as an architect and as a draughtsman is evident in his set of Halifax building studies, particularly in this unadorned elevation. The building had recently been completed, and architect John Merrick's working drawings might have been available for Woolford's use."

11. Whitelaw, 132.

12. Whitelaw, 137.

13. Whitelaw, 138.

14. Several sketches in the Woolford album relate very closely to works attributed to William Roebuck dated ca. 1820, in the NA collection. They are *The Long Sault, The Long Sault from the bottom, Passing down the Long Sault* and *View at the Cascades*. See W. Martha E. Cooke, *W.H. Coverdale Collection of Canadiana* (Ottawa: Public Archives of Canada, 1983), 169-171.

CHARLES RAMUS FORREST (ca. 1787-1827)

29. *Cape Diamond and Pointe Lévis, Quebec from the Chaudière River*, July 1823

Watercolour over pencil with scraping out on paper

32.4 x 42.4 cm

Inscribed in pen and brown ink, verso, c.: *Canadian Views. No. 48 / Cape Diamond & Point Levi, Quebec. from the heights of the Left bank / of the Chaudiere River, near its mouth / July 1823*

Purchased in 1987 with the assistance of a grant from the minister of Communications under the terms of the *Cultural Property Export and Import Act*

Accession no.: 1987-26-1

Negative no.: C-130700

From 1821 to 1823, Lt. Col. Charles Ramus Forrest served as aide-de-camp and assistant military secretary to Lord Dalhousie, governor-in-chief of Canada, 1820-1828.[1] While posted in North America, Forrest made numerous watercolour views, particularly around Quebec City. This view is one of these, and is taken from the mouth of the Chaudière River as it meets the St. Lawrence on the south shore, about six miles west of Quebec City.

Dalhousie had known Forrest during their service together at Bordeaux during the Peninsular War, 1812-1813, and in late December 1820 he sent orders requesting Forrest as his aide-de-camp. Dalhousie wrote in his diary that he feared that Forrest's "large family and natural turn for drawing and painting will prevent him coming to me...."[2] Forrest, however, responded to the call and arrived in Quebec City with his family on 16 June 1821.[3] Dalhousie had wanted Forrest not for his artistic talents but for his value as an officer. In fact, Dalhousie had since 1819 engaged John Elliott Woolford (Cat. no. 28) to act as his official artist, recording through his drawings the various tours the indefatigable Dalhousie pursued. Forrest's role as part of Dalhousie's personal staff was to contribute to the smooth operation of the vice-regal office. Nonetheless, Dalhousie did collect watercolours by Forrest, including a number that Forrest had apparently copied from works by Woolford.[4]

There is no evidence that Woolford and Forrest developed a relationship as brother artists, even though they were working in close contact as part of Dalhousie's household. However, Forrest apparently was acquainted with a fellow officer, James Pattison Cockburn (1779-1847), who was first posted to Quebec from November 1822 until June 1823. During this short time, according to Lord Dalhousie's diaries, Cockburn and Forrest were constant companions and often sketched together.[5] Apparently, Cockburn found his sketching companion to be a very odd fellow; Lord Dalhousie records in his diary that Cockburn found Forrest to be the "most unaccountable character he has ever met with."[6] Dalhousie too found him difficult, and his high expectations for Forrest were not realized after two years of service. As a result, Dalhousie relieved him of his duties effective 24 June 1823, and notes three main causes for Forrest's dismissal: his sullen and distant behaviour, the absence of himself and his family from church service and the fact that Forrest openly kept an English mistress at Quebec.[7] Forrest embarked for England in July 1823, the date of the present watercolour. It is possible that the watercolour was completed after his return to England.

Forrest, like Woolford and Cockburn, is one of the many soldier-artists who served in Canada with the British Army, and whose watercolours are highly valued as records of early Canada and as embodiments of the English landscape and watercolour traditions. Both Woolford and Cockburn are known to have received formal military training, which included instruction in drawing. While there is no documentation concerning Forrest's training, his extant drawings, maps and military journal make it clear that he had received formal instruction.

Although all three officers practised in the tradition of English topographical watercolour painting infused with elements of the picturesque, Forrest's controlled, meticulous workmanship is in striking contrast to the more fluid, spontaneous technique of either of his brother officers' Canadian work (Fig. 29.1). In fact, the most interesting comparison of Forrest's work can be made with that of Thomas Davies (ca. 1737-1812), who belongs to an earlier generation of British soldier-artists. Davies attended the Royal Military Academy, where he studied drawing some forty years before either Cockburn or Woolford, and was in Quebec ca. 1786-1790. Forrest and Davies have similar distinctive styles that make their work readily recognizable (Fig. 29.2, compare with Fig. 29.4). Forrest's finished watercolours, like those of Davies, are highly coloured, and layer light against dark in order to define shapes and create perspective. Forrest, however has a warm colour palette, while Davies tended to use cooler colours.[8]

Like Davies, Forrest stylized many of the natural elements in his compositions. The forces of nature are brought under control, reduced to their basic structure and recreated by the artist in patterns. A rocky outcropping is reduced to a neat pile of rounded boulders. Waterfalls are feathery undulating masses somewhat unaffected by the forces of gravity. Rivers are traced out in long regular strips of blue and white, and appear like sheets of glass. Trees are recreated with plume-like foliage. Hillsides tuck neatly one behind the other. Distant mountains become soft conical shapes marching quietly across the landscape. In all, nature is subdued and made neat and tidy in Forrest's vision.

Forrest's cityscapes are more conventional than are his interpretations of nature. His depictions of buildings – especially as seen in his ambitious but unfinished panoramic views of Quebec City[9] and in a very fine watercolour of Wolfefield (Fig. 29.3), a villa near Quebec City – attest to his proficiency as a draughtsman.

Forrest's Canadian work rarely contains the charming details of human activity that distinguish Davies' and Cockburn's compositions. As in the present watercolour, Forrest's figures appear more like stickmen and do not have the anecdotal quality of Davies' groupings. One might speculate that Forrest's alleged anti-social tendencies are somehow manifest in the lack of significant human presence in his Canadian compositions.

However distinctive Forrest's painting style, his watercolours are nonetheless accurate accounts of the locations he visited, in keeping with his role as a military observer. The present watercolour shows a view, looking north-north-east towards Quebec City from the mouth of the Chaudière River, depicting in the distance the promontory of Cape Diamond, the site of the Citadel fortifications with one of its two telegraph signal poles visible. Below are several ships at anchor along the shoreline, while the city itself is beyond the cape and out of view. Opposite Cape Diamond is Pointe Lévis with some of its buildings and wharves in evidence.

At the time Forrest was at Quebec, the timber and mercantile trades were prospering. Quebec was the gateway to the interior of Canada, and the transfer place for goods arriving and for the timber and furs being shipped to Europe (see Cat. no. 30, view of a Quebec shipyard). Navigation upstream past Quebec was risky, so most transatlantic shipping terminated at Quebec. The shoreline around Quebec was lined with wharves and warehouses, and although it is not obvious in the foreground of Forrest's watercolour, there was a wharf at the confluence of the Chaudière and St. Lawrence Rivers. However, he does show the buildings and warehouses, as well as the ferry crossing. The ferryman can be seen readying his flat-bottom boat, while a horse is being led to the landing in preparation for the crossing. A boat carrying human passengers is also shown at mid-crossing. A map, prepared in 1822,[10] a year prior to this watercolour, clearly indicates the wharf, the buildings and the ferry crossing, thus demonstrating that Forrest recorded these details of the location with a certain accuracy.

While the mouth of the Chaudière served as anchorage for ships and storage for lumber, flour and other goods, the famous Chaudière Falls, four miles from the mouth, attracted many visitors who often came by way of the ferry, crossing to the west side of the river where a path led to the falls. Though none is known to exist, it is very likely that Forrest did a watercolour of the Chaudière Falls, since it was one of the most popular natural attractions around Quebec City, along with St. Anne Falls (Fig. 29.4) and Montmorency Falls, both of which he recorded in watercolour and which are now in the collection of the National Gallery of Canada.

The present view was apparently a very popular one, since it offered an uninterrupted vista for some six miles looking toward Quebec City. Several other artists also chose to depict the St. Lawrence from this perspective. Among them was Daniel Wadsworth, founder of the Wadsworth Atheneum in Hartford, Connecticut, who accompanied Benjamin Silliman on an adventure holiday through Quebec in 1819. Silliman published an account of the trip, and included several engravings after drawings made by Wadsworth. One entitled *Quebec from the Chaudier* [sic] (Fig. 29.5) shows a strikingly similar view, with large ships at anchor in the foreground. Silliman's describes the view as follows:

> This scene, which we thought not to be exceeded in beauty by any that we saw in Canada, was sketched from the left bank of the Chaudiere river, at its mouth. Our road from Point Levi, conducted us to the foot of the precipise [*sic*] of rock, which is seen on the opposite side of the Chaudiere; and while a larger boat was getting ready to convey over carriage and horses, Mr. W [adsworth] had the good fortune to cross first, in a small boat, and occupied the few moments, before the rest of us arrived, in securing the outline of this grand and beautiful prospect.... This is the mouth of a very considerable river, the Chaudiere, which here, coming from the south east, pours its black waters into the deep green St. Lawrence, and is so imprisoned between abrupt, precipitous shores, principally of rock, but over hung in part by forest, that from the high back where the view was taken only a part of the river is seen.[11]

A few years after Forrest completed his watercolour, an elegant single-arch bridge was built over the Chaudière at the ferry landing to connect the road along the south shore of the St. Lawrence. While the exact date of the construction of the bridge is not known, it is represented in a pen and ink drawing by an unknown artist, dated March 1834 (Fig. 29.6). From the vantage point of the frozen St. Lawrence, several buildings are shown, along with ice-bound ships apparently moored at the wharf.

Upon his return to England, Forrest found himself in financial straits. He was receiving only half pay and attempted to capitalize on his watercolours. The London publisher Rudolph Ackermann published twenty-six aquatint views based on some of the extraordinary watercolours Forrest produced during his posting in India between 1807 and 1811. These prints were highly praised and were reissued with Spanish and Italian texts. There were also plans to publish a set of forty-eight Canadian views under the title "Picturesque Tour through the Provinces of Lower and Upper Canada." This project, announced in April 1825, was never realized; however, there is evidence that Forrest may have been preparing his watercolours with some thought of publishing them as coloured prints. The back of the present watercolour is neatly inscribed "Canadian Views. No. 48," followed by a full descriptive title and the date July 1823. At least three other Forrest watercolours bear similar inscriptions, each beginning with "Canadian Views" followed by a number and a full title, and all dated 1823. They are the view of St. Anne Falls, previously mentioned, which bears the number 50; a view of Quebec City as seen from the General Hospital, numbered 59 (National Gallery); and a view at Bay St. Paul on the St. Lawrence River, numbered 56 (Royal Ontario Museum). Whether Forrest began to prepare these in anticipation of his departure from Canada and with an eye to publishing them is uncertain. He was in the habit of numbering his watercolours, and several other works bear numbering schemes similar to the one noted above, but none are complete sequences.

At about the time Ackermann announced the Canadian prints, Forrest assumed a position at the Quartermaster General's Department, and by 29 June 1826 was again put on half pay; he died shortly thereafter. If the beauty of Forrest's watercolours had been realized in a print set, there is little doubt that it would have been one of the finest collections of Canadian views published in the nineteenth century.

L.F.

29.1 J.P. Cockburn
Cape Diamond from above the Chaudière River, 1828
Watercolour
NA C-12626

29.2 T. Davies
View on the River La Puce near Quebec, 1792
Watercolour
National Gallery of Canada 6274

29.3 C.R. Forrest
Wolfefield, near Quebec, ca. 1821-1823
Watercolour
Private collection
Photograph courtesy of Sotheby's, London

29.4 C.R. Forrest
St. Anne Falls, 1823
Watercolour
National Gallery of Canada 18509

29.5 S.S. Jocelyn, after D. Wadsworth
Quebec from the Chaudier, 1824
Engraving
NA C-18175

29.6 Unknown artist
Chaudière Bridge from Bordage, 1834
Pen and ink
NA C-89515

1. Charles Ramus Forrest joined the 3rd Regiment of Foot in 1802; served in India 1807-1811; served in the Peninsular War 1812-1813 and in the expedition against New Orleans 1814-1815; was posted to Canada 1821-1823; died 1827. For a more complete biography, see W. Martha E. Cooke, *W.H. Coverdale Collection of Canadiana* (Ottawa: Public Archives of Canada, 1983), 81-85.

2. Dalhousie papers, Journals, NA, MG 24 A12, microfilm, reel A-536, entry for 1 January 1821.

3. *Quebec Gazette*, 19 June 1821 and Dalhousie papers, Journals, 20 June 1821.

4. Seven watercolour views by Forrest of the French and Ottawa Rivers in the collection of the National Gallery and once belonging to Dalhousie are thought to be copies of works by Woolford. One of these watercolours is inscribed in Dalhousie's hand "copied by Lt. Col. Forrest from a sketch by Woolford."

5. The National Archives has a collection of over three hundred works by Cockburn; the Royal Ontario Museum has close to two hundred.

6. Dalhousie papers, Section 3, no. 372, NA, MG 24 A12, microfilm, reel A-533, letter to Col. Couper from Dalhousie, 22 April 1823.

7. Dalhousie papers, Section 3, nos. 59 and 372, NA, MG 24 A12, microfilm, reels A-329 and A-533, letter to Forrest from Dalhousie, Quebeç, 24 February 1823; letter to Col. Darling from Dalhousie, Quebec, 25 February 1823; letter to Col. Couper from Dalhousie, Quebec, 22 April 1823.

8. Dalhousie typified Forrest's autumn landscape, rather unenthusiastically writing that, "I have some drawings by Colonel Forrest trying to imitate them (autumn foliage), but gaudy and tawdry as they may appear to a critical judge, they do not come near the gaudiness & brilliancy of nature at the time...," Dalhousie papers, Journals, NA, MG 24 A12, entry for 7 October 1822.

9. Several of Forrest's panoramic views, one of which is over twelve feet long, are in the collection of the National Gallery.

10. John Adams, *Quebec and Its Environs from Actual & Original Survey, 1822*, engraved map, published 1826. The map has inset views of the Chaudière and Montmorency Falls, NA, NMC H2 / 349-Quebec-1826.

11. Benjamin Silliman, *Remarks made, on a short tour, between Hartford and Quebec in the autumn of 1819*, 2nd ed. (New Haven: S. Converse, 1824), 272-273.

GEORGE SETON (1819-1905)

30. *A Panoramic View of Quebec from Pointe Lévis*, 1847-1849

Watercolour over pencil with brown and blue washes and scraping out on paper

29.4 x 103.5 cm

Inscribed in pen and brown ink, verso, u.l.: *Quebec, Canada. From Point Levi. 17' Sept. 1847 / In 3 Sheets – No. 1*; l.l.: *7' July '49*; u.c.: *Quebec, Canada, – From Point Levi – 20 Sept '47/In 3 Sheets – No. 2*; l.c.: *3' July '49*; u.r.: *Panoramic Sketch of Quebec, Canada. 20 Sept '47/In 3 Sheets No. 3.*; l.r.: *26' June '49*

Purchased in 1985

Accession no.: 1986-15-2

Negative no.: C-96435

Judging by the large numbers of views of Quebec City taken from the vantage site of Pointe Lévis, the locale was a nineteenth-century hotspot for tourists, on a par with Niagara Falls. Indeed, the traveller was exhorted by no less avid an observer than James Pattison Cockburn to "cross the St. Lawrence, and visit the beautiful shore of Point Levi, where the roads are excellent and the scenery lovely."[1]

Following the tradition of a cadre of British military watercolourists, George Seton painted his panorama in the acceptable style of a tinted or stained drawing – an outlined subject with an almost monochromatic wash applied to afford weight in required areas. This method was particularly appropriate for working out-of-doors, where a fuller palette would have been more awkward to handle. In addition, Seton's watercolour was composed on three separate sheets joined with cloth. The division of the support in this manner facilitated the execution of panoramic views "on site" without the physical travail of a large single sheet. A further extension was added along the bottom.

George Seton was born in London, England, on 18 March 1819. *Burke's Landed Gentry of Great Britain* noted that he was descended from a branch of the Setons of Pitmedden. Lt.-Col. Alexander Seton of Mounie, the eldest brother and heir to the family seat, was a Scottish hero. An iron troopship under his command, the *Birkenhead*, foundered south of Cape Town on 26 February 1852. Alexander's selfless rescue of women and children in another boat disaster is memorialized by "Seton Lake" in British Columbia, so-named by A.C. Anderson during an early topographical survey expedition.[2]

On 28 July 1838, at the age of nineteen, George Seton purchased a commission as ensign in the 93rd Sutherland Highlanders. At the time, the majority of this regiment was stationed in North America, but Seton was initially attached to the headquarters depot, which remained in the United Kingdom. He was not posted abroad for almost six years. War Office records indicate that he arrived at Halifax on 14 April 1844, on board the troopship *Resistance*, having been promoted to the rank of lieutenant on 13 May 1842. His company proceeded to Quebec City two weeks later.

The 93rd Regiment was stationed in the Montreal region from May 1844 until July 1846. In the National Archives holdings are fourteen works that, originally ascribed to an unknown artist, were reattributed to George Seton.[3] This group of works includes sketches of Kingston, Niagara Falls, Beloeil and Trois-Rivières, executed between June and September 1844. Seton's regiment proceeded from Montreal to Quebec City in July 1846, where it would remain until August 1848.

The city that greeted Seton was, during the middle and late 1840s, enjoying the benefits of a thriving timber industry feeding the markets of Europe. Hand-in-hand came a booming ship-building trade, which would reach its apogee in the decade to follow. Timber exports set in place increasing demands for vessels to transport the supply to foreign markets. Records show that, in the year 1846, a virtual armada of 1,439 vessels arrived at the port of Quebec:

> The coves for miles on both sides of the river were sometimes like a forest of masts, so close were the ships lying to one another....[4]

Seton's rendition of these masts, in a watercolour in the holdings of the National Archives entitled *Sketch from Near the Old French Works* (Fig. 30.1), reminds one of a stand of leafless trees in winter. By the early 1850s, there were a record number of twenty-five ship-building yards and at least eight floating docks in and around Quebec and Pointe Lévis.[5] There were miles of dockage and dozens of boats loading pine at any one time, bound for European markets.[6]

In addition, Quebec, at the time Seton began this sketch, would have been rebuilding from the damage inflicted by two major fires in May and June 1845. The effects of an expanding economy were felt in all ancilliary communities. Obviously, George Seton was as impressed with the commerce as with the view. His watercolour does not portray the Lévis side as simply a bucolic retreat. Although a town would not officially be founded until about three years later, the artist depicted the bustle of the incipient community of Lévis. As well as rendering the majesty of Quebec City's ascending cliffs, he presents us with the accoutrements of the inseparable industries of lumber and ship-building.

The foreground is occupied by the Davie shipyard, the oldest in Canada, established by Allison Davie in 1830, and declared a national historic site in July 1990. A publication on the extended Davie family makes the claim that their dockyards were almost single-handedly responsible for the establishment of the city of Lévis.[7] Their ship-building enterprise would continue in operation for well over a century. The rows of standing posts indicate the supports used to hold ships' keels in place during construction or in the course of the repairs that were essential to many vessels after a few rough Atlantic passages. The timber commodity was an especially destructive export to transport. Loads were often placed on the decks – a dangerous locale during cold, icy autumn crossings. Ship-yards such as Davie's were often quite insular units that controlled their own saw-mills, timber-ranches and foundries.

The river is presented as a thriving source of transport. A ferry-boat parallels the shore, escorting sight-seers, businessmen and farmers to the tip of the Pointe Lévis shoreline. Cargo ships come and go as empty holds load up with the precious squared timbers. In the foreground are the loading docks and ships berthed for their short stays.

Across the St. Lawrence, Quebec City stands as the Gibraltar of North America. The *Illustrated London News* (29 September 1860) described it as "such a combination of the old and new... as makes it resemble no other place under the sun." Despite a city plan that an 1857 guide book describes as "the greatest enemy of symmetry," one is able to distinguish various architectural landmarks. To the left can be seen the Citadel and, below, the harbour of Cape Diamond. To the right of the enceinte is positioned the monument to Wolfe and Montcalm on Des Carrières Street. Behind and to the left of the obelisk stands the Ursuline Convent. The first spire, piercing the horizon to the left of centre, is the English Cathedral, built in 1804.

The dates of the work, 1847-1849, indicate that the finishing touches were completed when Seton returned to England. The 93rd Regiment left Quebec on 1 August 1848, embarking once again on the troop-ship *Resistance* to sail to Portsmouth. A short detachment with the 95th Regiment was followed by Seton's exchange to the Royal Canadian Rifles in November 1853. A month later, Captain Seton married Anne Lucy Wake of York in County Cumberland, England. Evidently, he returned to the colony shortly afterwards, as War Office records indicate that his two sons, Alexander, born in 1854, and William, in 1856, were baptized in Kingston, Ontario. Seton obtained his majority, by purchase, 14 December 1855. Numerous references to his later services can be found in the records of the Hudson's Bay Company, with which the regiment was associated.[8] A letter from William McTavish to George Simpson informed him that Major Seton wished to resign from his regiment and was planning to leave for England on 17 October 1858. The National Archives owns a sketchbook recording Seton's travels in the Red River colony in 1857-1858, indicating that he continued his sketching as he travelled further west during this second stay in Canada.[9]

George Seton's watercolours and drawings, executed during his stay in North America, have often been incorrectly attributed to a Charles Murray.[10] Curiously enough, two Charles Murrays have been documented as amateur artists working in the mid-nineteenth century.[11] The first was Charles Murray, Earl of Cathcart, whom Seton would have known while Murray held the position of commander-in-chief of the forces in British North America, and that of governor general of Canada from 1846 to 1847. Seton also belonged to the same regiment as another member of this family, the Hon. Augustus Murray Cathcart, from 1846 to 1848. Drawings and watercolours by Seton from the Royal Ontario Museum were formerly attributed to Charles Murray, Earl of Cathcart, because they may at one time have been owned by the Cathcart family.[12] A second Charles Adolphus Murray, Earl of Dunmore, served a short period in Canada in 1862 and is noted as exhibiting seventy-one works in 1894 at the Fine Art Society show in London, England.[13] It is difficult to link this C. A. Murray and George Seton, who retired from the armed services on 24 September 1858. Two watercolours in the collection of the Glenbow Museum, attributed to the Earl of Dunmore, show little or no stylistic similarities to Seton's work.[14]

The addition of this fine watercolour panorama complements a varied array of similar subject matter in the collection of the National Archives, as well as enhancing previously acquired Seton works. Many views of Quebec City from the Lévis shore are in the National Archives holdings. But George Seton, with his artistic eye on the commerce and industry of those bustling days, adds more than a topographical "lie of the land." He chose, instead, to give us an almost aural image of that far shore of Lévis, a testament to its lively din.

J.D.

30.1 G. Seton
Sketch from Near the Old French Works,
23 June-27 October 1847
Watercolour
NA C-96947

1. [James Pattison Cockburn], *Quebec and its Environs : Being a Picturesque Guide to the Stranger* ([Quebec] : T. Carey, 1831), 23.

2. Provincial Archives of British Columbia, A.C. Anderson papers, Correspondence Outward; see also an article in the *Ottawa Journal*, 26 January 1953, p. 6.

3. These works (NA, Accession nos. 1953-75-1 to 14) were reattributed, in 1981, by Mary Allodi, Royal Ontario Museum, and by Jim Burant, NA.

4. George Gale, *Quebec Twixt Old and New* (Quebec: The Telegraph Printing Co., 1915), 73.

5. Gale, 65.

6. Gale, 75. In addition, valuable information on the shipbuilding industry can be garnered from G.J.J. Tuchinsky, *The River and the Bush: the Timber Trade in the Ottawa Valley, 1800-1900* (Montreal: McCord Museum, McGill University, 1981).

7. Capt. G.W. Haws, *The Haws Family and their Seafaring Kin* (Dunfermline: J.B. Mackie & Co., 1932), 109.

8. Hudson's Bay Company Archives, Winnipeg, Governor's papers, D/43-D5/47, NA, MG20, microfilm, reels HBC 3M112, 3M114, 3M115, 3M116, Governor George Simpson – Correspondence Inward contains several letters from Seton to Simpson, most in the form of complaints concerning accommodations and pay.

9. Seton was in command of a company of volunteers from the Royal Canadian Rifles, who were stationed in Fort Garry at the request of the Hudson's Bay Company. Fearful of the potential erosion of their monopoly by the westward-expanding United States, Company officials persuaded the War Office to lend support by stressing the possibility of civil and Sioux nation unrest. For further information, see "A Soldier at Fort Garry," *The Beaver* (Autumn 1957), 10-15.

10. For an example, see Kennedy Galleries (New York), *The Kennedy Quarterly*, December 1973 (sale catalogue).

11. J. Russell Harper, *Early Painters and Engravers in Canada* (Toronto: University of Toronto Press, 1970), 61 and 234.

12. Mary Allodi, *Canadian Watercolours and Drawings in the Royal Ontario Museum*, vol. 2 (Toronto: The Royal Ontario Museum, 1974), nos. 1491 and 1507.

13. Jane Johnson and A. Greutzner, *The Dictionary of British Artists, 1880-1940* ([Suffolk, England]: Antique Collector's Club, 1976), 369.

14. Glenbow Museum, Cat. nos. DEM 61.95.3 and 61.95.4.

GEORGE ST. VINCENT WHITMORE (1798-1851)

31. *Aurora Borealis, Quebec*,
25 January 1837

Watercolour over pencil on paper

21.9 x 20.5 cm

Inscribed on mount, in the hand of the Earl of Gosford, in pencil, verso, u.l.: *By Capt Whitmore R E*; in artist's hand, in pen and brown ink, c.: *25 Jany 1837*

Purchased in 1987 with the assistance of a grant from the minister of Communications under the terms of the *Cultural Property Export and Import Act*

Accession no.: 1988-10-5

Negative no.: C-131918

This watercolour by Lt. George St. Vincent Whitmore depicts a spectacular occurrence of the aurora borealis, which could be seen in both Quebec and Montreal on the evening of 25 January 1837. The phenomenon was so extraordinary that it inspired extensive description in the newspapers:

> After some time, going into the street to see if the supposed fire had been subdued, we observed that the streak, or pillar of flame, was the Aurora Borealis, but unusually luminous in its appearance.... Immediately in the zenith it had the appearance of a star, such as is depicted by heralds, radiating downwards towards the horizon, forming a gorgeous canopy in the heavens, displaying, in folds, all the prismatic colours....
>
> [The] darting or evolving was accompanied by a sound as the rushing of wind through trees, or the distant murmur of a rapid stream.... Altogether it was the most brilliant and imposing appearance of this, yet undefined, phenomenon we have ever seen.[1]

There was also the following "flight of the imagination" by a Mr. T.J. Martin from Lower Town in Quebec:

> What are ye, O ye changing lights,
>
> ....
>
> Are ye the spirits of Warriors dead,
> Whose blood on mighty battles shed
>
> ....
>
> Are ye the dread infernal host
>
> ....
>
> Are ye malaria raised from swamps,
> Where lie the dead of thousand camps...?[2]

Whitmore's watercolour clearly shows the "canopy from heaven" effect, made very dramatic through being contrasted with the grey monochrome of the evening landscape and its silhouetted inhabitants. The view is taken looking northeast towards the St. Lawrence River along Des Carrières Street from the corner of Mount Carmel Street. On the right we can see the Jardin des Gouverneurs with the monument to Wolfe and Montcalm, and beyond, further to the right, the walls of the Citadel and Cape Diamond Redoubt.

Whitmore was not the only one fascinated by the aurora and its effects. At least two other sketches, one by Lt. Philip John Bainbrigge and another by Lt. A.F. Bowen, exist of the same subject.[3] All three watercolours had been in the collection of Archibald Acheson, 2nd Earl of Gosford, governor general of Lower Canada from 1835 to 1838, who managed to assemble an interesting selection of watercolours by various military officers. Included were several watercolours by Bainbrigge, such as Cat. no. 32 and others by Capt. Charles Wright.[4] In fact, the identification of Whitmore as the artist who executed this watercolour rests on Gosford's inscription on the verso of the mount.

George St. Vincent Whitmore (1798-1851), a newcomer to the known group of topographical artists active in Canada in the 1830s and 1840s, was the oldest son of Gen. George Whitmore, colonel-commandant of the Royal Engineers.[5] He joined the same regiment as second lieutenant in 1816.[6] He was a first lieutenant when he arrived in Quebec in August 1835 with his wife, Isabella Maxwell, five children – one of whom died within a month of their arrival – and three servants.[7] Three children were born during his time in Canada, Henry Ainslie in 1837 and Charles William in 1838 (died in 1839), both in Quebec; and Emily in 1840 in Kingston.[8] In June 1836, Whitmore was appointed adjutant to the commander of the Royal Engineers, Major General Nicolls, a position he occupied until 1839, in addition to being the district engineer in Quebec.[9] A major assignment as adjutant had been to put Quebec into a state of defence immediately after the first news of the 1837 uprising was received.[10] During the rebellion, Whitmore was commander of several militia regiments in Quebec City.[11] In addition to the work caused by the rebellion, Whitmore acted as expert for the Crown in a major land arbitration case, which lasted for three years and involved the ownership of land needed for military purposes.[12] He wrote a petition to receive remuneration for being adjutant:

> To accomplish these duties I gave up both night and day, nor was I once absent from my post... [and I had to go to] considerable expense for cariole hire during the winter 1837 and 1838. My one horse for which I was allowed forage being unequal to the work my duties required.[13]

He was promoted to captain in the Army in 1839. In 1840, Whitmore was posted to Kingston as district engineer.[14] Kingston was experiencing unprecedented construction activity at this time, because it was to become the new capital of the United Province of Upper and Lower Canada. Whitmore supervised the building of the commissariat stores of the advanced battery of Fort Henry. Because these were built one thousand pounds under the estimate, a brass tablet was installed to commemorate this achievement.[15] Whitmore was ordered to return to England in the late fall of 1841, but his order was postponed until the spring of 1842, because his expertise in land arbitration was needed and because of the difficulties of moving his large family of six children during the winter.[16] He was promoted to major in 1851 and died in the same year at Charlton in Kent.

Whitmore was in Canada at a time of unprecedented military activity, as large numbers of troops were stationed in the Canadas for the purposes of defence, to put down two rebellions and to carry out new construction.[17] His posting coincided with those of a group of artistically active officers, such as Lt. Philip John Bainbrigge, (Cat. no. 32) also of the Royal Engineers; Capt. Henry Francis Ainslie of the 83rd Regiment, Lt.-Col. James Hope-Wallace and Capt. Charles P. Wilbraham of the Coldstream Guards; and Lt.-Col. Henry William Barnard of the Grenadier Guards (Cat. no. 36). These officers have left a rich legacy of watercolours depicting their various postings and excursions. Oddly, however, despite the fact that Whitmore stayed in Canada for seven consecutive years, no other works by him were known prior to the acquisition of this watercolour. Yet the fact that his work was collected by Lord Gosford suggested that he was known for his sketches.

Among the holdings of works executed by British military officers, which forms such a significant part of the Documentary Art collection of the National Archives, was an album of twenty-four watercolours that fit the dates of Whitmore's arrival and early residence in Lower Canada.[18] The album was attributed to unknown artist "B," so-called because this initial is inscribed on some of the sketches. A stylistic comparison of *Aurora Borealis, Quebec* with these sketches showed promising similarities. The handling of details, such as the trees, fences and shadows in *The English Cathedral and Place d'Armes, Quebec City, Lower Canada* (Fig. 31.1), or the use of the silhouetted figure, as in *Indian Lorette from the Mill, Lower Canada* (Fig. 31.2) suggested the same hand as had worked on *Aurora Borealis*. But it was the extensive inscriptions on these watercolours that confirmed their new attribution (Figs. 31.3 and 31.4, both titled by the author on the verso). They matched exactly the examples of Whitmore's handwriting that were uncovered in the military records (Fig. 31.5). The flow of the writing, in addition to the similarity of words such as *the*, *Quebec* and *making*, and of letters such as the capital *B* and the *d* at the end of words, leaves no doubt that Whitmore inscribed these watercolours.

The problem remained with the initial "B." If Whitmore painted and inscribed them, why did he add the letter "B"? From the study of similar records in the Documentary Art collection, it is known that many of the officers and their circle of friends copied each other's pictures. For example, *The English Cathedral and Place d'Armes, Quebec City, Lower Canada* (Fig. 31.1) is known from two other versions, one in the Royal Ontario Museum drawn by Capt. Charles Wright, the other in a sketchbook by Mrs. Mary Millicent Chaplin, the wife of a Coldstream Guards officer, in the National Archives. Similarly, several sketches in the "B" sketchbook are replicas of watercolours by Philip John Bainbrigge, who served in the same regiment at almost the same time as Whitmore. The initial "B" appears on some of these copies. Whitmore must have used this notation to identify the sketches he copied from Bainbrigge. A discovery of a private collection of Whitmore sketches has confirmed this hypothesis.[19]

The other sketches in the Coverdale album consist of views taken around Quebec City and of the countryside, depicting all the picturesque spots that the British officers stationed in Canada regularly visited. Among the more unique are *St. Charles River near the Road to Indian Lorette, Lower Canada* (Fig. 31.6), because it likely shows a portrait of the Whitmore family; *Shadgett's Seminary on Lake Beauport*, a boys school where Whitmore's two older sons could have studied; and a scene showing a railway survey party entitled *Preparing for a Railroad through the Woods, Lower Canada*.

E.M.-M.

31.1 G. St. V. Whitmore

The English Cathedral and Place d'Armes, Quebec City, Lower Canada, ca. 1836

Watercolour

NA C-40362

31.2 G. St. V. Whitmore

Indian Lorette from the Mill, Lower Canada, 1836

Watercolour

NA C-40367

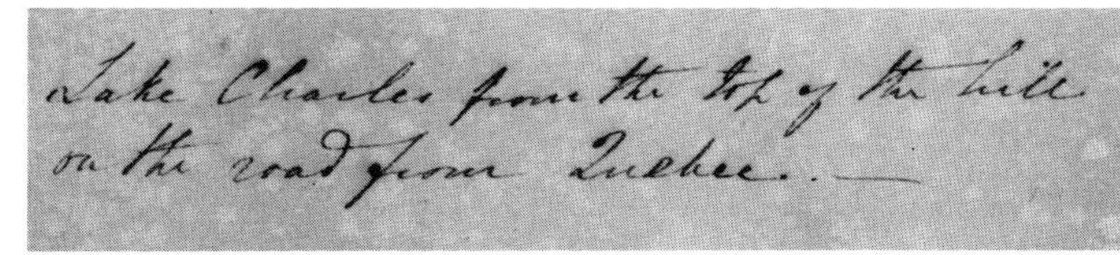
Lake Charles from the top of the hill on the road from Quebec. —

31.3 G. St. V. Whitmore
Inscription on verso of *Lake St. Charles from the Top of the Hill on the Road from Quebec*, ca. 1836
C-134701

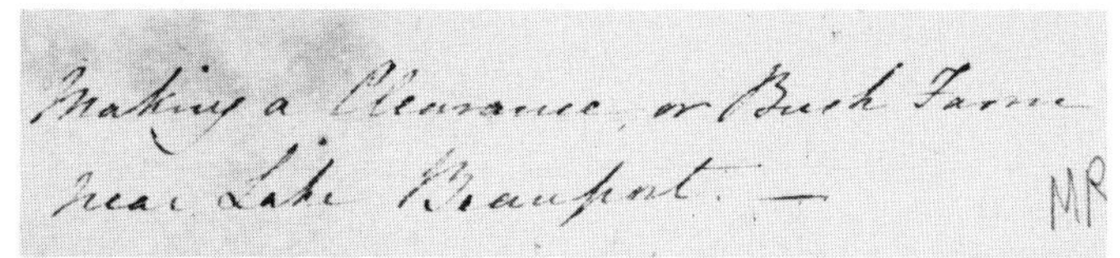
Making a Clearance, or Bush Farm near Lake Beaufort. — MR

31.4 G. St. V. Whitmore
Inscription on verso of *Making a Clearance on Bush Farm near Lake Beauport*, ca. 1836
NA C-85884

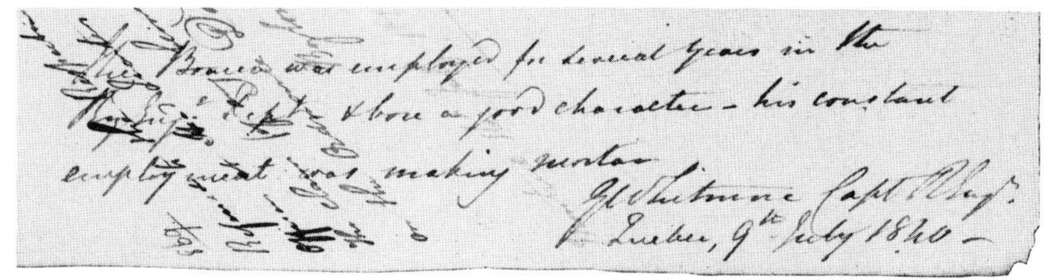
The Bearer was employed for several years in the ... Dept & bore a good character - his constant employment was making mortar
G Whitmore Capt R. Engrs
Quebec, 9th July 1840 —

31.5 G. St. V. Whitmore
***Recommendation of R. Molloy, Quebec, 9 July, 1840*,** 1840
NA RG 8 IA, vol. 218, p. 120 C-134605

31.6 G. St. V. Whitmore
***St. Charles River near the Road to Indian Lorette, Lower Canada*,** 1836
Watercolour
NA C-40324

---

1. *Quebec Mercury*, 26 January 1837.

2. *Quebec Mercury*, 26 January 1837.

3. Sotheby's (London), *Topographical Paintings, Watercolours and Drawings*, 4 November 1987, lots 44 and 53.

4. Sotheby's. Lots 41 through to 54 are all Canadian watercolours from Gosford's collection. In 1921, the 4th Earl of Gosford sold the contents of Gosford Castle, and the above lots were acquired by a private collector. This information was provided to the author by William A. Seaby, an acquaintance of the previous owner of the watercolours. The NA acquired lots 48, 49, 52 and 54.

5. Peter Townend, ed. *Burke's Genealogical and Heraldic History of the Peerage, Baronetage and Knightage*, 150th edition (London: Burke's Peerage Ltd., 1970), 2816-2817.

6. T.W.J. Connolly, "Skeleton Memoirs of RE officers," manuscript in the Royal Engineers Corps Library, Chatham.

7. *Quebec Mercury*, 22 August 1835, and letter to the author from Mrs. P. Whitmore, 24 March 1989.

8. *Burke's Peerage*, 2817.

9. NA, British Military and Naval Records, RG 8 IA, vol. 444, p. 74 (microfilm, reel C-2974), Col. Nicholls to the inspector of fortifications, 2 September 1836. There are a number of maps and architectural drawings in existence commissioned and signed by Whitmore during his years in both Upper and Lower Canada (see NA, NMC 1654, 1655, 3916, 3930, 4587, 4588, 5153, 11382, 11383, 22433).

10. Public Record Office, London, War Office Records, WO 55, vol. 875, p. 397, NA, MG 13, microfilm, reel C-2819, letter from Whitmore to the inspector general of fortifications, 30 May 1840.

11. *The Quebec Almanack and British American Kalendar*, 1838, 210; 1839, 223; and 1840, 251.

12. NA, RG 8 IA, vol. 450, pp. 70-72, 95-96, 159-160, 260-263, 281-283, 307-309; vol. 604, pp. 214-216.

13. Public Record Office, London, WO 55, vol. 875, pp. 397-398, NA, MG 13, microfilm, reel B-2819, letter from Whitmore to the inspector general of fortifications, 2 September 1840.

14. NA, Arthur Henry Freeling papers, MG 24 F72, diary entry for 24 December 1840. I would like to thank Tim Dubé of the Manuscript Division, NA, for his assistance.

15. Watson Kirkconnel, "Fort Henry 1812-1914," *Queen's Quarterly* (July, August, September, 1920), 84.

16. NA, RG 8 IA, vol. 451, p. 308, letter from Lieutenant-Colonel Ward to military secretary, 21 December 1841.

17. JIm Burant, "The Military Artist and the Documentary Art Record," *Archivaria* 26 (Summer 1988): 44.

18. W. Martha E. Cooke, *W.H. Coverdale Collection of Canadiana* (Ottawa: Public Archives of Canada, 1983), 8-14.

19. A sketchbook containing fourteen watercolours by Whitmore was subsequently donated to the NA (Accession no.: 1989-434) by descendants of the artist living in England. One image of the Capitol in Washington, D.C., is inscribed: *From an original sketch by P. Bainbrigge Esq. R.E.*

PHILIP JOHN BAINBRIGGE (1817-1881)

32. *Making Maple Sugar, Lower Canada*, ca. 1837

Watercolour over pencil with gum arabic and scraping out on paper

42.9 x 58.4 cm

Inscribed in pencil, verso, c.: *Making Maple Sugar, Lower Canada*

Purchased in 1987 with the assistance of a grant from the minister of Communications under the terms of the *Cultural Property Export and Import Act*

Accession no.: 1988-10-3

Negative no.: C-131921

Lt. Philip John Bainbrigge, a Royal Engineer in the British army, was posted in Canada between 1836 and 1842. Arriving in time to participate in the rebellions of 1837, he also travelled extensively throughout the Maritimes, Quebec, Ontario and New York State on special survey duties and reported on the nature of the country and the potential for its defence along the American frontier.[1] Like many of the soldier-artists whose works are represented in this exhibition, he recorded with his brush many of the places he visited; the National Archives alone has about 175 of his Canadian watercolours.

His depiction of maple sugar-making is distinguished not only because it is larger and more highly finished than many of his watercolours, but also because it depicts a subject other than the usual landscape or view of a town or settlement. Maple sugar-making, while a distinctly Canadian occupation, was rarely depicted by any of the early artists. Although there are many written descriptions dating as early as 1703, this watercolour by Bainbrigge is a rare early attempt to illustrate the process. There is no doubt that he meant his composition to be instructive, as he has included men performing all of the initial stages of the "sugaring off" and has made an inventory of the various utensils and containers used in the process.

The gathering and boiling of maple sap was introduced to European settlers by the native peoples, and by the late eighteenth century had became an important seasonal activity for farming families in north-eastern North America. Until the late nineteenth century, the sugar-makers produced only enough sugar and syrup to meet their own needs and to allow them to market it in local towns. For general consumption, sugar produced in the West Indies was preferred because it was readily available and was of a more consistent quality. Perhaps most importantly, it conferred a certain status on the household that could afford to serve it. By comparison, the supply of maple syrup and sugar was seasonal, and its quantity and quality depended on the spring weather, as well as the care taken by individual farming families in its preparation. While French Canadians and later British immigrants introduced improvements through the use of better, though usually home-made, implements, advances in the refining procedures were not seen until the beginning of the twentieth century.[2]

Then, as now, sap gathering began in the early spring, when cold night and warm daytime temperatures induced the flow or "run" of sap in the dormant trees. Once the run began, farmers would make their way to the sugarbush, either on their land or at greater distances in the forest where the highest concentration of maples could be found. There a sugar camp was established and a simple log shelter constructed. It accommodated the workers, who usually had to remain at the campsite for several weeks. Bainbrigge's watercolour depicts a log lean-to where a man sits enjoying his pipe, surrounded by the various activities that make up the operations of a sugar camp.

Sap was extracted from the tree by cutting with an axe a V-shaped gash in the trunk about 0.5 metre from the base of the tree. Once this "tapping" process was completed, sap would begin to flow from the wound. A "spile," made of a 15-25 centimetre piece of wood, either hollowed or concave, was inserted at the apex of the V and acted as a spout, guiding the sap to a trough that lay on the ground. There were variants on this technique, and eventually the gashing method of tapping was abandoned in favour of using an auger to bore a hole, a method that was thought to ensure the longevity of the tree.

The troughs were made from hollowed lengths of halved log about one metre long. Bainbrigge depicts the sap-collecting operation on the left of his composition, which shows a tree with the gash and the "spile" casting a shadow on the tree trunk. The trough is shown on the ground beside the tree. According to one account, the wooden troughs, although easily made and costing the farmer nothing, were often displaced by the effects of thawing and frost, or were frozen to the ground, both resulting in the loss of the valuable contents.[3] Wooden buckets were tried, but with similar results. Eventually, locally-made tin pails were used in place of the troughs, and a further innovation saw the pails hung on the tree below the spile or spigot.

At the extreme left of the watercolour is a man carrying a wooden bucket, presumably filled with sap gathered from the troughs. A wooden yoke was often worn over the shoulders with a bucket suspended from each end, which made the burden easier to carry, especially if the collector was making his rounds on snowshoes (Fig. 32.1). A large barrel was often mounted on a sledge drawn by either man or horse power. The sap from several trees could be poured into the barrel, thus making it possible to gather larger amounts of sap in one trip (Fig. 32.2).

Once gathered, the sap was brought to the sugar camp and deposited in a reservoir, usually a large barrel, as shown in the Bainbrigge watercolour, or a large hollowed log, where it was left to allow sediment to settle. From here the sap would be added to a large cauldron or kettle hung over a blazing fire. *The Canadian Settler's Guide* recommended that a large fallen tree be used as a back against which to build the fire. It also describes the method of suspending the kettles: " [Fix] two large stout-forked posts into the ground, over which a pole is laid, stout enough to support the kettles."[4] The kettles were then hung on hooked and notched poles above the fire as demonstrated by Bainbrigge. Two, and sometimes three, kettles of varying sizes were normally used, so that sap could be transferred to a smaller kettle once it had begun to thicken. Fresh sap then replenished the larger kettle. Once the sap had been reduced to the desired consistency, it could be used as syrup, or if further reduced it could be moulded into hard sugar loaves. It was also possible to make vinegar and spirits from the maple sap.

The boiling process was continuous and usually lasted well into the night. Careful attention at each phase of the refining process was necessary to ensure a good product. However, the clumsy methods often meant that a certain amount of the sap was wasted or spoiled. The fire, which had to be kept well stoked, often spewed ash into the boiling sap, and the heat and steam made it difficult and often dangerous for the attendant to remove syrup from the kettles. Bainbrigge's re-creation of the sugar camp includes not only the details of the operation, but also evokes some of its ambience. As a man pokes the blazing fire with a long pole, flaming embers rise in the smoke and steam that dominate the centre of the composition. Under this canopy, others chop wood and gather sap and add it to the large barrel. In the course of this continuous activity, there are periods of rest; in the left foreground a man sits on an up-ended bucket, a safe but comfortable distance from the fire. Surrounding all of this activity are the towering maples, whose trunks and still leafless branches weave a dense pattern on either side of the picture, creating a somewhat menacing presence. Bainbrigge was no doubt attempting to evoke for his English audience the exotic nature of this "primitive" operation carried out in the wilds of Lower Canada.

Bainbrigge gave this watercolour of maple sugar-making to the 2nd Earl of Gosford (governor-in-chief of British North America, 1835-1838) while both were serving in Canada. In all, Gosford received at least nine watercolours from Bainbrigge: three depicting Montmorency Falls in winter, two showing timber rafts at Quebec, single views of the aurora borealis at Quebec and of the Chaudière and St. Anne's Falls, and the present watercolour.[5] Gosford also acquired watercolours by Capt. George St. Vincent Whitmore, Capt. Charles Wright and Lt. Augustus Bowen. This collection of Canadian watercolours was sold in 1921 by the 4th Earl of Gosford, and the National Archives has subsequently been able to acquire the present watercolour and one by Whitmore (Cat. no. 31).

Bainbrigge did one other version of his maple sugar-making composition, which includes only the three central figures – the man tending the fire, the one resting in the lean-to and the one pouring sap into the barrel (Fig. 32.3). This variant watercolour is part of the James Du Pre Alexander, 3rd Earl of Caledon, collection deposited in the Public Record Office of North Ireland. Caledon served in Canada with the Coldstream Guards from 1838 to 1842 and, like Gosford, assembled a collection of watercolours by various soldier-artists as mementos of his years in Canada.

After returning to England in 1842, Bainbrigge went on to enjoy a long and very distinguished career, which included a long association with the Royal Military College, Woolwich. He retired in 1862 with the rank of major-general and from then until his death in 1881 he pursued charitable work among the "deserving poor of Greenwich."[6] He also lectured prospective emigrants to Canada, disseminating his knowledge of the country and perhaps enticing his audiences with tales of the sweet maple sugar made in the backwoods of Canada.

L.F.

32.1 J. Weston
Gathering Sap on Snow Shoes, 1880 (detail)
Wood engraving
In the *Canadian Illustrated News*, 17 April 1880
NA C-72948

32.2 H. Julien
Sugar Making in Canada, 1877 (detail)
Wood engraving
In the *Canadian Illustrated News*, 26 May 1877
NA C-65854

32.3 P.J. Bainbrigge
Making Maple Sugar, Lower Canada, ca. 1837
Watercolour
Public Record Office of Northern Ireland, Caledon Papers D.2433/B/25/13. Reproduced by permission of the Earl of Caledon and the deputy keeper of the Records of Northern Ireland.

1. For a detailed biography of Bainbrigge, see W. Martha E. Cooke, *W.H. Coverdale Collection of Canadiana* (Ottawa: Public Archives of Canada, 1983), 15; and Bainbrigge's obituary in *The Royal Engineers Journal*, 2 January 1882.
2. Much of the information regarding early maple sugar-making is derived from Marius Barbeau, "Maple sugar: Its Native Origin," *Transactions of the Royal Society of Canada*, 3rd series, vol. 40 (1946), section II, pp. 75-86, and Helen and Scott Nearing, *The Maple Sugar Book* (New York: The John Day Co., 1950); both have extensive extracts from early accounts.
3. Barbeau, 80.
4. C.P. Traill, *The Canadian Settler's Guide* (London: E. Stanford, 1860), 62-64.
5. The watercolour of St. Anne's Falls is inscribed in Gosford's hand "Given to me by Lt. Bainbrigge...," see Sotheby's (London), *Topographical Paintings, Watercolours and Drawings*, 4 November 1987, lot 45.
6. *The Royal Engineers Journal*, 2 January 1882.

MARY R. McKIE (active ca. 1840-ca. 1862)

33. *Military Prison, Melville Island, Nova Scotia*, 1849

Watercolour with scraping out on paper

13.2 x 18.2 cm

Inscribed on mount, in pen and black ink, recto, l.l.: *Nova Scotia 1849*; l.r.: *M.R. McK.*

From the Saunders album

Purchased in 1985

Accession no.: 1985-53-3

Negative no.: C-135453

Sometimes, as a result of the accidents of history, active and important members of a specific period in the past have disappeared from public view. Such is the case of Mary R. McKie, a woman artist working in Halifax, Nova Scotia, in the middle decades of the nineteenth century. Although she was patronized by the members of the colonial elite, taught drawing in the city for a number of years, and was awarded prizes for her skill as an artist in provincial competitions, she has sunk into obscurity. This watercolour, *Military Prison, Melville Island, Nova Scotia*, dated 1849, is one of the few signed works from her hand that has surfaced over the years, and it allows us to examine a number of aspects of nineteenth-century Canadian history, including the practice of compiling scrapbooks or commemorative albums, the difficulties of researching the careers of many women artists in the Victorian period, and an aspect of the British military penal system.

The watercolour originally formed part of an album compiled by a member of the family of Dr. William Sedgewick Saunders, a military surgeon stationed in Halifax, Nova Scotia, during the years 1849-1850.[1] The album was fortunately acquired by the National Archives from a dealer in 1984, thus enabling the National Archives to reunite the watercolour with the album.[2]

Mary R. McKie's career is known only because several watercolours executed and signed by her have turned up in commemorative albums or scrapbooks compiled by colonial and military officials in Halifax in the 1840s. Most of her known works are to be found in an album compiled by Lady Falkland, the wife of Viscount Falkland, the lieutenant-governor of Nova Scotia between 1840 and 1846. Lady Falkland, née Amelia Fitzclarence, was born 5 November 1803, the youngest daughter of the Duke of Clarence (later William IV) and Mrs. Dorothy Jordan, the well-known actress. Although in childhood she suffered the humiliation of being disowned, with the rest of her family, by the necessity of a legitimate ducal wedding to produce an heir to the throne, she became an important prize in the aristocratic marriage stakes when her father ascended the throne in 1830. She married Lucius Bentinck Cary, the 10th Viscount Falkland, in December of the same year; two days after the wedding, Falkland became a Lord of the Bedchamber. Lady Falkland accompanied her husband on his foreign postings, including his governorships of Nova Scotia from 1840 to 1846 and Bombay from 1848 to 1853. Lady Falkland was "possessed of considerable literary talent," and published a book on her experiences in India called *Chow-Chow* shortly before her death on 2 July 1858.[3]

While in Nova Scotia, Lady Falkland seems to have been at some pains to cultivate the local artistic community. Lady Falkland's album was acquired by the National Archives in 1922. Although the original source is unknown, it probably came from a member of the Cary family. The album consists of 75 folios in which 109 watercolours, drawings and small oil paintings by a number of different artists were originally preserved. Among these works are five by Mary R. McKie, as well as works by such other Nova Scotian woman artists as Ellen Nutting and Emma Haliburton. Two of the watercolours by Miss McKie are inscribed "Bought by Lady Falkland."[4]

No other mention of Miss McKie can be found in any sources on the development of the fine arts in Nova Scotia before 1848. In that year, she participated in the Halifax Mechanics' Institute art exhibition held at Dalhousie College in September, where she exhibited four works, primarily in the section devoted to the work of amateur artists.[5] She is supposed to have been awarded a prize for an entry in the Fine Arts section of the 1854 Nova Scotia Industrial Exhibition, and to have participated in the Halifax section of the 1862 International Exhibition held in London, England, but no evidence of this has been discovered. On 10 February 1857, Mary McKie announced in the Halifax *Morning Chronicle* that she would "reopen her drawing class on Tuesday the 13th inst at her residence No. 57 Hollis Street. Miss McKie will also give private lessons."[6] Thereafter, no further references to Miss McKie can be found; she disappears from sight and memory.

The watercolour is a distant view of a large wooden structure, painted red, which was originally built in 1808 on Melville Island by the British Admiralty for the accommodation of French prisoners of war.[7] The building is still standing today, and is being used as a sail loft and boat storage facility by a local yacht club. In 1849, however, the building and the island had not been used as a prison since the end of the Napoleonic Wars; it was to remain unoccupied until 1856, when the naval authorities transferred it to the Army. Nevertheless, the building was a well-known landmark in the Halifax vicinity, having been recorded by a number of other artists, including Alexander Mercer,[8] and it may have been because of this that Saunders acquired this watercolour as a souvenir of his brief posting in Halifax. The practice of acquiring souvenir watercolours from local artists and photographers was a common one in the nineteenth century, and it is thanks to this practice that many of the earliest views of Canadian towns and cities are preserved today. At the same time, such albums also reveal the efforts of early artists in Canada to support themselves. Without such records, their lives would probably have gone unrecorded in Canadian history. Happily for posterity, Mary McKie's delightful watercolours do survive, to hint at the talent of an otherwise obscure female artist.

J.B.

---

1. The provenance of the album can be identified from the numerous references to W.S. Saunders it contains, including a clipping from the *Illustrated London News*, 18 July 1876, concerning his appointment as medical officer of the city of London. The album also contains several watercolours by various artists, family photographs, poems and prints, all dating from between 1842 and 1898. For an obituary of Saunders, see the *London Annual Register 1901*, p. 109.

2. The Saunders album (Accession no. 1985-52) was acquired from a London dealer in 1984. Subsequently three watercolours, removed from the album before 1984, were purchased at auction at Christie's (South Kensington, London), 20 November 1984, lot 16. They are accessioned as 1985-53-1 to 1985-53-3, including the work under discussion here.

3. Biographical information on Lady Falkland is derived from the following sources: *Gentlemen's Magazine*, March 1831 and August 1858; *The Times* (London), 5 July 1858; W. Stewart, ed., *Macmillan Dictionary of Canadian Biography* (Toronto: Macmillan Company, 1978), 11:155-156; and NA, François Joseph Audet biographical notes, MG 30 D1, vol. 12. Research compiled by Sheila Powell, NA.

4. NA, Accession nos. 1990-207-31x and 33x.

5. Halifax Mechanics' Institute, *Catalogue of Paintings, other works of art and specimens* (Halifax: A.J. Ritchie, 1848), nos. 172, 190 and 232.

6. This reference was forwarded to me by Margaret Campbell of the Public Archives of Nova Scotia, to whom I would like to express my thanks.

7. Maj. H. Meredith Logan, "Melville Island, The Military Prison of Halifax," *United Services Institute of Nova Scotia Journal* (1933), 1:12-34, is the best record of the history of this institution.

8. The NA owns six watercolours by Alexander C. Mercer, all executed between 1840 and 1843.

JACQUES-FRÉDÉRIC DOUDIET (1802-1867)

34. *Sainte-Thérèse*, 1844

Pencil on paper

10.6 x 34.6 cm (double page)

Inscribed in pencil, recto, u.c.: *2.*; u.r.: *1844*; in pen and black ink, l.l.: *Sainte-Thérèse, 13 Juillet 1844.*; l.r.: *notre habitation – ouest*

In Doudiet sketchbook, on two pages

Purchased in 1985

Accession no.: 1985-175-2-3V/4R

Negative no.: C-127663

In June 1985, Christie's of London auctioned a book of sketches belonging to an Englishwoman. The subjects were Canadian, and the page reproduced in the catalogue suggested an artist of remarkable talent. The sketchbook bore the signature "F. Doudiet," but as this name does not appear in any reference book, the English experts attributed it to the "French School." The Archives acquired the sketchbook and undertook research on it.[1]

Jacques-Frédéric Doudiet was born in 1802 in Basel, Switzerland, where his father was a schoolmaster.[2] The family was Protestant, and Doudiet decided very early to become a clergyman. After theological studies undertaken in Lausanne in 1821, he graduated as a pastor from the University of Basel in 1829, and became a member of the "Compagnie des pasteurs de Neuchâtel," who were reformed Calvinists. After working for a few years in Montargis, France, he returned to Basel in 1823.

The young minister moved to Geneva after completing his studies, and there married Louise Batifolier in September 1829. He apparently lived in Geneva for many years, as his first three children were born there.[3] Perhaps it was during this time period that he was chaplain to a regiment.[4] He likely returned to work in France around 1834-1835, probably again at Montargis (where he painted between 1837 and 1839), in the service of the Société évangélique de France.[5] His next mission was in Tarbes, in the High Pyrenees, where his fifth son was born.[6]

After returning to Switzerland, Doudiet became acquainted with J.E. Tanner, a Swiss minister living in Montreal. After the unrest of 1837, a group of anglophone Protestants, who looked upon the conversion of French Canadians as an excellent way of assimilating them, had founded the French Canadian Missionary Society (FCMS) in 1839, and hired Tanner to strengthen the membership. His task proved to be too taxing, however, and the community sent him to Europe in the autumn of 1843 to recruit other francophone ministers and assistants.[7]

After arriving in Canada on 17 June 1844, the Doudiet family was assigned to the village of Sainte-Thérèse, northwest of Montreal. Doudiet, however, was above all a travelling missionary, whose territory stretched from Hawkesbury in the west to L'Industrie (now Joliette) in the east. The annual reports and the FCMS minutes,[8] along with the entries in our sketchbook, inform us in detail about his movements. In addition to his numerous pastoral rounds, he was sent to Upper Canada on several occasions to preach and to raise funds. At the request of the FCMS, he moved to L'Industrie in 1846 and then to Belle-Rivière, near Sainte-Scholastique (now Mirabel), in the autumn of 1847. Perhaps to ease his solitude during his missionary rounds, he always brought along his sketchbook.

The Doudiet family lived in Belle-Rivière until 1860, on a farm belonging to the FCMS. His salary, however, was not sufficient, and the Doudiets had to cultivate their farm.[9] The minister was away more and more often; his wife, who could not accompany him, assisted him by starting a Sunday school in their home. Their missionary work bore fruit: Several of the Québécois families in the region were converted," and in 1855 Doudiet requested permission to erect a chapel for his congregation.[10] He himself took on the responsibility for raising the necessary funds, and the building was inaugurated in October 1860.

His mission accomplished, the pastor could at last retire, and his family moved to Montreal a few weeks later. Being almost blind, Doudiet did not take up his ministry again, except on special occasions. But he did remain active, as the directories after 1864 refer to him as a "language teacher."[11] Doudiet died in July 1867.[12]

Although not a professional artist, Doudiet was an extremely gifted amateur. While we have no proof as yet that he took any art classes, certain facts link him to the Basel school: Pierre-A., his brother (1807-1872), a competent lithographer, was a protégé of the landscape artist Peter Birmann (1758-1844), a professor and art merchant from Basel. Doudiet's Swiss landscapes may also be compared to the engravings of Johann Jakob Biedermann (1763-1860), also an art teacher at Basel at the beginning of the nineteenth century. Doudiet glued two of his brother's small lithographs to the inside covers of his sketchbook, and the stylistic links are evident.

The sketchbook, which is horizontal, has ninety sheets, most of which have been used. Because the artist dated most of his drawings, we know that he began at the front, following, with a few exceptions, the natural order of the pages, while using the last pages for quick sketches of nature. Doudiet titled his sketchbook "Recueil de Vues prises au Canada 1844" [A Collection of Scenes of Canada 1844], but the inscriptions are dated from 12 July 1844 to 9 October 1848. Almost all the drawings bear the names of the locations depicted; naturally, the subjects are villages Doudiet visited in the course of his work. This sketchbook is therefore a vital source of visual information for the entire region north of Montreal – particularly for Sainte-Thérèse and L'Industrie and, to a lesser extent, for regions in southern Quebec and Ontario.

The subjects are exclusively landscapes; not a single figure enlivens them. But almost half of these drawings represent houses and farms, and Doudiet included the names of their owners. In cases where we have been able to verify, the families are Protestant and mostly francophone – undoubtedly the people who gave him lodging during his pastoral rounds. A number of Doudiet's French and Swiss watercolours also show houses and, it is interesting to note, include remarks about the families who lived in them.

The quality of the drawing is remarkable; it does not consist of quick sketches, but of studies that were a long time in the making. The drawings, always in pencil, indicate an excellent aesthetic sensibility. Colour is very sparse; watercolours were used on one page alone, and three others were given a brown wash; often, however, when the motif included water, such as a river or a pond, Doudiet emphasized this with a faint, light blue wash.

The two pages reproduced in Figs. 34.1 and 34.2 are among the most beautiful in the sketchbook. The view near L'Acadie (Fig. 34.1), found between pages dated June and August, 1846, could easily be enlarged; Doudiet has captured, within the small format, the feel of the vastness of the Quebec countryside.[13] Fig. 34.2, which represents the house of the peddler Joseph Vessot in L'Industrie,[14] is just one illustration of Doudiet's continued interest in architecture. In this connection, one may wonder what part he took in the planning and building of the evangelical chapel at Belle-Rivière (Fig. 34.3). While its broken pediment links it to the English neo-classical style, the proportions are not respected. The architect may have found inspiration in both the Saint Gabriel Presbyterian Church of Montreal and the traditional Québécois style.[15]

The pages chosen for the exhibition (Cat. no. 34) date from a few weeks after Doudiet's arrival in Canada, at the time of his move to Sainte-Thérèse. His house is seen at the far right, and the view spans the entire horizon, with the church on the left. The artist emphasized the panoramic effect by drawing the more distant buildings with a lighter stroke.[16]

The first church in Sainte-Thérèse was built in 1807, following the simple Conefroy plan. In 1834, the nave was lengthened and a new facade, modelled after that of Notre-Dame in Montreal, was begun. But while Montrealers had to wait until 1843 to see the towers erected to their full height, the churchwardens of Sainte-Thérèse completed theirs in 1836.[17] They even added spires, which disappeared in 1865 after a hurricane knocked one of them to the ground.[18] This church burned down early in 1885 and was replaced by the present-day church.

But were there ever two spires? With the exception of Doudiet's sketchbook, all known illustrations of the church at Sainte-Thérèse are dated later than 1865.[19] Now it is quite clear, according to the drawing exhibited, that only the left spire existed in 1844, and the 1846 watercolour sketch (fol. 41v-42r) does not indicate any change.

L.D.

34.1 J.-F. Doudiet
Grande Ligne, L'Acadie, 1846
Brown wash
NA C-127630

34.2 J.-F. Doudiet
L'Industrie, 1845
Pencil
NA C-127615

34.3
Church at Belle-Rivière
Photograph
In R.-P. Duclos, note 7

1. The NA corresponded in 1984 with a Swiss national who had just purchased, in Ottawa, some watercolours and panoramas signed "J.F. Doudiet" that featured Swiss and French motifs. In addition, a researcher contacted the Archives concerning the Doudiet family, and provided the NA with copies of correspondence with the Swiss collector, who, on returning to Switzerland, had been able to reconstruct the main outlines of Doudiet's European biography. Some of the research for this entry was carried out by Jennifer Trant, formerly NA staff.

2. Unless noted otherwise, biographical information concerning Doudiet was derived from private research provided to the NA; the reference to places where Doudiet painted in Europe were derived from the inscriptions on the works in the Swiss collection.

3. NA, Census Records, RG 31, 1861 Census for Montreal, Saint Lawrence Ward, microfilm, reel C-1243, fol. 9815a.

4. French Canadian Missionary Society (FCMS), *Sixth Annual Report* (Montreal, 1845), 8; inquiries directed to Swiss military have not been useful, their records being incomplete.

5. NA, RG 31, 1851 Census for Sainte-Scholastique, County of Deux-Montagnes, microfilm, reel C-1146, Nominal Census, fol. 31 and FCMS, *Sixth Annual Report*, 8.

6. NA, RG 31, 1861 Census for Montreal, Saint Lawrence Ward, microfilm, reel C-1243, fol. 9815a. The Doudiets also had a young daughter, but we do not know her date of birth, as she died shortly after the family's arrival in Canada and was therefore never enumerated. *Missionary Record* 4 (Montreal, December 1844), n.p.

7. R.-P. Duclos, *Histoire du protestantisme français au Canada et aux États-Unis* (Montreal: Librairie Évangélique, 1913), 1:150. On this subject, see also H. Finès, *Album du protestantisme français en Amérique du Nord* (Montreal: L'Aurore, 1972); D.T. Ruddell, *Le Protestantisme français au Québec, 1840-1919: "Images" et témoignages* (Ottawa: National Museum of Man, 1983); René Hardy, "La rébellion de 1837-1838 et l'essor du protestantisme canadien-français," *Revue d'Histoire de l'Amérique francaise* (Outremont, September 1975), 163-189.

8. University of Toronto, Victoria College, United Church Archives, FCMS, Minute Book.

9. NA, RG 31, 1851 Census for Sainte-Scholastique, County of Deux-Montagnes, microfilm, reel C-1146, Agricultural Census, fol. 1.

10. At the time of the census, the Doudiets and other converts were calling themselves "Christian Evangelicals." According to a report from a Protestant source, dated 1853, the region covered by Doudiet would have included between 135 and 162 converts or sympathizers (quoted in Robert Sylvain, "Aperçu sur le prosélytisme protestant au Canada français de 1760 à 1860," *Transactions of the Royal Society of Canada*, 3rd series, vol. 55 [1961], section I, p. 72.) The FCMS's annual report for 1861 mentions 222 converts and 262 sympathizers for the mission at Belle-Rivière alone, but the 1861 census includes far fewer! In this context, one must recall the religious awakening stirring Québécois Catholicism at that time, with the sermons of Mgr. de Forbin-Janson, the temperance crusades, and, above all, the zeal of Mgr. Bourget. Shortly after Doudiet's arrival, the charismatic preacher Chiniquy (still Catholic), who was passing through the region, obtained close to 12,000 adherents to his Society of Temperance: Marcel Trudel, *Chiniquy* (Trois Rivières: Éditions du Bien Public, 1955), 95.

11. *Mackay's Montreal Directory* for 1865-1866 and 1866-1867.

12. *Montreal Daily Witness*, 23 July 1867, p. 3.

13. This scene was drawn at Grande Ligne, an important centre for francophone Baptists, on Montreal's south shore; the FCMS had friendly ties with this group, and Doudiet had already visited them, as is witnessed by the two sketches dated 3 and 4 July 1844 (a few days after his arrival in Canada), glued to leaves 7 and 8 of his sketchbook.

14. Joseph Vessot was a "peddler," going from village to village to preach and sell Bibles. His diary was published in Ruddell, *Le protestantisme français*, 15-42.

15. One source tells us that "Xavier Trudeau began to build the temple in stone", but he was probably just the mason, not the architect, "1840-1940, Centenaire de l'église de Belle-Rivière," typed manuscript, 1940.

16. Two years later, Doudiet would take up this subject again, placing the church, this time, on the right (fol. 41v-42r of the sketchbook); it is the only drawing in the sketchbook enhanced with watercolour.

17. The completed model of Notre-Dame in Montreal, as drawn by James O'Donnell, was, however, made known via engravings: see Charles P. deVolpi and P.S. Winkworth, *Montreal, A Pictorial Record* (Montreal: Dev-Sco Publications Ltd., 1963), pl. 20 (1829), and above all pl. 28 (1834).

18. Société historique de Sainte-Thérèse-de-Blainville, *Histoire de Sainte-Thérèse* (Sainte-Thérèse?: L'étoile du Nord, 1940), 145.

19. Louise Voyer, *Églises disparues* (Montreal: Libre Expression, 1981), 139-140.

JOHN ARTHUR ROEBUCK (1802-1879)

35. *View from Cedar Island of the Dock Yard at Kingston*, ca. 1821-1824

Brown wash over pencil on paper

9.9 x 16.3 cm

Inscribed on mount, in pencil, recto, l.r.: *View from Cedar Island of the Dock Yard at Kingston*

In "Sketches in Canada," ca. 1821-1824

Purchased in 1984

Accession no.: 1984-3-41

Negative no.: C-121249

In 1828, George Ramsay, the 9th Earl of Dalhousie, left Canada after completing his term as governor general, which had begun in 1820. On this occasion, John Simpson, a private secretary in Dalhousie's employ, presented him with an album of fifty sketches of Canadian scenes executed by Simpson's step-son John Arthur Roebuck, perhaps as a farewell gift. The author of the sketchbook had himself left Canada only four years earlier, to begin a successful career in England that would bring him considerable acclaim as a British politician and statesman.

John Arthur Roebuck had already lived a colourful life by the time he left Canada in 1824. He was the fifth of six sons born to Zipporah Tickell and Ebenezer Roebuck, his father being a descendant of the Roebucks of Scotland, who were instrumental in the founding of the Scottish steel industry.[1] The first three children were left with their grandmother in England when Ebenezer moved with his wife to India to work with the East India Company. He was apparently on the verge of making a large fortune when, in 1807, the decision was made for Mrs. Roebuck to return home with the three youngest children, who had all been born in India. The day she set foot once again in England, her husband died. Shortly afterwards, word came that Mr. Roebuck's brother and partner had also died, leaving the family in an uncertain financial state.

Mrs. Roebuck took as her second husband a merchant named John Simpson. An unsuccessful businessman, Simpson has been described by John Roebuck as "a daring, sanguine man ... [who] indulged in schemes that would have terrified a sober-minded one."[2] After experiencing failures as both a merchant and farmer in England, a land grant enticed Simpson and his new family to emigrate to Canada in 1815. Mrs. Simpson had been given five hundred acres of land near Toronto after her brother's death in a boating mishap on the Niagara River. The gift was in recognition of his service as secretary to General Simcoe, lieutenant-governor of Upper Canada.

The family first settled at Augusta, located between Prescott and Brockville on the St. Lawrence River.[3] They lived there for four years, until Simpson joined Dalhousie's staff, prompting a move to Beauport and then to Coteau-du-Lac, where he was appointed inspector of merchandise and collector of customs in 1822. It is through this contact that Dalhousie came to possess watercolours and drawings by both John Roebuck and his older brother William.

In the years before the move to Canada, Roebuck said that he had experienced the "life of a child of polished society," because of the personalities he had seen in the house where his Aunt Eliza Tickell had lived. There, inspired by the actors he met, such as Charles Young and the famous Edmund Kean,[4] he developed a love for the theatre. In addition to early tutoring by his mother, he received formal schooling, once in Canada, under two famous educationalists who were both ordained clergymen, first at the school of Mr. Bethune at Augusta, and after the move to Quebec at the famous grammar school of Dr. Wilkie. He describes his years in Canada as "years of continuous steady study," during which time he absorbed the English classics, taught himself French and Latin, and was "constantly writing verse and prose." Another early pastime was drawing, from which he "derived great solace and pleasure."[5]

The refined sketches of the album reflect the love the artist felt for the country of his youth:

> The wild country, its great rivers, the vast scale upon which everything was framed, made on me a profound impression. The freedom in which we lived, the thorough liberty of going where we liked, the new scenes, brought with them a sort of enchantment.[6]

All the views in the album were taken along the St. Lawrence-Lake Ontario waterway from Quebec City to Niagara; there are scenes of La Malbaie, Sorel, Montreal, Lachine, Kingston and Fort Mississauga. The pencil drawings are of a very fine quality, and the monochrome wash studies have the same clean execution, precision and careful attention to detail. Many of the subjects are similar to those found in the Woolford album (see Cat. no. 28). John Roebuck's *The Fort of Coteau-du-Lac and Rapids from Prison Island* (Fig. 35.1) depicts the small fort and canal built by the British government where John Simpson moved with his family on becoming customs inspector. In *Fort Niagara from Fort Mississauga* (Fig. 35.2) the unusual perspective reveals a wonderful view of the interior of the courtyard at Fort Mississauga. Both sites were also treated by Woolford.

Views of Montreal, Quebec City, and smaller communities of the province are found in the Roebuck album. *Part of Montreal from the Hill on the Island of St. Helen* (Fig. 35.3) shows precise architectural detail of the barracks at Montreal, with a detailed background view of the city, its skyline punctuated by church spires. His *Indian Village and the Lake of Two Mountains from the Calvary at Oka* (Fig. 35.4) presents an unusual perspective of the shrine, with the looming crucifix and the church dominating the scene, and the faint outline of the village in the background. He also recorded scenes at Sorel on the Richelieu River, such as *Sorel from the Gate of Government House* (Fig. 35.5) and the vibrant pencil sketch *View on the Sorel Road Going up it* (Fig. 35.6). In other works he imparts his impressions of more unusual and out-of-the-way attractions such as *The Forges, Black River* and the charming scene of *Mrs. Nairne's House and the Church at Mal Baie from Point Fraser*, a spot Dalhousie has described in his diaries.[7]

One of the most interesting sketches from the Ontario group is that of the *View From Cedar Island of the Dock Yard of Kingston* (Cat. no. 35). The detailed scene of early nineteenth-century Kingston shows the partially constructed hulls of three ships, underlining the importance of this transshipment point as a flourishing shipbuilding centre. He also took views of *The Heights and Village of Queenstown*, where Brock fell during the War of 1812. A very successful sketch is his peaceful rendition of a rustic *Lundy's Lane* (Fig. 35.7), where little evidence remains of the bitter battle fought there on 24-25 July 1814.

Works by John Roebuck are rare. Although he was previously known to have worked as an amateur artist, this album appears to be the only example of his Canadian work to have come to light. He pursued his sketching very sparingly after his move to England, practising his hobby primarily when incapacitated by illness. Roebuck was aware of his talent, and acquaintances also thought highly of his skill, as evidenced by the following passages from his biography:

> I read the greater portion of our poets when a boy, and during my life have passed many hours in drawing from nature, and was, I may say, no mean amateur artist.... [The editor adds the following:] Part of the autumn of 1834 was passed in France, where...Mr. Roebuck was seized with a dangerous illness.... The convalescence was long, and the time was chiefly spent in drawing, for which a vigourous and graceful talent had already caused Mr. Roebuck's friends to say that he was an artist lost to the world.[8]

John Roebuck left Canada in 1824, two years after Mr. Simpson's move to Coteau-du-lac. He began an exciting new life in England, being called to the bar in 1831, and then launched into a political career after being elected to represent Bath. As an independent member of the House of Commons, his vigourous oratory and colourful antics earned him the reputation of a thorough-going radical, and the nickname "Tear'Em." He published *Pamphlets for the People* (in which he outlined his beliefs), which sold for a negligible sum. He caught the public's attention again when he fought duels in defence of his honour.

Canadian activities were again to become a large part of Roebuck's life when in 1835 he was appointed by the House of Assembly to act as the provincial agent for Lower Canada. He represented Canada in her plea for the privilege of self-government, at the request of Louis-Joseph Papineau,[9] and advised the British Parliament during the events leading up to the rebellion of 1837. He appeared at both the Bar of the House of Commons and the House of Lords to contest a bill proposed by Lord John Russell, calling for the suspension of the existing constitution of Canada, and his speech earned him acclaim by his contemporaries. He was again involved in Canadian affairs in 1843, when his efforts aided in the release of prisoners of the rebellion, who were in exile in Tasmania.[10]

Although defeated several times in elections, John Roebuck continued to devote the latter part of his life to English politics, representing the cities of Bath and Sheffield. He was a supporter of social reform and advocated legislation to improve the conditions of the working class. In 1878, in recognition of his services to the Crown, he was sworn in as a member of the Queen's Privy Council. He died in London on 30 November 1879.

John Roebuck's sketchbook is a wonderful pendant to the works of his brother William Roebuck (ca. 1797-1847), an officer and engineer who studied at Woolwich and later married and settled in Canada. The National Archives has several examples of William's work, some of which were produced for Dalhousie,[11] and one sketch, *Murray River at Malbay below Quebec* (Fig. 35.8), is almost identical to one of John's in the album (Fig. 35.9), attesting to the fact that they sometimes sketched together: "William and myself were given to drawing. William, having a genius for that art, became a very pretty artist".[12]

This album is significant in several respects. Sketches by the artist are few, and these Canadian subjects may be unique in his work. They help to complete the story of the Roebuck family and, perhaps most importantly, are charming and important records of early nineteenth-century Canada taken by an amateur hand.

M.M.

35.1 J.A. Roebuck

The Fort of Coteau-du-Lac and Rapids from Prison Island, ca. 1821-1824

Watercolour

NA C-121278

35.2 J.A. Roebuck
Fort Niagara from Fort Mississauga, ca. 1821-1824
Watercolour
NA C-121243

35.3 J.A. Roebuck
Part of Montreal from the Hill on the Island of St. Helen, ca. 1821-1824
Watercolour
NA C-121253

35.4 J.A. Roebuck
Indian Village and the Lake of Two Mountains from the Calvary at Oka, ca. 1821-1824
Watercolour
NA C-121244

35.5 J.A. Roebuck
Sorel from the Gate of Government House, ca. 1821-1824
Watercolour
NA C-121291

35.6 J.A. Roebuck
View on the Sorel Road Going up it, ca. 1821-1824
Pencil
NA C-121266

35.7 J.A. Roebuck
Lundy's Lane, ca. 1821-1824
Watercolour
NA C-121247

35.8 W. Roebuck
Murray River at Malbay below Quebec, ca. 1820
Watercolour
NA C-104266

35.9 J.A. Roebuck
Mal Baie Bridge from near the Church, ca. 1821-1824
Watercolour
NA C-121262

1. Arthur W. Roebuck, *The Roebuck Story* (Don Mills, Ontario: T.H. Best Printing Company Limited, 1963), 8.

2. Robert Eadon Leader, ed., *Life and Letters of John Arthur Roebuck* (London, New York: Edward Arnold, 1897), 15.

3. Leader, 14-15. Mr. Simpson bought the estate when the family stopped in Montreal. Roebuck's recollections of Augusta centre upon the "good stone house," the "capital orchard and garden," and the great breadth of the St. Lawrence River.

4. Leader, 4.

5. Leader, 12-19.

6. Leader, 20-21.

7. Dalhousie papers, Section 3, no. 552, NA, MG 24 A12, microfilm, reel A-537, diary of Lord Dalhousie, July 1828. Dalhousie describes the river dividing the two seigneuries of Dr. Fraser and "old Mrs. Nairne," apparently the only two seigneuries granted under British rule, by General Murray, following the province's conquest. He recounts the admiration the local populace held for her.

8. Leader, 37, 63.

9. NA, J.A. Roebuck papers, MG 24 A19, vol. 1, file 5, p. 7, Louis Joseph Papineau to J.A. Roebuck, January 1835, and p. 33, Louis Joseph Papineau to J.A. Roebuck, 25 March 1835. In January, Papineau requested that Roebuck agree to act as provincial agent for Lower Canada, and in March he confirmed that Roebuck had been officially appointed by the House of Assembly to act in that capacity.

10. NA, MG 24 A19, vol. 4, file 22, p. 56, group of freed exiles to J.A. Roebuck, 10 July 1839. In this emotional letter the former prisoners express their deep gratitude for Roebuck's efforts on behalf of their release.

11. A watercolour by William Roebuck, *Murray River at Malbay below Quebec*, ca. 1820, in the NA collection (Accession no. 1931-242, Fig. 35.8) bears the following typewritten note, l.c.: *Water-Colour Drawing of the Murray River, Circa 1820 from the collection George, 9th Earl of Dalhousie, G.C.B.*.

12. Leader, 21.

SIR HENRY WILLIAM BARNARD (1799-1857)

36. *Niagara Falls*, 1838

Watercolour over pencil with scraping out on paper
68.2 x 124.8 cm
Purchased in 1986
Accession no.: 1986-30-1
Negative no.: C-129774

This unusually large watercolour of Niagara Falls, with its accompanying certificate, is an excellent record of early nineteenth-century tourism in Canada.[1] The work was painted by Lieutenant-Colonel Barnard while he was posted to Lower Canada following the 1837 rebellion. An officer in the 2nd Battalion of the prestigious Grenadier Guards, Barnard arrived in Quebec City in May 1838. During the four years his battalion spent in Lower Canada, he was on duty one and a half years, from May 1838 until May 1839, and again from May to October 1841.[2] His most important military role in the aftermath of the rebellions was to be appointed to the court martial for the trial of political offences, which continued in session from the end of November 1838 until May 1839.[3] Moreover, as was expected from such a high-ranking military officer, Barnard was very active in Quebec high society. Jane Ellice, whose miniature portrait is also in this catalogue (Cat. no. 53), called him one of "the Lions of the town."[4]

Barnard made use of his North American posting in the same fashion as most gentleman travellers in the nineteenth century, and sketched the usual picturesque locations in and around Quebec city, such as the Chaudière Falls and the Indian Village at Lorette.[5] He may even have made use of the 1831 publication *Quebec and its Environs: Being a Picturesque Guide to the Stranger*, by fellow artist James Pattison Cockburn, since many of his sketches depict the scenes recommended in the booklet. He also did sketches of scenes with a more personal connotation, such as a view from the window of his room or of his commanding officer's house, both in Quebec. Most of his sketches are carefully labelled as to their location. As was usual for most British officers, Barnard was not a "war artist," and there are no references to the rebellion in his known watercolours.

Four months after his arrival in Quebec City, Barnard obtained leave from 6 September to 5 October to visit Niagara Falls.[6] This was his only major excursion while he was stationed in Canada. Given the fame of Niagara Falls, it is quite likely that Barnard had made plans to visit them even before arriving in Quebec. Sketches reveal that he travelled to the Falls from Montreal via the Richelieu River, crossing the border to the United States at Rouses Point. Sailing across Lake Champlain, he travelled down to Troy, New York, and then continued west on one of the horse-drawn barges on the Erie Canal. He made side-trips to various picturesque spots along this route, such as Trenton Falls and Genesee Falls, and also recorded some of the less picturesque surroundings of the canal. The route he took was well travelled, since it was part of the nineteenth-century American Grand Tour, which included the Erie Canal and Niagara Falls.[7]

Since its discovery in the seventeenth century, Niagara Falls has been the most frequently described and depicted natural wonder in North America.[8] No subject expressed better the most important aesthetic concept in the eighteenth and nineteenth centuries: the sublime. As defined in Edmund Burke's *Philosophical Enquiry into the Origin of our Ideas of the Sublime and Beautiful*, published in 1757, the sublime was a mode of experience consisting of fear and wonder, and a sublime subject in art or literature aroused the instinct of self-preservation. All visitors to North America who could afford it visited Niagara Falls. Travel accounts abound with references to the terror, pleasure and awe that the Falls aroused in the onlooker, and many were inspired to take brush in hand to depict this overwhelming scene.[9]

If tourists were busy flocking to Niagara Falls, entrepreneurs were just as busy marketing the falls by building various constructions, such as stairways and walkways, to "increase" the sublime aspect of the falls and to make them into "a commodity which could be consumed bit by bit."[10] There were numerous guide-books available, showing all the points from which the falls had to be viewed in order to experience their terrifying impact.[11] The sketches Barnard made at Niagara Falls reveal that "he did Niagara Falls" from the prescribed points of view. He sketched the falls from the distance, from below (Fig. 36.1), and from various vantage points on Goat Island, including the towers and walkways that "enhanced" the viewing (Fig. 36.2).

The National Archives' large watercolour shows both the American and the Canadian Falls, with Goat Island visible between them. The view also includes some of the structures, such as Biddle's Staircase, which led down to the foot of Goat Island, and the forty-five-foot Terrapin Tower, from which "the effect of the Falls upon the beholder is most awfully sublime and utterly indescribable."[12] The road in the immediate foreground descended to the ferry-landing, and the building visible at the extreme right was the Pavilion Hotel, one of two hotels on the Canadian side.

Barnard claimed that the painting was executed "on the spot." Because of its size, one would rather suspect that this was a studio piece, executed from sketches; however, there is no known sketch by Barnard from the same vantage point. The location from which the view was taken provides a clue. A slightly later lithograph, entitled *Falls of Niagara from Clifton House*, by Nathaniel Currier (Fig. 36.3), shows the same vista. The Clifton House Hotel was built in 1835 and was the most elegant and best-situated hotel on the Canadian side at the time of Barnard's visit. A watercolour by Barnard, taken from exactly the opposite view and entitled *Clifton House Hotel, Niagara* (Fig. 36.4), shows that the hotel had balconies that were convenient for sketching. It seems that Barnard stayed at the Clifton, where his friends could visit and admire his watercolours.[13] Therefore, he could easily have executed the watercolour while comfortably installed at the hotel.

Other known watercolours by Barnard are quite small, and were probably originally part of portable sketchbooks. A comparison with these smaller sketches reveals that the large watercolour is done with more care and finish.

The essence of watercolour technique is the building up of a work from light to dark by means of washes laid over one another.[14] Highlights are achieved by leaving areas of the paper blank or only thinly washed. Although Barnard used the wash technique in this work, he also used scraping out for his most brilliant highlights. This entails the dry removal of paint with, in this case, a penknife. The scraping is visible in the rocks in front of the American Falls and in all the white highlights that represent foaming water. Another interesting technique can be observed in the handling of the tree on the right side, where light leaves are painted on top of a dark background. This was done by means of a reductive technique. Barnard applied extra gum arabic to the dark tree shape, which slowed down the drying of the surface. Then, with a barely damp brush or sponge, he could pick up colour from desired areas in the tree. The latter technique was frequently used by artists trying to elevate watercolour to the status of oil painting.[15]

In choosing such a large format, almost three times the size of his other known pieces, Barnard indicated his high ambitions for recording the scene. In addition, the way it was displayed – presumably in Barnard's home, later in life – reveals the importance he attached to it. It was mounted on a cotton backing, stretched on a strainer, framed and glazed.[16] Such a presentation is more in keeping with a display of an oil painting than of a watercolour, but would have allowed the work to be placed permanently on view.

The certificate, which had been affixed to the back of the painting according to Barnard's wishes, was given to him for having "passed behind the great falling water to termination rock," one of the more thrilling adventures offered to the visitors. Dated 22 September 1838, it was signed by Isaiah Starkey, who had the concession to operate the stairs leading down to the falls and to take people behind Horseshoe Falls.[17] He also ran a bar called Starkey's Refreshment Rooms, where the drenched and overwhelmed visitors could be revived with lemonade, ice cream or liquor.[18] An approximation of Barnard's venture may be had from a description by Nathaniel Hawthorne, who visited in 1834:

> Leaning over the cliff, I saw the guide conducting two adventurers behind the falls. It was pleasant, from that high seat in the sunshine, to observe them struggling against the eternal storm of the lower regions, with heads bent down, now faltering, now pressing forward, and finally swallowed up in their victory. After their disappearance, a blast rushed out with an old hat, which it had swept from one of their heads. The rock, to which they were directing their unseen course, is marked, at a fearful distance on the exterior of the sheet, by a jet of foam. The attempt to reach it apppears both poetical and perilous to a looker-on, but may be accomplished without much more difficulty or hazard, than in stemming a violent north-easter. In a few moments, forth came the children of the mist. Dripping and breathless, they crept along the base of the cliff, ascended to the guide's cottage, and received, I presume, a certificate of their achievement, with three verses of sublime poetry on the back.[19]

The "sublime poetry" on Barnard's certificate was written in 1830 by Willis Gaylord Clark, American poet and editor of literary and religious periodicals. It is an excellent example of the response to Niagara Falls in the early nineteenth century, which had shifted from the aesthetic to the religious sublime.[20] It was believed that God communicated directly with man through natural grandeur, and Niagara Falls was the profoundest expression of this exchange.[21] The poem reads as follows:

> Here speaks the voice of God – let man be dumb,
> Nor with his vain inspiring hither come.
> That voice impels the hollow-sounding floods,
> And like a Presence fills the distant woods.
> These groaning rocks the Almighty's finger piled;
> For ages here his painted bow has smiled,
> Mocking the changes and the chance of time –
> Eternal, beautiful, serene, sublime!

Information concerning Henry William Barnard is scant. His family was of Irish origin with strong Church of England connections, as his great-grandfather, William Barnard (1697-1768) had been bishop of Derry.[22] His father was rector of two parishes in Buckinghamshire and also an amateur artist who was fond of picturesque travel and painted scenery in Wales and Ireland and on the Continent, especially in Italy.[23] He was likely Barnard's first artistic mentor. As for his profession, Barnard followed his uncles' examples in choosing the military. One of them, Sir Andrew Barnard, was a highly respected general and a close friend of the Prince Regent, later George IV.[24]

From 1807 to 1812, Barnard attended Westminster – an old Anglican public school that several members of his family had already attended – prior to enrolling in the Army.[25] While he was a cadet at the newly established Royal Military College at Sandhurst in 1813-1814, he studied, among other subjects, fortification and military drawing.[26] His drawing master was Scottish artist Andrew Wilson (1780-1848), who painted traditional, idealized landscapes in both watercolour and oils.[27] Barnard was commissioned ensign in the Grenadier Guards in 1814.[28] His choice of regiments suggests that he was socially ambitious. The Grenadier Guards had the highest percentage of titled officers in the early nineteenth century.[29] Reputed for their bravery and steadfastness in battle, they were usually employed in royal service, and were always on duty at important state functions, such as coronations, as well as all national pageants.[30] It was also one of the most expensive regiments to join, as a commission cost twice as much as in other, less exclusive regiments.[31] This may explain why Barnard's advancement in the regiment was fairly slow: He was promoted captain by purchase in 1822, and to lieutenant-colonel in 1831.[32] In 1846 he was promoted to colonel and, in 1854, to major-general. He served in the Crimean War as chief of staff, and subsequently received an award for distinguished service and was made knight commander of the Order of Bath.[33] In 1828, he had married Isabella Letitia Craufurd, the daughter of a brigadier-general.[34] They had at least one son, W.A.M. Barnard, who was his father's aide-de-camp in 1857 at the siege of Delhi, where Sir Henry died of cholera.[35]

A portrait of Barnard (Fig. 36.5) as a major-general in India, shortly before his death, shows him as a dashing officer, debonair despite the overwhelming military problems and the debilitating heat.[36] It seems that he remained a gentleman to the last:

> ... General Sir Henry Barnard, was 'a dear old gentleman' in more than one officer's opinion, 'always chatty and jolly'. He was said to be 'too fond of giving away to the opinion

of others, yet he endeared himself to all who came in contact with him by his gentlemanly conduct and desire to please everyone when it lay in his power'.[37]

Taken all together, the certificate, the size of the work, its presentation and its painstaking technique make this watercolour a unique reminder of Barnard's sublime encounter. It is also perhaps the most impressive of the many renderings of Niagara Falls held by the National Archives of Canada.

E.M.-M.

36.1 H.W. Barnard
Terrapin Tower, Niagara Falls, 1838
Watercolour
Royal Ontario Museum 949.41.19

36.2 H.W. Barnard
Clifton House seen from Goat Island, 1838
Watercolour
Royal Ontario Museum 949.41.38

36.3 N. Currier (1813-1888)
Falls of Niagara from Clifton House, before 1857
Handcoloured lithograph
NA C-114516

36.4 H.W. Barnard
Clifton House Hotel, Niagara, 1838
Watercolour
Royal Ontario Museum 949.41.26

36.5 O. Norie
Portrait of Major General Sir Henry William Barnard, 1857
Watercolour
Royal Ontario Museum 959.18

---

1. The full text of the certificate is as follows:
   Recto:
   Niagara Falls UC: This is to certify that Henry Barnard Esq Lieut-Col Grenadier Guards has passed behind the great falling sheet of water to termination rock. Given under my hand at the office of the General Register of the names of visiters [*sic*] at the Table Rock. This 22nd day of September, 1838. [Signed] Isaiah Starkey.
   Verso:
   The following lines were written by Willis Gaylord Clark, Esq. in the Register of Isaiah Starkey, for the names of visiters [*sic*] who have passed behind the great sheet of water, at Niagara Falls, UC. Tuesday morning, June 27, 1830. [See main text for poem] [Written below in Barnard's handwriting:] I wish this to be placed on the back of my water coloured drawing of the falls done on the spot. H.W. Barnard.
2. Barnard was in England from June 1839 until April 1841. He returned to Lower Canada in May 1841 but left again, for medical reasons, in October. His leave was extended so that he could rejoin the regiment when it returned to England in the fall of 1842. (Public Record Office, London, W.O. 17, vols. 1542-1546, NA, MG13, microfilm, reels B-1577 and B-1578, "Monthly Returns" for Canada from 1838 to 1842.) There are landscape drawings by Barnard dated 1840, the year he was on leave in England. Since he was one of a small group of amateur artists who seemingly sketched together and copied each others' works, it is likely that these are copies by Barnard of friends' sketches.
3. NA, British Military and Naval Records, RG 8 IA, vol. 173, pp. 104-105, microfilm, reel C-2775, Warrant appointing Barnard to General Court Martial, 21 January 1839, and vol. 174, pp. 31-32, letter from J. Clitherow to the Military Secretary, 16 April 1840.
4. Patricia Godsell, ed., *The Diary of Jane Ellice* (Ottawa: Oberon Press, 1975), 151.
5. Mary Allodi, *Canadian Watercolours and Drawings in the Royal Ontario Museum*, vol. 1 (Toronto: Royal Ontario Museum, 1974), Cat. nos. 63-119.
6. Public Record Office, London, W.O. 17, vol. 1542, p. 174, NA, MG13, microfilm, reel B-1577, Return of the General and Staff Officers, 1 October 1838.
7. John F. Sears, "Doing Niagara Falls in the Nineteenth Century," in *Niagara: Two centuries of changing attitudes, 1697-1901* (Washington: The Corcoran Gallery of Art, 1985), 103.
8. Jeremy E. Adamson, "Nature's Grandest Scene in Art," in *Niagara*, 11.
9. Charles Mason Dow, *Anthology and Bibliography of Niagara Falls*, 2 vols. (Albany, New York: J.B. Lyon Co., 1921).
10. Sears, "Doing Niagara Falls," 106-107.
11. Horatio A. Parsons, *A Guide to Travelers visiting the Falls of Niagara* (Buffalo: Oliver G. Steele, 1835) is a good example of such a guide-book.
12. Parsons, *Guide*, 29.
13. Godsell, *Diary*, 103.
14. Marjorie B. Cohn, *Wash and Gouache: A study of the development of the materials of watercolour* (Cambridge, Mass.: Center for Conservation and Technical Studies, Fogg Art Museum, ca. 1977). This is an excellent source for the history of watercolour technique.
15. Cohn, 46.
16. I would like to thank Geoffrey Morrow, former conservator of works on paper, NA, and now chief paper conservator at the National Gallery of Canada, for a discussion of the technical aspects of this work.
17. George A. Seibel, *Ontario's Niagara Parks 100 Years: a History* (Niagara Parks Commission, 1985), 9.
18. Seibel, *Niagara Parks*, 9.
19. Nathaniel Hawthorne, "My visit to Niagara," quoted in Dow, *Anthology* 1:193.
20. Adamson, "Nature's Grandest Scene," 42.
21. Adamson, "Nature's Grandest Scene," 42.
22. Information about the family from L. Stephen and Sidney Lee (eds.) *Dictionary of National Biography* (London: University of Oxford Press, 1921-1922), 1:1155-1162.

23. H.L. Mallalieu, *The Dictionary of British Watercolour Artists up to 1920* (Woodbridge, England: Antique Collectors Club, 1976), 1:24.

24. R.H. Gronow, *The Reminiscences and Recollections of Captain Gronow* (London: The Bodley Head, 1964), 46.

25. G.F. Russell Barker and Alan Stenning (compilers), *The Record of Old Westminsters* (London: Chiswick Press, 1928), 1:51.

26. Letter to the author from Central Library, Royal Military Academy Sandhurst, 7 May 1986.

27. Mallalieu, *Dictionary* 1:281.

28. H.G. Hart, *The New Army List* (London: John Murray, 1 July 1848), 39:44.

29. P.E. Razzell, "Social Origins of Officers in the Indian and British Home Army: 1758-1962," *The British Journal of Sociology* 14 (September 1963): 255.

30. Walter Richards, *Her Majesty's Army* (London: Virtue & Co., n.d.), Division 1, p. 143.

31. Hugh Thomas, *The Story of Sandhurst* (London: Hutchison, 1961), 17.

32. Hart, *New Army List* (1848), 44.

33. H.G. Hart, *The New Annual Army List and Militia List for 1857* (London: John Murray, 1857), 14 and 25a.

34. *Gentleman's Magazine* 98 (1828): part 1, 80.

35. Sir Henry Wylie Norman and Mrs. Keith Young (eds.) *Delhi – 1857* (London: W. & R. Chambers Ltd., 1902), 107-108.

36. G.W. Forrest, *A History of the Indian Mutiny* (London: William Blackwood and Sons, 1904), 1:100-101.

37. Christopher Hibbert, *The Great Mutiny: India 1857* ([London]: Allen Lane, 1978), 122.

WILLIAM GEORGE RICHARDSON HIND (1833-1889)

37. *Harvesting Hay, Sussex, New Brunswick*, ca. 1880

Oil on commercial board
27.5 x 47.1 cm
Purchased in 1982
Accession no.: 1982-204-9
Negative no.: C-103003

This extraordinarily beautiful harvest scene at Sussex, done during William G.R. Hind's last years in New Brunswick, has only recently been recognized as one of his finest oil paintings. How it was discovered and subsequently identified proves to be one of the stranger sagas in recent Canadian art history.

The picture first came to light in 1968 when the Kennedy Galleries in New York acquired it from a source in New Jersey along with four other landscapes, all attributed to one R.J. Best. No signature or other inscription had as yet been discovered, and where precisely the works were found remains unknown.[1] The name of the artist, along with the titles, was apparently supplied orally by the agent, presumably from the original owner. The present picture was then entitled *Haying Scene, St.John, New Brunswick*, while the other four were *Lake Scene, St. John, New Brunswick; On the Coast of St-John, New Brunswick; St-John, New Brunswick;* and *Cows Grazing, Nova Scotia*. All but *On the Coast* were listed and illustrated in *The Kennedy Quarterly* in 1973, where R.J. Best was described as unknown, "but he was perhaps connected in some way with a W.R. Best, who is recorded as having sketched various public buildings in St. John's, Newfoundland in the 1850's."[2]

When the present haying scene appeared at auction in Toronto in 1982, the artist had become William Robert Best, who was indeed active in Newfoundland in the mid-nineteenth century, but who has nothing whatever to do with the works attributed to R.J. Best.[3] The National Archives acquired the work at auction, because as soon as the picture was seen by Archives staff, they were convinced that it really was a major work by William Hind. Within the small format typical of the artist can be seen an astonishing perspective of trees carefully differentiated by type, and fields and tiny buildings all recorded with the minute, almost microscopic brush strokes, the dazzlingly brilliant, high-keyed colours and the decorative undulating rhythms that are all salient characteristics of Hind's mature work.[4] The picture was, moreover, executed on the same sort of commercial board with a matte grey verso that the artist favoured for his earlier oil panels, which are rarely, if ever, signed.[5] Once known, Hind's pictures are so distinctive that it seems impossible that another, totally unknown artist could produce works identical in syle and technique.

On purely stylistic grounds, J. Russell Harper, the organizer of the first Hind exhibition and a fervent champion of his art, immediately pronounced this harvest scene to be by Hind when he had the opportunity to examine it shortly before his death.[6] Another person intimately familiar with Hind's work, Kenneth Saltmarche, the director of the Art Gallery of Windsor, who hosted the first Hind exhibition, felt that the picture was "almost surely the work of Wm. G.R. Hind" on the basis of a black-and-white photograph.[7] Further research has confirmed the initial stylistic attribution.

After a peripatetic career that took him from Toronto to Labrador, the Cariboo gold fields, Victoria and Fort Garry, Hind moved to Shediac, New Brunswick, in 1870, where he worked for the Intercolonial Railway, probably as a draftsman. In 1879, he settled in Sussex, New Brunswick, an Intercolonial branch line station, and died there in 1889. It was always felt that the tiny church, with its distinctive architecture, in the middle distance of the haying scene would provide the vital clue to identifying the geographic location. Thanks to the superb resources of the Canadian Inventory of Historic Building, the structure was identified as Trinity Anglican Church in Sussex, New Brunswick,[8] which was built between 1874 and 1876 by Saint John architects McKean and Fairweather during the rectorate of the Rev. Charles S. Medley.[9]

It is a tribute to the artist's incredible powers of observation and description that such a small detail in his vast panorama, a mere 1.3 cm long, is so readily identifiable. Comparing an enlargement of the church in the painting (Fig. 37.1) with a photograph of Trinity Church as it is today (Fig. 37.2), we see the distinctive low side aisle only 2.6 m high at the eaves, the drop in the main roof level towards the east, the six lancet windows in the nave and the spire on the north side. The artist has even included a microscopic cross at the crest of the gable. Since Hind painted it, the side aisle has evidently been extended towards the east to create a small porch, and the spire has been covered with dark shingles. Otherwise the church in the painting corresponds exactly with the present structure.

A former rector of Trinity Church, the Rev. Canon F.H. Hazen, has very kindly confirmed that the church is definitely Trinity:

> The scene looks north from the hill up behind the Church. The Haying Scene is on the field next to the present rifle range. The building to the south and left of the church is the old rectory which was built in 1867. The rectory is still standing, although the outbuildings are gone.[10]

He goes on to point out that the hill to the left of the scene is "definitely what we call Smith Creek Hill." The streaming smoke in the far distance near the horizon might possibly depict a train, an entirely appropriate touch for an artist who was in the employ of the Intercolonial Railway and who lived at the Intercolonial Hotel in the main part of Sussex, which is off to the left outside the picture space. Canon Hazen notes that the smoke is in the right area of the present train track. The tiny, oddly shaped structure with a chute or slide near the left edge is probably some sort of mill.[11]

Once the stylistic conclusions have been added to the convincing evidence that the scene depicted is in fact Sussex, New Brunswick, it seems certain that the picture could not possibly have been painted by anyone other than William Hind. The painting is, therefore, not only a superb evocation of pastoral New Brunswick in the late nineteenth century, but also has the added autobiographical interest of being a loving depiction of the artist's home, where he spent the last ten years of his life.

The attribution to the mysterious R.J. Best remains more problematic. No artist of this name has been located in either Canada or the United States. As was mentioned above, no inscriptions of any kind were known on the five "Bests" when they were in the possession of the Kennedy Galleries. The National Archives subsequently purchased two more of the group, oil sketches on prepared paper, then entitled *Lake Scene, St. John, New Brunswick* and *On the Coast of St. John, New Brunswick* (Fig. 37.3), which are much more freely executed than the highly finished *Harvesting Hay*, but which reveal Hind's authorship in their brilliant colours and distinctive compositions. Conservation staff at the Archives have now removed these works from the backings to which they were laid down, thus revealing two interesting inscriptions on the verso of *On the Coast*. In the upper right corner is written in pencil: *Mr Best / Corners top Both alike* and in another hand in pencil in the lower right written along the side edge: *Jacquet River*. Although it is hard to decipher the exact meaning of the line following Best's name, it would seem to be the sort of framer's notations that are very frequently found on the verso of works along with the name of the owner who is ordering the framing.

During his years in New Brunswick, Hind was a frequent visitor to Sunnyside, the Windsor, Nova Scotia, home of his brother, Henry Youle Hind, who moved there in 1866.[12] By a strange coincidence, there was a Best family living at Horton, Kings County, Nova Scotia, which is very close to Henry Youle Hind's residence at Windsor. It is also worth noting that of the five pictures in the Kennedy group, four were described as views of New Brunswick and one of Nova Scotia, precisely the general areas of William Hind's later activities.

What is even more intriguing is the discovery that in the later nineteenth century one of the Best family at Horton was named John Richard.[13] Could John Richard Best, a near neighbour of Henry Youle Hind's, have been the original owner of the five pictures, who through the confusion of time became not only R.J. Best, but also the artist who painted them? The history of early Canadian art contains several instances where the original owners of pictures apparently became confused with the original artists. For example, the watercolours and drawings of George Seton (see Cat. no. 30) in the Royal Ontario Museum were originally attributed to Charles Murray, Earl of Cathcart, until Mary Allodi restored them to Seton with the suggestion that they may have at one time been owned by the Cathcart family.[14]

We have not been able to establish any positive connection between the Hind and Best families other than physical proximity, but they would not necessarily have needed close social connections for the one family to have acquired pictures from the other. As tantalizing as the possibilities are, the connection of the five pictures with the Best family of Horton, Nova Scotia, must remain pure conjecture.

As far as the second inscription on *On the Coast* is concerned, it reveals that the scene is not on the coast of Saint John as the Kennedy title suggested, but on the northern coast of New Brunswick at Jacquet River on the Baie des Chaleurs. This location would seem to fit well into William Hind's career dates, for it is known that his work on the railway took him to Matapedia on the Quebec-New Brunswick border in 1875, which is sufficiently close to Jacquet River to allow one to date the Jacquet view to that year.[15]

Of the four New Brunswick works in the original Kennedy group, two have, therefore, been more precisely documented within that province: the haying scene at Sussex and the coastal view at Jacquet River. It would appear that at least the provincial designations in the remaining Kennedy titles are correct, although the other three pictures might be much harder to locate precisely because of the lack of distinctive architecture and geographical features.

Harper has pointed out Hind's apparent debt to the English Pre-Raphaelites whose works he could have studied during his one documented visit to England during his Canadian years.[16] We do not know exactly when he went abroad, but he returned on the steamer *Arabian*, disembarking at Quebec in May 1861.[17] The small format of Hind's subsequent oils, their brilliant colour and minute transcription of nature all seem decidedly Pre-Raphaelite in inspiration.

His haying scene in Sussex is particularly reminiscent in colour, technique and subject matter of Ford Madox Brown's harvest landscapes such as *Carrying Corn*, 1854-1855, *The Hayfield*, 1855-1856 (both Tate Gallery, London; see Fig. 37.4) and *Walton-on-the-Naze*, 1859-1860 (Birmingham Museum and Art Gallery), which are all quite small, brightly coloured and microscopically detailed.[18] In both men's work, the minute details extending into a vast panorama of fields, trees and tiny buildings add up to a dreamlike pastoral vision of almost surreal intensity. The fact that Brown's small agricultural landscapes all date from 1854 to 1860, those years immediately preceding Hind's visit to England, further suggests that the latter had an opportunity to see some of them during his English sojourn.

It is also interesting to note that Ford Madox Brown was teaching at the Working Men's College in London from 1858 to 1860, where Ruskin and Rossetti also taught.[19] Since Hind himself served as a drawing master from 1851 to 1857 at the Toronto Normal School, he may have come in contact with Madox Brown through this common interest. Although the extant records at the Working Men's College for the years 1858 to 1861 do not list a William Hind among the students enrolled in the school, he could have met one of the professors there without necessarily being a full-time student.[20] At any rate, Ford Madox Brown's small haying scenes are so similar to Hind's Sussex landscape that some sort of influence seems evident, even though Hind's work was produced some two decades later. In very few other pictures does Hind come so close to Pre-Raphaelite ideals and quality as he does in this transcendent vision of the earthly paradise.

It is pleasant to report that all five of the Kennedy "Bests" are now in Canadian public collections. The spectacular autumn scene entitled *St. John, New Brunswick*, with its almost obsessive attention to botanical detail, is in the National Gallery of Canada.[21] *Cows Grazing, Nova Scotia*, a quintessential Hind subject that may perhaps have been painted near Windsor, is now in the Art Gallery of Ontario.[22] The superb collection of Hind's earlier work in the National Archives of Canada — some 130 paintings and drawings relating to his Labrador (see Cat. no. 5), Cariboo and Fort Garry visits, and including a wonderful self-portrait — has now been strengthened with two fine oil sketches and one outstanding oil panel from his later Maritime period, providing an almost coast-to-coast record of late nineteenth-century Canada through the eyes of this truly original artist.[23]

D.E.S.

37.1 W.G.R. Hind
Harvesting Hay, ca. 1880 (detail)
Oil on commercial board
NA C-103003

37.2
Trinity Church, Sussex, New Brunswick, 1973
Photograph
Canadian Inventory of Historic Building, National Historic Parks and Sites Directorate

37.3 W.G.R. Hind
Jacquet River, New Brunswick, 1875
Oil on paper
NA C-96621

37.4 F.M. Brown
The Hayfield, 1855-1856
Oil on canvas
Tate Gallery, London

1. Letter to the author from F. Frederick Bernaski, chief registrar, Kennedy Galleries, New York, 2 February 1983.

2. Kennedy Galleries (New York), *The Kennedy Quarterly*, December 1973, 223-226, 251 (sale catalogue). In the Kennedy titles, Saint John is always rendered as "St. John."

3. Sotheby's (Toronto) *Canadian Paintings, Drawings, Watercolours, Prints and Books*, 2-3 November 1982, lot 304 (illustrated). For William Robert Best, see Mary Allodi, *Canadian Watercolours and Drawings in the Royal Ontario Museum*, vol. 1 (Toronto: Royal Ontario Museum, 1974), no. 147, and also the Beaverbrook Art Gallery, *Recent Acquisitions Highlights 1978-1983* (Fredericton: Beaverbrook Art Gallery, 1983), no. 50, where his name is given as Robert William Best. At a subsequent Sotheby's (Toronto) sale (*Canadian Paintings*, May 3-4, 1983, lot 291), another oil on panel entitled *Atlantic Shore* appeared, attributed to William Robert Best, presumably based on a stylistic similarity to the distinctive haying scene of the year before. The presence of thatched cottages in this coastal scene suggests that the view is English. The panel support bears a lithographed advertising label on the verso: Finlayson, Bousfield & Co. Embroidery Thread Johnstone, Scotland. Lydia Foy, NA staff, examined the work and felt that there was sufficient similarity to the Kennedy group to make one suspect that it was also painted by Hind. In connection with the label on the verso, it is worth recalling that Hind's father was a lace manufacturer in Nottingham.

4. All of these characteristics may be seen in the superb little watercolour of sheep in the Art Gallery of Windsor's sketchbook of 1876, where the undulating rhythms of the foreground are particularly similar to the hay in our *Harvesting Hay*: see J. Russell Harper, *William G.R. Hind*, Canadian Artists Series (Ottawa: The National Gallery of Canada, 1976), plate 54.

5. The support seems identical to that which Hind used earlier in his career. Three small panels ca. 1870 in the NA (Accession Nos. 1937-278, 1937-279 and 1937-283), having been cut from the same larger sheet, bear between them the following label: ACADEMY BOARDS, / PREPARED / FOR OIL PAINTINGS, / BY / GEO. ROWNEY & CO., / 52, Rathbone Place, and 29, Oxford Street, / LONDON. Rowney occupied these addresses between 1862 and 1881; see Cathy Leach, "A Reference List of Firms Preparing Artist's Canvas in 19th Century London," unpublished typescript (Southampton: City Art Gallery, n.d.), 7.

6. J. Russell Harper, *William G.R. Hind (1833-1888): A Confederation Painter in Canada* (Windsor, Ontario: Willistead Art Gallery, 1967, exhibition catalogue) and Harper, *Hind*, 1976.

7. Letter to the author, 13 June 1985.

8. CIHB no. 04166000700857. Profound thanks are extended to Nathalie Clerk, head, Architectural Analysis Section, National Historic Parks and Sites Directorate, for her thorough search of all 659 wooden churches in Nova Scotia and New Brunswick, which resulted in the present identification.

9. G. Dallas Hawkes et al., *A History of Trinity-Anglican Church and its Rectors 1792-1974* (Sussex, New Brunswick: Trinity Anglican Church, 1974), 10-11. This publication was kindly brought to our attention by Rhonda Richardson, archives technician, The Anglican Church of Canada Archives, Toronto.

10. Letter to the author, 6 August 1985. The rectory is listed as no. 04166000700857A in the Canadian Inventory of Historic Building.

11. Regina Mantin, curator of fine arts, New Brunswick Museum, Saint John, was kind enough to inform us that "the date of the painting corresponds with the dates when Sussex had a train passing through and Sussex also had a mill at this time." Letter to the author, 2 July 1985.

12. George F.G. Stanley and Laurie C.C. Stanley, "The Brothers Hind," *Collections of the Nova Scotia Historical Society* 40 (1980): 121.

13. Public Archives of Nova Scotia, Best family papers.

14. Allodi, vol. 2, nos. 1490-1507.

15. Harper, *Hind* (1976), 25. Two of Hind's watercolours of Matapedia are in the Metropolitan Toronto Library, John Ross Robertson Collection, nos. 1947 and 1959.

16. Harper, *Hind* (1976), 7, 10.

17. Stanley, 111.

18. *The Pre-Raphaelites* (London: Tate Gallery and Penguin Books, 1984), nos. 61, 68 and 103.

19. Mary Bennett, *Ford Madox Brown* (Liverpool: Walker Art Gallery, 1964), 9. See also J.F.C. Harrison, *A History of the Working Men's College 1854-1954* (London: Routledge & Kegan Paul, 1954).

20. I would like to thank Anita Burdett, formerly of the NA London Office, for her research in the muniment room of the Working Men's College.

21. The same sort of minute treatment of foliage may be seen in the late watercolour *Wood Interior with Tree Stump*, ca. 1880 (Harper, 1976), cover illustration.

22. See for example *Pastoral Scene, Cattle in a Field*, ca. 1880 (Harper, 1976), plate 55.

23. I would like to acknowledge the assistance of Jennifer Trant, who undertook some of the research on Hind as a summer student with NA in 1985.

SIR HENRY WENTWORTH ACLAND (1815-1900)

38. *The Dying Daughter, St. Martin, Île Jésus, Quebec*, 25-29 August 1860

Watercolour and pen and brown ink with opaque white on paper

11.1 x 20.0 cm

Inscribed on mount, in pen and brown ink, recto, b.: *"I lost no opportunity of conversing quietly with the people, and used to try to see them alone. I strolled into the / interior of one of the small Farm houses in St. Martin. The deep chimney, with the oven in the recess – The crucifix / on the wall – the print of the Assumption – the French steeples – the looking glass – and the bird cage tell in plain characters, / the tale of life to be here as elsewhere – the dying daughter is set by her mother at the open window. Rose plants are / on the window sill"*

In "Montreal to London C.W.," volume 4 of the Acland collection

Purchased in 1985 with the assistance of a grant from the minister of Communications under the terms of the *Cultural Property Export and Import Act*

Accession no.: 1986-7-147

Negative no.: C-96919

While visiting Montreal in 1860 in the company of the Prince of Wales's tour, Dr. Henry Acland went to the small rural village of St. Martin on Île Jésus, just nine miles from the city. There he was the guest of Dr. Charles Smallwood,[1] who had a medical practice on the island, but whose avocation was the real reason for Acland's visit. Dr. Smallwood had set up an elaborate meteorological observatory of his own construction and was involved in a comprehensive program of record-keeping by which he studied environmental conditions and changes. Acland was fascinated by the operation and described it in great detail in his letters, including the fact that Dr. Smallwood was studying the effects of climate on health.[2] Acland would have found this of particular interest, since he himself had devoted a great deal of his time to the area of public health and sanitation.[3]

While in St. Martin, Acland visited the home of a young woman who was dying, probably with consumptive tuberculosis, which was prevalent in the nineteenth century. The purpose of his visit was no doubt to observe the care of such patients, for during the royal tour it had been his province to inspect hospitals, asylums, schools and orphanages. These he commented on at length in his letters, describing the buildings, the facilities and the quality of the care administered. In the case of the dying girl, he made this sketch and wrote below it the inscription as transcribed above. He notes the simple furnishings of the room and includes them in his drawing, which is a rare early view of the interior of a Canadian home. Though broadly sketched, it is easy to distinguish a number of features. On the floor are the narrow rag rugs, or "catalognes," which were sewn together to form a larger floor covering. The chair facing the girl is recognizable as a Capucine type, distinguished by its woven rush seat, splayed back legs and arched crosspieces. The mirror and the bird cage are the only touches of luxury, and the roses add the only dash of colour in the simple room. The crucifix and print of the Assumption hanging over the fireplace attest to the Roman Catholic faith of the inhabitants, while from the window can be seen the double spires of the parish church. This same church is featured in another of Acland's drawings, which also shows the priest's house (Fig. 38.1). The church was built in 1785 and was demolished in 1863, only three years after Acland's visit. It is therefore likely that these drawings are rare, if not unique, records of the village of St. Martin, made even more valuable by the fact that in 1868 a fire destroyed a number of its other buildings.[4]

While on Île Jésus, Acland also visited the home of a carpenter and drew a charming portrait of the man and wife (Fig. 38.2), writing below "Evening of life at a French Carpenter's. She knits – He chops his tobacco leaves on a shutter." Of the plain but comfortable life on Île Jésus, Acland also wrote that "both peasant and farmers seemed well to do in the struggle in a simple form – no unnecessary things – and the appliances of the country admirably adapted to their needs."[5] Acland had a great appreciation for the lives of ordinary people, and on several occasions during the tour he visited their homes, including that of a miller in London, Ontario, which he also sketched (Fig. 38.3).

In all, Acland made some 287 drawings during the tour, all of which he mounted into six albums and which are now in the collection of the National Archives. For a further description of the collection, see Cat. no. 23.

L.F.

38.1 H.W. Acland
St. Martin on the Île Jésus, Quebec, 25-29 August 1860
Pen and ink
NA C-96927

38.2 H.W. Acland
French Carpenter's Home, Île Jésus, Quebec, 25-29 August 1860
Pen and ink
NA C-96909

38.3 H.W. Acland
The Miller's Home, London, Ontario, 14 September 1860
Pen and ink
NA C 128141

1. *Dictionary of Canadian Biography* (Toronto: University of Toronto Press, 1972), 10:658-659, entry for Dr. Charles Smallwood.

2. NA, Sir Henry Wentworth Acland papers, MG 40 Q40, "Letters from North America," p. 73.

3. Acland's publications on the topic of public health include the following: *Health, Work and Play* (1856), *Fever in Agricultural Districts* (1858), *Forms for registering the sanitary conditions of villages* (1872), *Influence of Social and Sanitary Conditions on Religion* (1874) and *Health in the Village* (1884).

4. J.-Ad. Froment, *Histoire de Saint-Martin*... (Joliette: J.C.A. Perrault, 1915), 11, 17, 28.

5. NA, MG 40 Q40, "Letters," p. 78.

A Fancy Ball at the Victoria Rink

FRANCIS GEORGE COLERIDGE (1838-1923)

39. *A Fancy Ball at the Victoria Rink*, 1866

Watercolour over pencil with brush and black ink and opaque white on blue paper

22.8 x 36.1 cm

Inscribed in pen and black ink, recto, l.c.: *A Fancy Ball at the Victoria Rink*

In the Coleridge album

Purchased in 1983 with the assistance of a grant from the minister of Communications under the terms of the *Cultural Property Export and Import Act*

Accession no.: 1983-138-81

Negative no.: C-102533

This watercolour is one of ninety in the album held by the National Archives, all executed by Capt. Francis George Coleridge while he was stationed in Montreal in 1865 and 1866. He was an officer in the 25th Regiment, King's Own Borderers (KOB), and an amateur artist. The album was dedicated by Coleridge to Col. Francis Fane and the officers of the 1st Battalion of the regiment, and it features landscape views of the St. Lawrence valley, humorous depictions of garrison life, caricature portraits of his fellow officers, and events of the Montreal social scene. In these last respects, it resembles our contemporary high school yearbooks, recording as it does in-jokes, personal nicknames, amusing or embarrassing high-jinks and several inebriated escapades, as well as poking fun at superiors and equals alike. The album is also an interesting record of the social lives led by British officers while in Canada, in spite of the tension and martial preparations just prior to the Fenian raids of 1866. A caricaturist and cartoonist, Captain Coleridge was also a sensitive landscape painter, capturing the beauty of the countryside in its many seasonal variations.

Coleridge's background was typical of a nineteenth-century British army officer. Born in 1838 and a nephew of Lord Chief Justice Sir John Duke Coleridge, he was educated at Eton and was gazetted ensign in the 42nd Regiment in 1856 at the age of eighteen. The following year he was in India, where he took part in the capture of Lucknow.[1] He joined the KOB after his return from India and was a captain by 1864. Although the 1st Battalion of the 25th had been in Quebec City since June 1864, Coleridge himself did not arrive in Canada until 1865, after the regiment had moved to Montreal. The exact date of his arrival is still undetermined. The album dedication includes the date "May 5, 1865," but it also contains two sketches of Coleridge's passage that, according to their inscriptions, were done on the steamship *North American*, which did not arrive in Quebec City until 7 June.[2] Nevertheless, he was certainly in Montreal by 19 June, when he was recorded in the *Montreal Gazette* as one of the players in a local cricket game.[3]

Many of the events recorded by Coleridge in his album are also to be documented in contemporary newspapers, as is the one illustrated. There were at least three fancy dress balls at the Victoria Rink during the winter of 1865-1866.[4] Coleridge shows here (Cat no. 39) the one held in January 1866 and described in the *Montreal Gazette*:

> The characters on the ice, without being inconveniently numerous, were, in many instances, a decided improvement on those of last year, in the point of originality.... There was also a gigantic bottle of East India Pale Ale, refreshing to look upon when one reflected on the mediocre stature of the bottles in real life and their tall price.... Another well got up character was a Chinaman, who looked is if he had been nurtured in the celestial empire on green tea, so coppery was his complexion.... As for the ladies, they were not very numerous, and chiefly of tender years, the character [*sic*] most in vogue being Scotch lasses, Red Riding-hoods, old women, Vivandieres and Columbines....[5]

The beer bottle, Scotch lasses and Chinaman are visible in Coleridge's watercolour, as are the black imps, Jack Frost, snowshoer and Grenadier Guardsman that were also described in the newspaper article. Coleridge was obviously an enthusiastic participant in this type of event. The *Montreal Gazette* records the costumes of attendees of the fancy balls held that February. Our artist went first as a Highlander and then as Garibaldi.[6]

The KOB, like most regiments that served in Canada, participated in all the local winter sports, making up with bravado what they lacked in expertise. Several of the captain's sketches depict their attempts at skating, tobogganing, sleighing and snowshoeing. The last sport had been incorporated as a part of winter drill, reflecting a concern that the troops could be called upon to defend Canada in any season.[7] In Fig. 39.1, we can see that some caught on faster than others. The reporter for the *Montreal Gazette* also detected a variation in the degree of skill displayed:

> Yesterday morning the 25th Regt. was out on the Champ de Mars for exercise on snow-shoes. It must be said that these encumbrances like all other impediments are not very conducive to military precision. The men, however, appeared to be considerably at home in them.[8]

The concern for training, especially for the local militia, was a serious one, at least on the part of the commanders-in-chief. The movements and plans of the Fenian Brotherhood to the south were closely followed by the military authorities in the Canadas.[9] They were well aware that more than just British regulars, in spite of their increased numbers in Canadian garrisons, would be required to defend the border. In October of 1865, a three-week militia training camp was held at Laprairie. The cadets were drawn from both Upper and Lower Canada and were instructed by officers and non-commissioned officers from the British regiments in Montreal. While the militia were at the camp, the regulars went on an exercise to familiarize them with the Richelieu valley, one of the most vulnerable spots on the border. On 30 September, a "flying column" of the 25th, the 30th and the 60th Regiments and two batteries of artillery set out for Fort Chambly. They marched from there to St. Jean and then to Laprairie, arriving on 4 October. A grand review of both the cadets and the regulars by the commander-in-chief of the forces in Lower Canada, Major-General Lindsay, took place on 6 October. Captain Coleridge was present at this grand affair, which he recorded in at least two sketches. One shows Major-General Lindsay and his staff (Fig. 39.2). Another less serious sketch depicts an unfortunate officer being thrown from his horse at the review.

Shortly before or after the Laprairie review, our artist made an excursion south, travelling along the Hudson River where he sketched the Catskill Mountains and West Point. From the evidence of his watercolours, Niagara-on-the-Lake and the Thousand Islands (Fig.39.3) were also on his itinerary.

Captain Coleridge left Canada in the spring of 1866 on leave, before the Fenian raid in June (the album includes a sketch of the shore of Newfoundland, dated 13 May 1866).[10] Six companies from the KOB were sent to Prescott when Fenians invaded at Niagara. They patrolled along the St. Lawrence and then moved by rail to St. Jean to survey the Richelieu.[11] After events settled down, the regiment returned to St. Helen's Island, where they stayed until their departure for England in August of 1867. Coleridge must have rejoined them on St. Helen's, for he executed another album of watercolours very similar to the one exhibited here. During the course of research on the National Archives album, it was discovered that the 1866-1867 Coleridge album was in Massey Library at the Royal Military College in Kingston. Other similar albums by Coleridge, illustrating further adventures with the 25th on board the HMS *Himalaya* and in Paisley, are in the Regimental Museum in Berwick-upon-Tweed in Scotland.

Captain Coleridge remained with the KOB until 1872, when he sold his commission. Upon retirement, he took up painting as a profession, exhibiting in various London galleries and institutions. According to Algernon Graves, Coleridge began exhibiting in 1866; perhaps it was for this purpose that he was absent during that summer.[12] After his retirement, he painted mostly landscapes of the Thames and its rural villages, although he continued to recall the inspiration of his Canadian sojourn. Versions of an Indian woman on snowshoes painted in 1870s have turned up recently at auction in Britain. Captain Coleridge died in 1923 at the age of eighty-four, one of the last surviving veterans of the Indian mutiny of 1857.

His inimitable sense of humour continues to entertain and to remind us that history is not always serious.

S.N.

39.1 F.G. Coleridge
A Very Undignified Position that, Alas! our Acting Major is Far Too Fond of Assuming Upon the Most Unfitting Occasions, 1865-1866
Watercolour
NA C-102539

39.2 F.G. Coleridge
Our General and His Staff, 1865-1866
Watercolour
NA C-102478

39.3 F.G. Coleridge
***Thousand Islands of the St. Lawrence*,**
1865
Watercolour
NA C-102459

1. *The Times* (London), 26 July 1923, p. 9.
2. *The Quebec Gazette*, 7 June 1865, p. 2. Capt. Coleridge is not listed amongst the thirty-one cabin passengers.
3. *Montreal Gazette*, 19 June 1865, p. 2.
4. *Montreal Gazette*, 25 January, 6 and 14 February 1866, all p. 2.
5. *Montreal Gazette*, 25 January 1866, p. 2.
6. *Montreal Gazette*, 6 and 14 February 1866, both p. 2.
7. Robert Douglas Day, "The British Army and Sport," PhD thesis (University of Alberta, 1981), 114-115.
8. *Montreal Gazette*, 31 January 1866, p. 3.
9. Elinor Kyte Senior, *Roots of the Canadian Army: Montreal District 1846-1870* (Montreal: Society of the Montreal Military and Maritime Museum, 1981).
10. The diary of a fellow officer notes the following: May 3, 1866 – "Coleridge has got his leave to England. Went with him to take passage on 'Hibernian'.... and May 11, 1866 – Had dinner before with Coleridge & saw him off in the Quebec boat for England." Fort Henry Museum, Kingston, Ontario, Diary of Lt. John Talbot Coke, 25th Regiment, photocopy.
11. Capt. R.T. Higgins, *The Records of the King's Own Borderers* (London: Chapman and Hall, 1873), 352-353.
12. Algernon Graves, *A Dictionary of Artists* (Bath: Kingsmead Reprints, 1970), 59.

T. M. Richardson
1848

THOMAS MILES RICHARDSON, JR. (1813-1890), after Henry James Warre (1819-1898)

40. *Lake of the Woods, British North America*, 1848

Watercolour over pencil with opaque white and scraping out on paper

25.7 x 35.3 cm

Inscribed in pencil, recto, l.l.: *Lake of the Woods / B. / North America*; l.r.: *T.M. Richardson / 1848 / from a sketch by H.J.W.*

Purchased in 1983

Accession no.: 1984-8-1

Negative no.: C-120937

The English artist Thomas Miles Richardson Jr. is known primarily as a landscape watercolourist who exhibited extensively at the Old Water Colour Society in London between 1843 and 1889. Like several prominent watercolourists, he also worked with one of the large publishing and printing houses, producing both drawings and lithographs for illustrated travel books and print portfolios, which were popular in the late eighteenth and the nineteenth centuries.

These artists were often called upon to interpret landscapes and city views by other artists, usually amateurs. One such amateur artist was Henry James Warre, a British military officer who had been sent to the west coast of North America in 1845 on a secret reconnaissance mission. His job was to discover the extent of American settlement in the Columbia River and Puget Sound areas (then called the Oregon Territory), and to determine the feasibility of sending troops overland to the coast in defence of British interests. During his trip he kept extensive diaries, which are now in the National Archives of Canada, along with some 240 of his drawings.[1] In 1847, Warre asked for permission to publish a set of lithographs based on his western drawings, which would be accompanied by an account of his adventure. When the project was approved by the minister of state for foreign affairs, Dickinson and Company of London undertook to produce the sixteen-plate set of twenty views, entitled *Sketches in North America and the Oregon Territory* (London, 1848).[2]

Dickinson hired Richardson to copy Warre's sketches and watercolours, making improvements to the compositions and supplying "preparatory" drawings as a first step toward the creation of the prints. This he did by adding and changing elements of Warre's drawings to create more attractive and picturesque views.[3] An example of this process can be seen by comparing Warre's drawing of the Kakabeka Falls on the Kaministiquia River with Richardson's preparatory drawing and the final lithographic print (Figs. 40.1, 40.2 and 40.3). Richardson altered Warre's composition by bringing the point of view closer to the falls, making the water more agitated and dropping the horizon slightly to allow for more sky and higher mountains. Overall, these compositional changes create a more dramatic, if somewhat exaggerated, view of the falls, and with the addition of rising mist and clouds hanging over the mountains, also create a much more atmospheric effect. The most obvious change is the elimination of the foreground figure from the Warre composition, which would be too distracting and would reduce the scale and thus the grandeur of the falls.

In addition to improving the composition, Richardson's drawing of the falls also served to guide the lithographer in preparing the lithographic printing stone. The areas of opaque white on the drawing indicated highlights that would appear white. The washes and pencil work indicate shadows and outlines to be printed in black. The blue-green paper Richardson used is now sadly faded to brown, but it originally served to indicate the areas of colouring that would be achieved with the tint stone, which added an overall colour to the composition. The resulting lithograph relies heavily on Richardson's revised composition, but in all it is not a distortion of Warre's sketch. In fact, Richardson's drawing infuses the scene with elements, such as scale and atmosphere, that Warre was unable to capture.

The National Archives has nineteen of the twenty drawings that Richardson did for the Warre lithographs. They have been in the collection since at least 1925 and are of unknown provenance. For some time they were considered to be the work of Warre himself, thought to be his own preparatory drawings in his "studio" style. Once it was established that the drawings could not be the work of Warre, because of their sophistication and technical accomplishment, it was left to discover who had done them. There were no clues that would help identify the artist until this nineteenth-century watercolour of Lake of the Woods was offered for sale. While this in itself was enough to attract the interest of the National Archives, it was the inscription on the drawing that proved to be even more interesting. It read, "T.M. Richardson / 1848 / from a sketch by / H.J.W." It was clear that "H.J.W." was Henry James Warre, since the date corresponded to the publication date of the prints, and a view of Lake of the Woods could certainly have been based on a Warre composition, since he passed through the area during his journey to the Oregon Territory. It also became clear that Richardson was the artist responsible for all the preparatory drawings relating to the prints. In addition to the evidence of the inscription, there were also close stylistic comparisons to be made between the signed Richardson and the preparatory drawings, for example, the treatment of the tree and the mountains in the background. Particularly telling was Richardson's idiosyncratic way of drawing his figures, using small juxtaposed patches of black and white. Exactly the same schematic treatments appear in the preparatory drawings, especially in the view of the Willamette River valley (Fig. 40.4), and are also evident in Richardson's own sketches from nature.[4]

The Lake of the Woods composition was not made into a lithograph; Richardson apparently copied it for his own pleasure. He had sketched extensively in Europe and Britain, and no doubt found the North American landscapes interesting and picturesque. This drawing displays more of Richardson's palette and Turneresque technique than he was permitted in the preparatory drawings, the purpose of which was more utilitarian. A comparison between it and Warre's original sketch of the Lake of the Woods, although interesting to contemplate, is impossible, since the current location of Warre's drawing is unknown.

Further to the discovery that Thomas Miles Richardson was the artist responsible for the preparatory drawings is the notion that he may also have prepared the lithographic stones for printing. This idea must remain tentative, since the lithographs bear only Warre's name and that of the publisher-printer Dickinson and Company. However, Richardson is known to have prepared the printing stones for all twenty-six plates of a lithographic set after his own sketches entitled *Sketches on the Continent* (London, 1837).[5] Whoever the lithographer was, it is apparent from details in the prints that Warre's original drawings and Richardson's preparatory drawings were used side by side, since elements of both are incorporated into the final lithographic compositions.

The practice of using an intermediary artist, like Richardson, was common in nineteenth-century printmaking and is of particular note in the study of Canadiana prints published in England. Since this process has only recently been understood, it is not surprising that in the past preparatory drawings were assumed to be the work of the originating artist. Richardson's copy of Warre's Lake of the Woods composition provided the evidence needed to identify him as the artist of the nineteen preparatory drawings mentioned earlier. The present drawing also demonstrates how inscriptions on works of art can add new dimensions to our understanding of the work and of the artist.

L.F.

40.1 H.J. Warre
Falls of the Kaministakwia River, 1846
Brown wash
NA C-31267

40.2 T.M. Richardson, Jr., after H.J. Warre
Falls of the Kaministakwia River, 1848
Black and blue wash
NA C-82290

40.3 After H.J. Warre
Falls of the Kamanis Taquoih River, 1848
Lithograph
NA C-1616

40.4 T.M. Richardson, Jr., after H.J. Warre
Valley of the Willamette River, 1848
Black and blue wash
NA C-1612

1. The NA collection of Warre drawings and watercolours has been published with accompanying illustrative microfiches in *Archives Canada Microfiches* (Ottawa: Public Archives of Canada, 1985), microfiches 15-20.

2. For references to this print set, see: J.R. Abbey, *Travel in Aquatint and Lithography 1770-1860* (Folkestone: Dawsons of Pall Mall, 1972, reprint), no. 656; and R.V. Tooley, *English Books with Coloured Plates 1790 to 1860* (Folkestone: Dawson & Sons Ltd., 1978, revised edition), no. 500.

3. Richardson's preparatory drawings and the lithographic sets are discussed in *Archives Canada Microfiches*, microfiche no. 20.

4. For an example of Richardson's own compositions, see Martin Hardie, *Water-Colour Painting in Britain* (London: B.T. Batsford, 1967), 2: plate 219, "Mount Parnassus."

5. Abbey, *Travel*, no. 30.

Humboldt
Col A Wyndham 1885

ALFRED WYNDHAM (1837-1914)

41. *Humboldt*, 1885

Watercolour on paper

17.1 x 25.9 cm

Inscribed in brushpoint and black ink, recto, l.r.: *Humboldt / Col A Wyndham 1885*

Purchased in 1987

Accession no.: 1987-6-1

Negative no.: C-130085

At first glance, this charming watercolour of Humboldt, Saskatchewan, seems to be nothing more than a simple prairie landscape lying under a dreamy blue western sky. However, the two uniformed figures in the lower left corner and the inscription at the bottom right suggest that the subject is of historical significance. The work is identified as "Humboldt," and is signed and dated "Col A Wyndham 1885."

The watercolour dates from the year the Dominion government successfully quelled a second Métis uprising under the leadership of Louis Riel. Maj.-Gen. Frederick Middleton was commander of the Canadian militia and the North West Field Force assembled to subdue the rebels. When the Canadian militia mobilized for the Rebellion in April 1885, Lt.-Col. Alfred Wyndham went west with the York and Simcoe Provisional Battalion.

Middleton divided his forces into three, and the first column under his command took as their initial headquarters Fort Qu'Appelle in southern Saskatchewan, just north of the Canadian Pacific Railway line. With Batoche as their objective, the route followed by the general and subsequent reinforcement troops was from Fort Qu'Appelle, northwest past the Touchwood Hills to Humboldt, northwest to Clarke's Crossing on the South Saskatchewan River, and then northeast to Fish Creek and Batoche. Humboldt, situated some 55 miles southeast of Riel's headquarters at Batoche, and roughly 140 miles from the more easterly Fort Qu'Appelle, became a crucial provisioning and communications depot for the military during the rebellion.

Lieutenant-Colonel Wyndham came from a wealthy military family. His father was Capt. Alexander Wyndham of Blandford, Dorsetshire, England, an officer of the Scots Greys who fought at Waterloo. Following the family tradition, Alfred attended a naval academy. However, he subsequently chose an army career, joining the Wiltshire Militia. After the Crimean War and a tour of duty in the Mediterranean, he left the army and moved to Canada. In 1859, Wyndham married Caroline Elizabeth Stuart,[1] whose cousin Jane Seymour left this candid description of Alfred:

> ...my cousin Caroline Stuart married Mr. Alfred Wyndham, (afterwards Col.) a young Englishman who came out to Canada with a good deal of money, on hand, a truehearted Christian gentleman, but one of the many of that type, who seem to be born with a genius for muddling away wealth; but, if he lost money, he won respect and affection; and there is many a man up here today who has cause to bless the name of "The dear old Col...."[2]

The Wyndhams settled at Roches Point on Lake Simcoe, where they raised eleven children. Although Alfred undertook farming, he nevertheless remained involved with the militia at Simcoe, joining the 12th Battalion, York Rangers, and becoming a lieutenant-colonel in 1882.[3]

When the Canadian militia was preparing for the rebellion, a composite group called the York and Simcoe Provisional Battalion was formed from the 12th Battalion and 35th Simcoe Foresters. They left Yorkville on 2 April in such haste that little time could be devoted to appearance, one observer noting that their clothing was "old and rotten" and their knapsacks "ill-fitted."[4] Wyndham was commanding officer of the 12th, while Col. O'Brien was in command of the combined battalion. A photograph from the Glenbow Museum shows Wyndham in the uniform of the 12th, with stylish mutton chops (Fig. 41.1), looking surprisingly like the principal figure in the Humboldt sketch, which is possibly a self-portrait. Wyndham's presence at Humboldt during the rebellion is documented in family histories, military records and photographs, and by his few known sketches. In addition, a diary written by Lt. J.T. Symons, who was under Wyndham's command, establishes that he visited Batoche.

On 13 May, Wyndham's battalion started on a forced march from Fort Ou'Appelle to Humboldt to ready themselves as reinforcements for Middleton. However, since the capture of Batoche had taken place the day before, essentially ending the rebellion, they were too late to actively participate in the fighting; they arrived in Humboldt only on 19 May.

Humboldt, located in central Saskatchewan, was named after a German scientist and geographer, Baron Alexander von Humboldt, at the time of the 1870 Pacific railway survey.[5] In the Symons diary, the first impression of Humboldt is described as follows: "This flourishing City consists of one dirty Telegraph log house and some distance away a log stable."[6]

Lt.-Col. George T. Denison, of the Governor General's Body Guard, was the senior officer at Humboldt, having arrived there on 1 May, just as events were escalating at Batoche. When General Middleton, in dire need of assistance, became entrenched before Batoche, the telegraph lines linking him to reinforcements had failed between Clarke's Crossing and Humboldt to the east. If one looks closely at the watercolour, the telegraph wires can be seen extending from a curved pole in the left foreground across a pond to four other poles planted in a straight line that ends at the two-room log structure in the right background. Denison recalls in his memoirs that his main activity in Humboldt was communicating news to the eastern stations and ensuring messages were forwarded north by hand. He wrote:

> During those days, my time was principally spent in the telegraph station. Despatches came pouring in from all points, from General Strange, from Winnipeg, from Battleford, from Qu'Appelle, Swift Current, etc .... It took about two days to get despatches to the General at Batoche, and a reply back.[7]

There are other early visual records of Humboldt, among them a lithograph from *The Illustrated War News,*[8] and a photograph that shows a close-up view of the log structure with Colonel Denison in front of it (Fig. 41.2). In addition, a competent sketch of the cabin, as it looked in 1881 before the rebellion, was taken by Sydney Prior Hall during his western travels, and is inscribed "Humboldt. Mrs. Leggatt's Shanty" (Fig. 41.3).

Colonel Wyndham's drawing of this site is rather unique. His is not a view of just the building, but a view set back from it, showing the hilly terrain that extends into the background. Although his artwork reflects a charming amateur style, the pleasing composition demonstrates his talent for painting. His attention to detail, seen for example in the multitude of spindly tree trunks in the trees at the edges of the fields, suggests that he worked at the drawing with diligence. The abundance of foliage and the use of greens and browns indicate the scene is of late spring or early summer. The presence of the soldiers further narrows the date to sometime between 19 May and 9 July, when Wyndham's battalion was stationed at Humboldt. The group of six or more white tents in the centre background seem to be of the military type. A description of the camp by Colonel Denison corresponds to what is seen in the watercolour:

> The country around Humboldt in this early summer was perfectly beautiful. The ground was fairly carpeted with wild flowers of every variety. The country on one side of us for twenty miles was rolling prairie, with clumps of trees dotted about everywhere, with small lakes and ponds, the grass in the open stretches clean and fairly short, so that the whole place looked like an enormous old country park.[9]

Lieutenant-Colonel Wyndham also painted two watercolours of Batoche. One, held by the National Archives (Fig. 41.4), depicts in detail the buildings that were besieged by Middleton's forces, with several minuscule military figures with rifles over their shoulders, marching on a dirt road at some distance behind a Red River cart. The other, acquired by the Glenbow Museum in 1987, is virtually identical, although the two soldiers in the left foreground corner have been cropped. An inscription beside the figures in the Glenbow version identifies Wyndham as the artist and dates the sketch to June 1885. Although the rebellion was well over by June, his battalion did not return east until mid-July. Denison describes the time after the battle of Batoche as lax, and according to the Symons diary, Wyndham travelled to Batoche twice during this period. Both sketches of Batoche were likely produced sometime in June.[10]

After the rebellion, Wyndham decided to bring his family out west to live. He received a medal and clasp for his services as well as land in the Carseland district, south of the Bow River, as North West Rebellion scrip. When the allotment was first assigned, he obtained the deed and settled on Section 28. Afterwards, when the area was surveyed a second time, his land became part of Section 33, but he was allowed to remain in the same place. His predicament must have reminded him of the earlier Métis land disputes that had ironically led to his good fortune. He built his home and again took up farming, naming the homestead "Dinton" after his home in Wiltshire, England, and this area in Saskatchewan later assumed the name. He apparently painted a picture of his first home, a log structure with a sod roof.[11]

The Symons diary also documents Wyndham the artist. Symons comments on a "fine sunset" recorded during a stop on the Salt Plains, when his commanding officer made a sketch of "A sunset on the expanseless prairie."[12] In addition to the five works mentioned, according to family tradition Wyndham is said to have also produced a sketchbook with scenes of Muskoka and the Thousand Islands while living in Ontario. The talent was passed on to at least his eldest son Alexander, who, in a diary kept during his stay at school in England in 1875-1876, drew several cartoons.[13]

Colonel Wyndham's love for the military, his patriotism, and his love for the Canadian countryside are exemplified in the few known western sketches that have surfaced in recent years. A work like this watercolour of Humboldt gives us at least a small glimpse of an early Canadian soldier, pioneer and artist.

M.M.

41.1 W.A. McPherson
Lt. Col. Alfred Wyndham, 1885
Photograph
Glenbow Archives, NA-84-i

41.2
First Telegraph Station at Humboldt, Saskatchewan. Col. Denison seated in chair, 1885
Photograph
NA C-753

41.3 S.P. Hall
Humboldt, Ms. Leggatt's Shanty, 1881
Pencil
NA C-12962

41.4 A. Wyndham
Batoche, 1885
Watercolour
NA C-3124

---

1. Glenbow Museum Archives, Wyndham family papers, M4320, "The Wyndham Family," 1959, unpublished manuscript by Sheilagh S. Jameson prepared for the Glenbow Foundation, pp. 1-2. Caroline Stuart was the daughter of John Stuart, barrister-at-law in London, Ontario, and her family was very prominent in eastern Canada.
2. Glenbow, M4320, Memoirs of Miss Jane Seymour, 1922, p. 54.
3. Glenbow, M4320, appointment of Alfred Wyndham to lieutenant-colonel, 12th Battalion, York Rangers, 1882.
4. Capt. A.T. Hunter, *History of the 12th Regiment, York Rangers* (Toronto: Murray Printing Company, Limited, 1912), 60.
5. E.T. Russell, *What's in a Name?* (Saskatoon: Western Prairie Books, 1973), 145.
6. Archives of Ontario, MU-844, Lt. J.T. Symons diary, 19 May 1885, p. 8.
7. Lt.-Col. George T. Denison, *Soldiering in Canada* (Toronto: George N. Morang and Company Limited, 1901), 288.
8. *The Illustrated War News* (Toronto), 11 April 1885, p. 12.
9. Denison, *Soldiering*, 312.
10. Archives of Ontario, MU-844, Symons diary, pp. 10-13. The diary documents three trips made by Wyndham to Batoche: 23 May, 11 June and 21 June, 1885.
11. W.D.P. Wyndham, "The Wyndham Story," *Furrows of Time* (Calgary: Arrowwood-Mossleigh Historical Society, 1980), 644. Courtesy of Keith Stotyn, Provincial Archives of Alberta.
12. Archives of Ontario, MU-844, Symons diary, 17 May 1885, p. 8.
13. Glenbow, M320, Alexander Wyndam diary, October 1875-April 1876.

A PLACE IN HISTORY

Timeless Mementos

Portraits have a special role in documenting our history. They allow us to share an intimate meeting with both our renowned historical figures and our lesser-known, but equally interesting personalities from the past. The portraits featured in the exhibition are from the British colonial period, and are done in a variety of media, from small miniatures on ivory to large formal oil paintings. The National Archives makes a special effort to acquire important historical portraits, and over the years has established a national portrait collection whose scope encompasses all of Canadian history.

More recent portraits can be found in the twentieth-century section of the catalogue.

THOMAS HUDSON (1701-1779)

42. *Captain Philip Durell*, 1746

Oil on canvas

90.5 x 70.0 cm

Inscribed in brushpoint and black paint, recto, l.r.: *Tho: Hudson Pinxit / 1746*; in brushpoint and grey paint, recto, l.r.: *A Plan / OF/Louisburg / Harbour / 1745*

Bequest of J.H.P. Daman, 1979

Accesssion no.: 1980-22-1

Negative no.: C-117939

43. *Mrs. Durell*, 1746

Oil on canvas

90.7 x 70.0 cm

Bequest of J.H.P. Daman, 1979

Accession no.: 1980-22-2

Negative no.: C-117938

Having joined the British Navy at the age of fourteen, Philip Durell (1707-1766) served for the next five years on the Newfoundland, Nova Scotia and New England stations, experience that provided a solid foundation for his later distinguished naval career in Canada. His first military success came with the capture of Louisbourg in 1745, an event in which he played an important part and which directly inspired this handsome pair of portraits by the English artist Thomas Hudson.

In the decades following the *Treaty of Utrecht* (1713), in which Hudson's Bay, Newfoundland and Acadia were ceded to England, France began to fortify the settlement of Louisbourg on Cape Breton Island. From this outstanding harbour the French fleet could control the local fishery as well as transatlantic shipping. When King George's War (the North American phase of the European War of the Austrian Succession) broke out in 1744, Louisbourg became the focus for an English-French confrontation in the New World.

After repelling a French attack on Annapolis Royal, William Shirley, the governor of Massachusetts, proposed a major expedition to capture Louisbourg under Commodore Peter Warren of the British Navy and William Pepperrell, who commanded the land forces of about four thousand New England militiamen. Because he knew the area well and was an accomplished surveyor, Durell played a significant role in ensuring the success of the undertaking. While his ship the *Eltham* was wintering in Nantasket Roads, Massachusetts, he assisted in formulating Pepperrell's instructions, and his ship was the first to join the latter at Canso. During the siege that lasted from 1 May to 16 June 1745, Durell helped in the capture of the *Vigilant* (under the command of Capt. Alexandre de La Maisonfort Du Boisdecourt), which had tried to run Warren's blockade and bring supplies to the besieged fortress. A few months later, Durell was also instrumental in capturing two French East Indiamen, prize ships of enormous value.[1]

The surrender of Louisbourg was commemorated in a largely fanciful print engraved by Brooks after J. Stevens, entitled *A View of the Landing* [of] *the New England Forces in ye Expedition against Cape Breton, 1745*, published in London by R. Wilkinson, ca. 1747 (Fig. 42.1).[2] In October 1745, Durell returned to London with dispatches and his survey of Louisbourg harbour, about which Warren wrote: "Capt. Durell ... has taken a great deal of pains to make an exact survey of this garrison, harbour and careening place."[3]

One of the first things Durell must have done upon his arrival in England was to contact Thomas Hudson, then considered the most fashionable portrait painter in London, and to commission two half-length portraits of himself and his wife.[4] The conquering hero was depicted in his captain's uniform of blue coat and white waistcoat with gold braid, holding prominently in his left hand the plan of Louisbourg that he had taken such great care to make (Fig. 42.2). A similar document entitled *A Plan of the Harbour and Fortification of Louisbourg* survives in the British Library. It is dated 1745 and has a decorative cartouche around the title (Fig. 42.3). In the left background of the painting, a single ship, perhaps meant to be Durell's own vessel, symbolizes the naval siege at Louisbourg. As a man of action, Durell is shown outdoors under a cloudy sky.[5]

In the pendant portrait, Mrs. Durell, probably Captain Durell's first wife Madeline Saumarez, is shown indoors wearing a fancy blue and white "Van Dyck" dress decorated with lace and pearls. This portrait was probably painted by Joseph van Aken, Hudson's drapery painter, in what was a rather large studio operation. Like her husband, Mrs. Durell looks straight out at the spectator, but gestures towards her husband with her right hand. Since hands were considered difficult to paint, Hudson was probably glad to pose Captain Durell in the then-fashionable pose of tucking the hand into the waistcoat. To avoid painting both of Mrs. Durell's hands, however, the artist allowed her left wrist to slip off rather awkwardly at the bottom of the canvas.

Sometime after the completion of the pictures in 1746, a replica of Captain Durell's portrait was prepared, apparently for his wife's family in Guernsey (Fig. 42.4). This rather crude copy, certainly not created by Hudson or his studio, comes as something of a surprise, for Durell is shown wearing a different wig, a longer and fuller one that extends to his shoulder and ends with a big bow and queue. During the recent conservation of the Hudson portrait, it was discovered that Durell's wig had once been fuller and longer, just as it is shown in the copy, but that it had been shortened at some later date. It would appear that changes in fashion towards a shorter wig at mid-century caused Durell to return the portrait to Hudson, who obliged by painting out the old-fashioned hairpiece and replacing it with a more modish one, leaving the halo effect around the head that we see today.[6]

Other changes in the composition are also evident in the Durell picture. Hudson originally decided to close his composition on the right with a column and plinth that would balance the traditional drapery to the left behind Mrs. Durell. Like the longer wig, the column was later painted out, leaving the captain silhouetted against an uninterrupted expanse of sky. This pentimento, or change, evidently occurred at a fairly early stage in the work's creation, since no column was included in the Guernsey copy. Through time the overpaint of the sky has become somewhat transparent, exposing a ghost-image of the column standing on a veined marble plinth.

Durell was not the only hero of Louisbourg who wished to commemorate the event with a portrait. At the same time that he was sitting to Hudson, Governor Shirley, Peter Warren and William Pepperrell had all commissioned the New England artist John Smibert to produce impressive full-length portraits celebrating their achievements at Louisbourg.[7] The more expensive full-length format would have been appropriate for the commanders of the expedition, whose high ranks and elevated social status would be reflected in the larger size of the portraits.

According to the 1748 *Treaty of Aix-la-Chapelle*, the fortress of Louisbourg was returned to France, a decision that was not well received by the New Englanders who at considerable risk had captured it three years earlier. While Governor Shirley was in England trying unsuccessfully to reverse the terms of the treaty, he decided to have another portrait painted, and, following Durell's lead, chose Thomas Hudson. The resulting picture, dated 1750, continues to refer to the triumph at Louisbourg in the background. The following year, Peter Warren, who had returned to England, also showed up at Hudson's studio for another Louisbourg portrait.[8] The feeling seems to have been that since the victory was so short-lived, portraits (and the prints that were subsequently published after them) could be used for propaganda purposes to perpetuate the memory of the glorious enterprise and even perhaps to criticize the subsequent return of the fortress to the French.

It was only a matter of time before the English would retake Louisbourg. In 1758, Durell, now promoted to the rank of commodore, once again played an important part in its recapture by advising on the best place and time of landing. After the victory, Durell was promoted rear-admiral of the blue, remaining in North America as commander-in-chief for the winter, during which he built a dockyard for the navy at Halifax. In 1759, he sailed with Wolfe from Halifax to Quebec, successfully navigating the treacherous passages of the St. Lawrence River with the help of James Cook (later Captain Cook). As Saunders' second in command, Durell guarded the Traverse, the crucial passage south-east of the Île d'Orléans, during the battle for Quebec. Seven years later, he was named commander-in-chief of the North American station, but fell ill during the voyage to Halifax and, four days after his arrival, died "from eating dolphins," as the cause of death was diagnosed. He was buried under St. Paul's Church, Halifax, where his armorial hatchment may be seen to this day.[9]

As an older man, Durell had another portrait painted, which was apparently at one time incorrectly attributed to Sir Joshua Reynolds (Fig. 42.5). But Durell is best remembered as the younger hero of Louisbourg in Hudson's fine painting. For a man whose fame was largely won in Canada, it is very appropriate that these family portraits of Durell and his wife have now been presented to the Canadian people through the generosity of one of his descendants, to remind us of Durell's notable contribution to our history.[10]

D. E. S.

42.1 Brooks, after J. Stevens
A View of the Landing* [of] *the New England Forces in ye Expedition against Cape Breton, 1745, ca. 1747
Engraving
NA C-40989

42.2 T. Hudson
Philip Durell, 1746 (detail)
Oil on canvas
NA C-45907

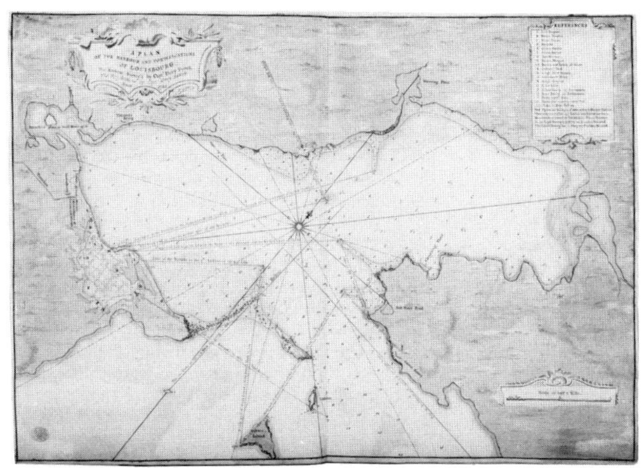

42.3 After P. Durell and H. Bastide
A Plan of the Harbour and Fortification of Louisbourg, 1745
Pen and ink
British Library

42.4 After T. Hudson
Philip Durell, ca. 1746
Oil on canvas
Formerly collection of Sir Havilland de Saumarez, Guernsey, present location unknown

42.5 Unknown artist
Philip Durell, ca. 1760
Oil on canvas
Plymouth Museum and Art Gallery, Plymouth, England

1. *Dictionary of Canadian Biography* (Toronto: University of Toronto Press, 1974), 3:208-210, entry for Philip Durell.

2. The event was also recorded in an oil painting by Peter Monamy (versions in the Royal Ontario Museum; the National Maritime Museum, London; and at Christie's [London], 18 November 1983, lot 55), which is related to a mezzotint printed for R. Sayer and J. Bennett, No. 53 Fleet Street, London, 1760 (copy at the Public Archives of Nova Scotia, Accession no. 1979-147.91; kindly brought to my attention by Jim Burant, NA staff).

3. Letter from Warren to Thomas Corbett, secretary to the Admiralty Board, dated at Louisbourg, 3 October 1745, as transcribed in Julian Gwyn, ed., *The Royal Navy and North America: The Warren Papers, 1736-1752*, Publications of the Navy Records Society 118 (1973): 172, letter no. 165.

4. See Ellen G. Miles and Jacob Simon, *Thomas Hudson 1701-1779, Portrait Painter and Collector: A Bicentenary Exhibition* (London: Greater London Council, 1979), an exhibition at the Iveagh Bequest, Kenwood. Both authors have generously assisted us with suggestions and information concerning our Durell portraits.

5. A copy of this portrait was made for John Clarence Webster while it was still in the J.H.P. Daman collection. It is now in the Webster Canadiana collection, New Brunswick Museum, Saint John, no. 503. Hudson's name was not connected with the Daman portrait until the signature was discovered upon its arrival at the NA.

6. Letter to the author from Jacob Simon, assistant curator, the Iveagh Bequest, Kenwood, 10 February 1981. Webster also had copies made of the Guernsey portrait (Webster Canadiana collection, New Brunswick Museum, nos. 499-501). Sir Havilland de Saumarez owned in addition what Webster calls the "first" portrait of Durell, showing him in a red coat and blue waistcoat with his right hand on a cannon and his left holding a telescope. Sea and ships are represented in the background (see Webster Canadiana collection, no. 502). Another portrait of Durell, attributed to Hudson and apparently deriving from the NA picture, is in the Royal Ontario Museum. This painting shows Durell three-quarter length to the knees with the plan of Louisbourg in his left hand and his right on his hip, the latter gesture similar to Peter Warren's in Hudson's 1751 portrait (the version in the National Portrait Gallery, London, and Faber mezzotint of the same year). The quality of the Royal Ontario Museum portrait is not sufficiently high to justify an attribution to Hudson.

7. Smibert's portrait of Shirley is now known only from a mezzotint after it by Peter Pelham. Warren's portrait is in the collection of the Portsmouth Athenaeum, Portsmouth, New Hampshire; Pepperrell's is in the Essex Institute, Salem, Massachusetts. See Ellen G. Miles, "Portraits of the Heroes of Louisbourg, 1745-1751," *The American Art Journal*, vol. 15, no. 1 (Winter 1983), 48-66.

8. Hudson's portrait of Shirley is in the National Portrait Gallery, Washington, and Warren's in the National Portrait Gallery, London (another version in the National Maritime Museum, London). See Miles, "Portraits," 61-64.

9. *Dictionary* 3:210, entry for Durell.

10. John H.P. Daman of Ipswich is thought to have been a descendant or collateral descendant of Durell's, but his closest surviving relatives at the time of the bequest did not know the genealogical details linking the two men. Mr. Daman also bequeathed to Canada some Georgian silver and a Chinese export porcelain service bearing Durell's coat of arms, which he apparently ordered soon after his return from the 1745 capture of Louisbourg (now in the collection of the National Gallery of Canada). See Ron Whate, "The Durell Service," *Canadian Collector*, vol. 20, no. 2 (March 1985), 48-50.

CATHERINE READ (1723-1778)

44. *Frances Brooke*, ca. 1771

Oil on canvas
72.4 x 60.0 cm
Purchased in 1981
Accession no.: 1981-88-1
Negative no.: C-117373

It is not uncommon for the National Archives to acquire from time to time eighteenth-century British portraits of important military, political or religious figures who made a significant contribution to the development of Canada (for example, Cat. nos. 45 and 52). These pictures of worthies invariably depict men, although portraits of their wives or sisters sometimes accompany them, but strictly as subordinate handmaidens to their heroic husbands or brothers (Cat. nos. 46 and 53). It is highly unusual to encounter a Georgian portrait of a person whose claim to fame in Canada is cultural or artistic, rather than military of religious; it is even rarer to encounter a portrait of a woman who excelled in the artistic sphere in the post-Conquest period of our history. There was therefore great excitement when we were able to acquire Catherine Read's charming oil portrait of Frances Brooke, who achieved fame by writing the first Canadian novel during her stay in Quebec City during the mid-1760s. The picture is also interesting because it was painted by a skilled woman artist who was a close personal friend of the sitter. The portrait of Mrs. Brooke is accompanied by one of her husband, the Rev. John Brooke (Fig. 44.1), who in this case is completely eclipsed in renown by his more celebrated wife.[1]

Frances Brooke, née Moore (1724-1789), was one of the leading literary figures of her day, moving in the circle of the famous Dr. Samuel Johnson. In about 1756, she married the Rev. John Brooke (ca. 1709-1789), the rector of Colney, Norfolk, who left for North America in 1757 as a military chaplain. In 1763, Mrs. Brooke published her first novel, *The History of Lady Julia Mandeville*, containing descriptions of Canadian scenery and discussions of Canadian issues evidently supplied by her husband, who had become garrison chaplain at Quebec in 1760. Evidently excited by the literary possibilities of the New World as subject matter for her novels, Mrs. Brooke joined her husband in Quebec in October 1763, where they lived for most of the next five years at the former Jesuit mission house at Sillery, a suburban settlement about four and half kilometres above Quebec. In August 1768, they returned to England.[2]

During her stay in Canada, Frances Brooke wrote *The History of Emily Montague*, published in London in 1769 with a dedication to Guy Carleton, the governor of Quebec, who had been a friend of the Brookes'. Comprising 228 letters dated between 10 April 1766 and November 1767, the epistolary novel tells the interlocking story of three sets of lovers: Ed Rivers, the handsome and compassionate officer on half pay who proposes to settle in Canada, and the divine Emily Montague, whose tenderness and delicacy make her a paragon of eighteenth-century decorum and sensibility; Arabella Fermor, a vivacious coquette who provides a foil to Emily, and the insubstantial Captain Fitzgerald; and Lucy Rivers, Ed's sister, and John Temple, a rich young bachelor who is also Ed's best friend.[3] Through the 228 dispatches, which are mainly written by Ed and Arabella, we follow the on-again-off-again romance of Ed and Emily, which ends in eternal married bliss on the last page.

By making her first two pairs of lovers newcomers to Canada and leaving Lucy and Temple in England, Frances Brooke provided her principal Canadian correspondants with the opportunity of sending back to their friends in England both frequent and lengthy descriptions of Quebec society, politics, religion and natural surrounds, based, of course, on the Brookes' own experiences. Until she discovers the redeeming social pleasures of a Canadian winter, the high-spirited Arabella is particularly severe on our climate:

> Silleri, Jan. 1: It is with difficulty I breathe, my dear; the cold is so amazingly intense as almost totally to stop respiration....
>
> The strongest wine freezes in a room which has a stove in it; even brandy is thickened to the consistence of oil: the largest wood fire, in a wide chimney, does not throw out its heat a quarter of a yard....
>
> I no longer wonder the elegant arts are unknown here; the rigour of the climate suspends the very powers of the understanding: what then must become of those of the imagination? Those who expect to see "*A new Athens rising near the pole*," will find themselves extremely disappointed. Genius will never mount high, where the faculties of the mind are benumbed half the year.[4]

Although it enjoyed only a moderate success in England, *Emily Montague* became required reading for travellers to Canada and was still a current reference in Quebec over a century after its publication. For example, in 1829 the military artist James Pattison Cockburn made a watercolour of the Jesuit house at Sillery in which the Brookes lived in Canada, entitling the view: *Emily Montague's House at Sillery Cove* (Fig. 44.2).[5] In his little guidebook to Quebec, Cockburn also advised the picturesque traveller to read the novel because it furnished "a faithful picture of the manners and situation of the colonists at the time when Canada first became a British Colony."[6] As late as 1880, Alfred P. Wheeler, a customs official at Quebec, named his house at Sillery "Montague Cottage."[7] For the modern Canadian, Frances Brooke's achievement may be summed up in the words of her recent biographer, Lorraine McMullen:

> Her major contribution to Canadian literature remains the first novel written in North America, *Emily Montague*, which conveys with grace, wit, intelligence and perception what it meant to experience Canada in the 18th century.[8]

On her return to London in 1768, Mrs. Brooke resumed her literary career, writing at least two more novels, a tragedy and the libretti for two comic operas, including *Rosina* (Covent Garden, 1782), and becoming joint manager with the great tragic actress Mary Ann Yates of the Haymarket Opera House. A few years after her return she had her portrait painted by her friend Catherine Read.

Although now almost totally forgotten, the Scottish-born Catherine Read was one of the most fashionable portraitists of the generation of Sir Joshua Reynolds, who was in fact her exact contemporary.[9] Although she also worked in oils and in miniature, Read was especially esteemed as a pastellist, earning the nickname the "English Rosalba," since her work in that medium was deemed to equal that of the famous Italian pastellist Rosalba Carriera. Her work has been neglected in modern times mainly because almost all of her portraits are still in private English and Scottish country houses, and because she rarely signed her work. Only with the recent re-examination of art history from a feminist perspective has Catherine Read's name emerged once again from obscurity.[10]

Between 1745 and 1751, Read studied with the well-known pastellist Maurice Quentin de la Tour in Paris, and completed her artistic education under Louis-Gabriel Blanchet in Rome, ca. 1751-1754. On her return to England in 1754, Thomas Hudson was the most popular portrait painter of the day (Cat. nos. 42 and 43). Read quickly achieved fame as a portraitist. Between 1761 and 1765, one Royal commission followed another for portraits of Queen Charlotte and the Prince of Wales. But by 1777, with her popularity dwindling, she set out for India to join her brother at Madras, where she is known to have made a number of portraits of Indians. Read died at sea on 15 December 1778 en route to the Cape of Good Hope, having decided to go there for the sake of her health.[11]

During the decade of her greatest popularity (1761-1771), Read commanded as high a price for her work as any but one or two of the leading artists of her time. From 1760 on, she exhibited almost annually with the Society of Artists, the Free Society, and the Royal Academy, although her portrait of Mrs. Brooke did not figure in any of these exhibitions. She specialized in portraits of beautiful women, including aristocratic ladies, blue stockings like Mrs. Brooke, actresses and famous courtesans.[12] Children were also favourite subjects.

Although the picture is not signed, our portrait of Frances Brooke may be securely attributed to Catherine Read on the basis of an engraving after it by Mariano Bovi inscribed "Catherine Read pinx." and dated 1790, and apparently published to commemorate Mrs. Brooke's death the year before (Fig. 44.3). In her *Connoisseur* articles on Catherine Read, however, Lady Victoria Manners states, without revealing her source, "In 1771, M. Bovi made stipple plates of Mrs. Brooke."[13] No impression of the print is known before the 1790 one, and since Mariano Bovi was born in Naples in 1757 and only came to London in 1781, it seems impossible that he could have engraved anything in London as early as 1771.[14] While Lady Victoria is almost certainly wrong about the publication date of the print, the year she gives may very well be correct for the painting. In 1771, Frances Brooke would have been forty-seven years old, an age which would agree well with the painted likeness.

Perhaps the most interesting aspect of the present picture is the fact that it is a portrait of a gifted woman author by another talented woman artist from an age in which very few women made their mark in the male-dominated world of the arts and literature. It is not surprising that the two successful women should become close friends. Looking at Read's portrait of Mrs. Brooke, one sees a charming and cultured woman whose lively intelligence and wit are suggested by the hint of a smile that she seems to exchange like a confidence with the artist herself. This warm bond of sympathy between artist and sitter is quite different from the icy formality that often obtains in the professional portraiture of the day. One has only to compare Mrs. Brooke's portrait with Mrs. Durell's (Cat. no. 43) to understand the intimate rapport established in the former. Mrs. Brooke's costume is particularly attractive in colour and style, characteristic of the picturesque and romantic dress in which Catherine Read often depicted her sitters.

In the eighteenth century, paintings were ranked in a qualitive hierarchy according to their subject and style. History painting in the grand manner of Raphael was the ideal to which all serious artists aspired, and was given pride of place. In a descending order of merit followed genre painting, battle pieces, fêtes galantes and landscapes. In Sir Joshua Reynolds' view, portrait painting came at the very bottom of the list.[15] Since the lowly portrait had so few pretensions to high art, painters sometimes sought to elevate their portrait work by deliberately quoting or borrowing from well known and approved pictures by the Old Masters. One such example in the work of Reynolds himself is his famous portrait, *Mrs. Siddons as the Tragic Muse*, in which he cast the actress as a prophet or sibyl from Michelangelo's Sistine ceiling, thus elevating both his painting and his sitter by this flattering association.[16] Catherine Read has followed the same tradition in her portrait of Frances Brooke, basing the figure and pose on Guercino's *Libyan Sibyl* (Fig. 44.4), which George III had acquired for the Royal Collection, probably in the 1760s.[17] From Guercino Read appropriated the motif of the model's right hand supporting her head with her elbow resting on a closed book, while her left hand holds an open book. Guercino's sibyl is intently reading, while Mrs. Brooke has just raised her eyes from her book to acknowledge the viewer. Although the two poses are not exactly the same, there are enough subtle echoes to indicate that Catherine Read intended the connoisseurs of her day to make the connection between her portrait of her authoress friend and Guercino's *Sibyl*, a comparison that again compliments both painter and sitter.

Several interesting records survive to document the friendship between Miss Read and Mrs. Brooke. In 1774, Fanny Burney recorded in her diary a visit to the studio of Miss Read, "the celebrated paintress, to meet Mrs. Brooke, the celebrated authoress." Soon to become a celebrated authoress herself, the delightful Fanny Burney left us these amusing, if somewhat catty, character sketches of the two women:

> Miss Reid [*sic*] is shrewd and clever, where she has any opportunity given her to make it known; but she is so very deaf, that it is a fatigue to attempt conversing with her. She is most exceeding ugly, and of a very melancholy, or rather discontented, humour. Mrs. Brooke is very short and fat, and squints; but has the art of showing agreeable ugliness. She is very well bred, and expresses herself with much modesty upon all subjects; which in an authoress, a woman of known understanding, is extremely pleasing.[18]

By chance a letter has survived from Frances Brooke to her friend the Rev. Richard Gifford, in which she makes specific reference to her portrait:

> ...I will give you my picture, of what size you please, by my friend Read, who is retired to Marlybone, where she paints less, & is better in health. I sometimes see her, & often your old acquaintance Mrs. Stanhope (once Miss Peters) who you used to see at Read's.[19]

Although the letter is undated, Lorraine McMullen dates it ca. 1772;[20] the reference to Read's recent move to Marlybone is documented in one of her own letters of 1771 to the Duchess of Argyll in which she specifically mentions her intention to move from Jermyn Street to "next door to Marybone [*sic*] Church."[21] It would therefore appear that ca. 1771 is quite possibly the date at which Read painted the portrait of Mrs. Brooke.

As to the portrait of the Rev. John Brooke, which was acquired with that of his wife (Fig. 44.1), there is no certainty that it was also painted by Catherine Read. Although it is of approximately the same size, there are enough differences between the two portraits to raise a doubt that they were conceived as a matching pair, as were, for example, the Hudsons (Cat. nos. 42 and 43).[22] One notices that the Rev. Brooke is set into a painted oval, while the composition of Mrs. Brooke's portrait fills the entire rectangular field, but it should be noted that the print after it was engraved, perhaps coincidentally, as an oval (Fig. 44.3). Mrs. Brooke, moreover, is shown half-length, seated, holding a book in one hand and propping her head up with the other; her husband is depicted as only a handless bust. Since Catherine Read specialized in portraits of women and children, portraits of adult men are almost, but not completely, unknown in her work.[23] Read might have agreed to paint the husband of a friend, but then one would expect the two likenesses to have a greater visual rapport than the present pictures have. It is therefore quite possible that the Reverend Brooke was painted by another hand, although his very florid complexion is somewhat similar to the high-keyed flesh tints of his wife, which are characteristic of an artist who worked principally in coloured chalks. No matter who painted him, the Rev. John Brooke is principally remembered because he was Frances Brooke's husband and the reason for her visit to Canada.

Catherine Read's portrait of Frances Brooke obviously has considerable importance to the cultural history of Canada. Instead of being a mere literary statistic, the author of the first Canadian novel is now materialized before us in her portrait. The picture therefore serves as a charming memorial to the "ingenious" Mrs. Brooke from her friend the "graceful" Miss Read, eighteenth-century epithets with which a twentieth-century observer can heartily agree.

D. E. S.

44.1 Attributed to C. Read
The Rev. John Brooke, ca. 1771
Oil on canvas
NA C-117375

44.2 J.P. Cockburn
Emily Montague's House at Sillery Cove, 1829
Watercolour
Royal Ontario Museum

44.3 M. Bovi, after C. Read
Mrs. Brooke, 1790
Engraving
British Museum

44.4 Guercino
Libyan Sibyl, ca. 1650
Oil on canvas
Royal Collection, Reproduced by gracious permission of Her Majesty the Queen;
© Her Majesty the Queen

1. We are deeply grateful to Lorraine McMullen, professor at the University of Ottawa and the outstanding Frances Brooke scholar, for bringing the portraits to our attention.

2. For biographical details on the Brookes, see the following: *The Dictionary of National Biography* (London: Oxford University Press, n.d.), 2:1328-1329, entry for Frances Brooke; *Dictionary of Canadian Biography* (Toronto: University of Toronto Press, 1979), 4:103-105, entry for John Brooke; *Dictionary of Canadian Biography* (Toronto: University of Toronto Press, 1979), 4:553-555, entry for Frances (Brooke) Moore; Lorraine McMullen, *An Odd Attempt in a Woman: The Literary Life of Frances Brooke* (Vancouver: University of British Columbia Press, 1983).

3. Two of the central characters of the novel were modelled on real persons Mrs. Brooke knew at Quebec. Anna-Marie Bondfield was apparently the model for Arabella Fermor, and Henry Caldwell the model for Ed Rivers. See McMullen, 106-110.

4. Frances Brooke, *The History of Emily Montague*, New Canadian Library, no. 27 (Toronto: McClelland and Stewart, 1961), letter 49, p. 90.

5. Mary Allodi, *Canadian Watercolours and Drawings in the Royal Ontario Museum* (Toronto: The Royal Ontario Museum, 1974), vol. 1, no. 311; Christina Cameron and Jean Trudel, *The Drawings of James Cockburn: A Visit through Quebec's Past* ([Agincourt, Ontario]: Gage Publishing, 1976), no. 137, p. 150.

6. [James Pattison Cockburn], *Quebec and Its Environs: Being a Picturesque Guide to the Stranger* (Quebec: Thomas Cary & Co., 1831), 12.

7. McMullen, 109-110.

8. *Dictionary of Canadian Biography* 4:555.

9. The main sources of information about Catherine Read are three articles by Lady Victoria Manners, "Catherine Read: the 'English Rosalba,'" *The Connoisseur*, vol. 88, no. 364 (December 1931), 376-386; "Catherine Read and Royal Patronage," *The Connoisseur*, vol. 89, no. 365 (January 1932), 35-40; "Catherine Read: The Last Phase," *The Connoisseur*, vol. 89, no. 367 (March 1932), 171-178.

10. See, for example, Germaine Greer, *The Obstacle Race* (London: Secker & Warburg, 1979), 277-279.

11. Mildred Archer, *India and British Portraiture 1770-1825* (London: Sotheby Parke Bernet, 1979), 118-121.

12. Read's portrait of Mrs. Brooke can be compared to her picture of another literary woman, Catharine Macaulay, who is similarly depicted surrounded by books. See Manners, "Catherine Read: the 'English Rosalba'," plate VI, p. 381.

13. Manners, "Catherine Read: the 'English Rosalba'," 382.

14. Letter to the author from Paul Goldman, research assistant, Department of Prints and Drawings, The British Museum, 19 January 1982.

15. Sir Joshua Reynolds, *Discourses on Art*, Robert R. Wark, ed. (San Marino, California: The Huntington Library, 1959), 51-52.

16. Robert R. Wark, *Ten British Pictures 1740-1840* (San Marino, California: The Huntington Library, 1971), 46 and 48.

17. *Treasures from the Royal Collection* (London: The Queen's Gallery, Buckingham Palace, 1988), Cat. no. 27, p. 45. Since Bartolozzi published an undated engraving of the Guercino, artists such as Read may have known the picture through the print rather than in its original form. See Michael Levey, *The Later Italian Pictures in the Collection of Her Majesty The Queen* (London: The Phaidon Press, 1964), Cat. no. 521, p. 84.

18. Fanny Burney, *The Early Diary of Frances Burney 1768-1778*, Annie Raine Ellis, ed. (London: G. Bell, 1913), 1:283.

19. McMullen, 135.

20. Private communication to the author.

21. Manners, "Catherine Read: The Last Phase," 171.

22. The portrait of the Rev. John Brooke is slightly larger than that of Mrs. Brooke, measuring 73.3 x 60.6 cm.

23. Read exhibited a "head of Mr. Ferguson, the astronomer; in oil" at the Society of Artists in 1767 (no. 133). See Algernon Graves, *The Society of Artists of Great Britain, 1760-1791* (Bath: Kingsmead Reprints, 1969).

JOHN DOWNMAN (1750-1824) and CHARLES TURNER (1773-1857), after Henry Edridge (1768-1821)

JOHN DOWNMAN (1750-1824)

45. *Jacob Mountain*, 1778

Oil on copper
22.9 x 19.1 cm
Purchased in 1982
Accession no.: 1982-92-1
Negative no.: C-100660

JOHN DOWNMAN (1750-1824)

46. *Sarah Mountain*, 1778

Oil on copper
23.1 x 18.8 cm
Purchased in 1982
Accession no.: 1982-92-2
Negative no.: C-100661

When Jacob Mountain landed at Quebec City on 1 November 1793 to take up his position as first Anglican bishop of Quebec, he brought with him twelve members of his family. Not only did he establish the official administration of the Anglican Church in Upper and Lower Canada, he also founded a branch of the Mountain family in Quebec. His brother, his sons and his nephew were to continue the family influence on church affairs.

Up until 1787, the Anglican Church in North America was under the jurisdiction of the Diocese of London. The church duties were carried out by military chaplains, and the missions were founded and run by the Society for the Propagation of the Gospels in Foreign Parts (SPG). The first Anglican diocese in British North America was established in 1787 in Nova Scotia. Charles Inglis was bishop, and he had jurisdiction over all remaining English colonies in North America. With the *Constitution Act* of 1791, local colonial governments were set up to levy taxes and administer affairs with a limited degree of responsibility. There were also provisions in the Act for the administrative and financial support of Protestant clergy. The spiritual demands of the incoming Loyalists and the requests of Lt. Gov. John Graves Simcoe for Anglican bishoprics in the Canadas brought about the creation in 1793 of the Diocese of Quebec to include both Upper and Lower Canada.

Jacob Mountain was born in 1749 at Thwaite Hall in Norfolk England. He was educated at Caius College, Cambridge, and between the years 1783 and 1793 he worked in various English parishes. Jacob Mountain was not only considered a man of promise in the Church, he was well-connected by virtue of his friendship with William Pitt, the British prime minister, and George Pretyman Tomline, bishop of Lincoln.

The portraits of Jacob Mountain and his sister Sarah were painted by John Downman when Jacob was at Cambridge in 1778. Downman was just beginning his career as a portraitist and painted many members of society in Cambridge in 1777 and 1778. At the same time as he painted Jacob and Sarah's portraits, he also made portraits of their brother Jehoshaphat (who become the rector of Three Rivers, and later, Montreal) and their sister Mary. Another sketch of this period depicts Jacob Mountain with a friend, Mr. Brundish.[1] Downman was to paint a portrait in 1783 of Jacob Mountain and his bride Eliza Kentish.

Downman kept preliminary sketches of many of the portraits he made, and these he put together in a series of volumes. He also annotated many of them with remarks (not always complimentary) about the sitter. Concerning Jacob Mountain he wrote: "Jacob· Mountain, of Caius College, Cambridge, 1778. Was soon afterwards bishop of Quebec and truly a man in every sense of the word."[2]

The two portraits in the National Archives are oil on copper, which is typical of Downman's finished portraits, although he usually worked in an oval rather than a rectangular format. In fact, the preliminary drawings for the Mountain portraits show an oval composition (Figs. 45.1 and 45.2). Downman's oils are distinguished by their sombre colouring, well-defined lines and polished finish. His profile portraits are particularly successful, as can be seen in these examples. Downman's facility for rendering a flattering yet convincing likeness made him an extremely popular portraitist. He had studied at the Royal Academy school from 1767 to 1770, and under Benjamin West the following two years. After Cambridge, Downman moved to London and set up a studio. He became an associate of the Royal Academy in 1795. During his forty-year career, he painted most of the English aristocracy, including several members of the royal family.

Jacob Mountain was consecrated bishop of Quebec at Canterbury on 7 July 1793, and set sail for the Canadas on 13 August. In the Canadas there was a well-established population of Roman Catholic faith, a French culture, and a small but increasing English-speaking population coming in from the new United States. This cultural combination was unprecedented in British colonial history. The *Quebec Act* of 1774 had given the Roman Catholic church far greater freedoms than it had in England. As well, the 'Dissendent' churches (mainly Presbyterian) were represented in the colonies. The privileges and jurisdictions of each were not clearly defined. Although the Church of England was the official church, the Roman Catholic one was much larger and older. Bishop Mountain arrived in Quebec with the conviction that the Anglican Church would occupy the dominant position in the Canadas that it had in Britain. He became embroiled in a power struggle with the Roman Catholic Church; however, his success was largely dependent upon the support of the governor, and his influence varied according to their relationship.

The first years in Lower Canada were difficult. There were delays in sending the documents giving Bishop Mountain his seat on the Executive Council. He received little support from Lord Dorchester (governor of the Canadas, 1786-1796), who was more interested in securing the loyalty of the French-Canadian, Roman Catholic population than in the establishment of the Anglican Church.

CHARLES TURNER (1773-1857), after Henry Edridge (1768-1821)

47. *The Rt. Revd. Jacob Mountain, D.D., Lord Bishop of Quebec*, 1820

Mezzotint

28.8 x 22.5 cm (image), platemark cropped

Inscribed in the plate, b.: *THE RT. REVD. JACOB MOUNTAIN, D.D. | Lord Bishop of Quebec.*; l.l.: *Painted by H. Edridge Esqr. 1819*; l.r.: *Engraved by C. Turner.*

Donated in 1982

Accession no.: 1983-5-2

Negative no.: C-127092

Bishop Mountain made his first visitation of his see in 1794. He was impressed with the rapidly developing settlements and the potential prosperity of the colonies. But in his report of 15 September 1794 to the colonial undersecretary, Henry Dundas, he wrote: "With respect to Religious Instruction the state of these settlers is, for the most part, truly deplorable."[3] The bishop requested funds to build churches at Cornwall and Johnstown, and that clergymen be sent for them as well as for Detroit, York (Toronto) and the Bay of Quinte.

Funding was one of Bishop Mountain's biggest and most enduring problems. He realized immediately that the Anglican populace was not yet large and prosperous enough to be able to provide the sums required for the number of churches and clergy needed. He discovered very quickly that the meagre amounts of money sent from London were not sufficient. Tithing, he felt, was a most inappropriate means of raising money, since the majority of the population were not of the Anglican faith.[4] The clergy reserves were given in lieu of salary, but no money could be made in renting them to immigrants when land was so cheap and freely available. Most of the reserves remained unused until the 1820s, when the exclusivity of ownership by the Anglican Church was called into question.

The situation improved for Bishop Mountain under Governors Sir Robert Shore Milnes and Sir James Craig, for both of whom he was a trusted advisor.[5] On his first return to Britain, from 1805 to 1808, he met Charles James Stewart, an Anglican missionary whom he persuaded to return with him to Quebec. Stewart, who provided invaluable assistance in the establishment of missions, especially in the Eastern Townships,[6] succeeded Jacob Mountain as bishop of Quebec upon the latter's death in 1825.

Another of Bishop Mountain's colleagues was John Strachan, who was to become bishop of Toronto when the Diocese of Quebec was finally divided in 1839. Their personalities were not sympathetic, but they had similar views concerning the goals of the Anglican Church in the Canadas and its relationship to the colonial and home governments.[7] As members of the "establishment," their views were reactionary and eventually rejected by the populace. What they were reacting against was the American Revolution, the War of 1812 and the democratic ideals of the United States, whose influence was considered dangerous. One of the driving forces behind Bishop Mountain's concerns for education in the Canadas was "the mischief that may eventually arise from the necessity of sending our youth for education to the Schools of Foreign America."[8] His dedication to the promotion of education in the Canadas was sometimes thwarted by his rivalry with the Catholic Church. In 1801, Bishop Mountain promoted the passage of the Royal Institute of Education. The Catholic bishop refused to participate on the governing board, and the institute achieved nothing.[9] Nevertheless, in 1818, it was revived as the Royal Institution for the Advancement of Learning to establish a university with the bequest from Andrew McGill. Bishop Mountain became president in 1819, and eventually McGill University was created after much delay and litigation and not before the bishop's death.[10]

The worst of Bishop Mountain's political problems came during the administration of Sir George Prevost. The latter governor was singularly unsympathetic to the bishop's attempt to have the Church of England declared the official church of the Canadas. In fact, Prevost went out of his way to woo the Roman Catholic Church and the predominantly French Assembly. In doing so, he alienated the English Executive Council, which included Bishop Mountain. A letter of complaint was sent to Lord Bathurst, the colonial secretary. The latter was infuriated by such insurrection and rebuked the bishop, whom Prevost had accused of being the ringleader of the cabal.[11] After this unfortunate affair, Bishop Mountain largely withdrew from provincial affairs. Because of the length of his second visit to England, he had little contact with the next two governors, and his relationship with Lord Dalhousie was more congenial.[12]

In spite of his political problems, Bishop Mountain did achieve several things. He made eight visitations during his episcopate, travelling to the Anglican churches and missions throughout Upper and Lower Canada. The first was made within a year of his arrival in British North America, the last at the age of seventy-one.

The number of clergy under his jurisdiction increased from nine to sixty, while sixty new churches were built between 1793 and 1825. It was his determination that was behind the building of the Anglican Cathedral (known as the Metropolitan Church) in Quebec City. Begun in 1800, it was based on the design of St. Martin-in-the-Field, London, and was the second cathedral to be built since the Reformation.[13] The church was consecrated in 1804, but not completed until 1819.

With the help of Charles Stewart and the SPG, thirty-five new missions were established throughout Upper and Lower Canada.

Bishop Mountain also concerned himself with the lack of theological education in

Upper and Lower Canada. On the suggestion of John Strachan, he arranged for SPG scholarships to be given to four Canadian candidates to study theology in preparation for ordination.[14]

During Bishop Mountain's 1816-1819 sojourn in Britain, his portrait was painted again, this time by Henry Edridge. In this later work, Jacob Mountain is presented in his official role with wig and robes, seated at his desk, surrounded by his work. The original oil portrait was exhibited at the Royal Academy in 1820, and now hangs in Bishopthorpe, the official Anglican bishop's residence in Quebec City.

Like Downman, Edridge was an accomplished portraitist who recorded the leading personalities of his time. He made many portrait miniatures on ivory as well as painting landscapes. Bishop Mountain probably met Henry Edridge through Joseph Farington, associate and academician of the Royal Academy and a good friend of Edridge. Farington and Jacob Mountain had first met in Houghton, Norfolk, in 1775 and maintained contact during the bishop's return trips to Britain.[15]

In 1820, Charles Turner engraved Edridge's portrait of Mountain, using the mezzotint technique (Cat. no. 47). Copies of the resulting prints were offered for sale by the print dealers A.E. Evans and Son in their catalogue of famous personalities.[16] The medium of mezzotint is particularly well-suited to engravings after oil paintings, for it allows an extremely wide range of tonalities. The rich shadows of the background highlight the face of the bishop, and the deep black of the stole is in stark contrast to the white of his robes. Turner has beautifully rendered the intricate pattern of shadows in the sheer material of the bishop's sleeves.

The National Archives' copy of this print was donated by a descendent of the Mountain family. It arrived mounted in an elaborate ornate frame, the top edge of which is decorated with a miniature bishop's mitre. As a tribute to the accomplishments of Bishop Mountain, this portrait in its extravagant frame no doubt enjoyed a special place in the Mountain family homes through which it descended.

About Sarah Mountain, we know very little. She and her sister Mary came with their brother to Quebec in 1793, along with his wife and her sister Miss Mary Kentish and Jacob's three children. Neither of the Mountain sisters married, and they seem to have left very little mark on history.

The incidence of unmarried gentlewomen increased throughout the eighteenth century, and their options in life were limited.[17] Class expectations forbade them to work, and few had sufficient inheritance to allow them to live alone. Most found a home with a married brother or sister, looking after the children and helping in any way required. Charitable works were the only acceptable occupations outside the home.

This seems to have been the fate of Sarah and Mary Mountain. Sarah is recorded as a contributor to the Quebec Fire Society and Mary contributed to the newly formed Ladies Compassionate Society in January 1821, just a few months before her death.[18]

Jacob had seven children, his brother Jehoshaphat had three; there would have been ample occasion for their sisters to assist in the children's upbringing. A group of letters written by the wife of Rev. Jehoshaphat Mountain and her daughter, Maryanne, to their relations in England in the years just after the family's arrival in Quebec, gives a few clues to the lives of the Mountain sisters.

> ... my sisters [in-law] and Maryanne are with us but I fear we shall soon lose my sister [in-law] Mary as Mrs. M[ountain] expects every day to be confined when that happens M[ary] M[ountain] goes to her.[19]

Sarah's poor health is noted a few times:

> I am sure I shall give you pleasure when I tell you that my Aunt Sarah's complaints are much slighter and her general health better....[20]

And later:

> Miss Mountain's complaints are more frequent than they used to be but not so violent. My sister[in-law] Mary's spirits I think much altered by constant anxiety about her sister.[21]

Sarah Mountain died on 18 May 1808, and her obituary states that she had suffered "for many years, a lingering affliction."[22]

Bishop Mountain died on 16 June 1825. He had contributed much to the growing colonies and in particular to the Anglican Church. After his death, his descendants carried on his work. Both his son and his grandson became Anglican ministers. The latter, Armine W. Mountain, was the incumbent of St. Michael's Chapel in Quebec City. George Jehoshaphat Mountain followed his father's footsteps as third bishop of Quebec and sponsor of Bishop's University, Lennoxville, Quebec.

S.N.

45.1 J. Downman
Jacob Mountain, 1778
Black chalk
Fitzwilliam Museum, Cambridge

45.2 J. Downman
Sarah Mountain, 1778
Black chalk
Fitzwilliam Museum, Cambridge

1. G.C. Williamson, *John Downman, A.R.A.*, (London: Otto Ltd., 1907), lvii. The Brundish-Mountain sketch is in vol. 4, series 3 of the Butleigh Court sketchbooks. The inscription reads: "Mr. Brundish and Mr. Mountain, two friends, of Caius College, Cambridge, 1778; the latter soon after was Bishop of Quebec."

2. Williamson, liii. The four Mountain family sketches are in vol. 3, series 2 of the Butleigh Court sketchbooks.

3. Public Record Office, London, Colonial Office records, C.O. 42, vol. 100, p. 396, NA, MG 11, microfilm, reel B-60, Bishop Mountain to Henry Dundas, 15 September 1794.

4. Canon A.R. Kelley, "Jacob Mountain: First Lord Bishop of Quebec, A summary of his Correspondence and of Papers Related Thereto for the Years 1793 to 1799 Compiled from Various Sources," *Rapport de l'Archiviste de Province de Quebec pour 1942-1943*, p. 219.

5. Helen Taft Manning, *The Revolt of French Canada 1800-1835* (Toronto: Macmillan Co., 1962), 4.

6. Philip Carrington, *The Anglican Church in Canada* (Toronto: Collins, 1963), 57-58.

7. T.R. Millman, *Jacob Mountain: First Lord Bishop of Quebec*, History and Economics Series (Toronto: University of Toronto, 1947), 10:144 and 265.

8. Public Record Office, C.O. 42, vol. 100, p. 402, NA, MG 11, microfilm, reel B-60, Bishop Mountain to Henry Dundas, 15 September 1794.

9. Manning, 19.

10. Millman, 173-178.

11. Manning, 97-105, describes the clash with Prevost.

12. Millman, 272.

13. William Bertal Heeney, *Leaders of the Canadian Church* (Toronto: Ryerson Press, 1918), 59.

14. Millman, 186-188.

15. Joseph Farington, *The Diary of Joseph Farington*, James Greig, ed., (London: Hutchinson & Co., 1924), 8:123.

16. Edward Evans published vol. 1 of the *Catalogue of Engraved British Portraits Comprising Thirty Thousand Portraits of Persons Connected with the History and Literature of Great Britain, the British colonies and the United States*, and vol. 2 was published by A.E. Evans & Sons. The dates of publication are unknown. The Turner mezzotint of Edridge's portrait of Bishop Mountain was advertised in the second volume at the price of five shillings.

17. Lawrence Stone, *The Family, Sex and Marriage in England, 1500-1800* (London: Weidenfeld and Nicolson, 1977), 381.

18. *Quebec Gazette*, 9 July 1807 and 18 January 1821, both p. 3.

19. Norfolk Record Office, Norwich, England, Accn. Freemen 27/8/62, T169A, Mrs. Mary Mountain to Mrs. Salter, 6 September 1795.

20. Norfolk, Accn. Freemen 27/8/62, T169A, Maryanne Mountain to Mrs. Salter, 15 September 1794.

21. Norfolk, Accn. Freemen 27/8/62, T169A, Mrs. Mary Mountain to Mrs. Salter, 5 July 1795.

22. *Quebec Gazette*, 19 May 1808, p. 2.

MARY ANN KNIGHT (1776-1851)

48. *Major John Norton, Teyoninhokarawen, the Mohawk Chief*, 1805

Watercolour on ivory

9.2 x 7.3 cm

Inscribed on backing paper attached to verso of ivory, in pen and brown ink: *Teyoninhokarawen / Mohawk Chief / Major Norton / painted 1805*

Purchased in 1984

Accession no.: 1984-119-1

Negative no.: C-123832

Major John Norton, known as Teyoninhokarawen and Snipe,[1] the Mohawk chief who was the adopted nephew of Joseph Brant, was painted in miniature by Mary Ann Knight during his visit to England in 1805. Although by 1805 Major Norton had become an adopted Mohawk, he originated from Salen, Scotland, and was likely born sometime in the 1760s. His father was a Cherokee Indian who had been adopted and taken to Scotland by an officer serving with a Scottish regiment in North America, while his mother was a Scottish woman named Anderson.

According to military records, John Norton Jr., like his father, joined the 65th Regiment of Foot. He went to Quebec in 1785, and Niagara in 1787, where he deserted; he was discharged in 1788. He then went to live with the Grand River Mohawk Indians, and under Joseph Brant learned to speak and write their language. He soon adopted their lifestyle, "associated with the young Indians...and became at once as perfect an Indian as ran in the woods, having his ears cut and his nose bored."[2]

In 1796, Norton accepted Joseph Brant's invitation to become an interpreter of the Grand River Indians, working for the government's Indian Department. Thus began his involvement in the political disputes between the Grand River Mohawks and the colonial government. Acting on Brant's behalf as an interpreter, emissary and deputy, Norton went to England in 1804 to make direct appeals to the British government to settle land ownership disputes with the colonial government. The Grand River Indians wanted deeds for the land given to them after the American Revolution, under the authority of the Haldimand Proclamation. Norton's mission was seen as a way to circumvent the colonial government, to whom fruitless appeals had been made for years.

In England he was politely received by various officials, and presented his "Memorial for the Six Nations," which outlined the grievances and proposals of the Indians. Reaction to his efforts was slow, and as if to hamper any success, a copy of the Haldimand document could not be found in England. To his chagrin, by July 1805 letters arrived from Upper Canada declaring that two recent councils of the Six Nations had disavowed Norton's actions and announced Brant's deposition as head of the Confederacy.[3]

In spite of the political failure of the mission, Norton had become somewhat of a celebrity. Because of his humanitarian sentiments, he attracted the attention of many who had been swept along in the evangelical movement. At the request of a friend, the Rev. John Owen, secretary of the British and Foreign Bible Society, Norton began a project to translate the Gospel of St. John into Mohawk, which he would eventually distribute in Upper Canada. Reverend Owen brought Norton to speak at Corpus Christi College, where he charmed his audience with anecdotes of Indian life in Upper Canada. Owen may also have introduced John Norton to Mary Ann Knight, since she appears to have painted the reverend's portrait as well. The miniature of Norton was actually a gift from a Miss Mary Ansted to the Rev. John Owen, and a much treasured present, as a letter from Owen to Miss Ansted of 20 January 1806 implies:

> A Letter which I lately opened, announced to me that a Petition which I preferred to Miss Knight had been granted by Miss Ansted. The intelligence afforded me very considerable pleasure... an accommodation to my wishes in this instance must have cost the Possessor of the Portrait a painful conflict. She knew (it is sure) less of the extraordinary man whom it so faithfully represents than I did; and therefore may be supposed to have valued him less. I am however well convinced that she saw & knew enough of him to make the preservation of his memory, & consequently the possession of his image an object of peculiar interest.... I am deeply affected with her kindness in sacrificing to my ardent wishes so important a treasure; that I shall always connect the generosity by which I acquired the Portrait with the memory of the great original; and that I shall ever consider myself as in the highest degree.[4]

The striking image is protected by a convex crystal and set within an oval gold frame. The whole is set within a larger, dark brown, square wooden frame. It is an example of a "cabinet miniature," made to hang on a wall.[5] There is an inscription on a paper label attached to the back of the ivory (Fig. 48.1). Such inscriptions are not always found with miniatures, but when present often provide invaluable information.

The brown background area of the painting is textured by minute cross-hatching, a characteristic of the artist's work,[6] while curvilinear brush-strokes define the flesh and the dark hair. Topped by rather unruly eyebrows, the soft brown eyes of the sitter gaze with quiet confidence at the viewer. The tight curls of the sideburns and at the nape of the neck suggest the type of hair that might be found if the exotic headdress were removed. The head is crowned by the horizontal sweep of a white ostrich feather, which is fastened at the left side. The long graceful nose and slightly pursed lips lead down to the black cravat, over which dangle what seem to be trade silver earrings, possibly of the "wheel-star" pattern that was worn by the Mohawks.[7] The shoulders are draped in a coarse-looking piece of red cloth. Underneath is a mottled brown upper garment covered with nearly one hundred small ring brooches popular with the Mohawks. They were symbols of the sitter's status and wealth.

While Norton usually wore European-style clothing abroad, he occasionally appeared in Indian dress. The following description by Headley (probably Lord Headley), who met Norton while he was in England, compares favourably with Knight's portrait of Norton:

> He is tall about 6 feet high well made, very active rather dark complexion, but by no means sallen [sallow?] not so dark as many Englishmen, who have lived in hot climates, his countenance is remarkable mild and pleasing; his manners are perfectly surprising... a chintz Handkerchief was bound about the head under which was a piece of red silk of the same texture as our officer's sashes on one side was put an ostrich feather... his shirt... was made of blue Calico.... All the forepart... was closely studded with silver broaches this I conclude is limited to the chief... over the shirt upon state occasion is thrown loose unornamented & unhemmed peice [*sic*] of Cloth...depending from his ears [were] large silver earrings....[8]

Two other portraits of Norton were painted in England. A close friend named Robert Barclay — a wealthy industrialist — introduced him as an honorary member of the Bath and West England Agricultural Society at their meeting on Christmas Eve in 1804. A "valuable painting...by Williams," now lost, was presented to the society after his appearance there. Another portrait of Norton in Syon House, the Northumberland family seat in Brentford, England, was painted by Thomas Phillips (Fig. 48.2), and fittingly hangs next to a portrait of Joseph Brant by Gilbert Stuart. Thomas Phillips was the favourite portrait painter of the second Duke of Northumberland, who served in North America during the War of Independence, where he was acquainted with Norton.[9] The simplicity and ruggedness of the miniature is quite different from the more polished and romanticized Phillips portrait, in which the features of the "noble savage" have been anglicized to some extent.

The subject must have been a refreshing change for Mary Ann Knight, since affectations used to enhance the sitters in other portraits were not necessary for a genuine Mohawk chief. The miniature of Norton was exhibited at the Royal Academy in 1805 as Cat. no. 403, but does not appear in the records of over 696 of her own works that the artist kept until the year 1836.

Mary Ann Knight was a student of the renowned miniaturist Andrew Plimer (1763-1837), who was also her brother-in-law. To help her parents financially, she started portrait painting in 1802. When she began, her records show that she was receiving from two to four guineas for a work, but she must have gradually received recognition of her talent, for she was obtaining as much as ten guineas per work in 1805, and fifteen to twenty guineas in 1836, near the end of her career.

Knight appears to have been most successful in her portraits of children, although those where she used classical allusions and affected poses are less appealing.

> The success which Miss Knight obtained in her portraits of children appears to have been the result of her own engaging Charm, quiet soft voice, merry vivacious manner, and great kindliness of disposition.[10]

Her work often reflected the influence of Plimer, in the wiry treatment of the hair and the faulty modelling. Those who have studied her work feel that where she used a rich palette the result was more pleasing, and it is into this category that the Norton miniature falls.

> Her portraits are generally of large size, and as a rule pale, even somewhat washy in colour, but there are cases in which she has employed a dark and rich scheme of colouring....[11]

When Norton returned home, early in 1806, he brought with him five hundred copies of the Gospel he had translated in England, as well as a renewed zeal for helping his people. In spite of some differences of opinion, he remained a close friend of Joseph Brant up until the latter's death in 1807. He continued on as a deputy head of the Mohawks appointed by the Councils, and was asked by General Brock to lead the Grand River Indians during the War of 1812, where once again they proved their loyalty by gallant fighting. Although spurned by the Indian Department, Norton received honours from the military, such as the presentation of a sword and pistols, and a pension from the government in 1815, ending his tenure as official representative of his people.

The last years of his life were no less extraordinary than the first. In 1823, an indiscretion involving his wife led him to kill a man during a duel. He was tried and found guilty of manslaughter, but in the end was fined only twenty-five pounds. Nevertheless, the incident caused him great personal turmoil and resulted in the break-up of his marriage and home. He left his life of agricultural bliss at the Grand River, and it is thought he may have spent his last years on the Sante Fe Trail, seeking new western lands for the American Indians. As a brevetted major, he received a last military pension payment in 1826, and then passed into oblivion, dying in October 1831, according to accounts left by a nephew.

Norton has left behind a journal with accounts of his exploits, a copy of which is now in the Duke of Northumberland's collection at Alnwick Castle. John Richardson (1796-1852), one of Canada's early novelists, had known Norton and loosely modelled the principal character of the book *Wacousta* after him.[12] Below a memorial window at the Mohawk Chapel in Brantford, Ontario, words from his "Preface to the Gospel of St. John" are quoted, a reminder of the part he played in bringing the Mohawk translation home. The miniature is yet another tribute to the life of Teyoninhokarawen, "a man who ...[made] you almost wish to be an Indian chief."[13]

M.M.

48.1 M.A. Knight
***Inscription on backing paper attached to miniature of Major John Norton*, 1805**
NA C-123837

48.2 T. Phillips
***Major John Norton*, 1817**
Oil on canvas
Collection of the Duke of Northumberland

---

1. John Norton, "The Journal of Major John Norton 1816," Carl F. Klinck and James J. Talman, intro. and eds., *The Publications of the Champlain Society*, no. 46 (1970), xxxviii-xxxix. Norton's Mohawk title, Teyninhokarawen, meant "'open' door importing, frankness, and an open heart." Although Norton was seen as a potential successor, he apparently was never thought to be a rival to Joseph Brant's sons. Much of the biographical information about Norton used in this text has been derived from this publication. See also *Dictionary of Canadian Biography* (Toronto: University of Toronto Press, 1987), 6:550-553, entry for Norton.

2. From the *Missouri Gazette*, 16 June 1816, as quoted in Norton, xxxiii.

3. William L. Stone, *Life of Joseph Brant-Thayendanegea* (New York: H. & E. Phinney, 1844), 2:414-415. The Council held at Buffalo Creek was "illegal, according to the ancient usages of the Confederacy."

4. Newberry Library, Chicago, Ayer manuscript 654, Norton papers, letter from Rev. Mr. Owen to Miss Ansted, 20 January 1806.

5. Daphne Foskett, *British Portrait Miniatures* (London: Methuen and Co. Limited, 1963), 34.

6. George C. Williamson, *Andrew & Nathaniel Plimer* (London: George Bell & Son, 1903), 76.

7. N. Jaye Fredrickson and Sandra Gibb, *The Covenant Chain: Indian Ceremonial and Trade Silver* (Ottawa: National Museums of Canada, 1980), 52, 56, 131.

8. Norton, 1.

9. Letter to the author from Colin Shrimption, Northumberland Estates, Alnwick Castle, Northumberland, England, 10 September 1986.

10. Williamson, 77.

11. Williamson, 77.

12. *Dictionary* 8:743-744, entry for Richardson. "In *Wacousta*, Sir Reginald Morton, an English nobleman, comes to British North America to seek revenge for the loss of his fiancé...Disguised as an Indian and adopting the name Wacousta...."

13. Norton, xx.

HENRIETTA MARTHA HAMILTON (ca. 1780-1857)

49. *Mary March*, 1819

Watercolour on ivory

7.5 x 6.5 cm

Inscribed on backing paper attached to verso of ivory, in pen and brown ink: *Mary March / a Female Native / Indian of the / Red Indians who / inhabit Newfound / land painted by / Lady Hamilton / 18* [?]

Purchased in 1977

Accession no.: 1977-14-1

Negative no.: C-87698

This beautiful little painting is a testament to the tragic death of its subject, Demasduit, or Mary March, as she was called in captivity, and the subsequent extinction of her tribe, the Beothuks.

The native inhabitants of Newfoundland lived and hunted along the Exploits River from the interior down to Notre Dame Bay. Many early accounts of the Beothuks report their use of red ochre on their bodies, clothing and possessions, for which they were named "Red Indians." Their first encounters with Europeans in the sixteenth century were hostile, as a result of either misunderstanding or actual treachery. Fearing and mistrusting the white settlers and fishermen, the Beothuks and the latter fell into a pattern of hostility and revenge, from which the natives suffered the worst. For reasons unknown, they never adopted the white man's gun for either hunting or warfare, unlike other native North American tribes. As the European settlements began to encroach on Beothuk lands, particularly in the Notre Dame Bay region, the theft of articles such as knives, fishing hooks, sails, etc. (items on which the fisherman depended for survival) by the natives was avenged by the murder of the Beothuks on sight by the white men. Retaliation by the Beothuks was met with continued violence.

This situation was never addressed by any authority, because up until 1713 many European countries (England, France, Spain and Portugal) used Newfoundland as a fishing base. Also, it was a haven for pirates. Haphazardly settled by France and Britain, the island was claimed by both but governed well by neither. After the *Treaty of Utrecht* in 1713, Newfoundland became a British possession. But the state of lawlessness continued throughout the eighteenth century. There was no policing body, like the RCMP a century later in Canada's West, to maintain peace amongst the settlers and between them and the native inhabitants. Furthermore, no missionaries were sent to Newfoundland during this period. However questionable the value of Christian conversion, the missionaries cared for the people they sought to redeem. They would not have allowed the Beothuks to be murdered and would have saved those they could from the ravages of European disease, which decimated the native population.[1]

Another factor contributing to the reduction of the Beothuk population was the expansion of the Micmac tribe from the Nova Scotia-New Brunswick area into the southern part of Newfoundland. Whether Beothuk-Micmac relations were friendly or not is difficult to ascertain. What is known is that the presence of the Micmac gave Beothuks competition for the caribou, upon which they depended for food, clothing and shelter. With the additional reduction of hunting grounds due to European settlement, starvation became an increasing problem for the Newfoundland natives.

With all these factors against them, the Beothuk population (which could not have exceeded 2,000 at its peak[2]) was drastically reduced by the end of the eighteenth century. By the 1760s, the British authorities in Newfoundland began to realize the extent of the devastation, and a proclamation was issued forbidding murder of the Beothuks and encouraging the establishment of friendly contact.[3] In 1768, an expedition led by Capt. John Cartwright was conducted up the Exploits River in an attempt to establish contact with the Beothuks. Unsure, however, of the intruders' intentions, they kept well out of sight.

Further expeditions and proclamations had little effect. A committee examining the state of trade in Newfoundland in 1793 brought to light many of the depredations against the Beothuks; some potentially worthwhile recommendations were made, but not followed up. Another expedition to the interior was made in 1811, led by Lt. David Buchan, a naval officer. Contact with the Beothuks was established, but with no interpreter, misunderstandings arose between the naval party and the Indians, which led to the murder of two marines by the latter.

A reward of a hundred pounds was offered in the 1810 and 1813 proclamations to anyone successful in establishing friendly contact with the Beothuks. However, the methods by which this contact was to be made were not stipulated, and greed rather than humane intention led to the capture of the subject of our miniature, Demasduit. In March of 1818, a group of fishermen from Notre Dame Bay led by John Peyton set out to recover some articles stolen from them by the Beothuks over a period of time. After travelling up the Exploits River to Red Indian Lake, they managed to surprise an Indian encampment at daylight. The Beothuks fled, as usual in such encounters, and might have escaped the fishermen entirely had Demasduit, still weak from childbirth, not fallen behind. Peyton caught up to her easily and, with the reward of the 1813 proclamation in mind, made to bring her back with him. Her husband, Nonasbawsut, attempted to free her. In the ensuing scuffle, Nonasbawsut was killed and possibly another Beothuk as well.[4] In spite of or perhaps ignorant of her newborn, the fisherman brought Demasduit alone to Twillingate, where she was placed in the care of Rev. John Leigh. (Bereft of his mother, her baby died a few days after the incident.)

Demasduit was named Mary March, her second name referring to the month in which she was captured.

Later that spring, Mary March was taken to St. John's to be presented to the governor, Sir Charles Hamilton. It was here that her portrait was painted by the governor's wife, Lady Hamilton.[5] Mary March excited much interest in St. John's, and numerous descriptions of her were recorded.[6] Sir Charles was anxious that she be returned to her people, and efforts were made during the summer of 1819, but with no success. In September, David Buchan (leader of the ill-fated 1811 expedition and now a captain) was instructed to take her up the Exploits to rejoin her tribe. He met Mary at Twillingate in November, but by this time she was seriously ill with tuberculosis and Buchan, shocked at her state of health, realized it was impossible for her to travel. While Buchan and his party made plans to contact the tribe and bring them to her, Mary March died on 8 January 1820, the unfortunate victim of the colonists' and authorities' well-meant but tragically clumsy attempts at reconciliation with her people. Her body was returned to the spot where she had been captured and was later placed by the Beothuks in the grave where her husband and infant lay.

By virtue of her genial and vivacious personality, Demasduit was much loved by her captors and on her death, Lt. Buchan wrote: "Her mild and gentle manners and great patience under much suffering endeared her to all, and her dissolution was deeply lamented by us."[7]

Three more Beothuk women were captured in Notre Dame Bay and taken by John Peyton to St. John's in June 1823. As with Mary March, they were ordered returned to their tribe, but again two women, mother and daughter, died of consumption before their people were contacted. The remaining daughter, Shanawdithit, lived in John Peyton's household until her death from the disease in 1829.

In 1828, Shanawdithit was introduced to William Epps Cormack, a young Newfoundlander who had made the Beothuk plight his cause. Two journeys on foot across the island (one in 1822 and one in 1827) had yielded him no contact with them, although Cormack recorded copiously every detail he observed about their habitation, burial sites, deer fences, etc. In between his expeditions, Cormack founded the Beothuck Institution, for the purpose of "opening a communication with, and promoting the civilization of the Red Indians of Newfoundland."[8] However, Shanawdithit's assertion that at the time of her capture in 1823 there were only twenty-seven remaining Beothuks, many starving or suffering from tuberculosis, confirmed Cormack's conviction that she was the last of her race. He set about learning as much from Shanawdithit as possible about her people and their culture. With her artistic skill and superb memory, she related many details about the events of Lieutenant Buchan's 1811 journey and the aftermath of the capture of Mary March (Shanawdithit's aunt). In addition, she described aspects of Beothuk culture, which Cormack recorded. Included in his notes are a series of drawings by Shanawdithit. Unfortunately, her death in June 1829, just months after her introduction to Cormack, and the subsequent loss of some of his papers have reduced our knowledge of the extinct Beothuks.

What we do know we owe to Cormack and other concerned scholars who collected archeological evidence and documentary material about the natives of Newfoundland. Rev. George Patterson published a long article about the Beothuks in the *Transactions of the Royal Society of Canada* in 1891.[9] By far the most comprehensive work was compiled by James P. Howley, a Newfoundlander and a geologist. His book, *The Beothucks or Red Indians*, published in 1915, includes transcriptions of many historical documents as well as interviews with the people involved with the events of the 1820s. Recent scholarship has focused on interpretation of these documents and on an objective analysis of the factors affecting the demise of the Beothuks. Frederick Rowe's *Extinction, The Beothuks of Newfoundland* is a particularly incisive example of the latter. The Mary March Regional Museum in Grand Falls, Newfoundland, is dedicated to the memory of Demasduit and her people.

Information about the artist of our miniature, Henrietta Martha Hamilton, is very scarce. The daughter of George Drummond, she was probably born about 1780 and married Charles Hamilton in 1803.[10] She accompanied her husband to Newfoundland on his appointment as governor, staying six years. Nothing is known of her artistic training, which is a pity given the skill evident in the Mary March miniature. Lady Hamilton's sensitive rendering of Demasduit's face, especially her large dark eyes and delicate mouth, still touches our hearts a century and a half later.

Ingeborg Marshall has written two articles for *The Newfoundland Quarterly* about this miniature and the many copies made after it.[11] At one point a copy of the Mary March miniature was thought to be a portrait of Shanawdithit, and several reproductions were printed as such. However, as Ms. Marshall's research has ascertained, there was only one portrait executed. The miniature on display is the only known original portrait of any of the lost Beothuks, and as such is a national treasure of the first magnitude.

S.N.

---

1. Frederick W. Rowe, *Extinction, The Beothuks of Newfoundland* (Toronto: McGraw-Hill Ryerson, 1977), 116.
2. Rowe, 134.
3. Proclamation issued by the governor, Capt. the Hon. John Byron in 1769. Reissued by subsequent governors in 1775 and 1776. James P. Howley, *The Beothucks or Red Indians* (London: Cambridge University Press, 1915), 45.
4. The testimonies of John Peyton and other members of the party claim only Nonasbawsut was killed. Shanawdithit, recalling the incident later to Cormack, attested that another Beothuk was shot as well. Howley, 100 and 228.
5. Henrietta Martha Hamilton – not to be confused with the other, notorious Lady Hamilton, Emma. Sir Charles Hamilton, governor of Newfoundland, was distantly related to Sir William Hamilton, ambassador to Naples, the husband of Emma.
6. The report of Lieutenant Buchan gives us a good description of Mary's character. A naval officer, Sir Hercules Robinson, met Reverend Leigh shortly after Mary's death and recorded a description of her as related by the minister. He noted "her miniature taken by Lady Hamilton, is said to be strikingly like her...." Howley, 128.
7. Letter from Buchan to Sir Charles Hamilton, 10 March 1820, as transcribed in Howley, 121.
8. Howley, 184.
9. Rev. George Patterson, "The Beothiks [*sic*] or Red Indians of Newfoundland," *Transactions of the Royal Society of Canada*, 1st series, vol. 9, section II (1891), 123-171.
10. Ingeborg Marshall, "The Miniature Portrait of Mary March," *The Newfoundland Quarterly*, vol. 73, no. 3 (Fall 1977), 5.
11. Ingeborg Marshall, "The Miniature Portrait of Mary March," *The Newfoundland Quarterly*, vol. 73, no. 3 (Fall 1977), 5-7; Ingeborg Marshall, "A New Portrait of Mary March," *The Newfoundland Quarterly*, vol. 76, no. 1 (Spring 1980), 25-28.

JOHN COX DILLMAN ENGLEHEART (1782/4-1862)

50. ***Joseph Bouchette*****, 1815**

Watercolour on ivory

10.0 x 8.0 cm

Inscribed in pen and ink, recto, l.r.: *DE*; on backing paper, in pen and brown ink: *This is / Lt. Col. Joseph Bouc*[hette] */ Surveyor General o*[f] */ Lower Canada / This was painted in London / in 1805 by Englehart / Property of / R.S.M. Bouchette*

Donated in 1976 by Meeta Myers Bouchette in loving memory of her late husband Alfred Henri Bouchette

Accession no.: 1976-104-5

Negative no.: C-112049

Facsimile in exhibition

This superb miniature was painted by John Cox Dillman Engleheart and engraved for the frontispieces of two books on the geography of Canada written by Joseph Bouchette, surveyor-general of Lower Canada, 1803-1840.[1] A dedicated civil servant and soldier, and a distinguished artist, author and cartographer, Bouchette's career has been documented most recently and most extensively by Claude Boudreau.[2]

Born on 14 May 1774 in Quebec City, the eldest son of Jean-Baptiste Bouchette and Marie-Angélique Duhamel, Joseph Bouchette's career began as a draftsman in the office of his uncle, the Hon. Maj. Samuel Holland, in 1790. A year later, he joined the Provincial Marine, where he served for five years. After the reduction of the Great Lakes naval force, Bouchette returned to the office of his uncle in July 1801. When Samuel Holland died in December, Joseph became deputy surveyor-general and was promoted to surveyor-general in 1803. The next nine years were devoted to surveying, mapmaking, granting land and providing evidence to help settle land disputes.

When hostilities broke out between the United States and Britain in 1812, Bouchette, by now a major, joined a militia regiment, where he was assigned reconnaissance duties for the duration of the war. In March 1813, he was promoted to lieutenant-colonel.

Towards the end of the war, Bouchette returned to his civilian duties and a project of particular importance. In August 1814, he sailed to London to publish his *Topographical Description of the Province of Lower Canada*, with public support from the House of Assembly of Lower Canada. This was an ambitious project involving descriptions of the history, topography, and industrial and agricultural outputs of the seigneuries of the province, using material from the Surveyor-General's Office and information collected on his many surveys, illustrated with maps and his own sketches. The work was published in English and in French in 1815.

The frontispiece included an engraving by Francis Engleheart of this miniature by his nephew John Cox Dillman Engleheart. They were both members of the Engleheart family of artists, which included sculptors, miniaturists and engravers. John Cox Dillman had been trained in the studio of his uncle George and later at the Royal Academy schools. By 1807, he had a studio of his own and continued to paint until 1828 when he retired from the profession, although he lived until 1862.

How Joseph Bouchette came to commission Engleheart is not known.[3] Although the artist kept lists of his clients in his early years, they were not continued after 1803, and we have no record of his painting Bouchette's portrait.[4] Typical of Engleheart's work is the dark palette and the use of accessories such as the globe as an attribute of Bouchette's profession. Engleheart's rendering of the surveyor general's face is particularly fine. Bouchette's features are minutely delineated from the faint lines of the forehead to the highlight of the pupils. The shadows of the face have been intensified by red colouring on the reverse of the translucent ivory.

Bouchette's publication was dedicated to His Royal Highness the Prince Regent, and on 27 April 1816, the author was presented at court. He received five hundred pounds from Lord Bathurst towards the expenses of his publication as well as a gold medal from the Society for Encouraging Arts, Manufactures and Commerce in recognition of the importance of his book.

During the summers of 1817 and 1818, Bouchette served with the British surveying team in the Maine-New Brunswick boundary dispute between Britain and the United States, after which he returned to the post of surveyor-general in Quebec. He continued his provincial surveying duties throughout the twenties, performing survey tours of the province in 1824 and 1827. Throughout this period, Bouchette continued to collect up-to-date information about the topography, demography and industry of the British North American colonies in preparation for his second and third publications, *The British Dominions in North America* and *A Topographical Dictionary of Lower Canada*. The two volumes of the former were published in 1831 in London by Henry Colburn and Richard Bentley. The following year, Longman, Rees, Orme et al. published the topographical dictionary and reissued *The British Dominions* in a single binding. Bouchette's son, Robert-Shore-Milnes (Cat. no. 57), accompanied him to England, helped prepare the texts and contributed some of the illustrations in *The British Dominions*.[5] The Engleheart miniature was engraved again for the frontispiece of both editions of *The British Dominions*, this time by J. Thomson. Indeed, the miniature is the only known portrait of Bouchette; all subsequent engravings and even a sketch by Robert-Shore-Milnes Bouchette used either the original miniature or one of the two engravings from his books as a model.[6]

The British Dominions was a more extensive edition than Bouchette's 1815 book, encompassing all the British North American colonies, and was accompanied again by maps and illustrations. It was well received critically, and Bouchette had the opportunity to present a copy to the Duchess of Kent and to meet her daughter, Princess Victoria, the future Queen.

The years following Bouchette's return to Lower Canada in 1833 were troubled by financial difficulties and legal problems. In 1837, when the Lower Canada Rebellion broke out, Bouchette's son, Robert-Shore-Milnes, was one of the leaders of the insurgents and was subsequently exiled to Bermuda in 1838. The union of Upper and Lower Canada which Bouchette had supported in 1822 resulted in the merging of the provincial surveyor-general's offices and his forced retirement.[7]

Joseph Bouchette died in Montreal, on 9 April 1841. The miniature remained in his family and was handed down to his great-grandson, Alfred Henri Bouchette, whose widow donated it along with other items to the National Archives of Canada in 1976. A very welcome addition to several collections of manuscripts, maps and drawings concerning Joseph Bouchette now held by the National Archives, this portrait is further evidence of his contribution to Canadian history.

S.N.

---

1. His published topographic books were: *A Topographical Description of the Province of Lower Canada* (London, 1815), also published in French under the title *Description topographique de la Province du Bas Canada* (London, 1815); *The British Dominions in North America*, 2 vols. (London, 1831-1832) and *A Topographical Dictionary of the Province of Lower Canada* (London, 1832).

2. Claude Boudreau, "L'analyse de la carte ancienne: essai méthodologique; la carte du Bas-Canada de 1831 de Joseph Bouchette," *Rapports et Mémoires de recherche du Celat*, no. 7 (December 1986), 1-117.

3. There is some uncertainty about the date of the miniature. A sheet backing the frame in which the miniature was kept records the date 1805. However, Bouchette did not make his first trip to London until 1807, although it is possible the miniature was painted then. Since it relates directly to Bouchette's publications and the engraved frontispiece, it seems more likely that the miniature was executed sometime after Bouchette arrived in London in August 1814 and before the publication of *A Topographical Description* in 1815. An inscription on a card backing the miniature has been obliterated. Possibly the note on the frame backing is a transcription of the miniature backing, and 1815 was misread as 1805.

4. George C. Williamson and Henry L.D. Engleheart, *George Engleheart 1750-1829 Miniature Painter to George III* (London: George Bell and Sons, 1902), Appendix III.

5. Bouchette's other sons also contributed illustrations to *The British Dominions* — Joseph Jr., who had accompanied his father on the Boundary Commission survey, and Jean-François, who later obtained a commission in the British Army and served with the 68th Light Infantry. While in London, Bouchette also published an album of lithographs entitled *Canadian Views*, printed by Day and Haghe and based on his own drawings and those of his sons and other artists.

6. Engleheart's miniature was engraved by Francis Engleheart in 1815 and by J. Thomson in 1831. A lithograph by an unknown artist after the 1815 engraving appears in *Notice sur la famille Guy et sur quelques autres familles* (Montreal, 1867). In 1839, Robert-Shore-Milnes did a watercolour portait of his father based on the Engleheart miniature, now in the NA, Accession no. 1976-104-1.

7. See Bouchette's speech in support of the *Act of Union* in the *Quebec Gazette*, 5 December 1822, p. 2.

SIR WILLIAM CHARLES ROSS (1794/5-1860)

51. ***Edward Ellice Sr.***, 1838

Watercolour on ivory
12.2 x 8.6 cm
Purchased in 1983
Accession no.: 1983-88-1
Negative no.: C-104372

52. ***Edward Ellice Jr.***, 1838

Watercolour on ivory
10.5 x 8.2 cm
Purchased in 1983
Accession no.: 1983-88-2
Negative no.: C-104373
Facsimile in exhibition

"I never liked Ross['] miniature of him, but now it is my greatest pleasure."[1] So wrote Jane Ellice (ca. 1814?-1864)[2] about this miniature of her husband, Edward Ellice Jr., while she was held hostage by the patriotes of 1838 at the seigneury of Beauharnois. Though the Ellice family had long been involved in business in Upper and Lower Canada (Ontario and Quebec) and influential in its governing, the events of November 1838 included them in a manner that none would have imagined.

Edward Ellice Sr. (1781-1863) inherited a large business empire from his father, Alexander Ellice, in 1805. With the disappearance of his brother George about 1810 (lost at sea), he also acquired the seigneury of Beauharnois on the banks of the St. Lawrence, south of Montreal. A shrewd businessman and politician, Edward Sr. capitalized on his father's assets and greatly increased the family wealth. His marriage to the sister of Earl Grey and his seat in British politics for over forty years gave him the opportunity to play an important role in decisions concerning the British North American colonies. His nickname, "Bear," has been ascribed to both his involvement in the fur company and his unctuous manner.[3]

In the complex scene of Lower Canadian politics in the 1820s and 1830s, the Ellice sympathies were firmly with the Montreal merchants, or the Constitutionalists, who were pressing for the union of Upper and Lower Canada and the revocation of French civil law. This was due to the part played by Ellice Sr. in the Hudson's Bay-North West Company merger and his concerns at Beauharnois. He wanted to sell parts of the seigneury to settlers, but was prohibited by the laws of Lower Canada. Ellice was also concerned about the general economic climate of the colony. Having lands and business interests in the United States, he could not help but compare the British colonies unfavourably to the prosperity and economic expansion in her southern neighbour. As a capitalist and entrepreneur, Edward Sr. saw the future of the Canadas in their union under a representative government and English civil law. For these reasons, he was highly critical of the "Château Clique" who monopolized the governing of Lower Canada, and he was mistrusted by the parti canadien, whose leader Louis-Joseph Papineau regarded him as an enemy.[4] It was Edward Ellice Sr. who introduced the Union Bill of 1822, which was the catalyst for French-Canadian opposition in Lower Canada.

Edward Ellice Jr. (1810-1880) was the private secretary to Lord Durham and had accompanied him to Russia in 1832. When Durham was given the task of preparing a report on the Canadas after the rebellions in 1837, he brought Ellice Jr. with him in the same capacity, an appointment not without its detractors on both sides of the ocean.[5] It was an opportunity for Edward Jr. to check on the progress at Beauharnois and to keep his father informed of events in Canada.

The younger Ellice, with his wife Katherine Jane and her sister Eglantine (Tina) Balfour, departed from England with Durham and his family on 24 April 1838. The correspondence between father and son during the ensuing months gives an excellent account of their opinions on Canadian affairs.

After spending several weeks at both the Canadian and American properties, Edward Jr. compares the habitants of Beauharnois with the English settlers of both Lower Canada and the United States:

> Look at our people in the Chateauguay – they are exactly the same class as in Vermont – people who have made their property by their own industry and also are independent in the fullest extent of the word. What a contrast between them and the French Canadian – a poor devil, who can't call his soil his own.[6]

As men whose wealth depended on property ownership, they found the seigneurial system of Lower Canada intolerable. Ellice Jr. goes on to deplore the lack of education amongst the canadiens, accusing the Church and the upper-middle class of the province of deliberately keeping them ignorant:

> This is the idea of all who have influence among the French. They amount to 200 talented individuals such as W. Nelson, Papineau, Lafontaine etc. It is their interest to keep the people in this present state to prevent them mixing with British & as long as they are allowed this power they will succeed in their object.[7]

The two Ellices were also concerned about the political future of the Canadas. They worried that the British population would turn to the United States if their grievances were not addressed.[8] Durham's proposal for a union of all the British North American colonies was discussed and rejected by them both.[9]

On the difficulties in reconciling the interests of French and English Canadians, father and son differed sharply. The latter wrote about Durham's recommendations:

> ...it...tends to the annihilation of the nationality of the French Canadians. That in any sense must be a sine qua non (we may as well talk of keeping up a horde of Indians in the middle of Middlesex) & certainly is the best proposition I have yet heard on the subject.[10]

53. *Jane Ellice*, 1841

Watercolour on ivory

4.7 x 3.9 cm

Inscription on the inside of the locket case: *Janie Ellice / July 14th 1841*; on back of case: *EE*

Purchased in 1987

Accession no.: 1987-97-1

Negative no.: C-131638

His father, a wiser, more experienced man, knew that the subjugation of either race was not the solution to the problem:

> ...the French ought not to be left to the ascendancy of a vulgar English faction who will in their time treat them with at least as little feeling as they have shown for their English fellow colonists.[11]

Edward Jr. confesses to a lack of understanding of the French Canadians in a letter to Major Clitherow concerning the activities of the Chasseurs (the society of insurgents organized in Lower Canada and the United States during the summer of 1838). Less than two days before the outbreak of the rebellion, he was confident that "the very fact of Volunteers being drilled and ready for defence may be the means of preventing an intended outbreak."[12]

How wrong he was! On 4 November 1838, the household at Beauharnois was awakened at 4 a.m. by shouting and the sound of gun-shots. The manoir was surrounded by rebels. Ellice Jr., his agent Lawrence Brown and other employees of the family were sent under guard to Châteauguay, where they were imprisoned. Jane Ellice, her sister, Mrs. Brown and her children were transferred to the house of the local curé, M. Quintal, later that day. Jane recorded the events of her captivity in a diary that had been given to her by her father-in-law, Ellice Sr., before she left in April. Her fears for the lives of her husband and sister are vividly described, as is the comfort she took in the once-maligned miniature.

The rebellion was quickly put down. Distressed but unharmed, Jane was released from captivity on 10 November, shortly before Edward and the other prisoners at Châteauguay were allowed to escape and make their way back to Beauharnois.

Needless to say, the Ellices' enthusiasm for the New World and Beauharnois was somewhat cooled. Edward, Jane and Tina left Quebec on 19 November and the seigneury was put up for sale.[13] However, the Ellice influence on Canadian affairs continued. Edward Sr. is known to have discussed and advised Lord Durham prior to the latter's completion of his famous report.[14] In fact, at Lord Russell's request, Ellice drew up his own list of proposals for the Canadas, entitled "Suggestions for a Scheme for the Future Government of the Canadas." He recommended the union of Upper and Lower Canada under a type of government similar to that of the United States. He also advocated the designation of Montreal as a "congressional district." The abolition of the seigneurial system by the adoption of English civil law, the dissolution of the clergy reserves and representative government were amongst his proposals, and, ironically, similar to many of the proposals the Chasseur leader Robert Nelson had published in March 1838.[15]

There are indications that the Ellices may have been influential in securing clemency for some of the insurgents sentenced to death for their participation in the 1838 rebellion. François-Xavier Prieur, one of those condemned, wrote in his memoirs of his exile:

> During the course of our trial, one of my generous defending counsel, Mr. Hart, told me that he had it on good authority that some disinterested persons had presented a petition to His Excellency the Administrator, Sir John Colborne, recommending me personally to the Royal clemency, in whose powers it lay, as the King's representative.
>
> This request was due, I was informed, to the efforts and the entreaties of the excellent ladies of the Ellice family, who in this wise, wished to recognise the kindnesses which I had shown them formerly, when in command of the troops in the village of Beauharnais [*sic*].[16]

Louis-Joseph-Amédée Papineau (Cat. no. 59) recorded in his journal that Dr. Brien, one of the insurgents, had been visited by Edward Jr., and he had promised to help him.[17]

The miniatures of the Ellices, father and son, were painted by William C. Ross in 1838, sometime before April. Ross was a well-known miniaturist; during his career he painted over two thousand portraits, and was a favourite artist of Queen Victoria's. He was reknowned for his rich colouring, accomplished draughtsmanship and accurate likenesses. But it is easy to see why Jane Ellice disliked his rendering of Edward Jr. While the drawing is good, the sharp contrast of muddy brown and bright blue is quite harsh. However, the pair illustrates the private and public purposes that miniatures served before they were eclipsed by photography, invented a year later. The portrait of Edward Ellice Jr. was treasured as a private memento; the portrait of Edward Sr. was engraved by J.S. Agar later in the same year.

Three years after their eventful sojourn in the Canadas, Jane Ellice presented her husband with a miniature of herself, also by William Charles Ross, who seems to have responded better to Jane's vivacious beauty. Engraved on the encasing locket is the date 14 July 1841, which we know from Jane's diary was the eve of their wedding anniversary. So the portraits of these three important participants in Canada's history, all executed by the same artist, are now reunited as part of the National Archives collection.

S.N.

1. NA, Edward Ellice family papers, MG 24 A2, vol. 50, diary of Jane Ellice, entry for 9 November 1838. The diary has been published: Patricia Godsell, ed., *The Diary of Jane Ellice* (Ottawa: Oberon Press of Ottawa, 1975).

2. Jane Ellice's birthdate is as yet unknown. Although she is mentioned in *Burke's Landed Gentry* (London: Harrison and Son, 1886), 1:77, as the second daughter of Robert Balfour of Balbirnie, the birthdates of daughters are not given in this authority. Her death was noted in the London *Times* and *Gentlemen's Magazine*, but neither mention her age or her date of birth. Jane notes in her diary on 15 July 1838, her wedding anniversary, that she has been married four years, putting the year of her wedding at 1834. Assuming she was about twenty years old when she married, she could have been born ca. 1814. However, she was possibly older or younger on her wedding, and her birthdate could range from 1810 or earlier to 1818.

3. James Colthart, "Edward Ellice and North America," doctoral dissertation (Princeton University, 1971), p. 3, credits the nickname to Ellice's Hudson's Bay Company association, while Dorothy E.T. Long, "The Ellusive Mr. Ellice," *The Canadian Historical Review* 23 (1942): 42, refers to Thomas Carlyle's description of Ellice's personality.

4. NA, Papineau family papers, MG 24 B2, vol. 2, p. 2798, Edmund B. O'Callaghan, member of the parti patriote, to Papineau, 20 March 1838, concerning the impending visit of Ellice Jr.:

> You will see by the late arrivals from England that Ellice is on his way again to Canadas on a mission. What is now to intrigue about? Have they not it all their own way?

5. NA, Lord Durham papers, MG 24 A27, vol. 25, p. 495, an anonymous letter to Lord Durham, April 1838 just before his departure for Quebec:

> Finding that the same parties whose machinations have brought Canada to its present state are now engaged and with some appearance of smugness in plans to render your Lordship's Administration subservient to their purposes I address Your Lordship in the hopes that it may tend to frustrate their designs....

6. NA, MG 24 A2, vol. 12, p. 4216, Edward Jr. to Edward Sr., dated at Albany, New York, 28 August 1838.

7. NA, MG 24 A2, vol. 12, p. 4319, Edward Jr. to Edward Sr., dated at Beauharnois, 11 October 1838.

8. NA, MG 24 A2, vol. 12, pp. 4215-4216, Edward Jr. to Edward Sr., 28 August 1838.

9. NA, MG 24 A2, vol. 12, pp. 4215-4216, Edward Jr. to Edward Sr., 28 August 1838:

> These smaller colonies have no interest common with Canada, are not likely to be more important than they are now; & if they were, then interests would probably clash directly with the Canadas.

10. NA, MG 24 A2, vol. 12, p. 4339, Edward Jr. to Edward Sr., dated at Quebec, 10 October 1838.

11. NA, MG 24 A2, vol. 12, p. 4141, Edward Sr. to Edward Jr., 9 August 1838.

12. NA, Sir John Colborne papers, MG 24 A40, vol. 40, pp. 5428-5429, Edward Ellice Jr. to Major Clitherow, 2 November 1838.

13. Beauharnois was sold to the North American Colonial Association of Ireland in 1839. However, the company failed to uphold the terms of their agreement and the property was repossessed by the Ellices. It was not until 1854 that it finally left the family. Long, 50.

14. Colthart, 244.

15. Robert Christie, *History of the Late Province of Lower Canada, Parliamentary and Political from the commencement to the close of its existence as a separate province*, 2nd edition, (Montreal: Richard Worthington, 1866), 5:44-47.

16. François-Xavier Prieur, *Notes of a Convict of 1838*, Gerald Mackaness, trans., Australian Historical Monographs Series, no. VI (Sydney: D.S. Ford, 1949), 39.

17. NA, MG 24 B2, vol. 32, "Journal d'un Fils de la Liberté," vol. 2, p. 34, entry for 21 January 1839:

> Dr. Brien of St. Martin, who had been at Châteauguay, pleaded guilty. He had taken Ellice and Brown prisoner, but had treated them well. Ellice went to see him in prison and promised to help him, but where will that lead? Ellice has left and probably his promise with him....

Whether or not the Ellices had any direct influence on the commutation of Prieur's sentence is difficult to prove. There is no evidence of such a request in either the correspondence of the Ellice family or that of Sir John Colborne, the governor-in-chief at the time. There is mention in the latter's dispatches to London in January 1839 of another prisoner being given a reprieve because of family connections (Public Record Office, London, Colonial Office records, C.O. 42, vol. 293, NA, MG 11, microfilm, reel B-266). By the time of Prieur's trial, however, Colborne is already contemplating clemency for the majority of those convicted. In his dispatches, he argues that an example of severity has already been set with twelve executions, and that the example of clemency would be more expedient (Public Record Office, C.O. 42, vol. 295, NA, MG 11, microfilm, reel B-267, dispatch of May 1839). That Ellice visited the prisoners is clear; Jane records it in her diary entry for 16 November 1838 (see note 1). However, his efforts cannot be distinguished from a general tendency towards leniency on the part of the courts and Sir John Colborne.

WILLIAM BERCZY SR. (1744-1813)

54. ***Pierre de Rastel de Rocheblave*,** ca. 1806-1807

Oil on canvas
69.0 x 53.1 cm
Purchased in 1988
Accession no.: 1988-42-1
Negative no.: C-132756

At a time when most successful French Canadians tended to establish themselves in the clergy or in the professions, Pierre de Rocheblave was one of the few to make his mark in the fur trade. And what is more, his success came early. Unlike some of his colleagues, he did not establish his reputation by opening new routes to the West; instead, it was his business sense, diplomacy and good nature that won him the respect of those who had the pleasure of meeting and working with him throughout his long career as a trader and politician.[1]

Rocheblave was born in 1773 in Kaskaskia, Illinois; his father, Philippe-François, who was an adventurer and the son of a marquis, had married Marie-Michelle Dufresne, a native of Kaskaskia.[2] The family arrived in Canada after the American War of Independence and spent a few years in Quebec before settling in Varennes, near Montreal, around 1789. Philippe de Rocheblave became interested in the fur trade and politics, and his two sons followed in his footsteps.[3]

Pierre began his career at an early age, working for a few years in Detroit as a clerk, first for his father, then for the merchant Grant. During the winter of 1797-1798, after returning to Montreal, he hired voyageurs on his own account to travel to Michilimackinac, Michigan. He became one of the founding members as a wintering partner of the XY Company, which was established in October 1798 to compete against the North West Company. He wintered successively at Lake Athabasca and at Fort Augustus (present-day Edmonton). In the end, the competition between the two companies proved too severe for the men and the trade; they merged in November 1804. Rocheblave became a wintering partner, or "bourgeois," of the North West Company, which was from then on the only rival of the Hudson's Bay Company. At that time, he and Charles Chaboillez were the only French-Canadian partners.

In 1805, Rocheblave was assigned to the Red River department, and two years later found himself again at Lake Athabasca, at the Company's most important post, Fort Chipewyan (Fig. 54.1). From 1810 to 1812, he was responsible for the Pic department, north of Lake Superior. He took part in the War of 1812 as captain of the Corps of Voyageurs. In 1813, he went west again to take charge of the Saskatchewan River department, but returned to Montreal by the following summer. He then made a start in some new commercial enterprises associated with the fur-trading business, and frequented the Beaver Club.[4] Having become a North West Company agent in April 1817, Rocheblave was obliged to travel to Fort William each summer in order to meet the wintering partners, or "winterers." He never again ventured further west than this company post.

In Montreal, at the age of forty-six, he married Anne-Elmire Bouthillier, daughter of a prosperous merchant, and the couple settled on Beaver Hall Hill. The honeymoon was brief: in May, the young groom left again for Fort William. In addition to his clerk and Abbé Tabeau, a missionary, he was accompanied in his "canoë de maître," or lead canoe, by John Jeremiah Bigsby (1792-1881), an English geologist and physician, who informs us that Rocheblave was "a tall dark Frenchman, with a stoop," charming but quiet because of his recent marriage.[5]

When the North West Company was taken over by the Hudson's Bay Company in 1821, Rocheblave was nominated to take inventory of his former company's goods. This task left him with enough leisure time to immerse himself with renewed ardour in commerce and real estate. He subsequently devoted himself to the service of his fellow citizens as a member of Parliament for Montreal West from 1824 to 1827, as a member of the Legislative Council in 1832, and then, from 1838 to his death, as a member of the Special Council (he voted for the Union of the Canadas, after having at first opposed it). He sat on a number of committees, was Justice of the Peace for the District of Montreal and churchwarden of Notre-Dame, in addition to holding other public posts. He died in October 1840.

Looking at his portrait, it is difficult to imagine Rocheblave's daily life in the Northwest.[6] Each wintering partner was responsible for a large territory, and was assisted by a clerk, voyageurs (who plied the canoes) and sometimes an interpreter. It was mainly the clerks stationed at secondary posts who came into contact with the native people. In exchange for their beaver skins, the Indians were offered blankets, implements and, unfortunately, plenty of alcohol – especially if it meant winning their collaboration before a clerk from the rival company did. Travelling was done in light canoes along a network of rivers and lakes and over a series of portages; in winter, snowshoes were used.

Many of the men had Indian wives, but the company discouraged such unions, as the upkeep of families was too expensive. To prevent loneliness, especially in winter, the company made books available. The men could also visit colleagues in neighbouring posts. Apart from the annual assembly at Fort William, however, the event of the season was the visit by the "winter express," two couriers who travelled on horseback throughout the territory from January to April. According to many accounts, food was sometimes a problem, especially in winter when the men could not hunt or fish, let alone tend a garden. The main forts kept a stash of pemmican but, as transportation was hazardous, regular distribution to secondary forts was not guaranteed; sometimes the winter partners and their clerks endured starvation.

Given the great distance separating Montreal from the Northwest, the annual meeting of agents and wintering partners was at a halfway point at the western end of Lake Superior – first at Grand Portage, then, after 1803, at Fort Kaministiquia, which became Fort William in 1807 (now Thunder Bay) (Fig. 54.2). The brigades coming from Montreal loaded themselves with trade goods from England and returned with furs transported to the fort by the wintering partners, who in turn left at the end of July for the posts assigned to them by the general assembly; their journey could take up to two months.

Leave periods for wintering partners, which lasted from one summer to the next because of distances, had to be strictly regulated.[7] From time to time the partners and agents established a rotation list for leaves. In 1805, after the merger with XY, the list drawn up in 1802 was modified; the wintering partners of the XY Company were placed at the end of the list, and Rocheblave's leave was scheduled for 1808, ten years after his departure from Montreal. A note in the margin of the list states, however, that he went down on rotation in 1806 in place of John McGillivray, who had to wait one more year. Rocheblave returned to Fort William in July 1807 and did not return to Montreal until 1812, as his 1808 leave was given to A.N. McLeod.[8]

It is apparent from this information that Rocheblave had only two leaves between 1798 and 1814, both of which he spent in the Montreal area: September 1806 to May 1807 (allowing about two months for the journey to and from Kaministiquia), and 1812, when he was thirty-nine. It is unlikely that he sat for his portrait during the 1812 visit, since he was involved in war service at the time and was older than the man who appears in the portrait. Examining the sitter's costume helps us to be more precise in determining the date of the portrait. The indigo tailcoat, with its round cut-in and low collar, as well as the cream-coloured vest cut above the waistline, were more typical of the early nineteenth century than the late eighteenth.[9] In addition, the hairstyle, which overpainting has exaggerated in a somewhat ridiculous manner, is a variant of the Titus style, which was particularly popular after General Bonaparte adopted it around 1800.[10] In *The Woolsey Family*, painted by William Berczy in 1808-1809, Benjamin Lemoine wears his hair in the same style as Rocheblave, and his costume, except for the colour, is identical (Fig. 54.3). This similarity enables us to date the Rocheblave portrait as 1806-1807, rather than to a date prior to his departure for the west in 1798.

The comment added in 1806 to the rotation list does not mention the reason for Rocheblave's early leave. However, his father had died in 1802, and his brother Noël, who had succeeded the father as member of Parliament in 1804, died suddenly in December 1805. Because of the slow means of communication, Pierre learned about this only at the annual assembly in July 1806. He no doubt returned home to comfort his mother, for whom he was now the sole support, and to assist her in settling the estate. If, in addition, he was, as his friend Larocque would lead us to believe, "very sick" when he left the post at La Souris for Kaministiquia, the early leave is even more understandable.[11] It was perhaps more to leave his mother a memento in case something unfortunate should happen to him, rather than to emphasize his success in business, that he left her his portrait before returning to the west in the spring of 1807.[12]

He was only following current fashion. Indeed, one of the results of the considerable demographic and economic growth that followed the Conquest was the increasing number of English and French Canadians who were joining the bourgeoisie. From the time of the Renaissance, the rise of the bourgeoisie has always been accompanied by a proliferation of portraits, which are concrete evidence of success, and Canada at the turn of the nineteenth century was no exception. The Montreal and Quebec elite kept a number of resident artists and many itinerants busy. The least expensive portrait was the silhouette, followed by miniature portraits on paper or ivory. Certain artists also offered to do oil paintings, which varied in price according to whether the subject was shown with hands (requiring more work), or with an appropriate background decor (again more costly).[13]

At the time Pierre de Rocheblave commissioned his portrait, two immigrant artists, the Frenchman Louis Dulongpré (ca. 1759-1843) (Cat. no. 55) and the German William Berczy Sr. shared the Montreal bourgeois portrait market. Because Dulongpré was absent for long periods of time filling orders for religious paintings, the field was left open to his friend and competitor, Berczy.[14]

Born in Germany as Johann Albrecht Ulrich Moll, Berczy arrived at York (Toronto) in 1794, as the head of a group of German immigrants.[15] An initial attempt at colonization in the state of New York had not succeeded, and the undertaking at Toronto was to be only a partial success. Disillusioned and financially ruined, Berczy was obliged to return to his first calling as miniature-portrait painter, a craft he had learned and practised in Europe. The few watercolour portraits that he painted in Toronto in 1803 renewed his confidence in his talent, but he quickly exhausted the potential commissions among the tiny clientele in early Toronto. He then settled in Montreal in October 1804, rejoining his wife, who had been there since 1798 (Berczy went to London in 1799, and did not return to Canada until 1802). Except for a one-year stay in Quebec City, where he painted *The Woolsey Family* from July 1808 to July 1809, Berczy remained in Montreal until May 1812, when he travelled to New York in an attempt to have a book on Canada published. He died there a few months later.

Berczy was a cultivated and educated man who had no difficulty finding clients in Montreal, particularly in fur-trading circles. His wife's best friend was the wife of Daniel Sutherland, who, like Rocheblave, had been a partner of the XY Company.[16] Berczy did a drawing of the widow of Simon McTavish and her children (1804, Royal Ontario Museum; perhaps in preparation for a canvas now lost) and an oil portrait of William McGillivray and his family (1806, McCord Museum, Montreal). Berczy had also painted a life-sized portrait of Admiral Nelson (1805) and a depiction of the Battle of Trafalgar (1806), both commissioned for the Fort William depot. Today these two canvases still belong to the Hudson's Bay Company. Finally, among the numerous profiles in miniature attributed to him, we notice the names of some of the wintering partners of the North West Company.[17]

There is no document confirming the attribution of the portrait of Pierre de Rocheblave to William Berczy Sr.; however, Berczy appears to have been the only artist working in Montreal at the time of Rocheblave's visit in 1806-1807 who would have been capable of producing such a skilfully modelled face.

L.D.

54.1 G. Back
Fort Chipewyan — a N. W. Co. Post on Lake Athabasca, ca. 1821
Watercolour
NA C-15251

54.2 R. Irvine
Fort William, ca. 1812
Watercolour
Archives of Ontario

54.3 W. Berczy
The Woolsey Family, 1808-1809 (detail)
Oil on canvas
National Gallery of Canada 5875

---

1. Eva Major-Marothy carried out part of the research presented here.

2. *Dictionary of Canadian Biography* (Toronto: University of Toronto Press, 1988), 7:735-739, entry for Pierre de Rastel de Rocheblave.

3. Philippe de Rocheblave, having come to America around 1755, served the English, the Spanish and the English successively on either side of the Missouri River before he was taken prisoner and brought to Virginia in 1778; after his escape in 1780, the family spent some time in New York, then in Quebec City. Rocheblave chose to settle in Varennes near Montreal after having attempted unsuccessfully to obtain the land concession of York (Toronto); he hoped to have the traditional route to the west via the Ottawa River modified to benefit the Lake Ontario area, and to obtain a transportation monopoly through York for trade goods and furs. He was the member for Surrey in the House of Assembly of Lower Canada from 1792 until his death in 1802. See Percy Robinson, *Toronto During the French Regime... 1615-1793* (Toronto: Ryerson Press, 1933), 159 ff. and Appendix III, E. Fabre Surveyer, "Philippe François de Rastel de Rocheblave," 233-242.

4. The Beaver Club was reserved exclusively for the bourgeois of the North West Company who had spent at least one winter west of Lake Superior; members were obliged to be present at the banquets if they were in Montreal. Rocheblave was made a member in January 1807, along with his old XY Company partners. NA, Beaver Club papers, MG 19 B3, Minutes, fol. 76; Rocheblave's name appears on this 1814 membership list, which also states that he became a member in 1807, and fol. 78 ff. notes Rocheblave's presence during the winters of 1814-1815 and 1815-1816.

5. John J. Bigsby, *The Shoe and Canoe* (New York: Paladin Press, 1969), 1:129, reprint of 1850 edition. The NA owns a number of sketches done by Bigsby, one of which is dated 22 May 1819 and shows the Rideau Falls (C-11627); however, the artist has not included depictions of his travelling companions in the view.

6. For information concerning the North West Company, see Marjorie W. Campbell, *The North West Company* (Toronto: Macmillan Co., 1973) and Robert Rumilly, *La Compagnie du Nord-Ouest, une épopée montréalaise*, 2 vols. (Montreal: Fides, 1980). Several documents, including various first-hand accounts and clerks' diaries, have been published in L.R. Masson, *Les Bourgeois de la Compagnie du Nord-Ouest* (Quebec: A. Côté et Cie., 1889-1890) and in W.S. Wallace, ed., *Documents Relating to the North West Company*, Champlain Society Publications, no. 22 (1934). For the XY Company, see R. A. Pendergast, "The XY Company 1798 to 1804," doctoral thesis (University of Ottawa, 1957).

7. See Wallace, Document 19, "Minutes of the Meetings of the North West Company at Grand Portage and Fort William, 1801-1807," and Document 20, "Minutes of the Transactions of the North West Company at Fort William, 1807-1821." As for the XY Company, Pendergast does not discuss the subject of leaves, but one can imagine that with only six winterers to cover a territory that was growing larger because of competition, none of them had the opportunity to return to Montreal during the six years of the Company's existence. Rocheblave's presence in the Northwest is noted in the following accounts: winters of 1801-1802 – John Macdonald of Garth, "Autobiographical Notes 1791-1816" in Masson, 2:25; 1802-1803 and 1803-1804 – Elliott Coues, *New Light on the Early History of the Greater Northwest: The Manuscript Journals of Alexander Henry the Younger... and David Thompson* (New York: F.P. Harper, 1897), 214. In November 1804, all the XY winterers, including Rocheblave, who was still in the West, signed the agreement between the North West Company and the XY Company, by Sir Alexander Mackenzie's proxy (Wallace, 144).

8. Wallace, 210, minutes of the general assembly of 1805, "Rotation List," with a margin note dated 19 August 1806, and 258-261, minutes of 1808, "Review of Rotations."

9. C. Willett and Phillis Cunnington, *Handbook of English Costume in the Nineteenth Century* (Boston: Plays Inc., 1970), 33, 55-65.

10. Richard Corson, *Fashions in Hair* (London: Peter Owen, 1980), 423, plate 89, illustrations E (ca. 1800) and I (1802), illustrate two examples of the "incroyable" hairstyle in which the hair at the crown of the head was puffed up.

11. François-Antoine Larocque, *Journal of Larocque from the Assiniboine to the Yellowstone, 1805* (Ottawa: Government Printing Bureau, 1910), 74; but on p. 76 Larocque gives us the reason for Rocheblave's departure for Montreal: "Mr. Rocheblave having heard at Caministiquia [*sic*] of the death of his Brother Noel went down." Noël died in Montreal, following a shipwreck on Lake Champlain, as reported in the *Quebec Mercury*, 16 December 1805, pp. 398-399.

12. She already had a portrait of her son Noël; the two portraits were published for the first time in Pinney's (Montreal) auction catalogue for 22 March 1988 (lots T138 and T140, property from Manoir de Bleury). The family of owner Randolph Routh is connected to the Bouthillier and the Sabrevois de Bleury families on the female side (the wife of Pierre de Rocheblave was a Bouthillier). The portrait of Noël, attributed to Dulongpré in the sale catalogue, was bought by the McCord Museum, Montreal; it is now attributed to an anonymous artist: See Robert Derome, Paul Bourassa and Joanne Chagnon, *Dulongpré De plus près / A Closer Look* (Montreal: McCord Museum, 1988), 13, illustration.

13. Mary Allodi, "Canadian Faces. Some Early Portraits," *Rotunda*, vol. 11, no. 1 (Spring 1976), 22.

14. See Derome, 89. Eleven religious canvases are mentioned for 1806-1807, notably at L'Islet, Rivière-Ouelle and Trois-Rivières.

15. For Berczy's biography, see John André, *William Berczy, Co-founder of Toronto* (Toronto: Borough of York, 1967).

16. Their friendship was mentioned for the first time in one of Berczy's letters to his wife Charlotte, 6 February 1899. "William von Moll Berczy," *Rapport de l'Archiviste de la Province de Québec pour 1940-1941*, p. 22.

17. André, 85-100.

LOUIS DULONGPRÉ (ca. 1759-1843) and JEAN-BAPTISTE ROY-AUDY (1778-ca. 1848)

LOUIS DULONGPRÉ (ca. 1759-1843)

55. *Jean-Baptiste Dumont*, 1821

Oil on canvas

57.4 x 46.7 cm

Inscribed in black ink, verso, l.l.: *Peint par / Dulongpré-*; l.c.: *-Jean Baptiste Dumon agée de 72... / Le 13 Juillet 1821 / Née le 23 Janvier 1749 mort le 4 Novembre 1830*

Gift of Alfred F. and Eileen Greenwood in memory of Dumont and Frances Huot, 1982

Accession no.: 1984-1-1

Negative no.: C-136657

JEAN-BAPTISTE ROY-AUDY (1778-ca. 1848)

56. *Alphonse Montaigu Dumont*, 1834

Oil on canvas

58.0 x 50.0 cm

Inscribed in pen and black ink, verso, l.c.: *Alphonse Dumon agée de 47 ans et un mois le 27 Février 18... / 1834 / Décédé 2 Sept 1858 – 71 em ane* [?]; l.l: *Peint par / Oudy-*

Gift of Alfred F. and Eileen Greenwood in memory of Dumont and Frances Huot, 1982

Accession no.: 1984-1-2

Negative no.: C-136468

In 1982, a family donated its collection of family portraits to the National Archives. It consisted of portraits of the male ancestors of the Dumonts and the Huots. Although these families did not figure prominently in our nation's history, this unique collection of portraits spanning five generations, along with the family papers also donated, have provided us with almost all the information necessary to reconstruct the lives of these people, who were typical members of middle-class Quebec society in the nineteenth century.[1]

The subjects of the two oldest portraits, Jean-Baptiste and Alphonse Dumont, are identified by the inscriptions on the back of the canvases. Each also bears another inscription, in a different handwriting, which attributes the portraits respectively to Louis Dulongpré and Jean-Baptiste Roy-Audy, two of Quebec's best-known portrait painters at the beginning of the nineteenth century.[2]

The earliest ancestor, Jean-Baptiste Dumont, was born in Quebec in 1749. His father, Jean-Baptiste Sr., had come from France before his marriage in 1742, and owned the land on which the battle of Sainte-Foy had been fought in 1760, during which Commander Lévis' forces overcame those of Commander Murray.[3] Like his father, Jean-Baptiste Jr. became a merchant. Perhaps in order to improve the family business, he settled at Beloeil, on the banks of the Richelieu River, around 1774.[4] In 1777, he returned to Quebec to marry Marie LeBlanc, an Acadian.[5] The couple returned to Beloeil, where all their children were born.

Jean-Baptiste Dumont Jr. acquired land on the shore of the Richelieu River in 1796, but the exact date when he built the stone house (known today as "Villebon"),[6] is not known. In 1803, a niece's marriage settlement referred to him as a "former merchant," but he was still living at Beloeil and would remain there until at least 1810. Four years later, in 1814, the entire family was living in the agricultural parish of Saint-Joseph-de-Chambly when his daughter Clémentine married a farmer, Charles Huot, from the same village. In 1825, at the time of the census, Jean-Baptiste lived with a bachelor, probably his son Alphonse.[7] Marie LeBlanc had died in 1816, and her husband's death would follow in 1830.

Born in 1787, Alphonse Dumont had at first been destined for a career in business. When his father retired, Alphonse was sent to train for a few years with the Quebec merchant Louis Dunière. But in 1808, when war threatened between the United States and Great Britain, Col. J.-B. Melchior Hertel de Rouville (1748-1817), owner of a neighbouring seigneury, named him sergeant of a militia company. Alphonse found his calling, and the War of 1812 gave him the opportunity to advance his military career. He took part in the Battle of Châteauguay as lieutenant of the 2nd Select Embodied Militia Battalion of Lower Canada (active militia), although as a member of the reserve. This action won him a medal, awarded in 1847,[8] and probably his appointment to the rank of captain a few months later. In 1818, he was promoted to major in a division of the sedentary militia at Chambly, commanded by Jean-Baptiste-René Hertel de Rouville (1789-1859), who had succeeded his father as seigneur and colonel.

Alphonse became a leading citizen of his village, and was named justice of the peace for the district of Montreal in 1820.[9] He apparently did not take up his father's business again, preferring to develop the lands he owned at Saint-Hilaire and in the neighbouring parish of Saint-Jean-Baptiste. A ledger kept from 1825 indicates that he regularly paid his dues and obligations to the Seigneur Rouville, for whom he was also the estate manager.[10]

Dumont subsequently became involved in real estate speculation. At the time when lands were awarded to veterans of the War of 1812, he was given eight hundred acres at Acton in the Eastern Townships, and immediately settled a man named Duval there to begin clearing the land. Four years later, all conditions having been fulfilled, the land was officially granted to him.[11] He resold it almost immediately to the Seigneur de Rouville.[12] In 1833, he acquired land at Beloeil. He returned to live in the village of his birth by 1841, the year he was elected churchwarden of the parish.[13] He settled on his father's land instead of his own, for the 1851 census indicates that he lived in a stone house ("Villebon") with his niece Adeline Huot and two domestics.[14] He never married. The wooden house he built in 1842 was probably located on the land purchased in 1833, land which was set aside for cultivation. Moreover, as a little notebook records, between 1844 and 1851 he took a very close interest in his agricultural activities, and his success enabled him to take on farm hands and servants.

Even though Alphonse Dumont lived in one of the regions most affected by the rebellion of 1837, we don't find his name among those of the patriotes. But he might have been sympathetic. We only know that, one week before the battle of Saint-Denis, he resigned his post as major in the militia. As was often the case, however, during these unsettled weeks, his resignation was not accepted.[15] In 1845, when the militia was reorganized, he was asked to set up a company and was named lieutenant-colonel of the 2nd Regiment of the militia at Verchères. He was then fifty-eight years old, and he did not retire until 1855, three years before his death.

Louis Dulongpré and Jean-Baptiste Roy-Audy both worked from time to time as itinerant painters, moving about as required by their commissions for either religious art or portraits. In response to a rapidly developing middle class, other artists were equally hard at work in Quebec at that time. Unfortunately, they signed very few of their portraits, and, in the past, most of these paintings were attributed without hesitation to either Roy-Audy or Dulongpré. Research has progressed a great deal during the last few years, but it is still difficult, much of the time, to attribute a portrait with certainty to a specific artist. In the case of Roy-Audy, the task is relatively easy, as his signed portraits reveal a very particular style around which it has been possible to group other works, but Dulongpré's artistic personality is less distinct, which somewhat complicates the task of attribution.

Our portraits of the Dumonts are not signed, but the inscriptions on the backs date to the nineteenth century, and we have no reason to doubt these attributions.[16] Like many of the portraits of the period, the inscriptions also mention the precise date when the work was painted.

Although already in his sixties, Louis Dulongpré was still painting in 1821. Did Jean-Baptiste Dumont approach him because of his renown or because they were already acquainted? In 1800 and 1811, the artist had painted two religious pictures for the church of Saint-Matthieu at Beloeil.[17] He visited Chambly during the War of 1812 to sit on a court martial.[18] If the two men were acquainted, one would wonder why Dumont waited so long to have his portrait painted, and why he did not have it done while his wife was still living, as was more usual.

Dulongpré portrayed Dumont as a man of austere bearing, tempered by a benevolent expression. This is much as one would expect him to be, judging from a letter he sent to Alphonse, in July 1802, when the latter was spending time in Quebec: After lengthy advice on good manners and work, he adds: "Mr. Dunière wants to make a man of you," as if he himself had not entirely succeeded in doing so.

The portrait of Alphonse by Roy-Audy conveys precisely the air of solemn authority and strictness that perfectly suits a career militiaman. The yellow vest and brooch are the trappings of a very elegant man, but the stiff collar, cravat and shirt-front bespeak a rigid temperament. Roy-Audy's style, which is linear and filled with detail (he learned his craft by painting carriage decoration), is evident in the vivid colours, which he knew how to use with flare; the contrast offered by the yellow vest and black coat and cravat is very successful.[19]

We do not know the circumstances surrounding the commissioning of this portrait, but we have a hypothesis. We have shown earlier the professional ties that linked Alphonse Dumont and the fifth Seigneur de Rouville, Jean-Baptiste-René. We presume that Alphonse frequented the Rouville manor in Saint-Hilaire. The Rouville family kept a gallery of ancestral portraits, and when Jean-Baptiste-René decided to add his own and that of his wife, he approached Roy-Audy.[20] Dumont, who already owned the portrait of his father (Cat. no. 55), may have wanted to do the same as his friend, and he may have commissioned Roy-Audy to do his portrait while the painter was visiting Saint-Hilaire (Fig. 55.2).[21] Better yet, Alphonse seems to have suggested that Roy-Audy use the portrait of Jean-Baptiste-Melchior, the father of Jean-Baptiste-René (a painting attributed to William Berczy Sr.) as a model; the pose is exactly the same, and both wear brooches on their shirts (Fig. 55.1).

These two magnificent portraits may be attributed with near certainty to two well-known painters whose production is still not very well understood. They are among the most significant recent acquisitions, not only for the portrait collection of the National Archives, but also for the study of nineteenth-century portraiture in Canada.

L.D.

55.1 W. Berczy Sr.
Jean-Baptiste-Melchior Hertel de Rouville, ca. 1810
Oil on canvas
McCord Museum, Montreal M966.62.3

55.2 J.-B. Roy-Audy
Jean-Baptiste-René Hertel de Rouville, ca. 1830-1840
Oil on canvas
McCord Museum, Montreal M966.62.5

1. NA, Charles Henri Villebon Huot family papers, MG 24 K65. Except for the sources cited hereafter, all details pertaining to the Dumont biographies are derived from these papers.

2. The biographical data in the inscription on Jean-Baptiste's portrait is likely in Alphonse's handwriting (notable for poor spelling) along with the details of birth on his own portrait. The names of the artists (probably passed down orally) and Alphonse's death date may be in Adeline Huot's hand. She was Alphonse's niece and inherited all his possessions. When she died in 1894, she left her "family portraits" to her nephews Lucien and Arthur Huot.

3. P.-B. Casgrain, "Le Moulin de Dumont," *Bulletin des recherches historiques* 11 (March 1905): 65.

4. *La Petite Histoire. Paroisse Saint-Matthieu de Beloeil 1772-1972* (Beloeil: Comité des Fêtes du deuxième centenaire, 1972), 42.

5. A certain "Jean-Baptiste Dumont" was appointed lieutenant-colonel of the Canadian Militia in Quebec City at the time of the American invasion in 1775. Mentioned in the nominal roll on 13 October 1775, he had already been replaced by LeComte Dupré in the 16 December roll, and he did not serve during the American blockade. NA, British Military and Naval Records, RG 8 ID, Miscellaneous Records Relating to the Militia of the Town of Quebec 1775-1776, vols. 1714-1714A, microfilm, reel C-3840. Because of his high rank, we believe he is the father of our Jean-Baptiste, then aged twenty-six and living in Beloeil. Dumont Sr. resigned perhaps because of his age, but he was above all sympathetic to the American cause, even going so far as to lend money to the enemy army; his descendants would request reimbursement many times but without success.

6. André Giroux and Christina Cameron, "Du nouveau sur la maison Villebon," *Cahier no. 13 de la Société d'Histoire de Beloeil-Mont-Saint-Hilaire* (February 1984), 19. The name of the house is derived from the name of Clémentine Dumont's son, Charles-Henri-Vilbon Huot.

7. NA, Census Records, RG 31, 1825 Census for Saint-Joseph-de-Chambly, County of Chambly, p. 950, microfilm, reel C-717.

8. NA, RG 8 ID, List of Veterans of the War of 1812, vol. 1202, pp. 18 and 30, microfilm, reel C-3519.

9. *La Gazette de Quebec*, 6 March 1820, p. 1 and 5 July 1821, p. 2; Saint-Hilaire, and not Chambly, is given as his place of residence.

10. In 1828, he wrote to a local merchant on Rouville's behalf. Université de Montréal, Baby collection, NA, MG 24 L3, transcripts, p. 10546, A. Dumont to Eustache Soupras, 14 February 1828. During this period, Hertel de Rouville was a member of Parliament and was often absent. Dumont's title of manager is confirmed by Robert de Roquebrune, *Testament de mon enfance* (Montreal: Fides, 1979), 155, which sheds some doubt on Dumont's honesty.

11. NA, Lower Canada Land Petitions, RG 1 L3, vol. 3, General List of Petitions, p. 900, microfilm, reel C-2493; vol. 7, Scrip Book, p. 2230, microfilm, reel C-2494; vol. 77, Petitions, pp. 38754-38760, microfilm, reel C-2523.

12. Marie-Paule LaBrèque and Albert Rémillard, *Acton, Acton Vale, Saint-André d'Acton* (Acton Vale: Société d'Histoire des Six Cantons, 1984), 24.

13. *Petite Histoire*, 191.

14. NA, RG 31, 1851 Census for Beloeil, Verchères County, p. 7, microfilm, reel C-1149.

15. NA, Quebec and Lower Canada, S Series, RG 4 A1, vol. 524, letter from Jean-Baptiste-René Hertel de Rouville to Louis Juchereau Duchesnay, 16 November 1837. Colonel de Rouville sends the resignations of Alphonse Dumont and his brother-in-law, Charles Huot, a captain, but he adds that their letters were dictated to them. The reason they give is fear of reprisal if they refuse to conform to the people's orders. A general militia order, also dated 16 November, informs us that many resignations were the result of intimidation and as a result were not accepted. This was probably the case for Dumont and Huot, as no subsequent general order mentions their resignations. NA, Records of the Department of Militia and Defence, RG 9 IA 3, vol. 10, General Orders 1837-1839, microfilm, reel C-1528.

16. The portrait of Abbé Boissonnault at the Musée du Québec bears a similar old inscription, and this is sufficient for it to be considered an authentic work by Dulongpré. *Le Musée du Québec: 500 œuvres choisies* (Quebec: Gouvernement du Quebec, 1983), 57.

17. *Petite Histoire*, 60: excerpts from the parish accounts; these canvases disappeared when the church burned down in 1817.

18. NA, RG 8 ID, Order Books 1764-1894, vol. 1203, p. 23, microfilm, reel C-3521. Dulongpré was then major of the 3rd Select Embodied Militia.

19. Roy-Audy employed a similar contrast in his *Portrait of a Man*, n.d. (Art Gallery of Ontario 76/147).

20. J. Russell Harper, "La galerie de portraits de la famille Hertel de Rouville," *Vie des Arts* 47 (Summer 1967): 50 and 20 (Figs. 7 and 8).

21. We do not have proof of this visit, but we know that the painter moved around in order to fill orders, taking advantage of the hospitality of his clients. Michel Cauchon, *Jean-Baptiste Roy-Audy* (Quebec: Ministère des Affaires culturelles, 1971), 90.

R. S. M. Bouchette

LaFontaine

JEAN-JOSEPH GIROUARD (1794-1855)

57. *Robert-Shore-Milnes Bouchette*, ca. 1838

Pencil and charcoal, with stumping, on paper

23.5 x 19.0 cm

Inscribed in Bouchette's hand in pen and black ink, recto, b.: *R.S.M. Bouchette*

Purchased in 1984

Accession no.: 1984-81-13

Negative no.: C-18409

58. *Louis-Hippolyte LaFontaine*, ca. 1838-1839

Pencil and charcoal on paper

27.0 x 21.2 cm

Inscribed in LaFontaine's hand, in pen and black ink, recto, b.: *LaFontaine*

Purchased in 1984

Accession no.: 1984-81-50

Negative no.: C-18454

Jean-Joseph Girouard, a notary and patriote leader, has left us an unequalled visual testimony of the rebellions of 1837-1838 in Lower Canada, in the form of a series of portraits of the patriotes done, for the most part, in prison. Although some drawings were given to the patriotes or their families, most were carefully kept by the Girouard family.[1]

Girouard was born in Quebec City on 13 November 1794.[2] He lost his father when he was five, and spent part of his childhood with his maternal grandfather, the architect Jean Baillairgé, at whose side he learned the "rules of cubage and other things."[3] His cousins, François and Pierre-Florent Baillairgé, were both artists and may also have contributed to his artistic training. When Girouard was ten years old, his family left Quebec City for the Île d'Orléans, and then for Saint-Eustache near Montreal. Here he studied to become a notary and received his commission in 1816. He established a practice in the neighbouring village of Saint-Benoît, and in 1828 began to take an interest in politics.

When the rebellion of 1837 broke out, Girouard had been a member of Parliament for the constituency of Deux-Montagnes for six years. An admirer of Papineau and a friend of A.-N. Morin, he had helped draft the ninety-two resolutions, and had actively participated in the patriote movement. Girouard found the devastating defeat of the patriotes at Saint-Eustache abhorrent, and advised his fellow citizens at Saint-Benoît to return home rather than take part in another futile confrontation with government troops. So there was no battle at Saint-Benoît, but the village, including Girouard's house and office, was set on fire. With the threat of arrest hanging over him, he tried to escape to the United States, but on learning that most of his friends had been imprisoned, he in turn surrendered. He was imprisoned in Montreal on 26 December 1837, and was not freed until 16 July 1838, when Durham granted a general amnesty.

Girouard was imprisoned once more at the beginning of the abortive uprising of November 1838, and was not released until 27 December. These two incarcerations discouraged him from pursuing a political life, and he never again sought public office. He devoted the rest of his life to his legal profession and charitable works.

In addition to his portraits of the patriotes, Girouard has left us valuable testimony regarding conditions at the new jail at Pied-du-Courant in Montreal.[4] Conditions were not easy; writing of any kind, communication with other prisoners and visits were all forbidden. Many of the imprisoned patriotes, including Girouard himself, fell ill, and suffered anxiety and low morale in the face of their uncertain future. Later, when the rules were relaxed, Girouard lifted his spirits by keeping notes and drawing the portraits of his prison companions, at the same time preparing a defence for some of them.

We know the internal layout of the prison through a plan drawn by Girouard.[5] The cells in the central area, assigned to the patriote leaders, were the most spacious, and Girouard's adjoined that of R.-S.-M. Bouchette. The latter had painted several watercolours of his cell, and one would almost think he had a pleasant stay (Fig. 57.1). In his prison notes, however, Girouard speaks of some cells that had no bed or blankets, and of dark cells that were filthy and badly ventilated.[6]

The Girouard collection acquired by the National Archives consists of ninety-five items. There are ninety portraits by Girouard: eighty-seven of patriotes, plus portraits of the jailer, the prison bookkeeper, and a publisher of engravings from New York.[7] Included as well is a view of the ruins of Saint-Benoît, also by Girouard, and a portrait of Dr. J.-O. Chénier by the notary André Jobin, and two lithographs by patriote publisher Napoléon Aubin.

Having established the incarceration dates of the sitters, we are able to place the ninety portraits by Girouard into three distinct groups.[8] The first group, comprising sixty-seven drawings, can be linked to his first imprisonment, from December 1837 to July 1838. The second group consists of twelve drawings made during his second confinement, from November to December 1838. In the third group of eleven drawings, most of the subjects were either never in prison or were jailed at Quebec City and not with Girouard at Montreal.[9] Most of these portraits show a more careful workmanship than the "prison" ones.

Most of the drawings from the first stay bear the date of the sitter's imprisonment, his age, and his profession. The sitters are all identified on the drawings, whether by their signatures (as in the case of Cat. nos. 57 and 58) or by Girouard. Additional inscriptions written after the notary's death can be attributed to Judge Berthelot.[10]

We have attempted to establish the chronology of the portraits done during Girouard's first imprisonment by taking into account the incarceration dates of the sitters, and by analyzing the drawing paper, the compositions and the watermarks. While the chronology could not be established conclusively because many of the subjects and the artist were in prison for a long period (December

1837-July 1838), it is possible to offer a few hypotheses.

Girouard may have begun this group of portraits in January 1838. On the 13th of this month, he wrote his wife and asked her for his pastels and gray paper, but he never received the package.[11] As a result, all the drawings are done in pencil, most heightened with charcoal, a few with conté crayon, and one with red chalk. In many cases the charcoal was stumped, especially on the clothing. Twenty-five of these portraits, all from the first imprisonment, are on tracing paper, and all except one could date from January or February: the portrait of the jailer, Charles Wand, dated 7 February, is on this type of paper. Of the other drawings in this group, several are on coloured or heavy paper, although most of them are on good quality drawing paper, some with watermarks. We believe the artist first used tracing paper because that was all he had on hand, then found or received better quality paper. The drawings from the second prison stay are all on better quality paper.[12]

Most of the portraits depict the sitter's left profile. It is indeed easier to draw a subject in profile, and a right-handed person would more naturally draw a left profile than a right one. An examination of the original drawings reveals, in several cases, a faint pencil outline that is slightly shaky. The artist probably had his subjects sit in front of the wall, to which he had attached a sheet of paper, and then quickly drew the profile projected by their shadows. Many of the drawings still have pin marks, and we believe that badly placed lighting explains the elongated shape of many of the heads.

The two portraits featured here illustrate the two styles that are found in the Girouard collection. The portrait of R.-S.-M. Bouchette (Cat. no. 57), with its elongated profile, is typical of the "prison portraits," particularly those done during Girouard's first stay. That of LaFontaine (Cat. no. 58) is in the more accomplished style of portraits done outside prison, although LaFontaine's stay in prison overlaps Girouard's second imprisonment by a few weeks.

Robert-Shore-Milnes Bouchette (1805-1879), the fourth son of Joseph Bouchette, surveyor general for Lower Canada (see Cat. no. 50), was, like Girouard, as keenly interested in drawing as in law, and he had also studied cartography in New York.[13] After practising law for a few years in Quebec City, he became a professional cartographer and accompanied his father to Europe. It was only after his return from this trip that he became interested in politics and founded, in June 1837, the paper *Le Libéral-The Liberal.*

Arrested for the first time when unrest broke out, Bouchette was quickly released on bail and made his way to Vermont, where other patriotes had sought refuge. He was arrested on 6 December 1837 during the battle of Moore's Corner. Wounded in the foot and ill, he was sent to Montreal on a cart. On account of his poor health, he was given one of the best cells in the prison, and he spent his enforced leisure time painting his walls and ceiling.[14] He also painted several watercolours depicting the interior of his cell; one version belongs to the National Archives (Fig. 57.1), and two others to the Musée du Québec.

Condemned, along with seven other leading patriotes, to exile in Bermuda, Bouchette spent only a few months on the island. Then, still prohibited from returning to Canada, he practised law for a few years in Vermont. The amnesty of 1845 finally permitted him to return home, and he undertook a brilliant career as a public servant.

A second portrait of Bouchette by Girouard (Fig. 57.2) is in the collection of the Musée du Québec. Although it is slightly more polished than the National Archives portrait, it is difficult to confirm if one is a copy of the other, as both exhibit traces of the light, shaky outline mentioned earlier. While the Archives drawing bears Bouchette's signature, the other drawing was likely inscribed by Judge Berthelot.

Unlike Bouchette and Girouard, Louis-Hippolyte LaFontaine (1807-1864) did not take up arms during the rebellion. A lawyer and a member of Parliament for Terrebonne since 1830, he preferred the tools of democracy to violent action.[15] He went to London in December 1837 to seek a compromise with members of the British Parliament. On returning home, he defended his imprisoned friends, one of whom was Girouard. Arrested at the same time as Girouard, on 4 November 1838, he was freed a month later, as the authorities could find nothing with which to charge him.

LaFontaine continued his political career with even greater energy, fighting for, among other things, the pardon of the partriote leaders, which was finally granted in 1845. Four years later, he obtained for them pecuniary compensation for the losses they suffered. LaFontaine was then at the height of his career, having served as attorney-general and prime minister of Canada for a year. He resigned in 1851, however, only to be named chief justice two years later.

His contemporaries all noted his surprising physical resemblance to Emperor Napoleon I. Already aware of this when Girouard did his portrait, LaFontaine arranged his hair "à la Titus," as had his illustrious double.

L.D.

57.1 R.-S.-M. Bouchette
R.-S.-M. Bouchette in Prison,
ca. 1837-1838
Watercolour
NA C-21554

57.2 J.J. Girouard
Robert-Shore-Milnes Bouchette, ca. 1838
Pencil
Musée du Québec A 59.350 D

1. These drawings have had much public exposure. L.O. David chose several, reproduced as engravings, to illustrate his series of articles on the men of 1837-1838 in *L'Opinion publique*, 15 February to 27 September 1877 (Saturday editions). The collection then belonged to Judge Joseph-Amable Berthelot (1815-1897), Girouard's friend and brother-in-law. Following Berthelot's death, the collection was apparently remitted to the notary's descendants. In 1924, several reproductions of the drawings accompanied Louis-Joseph-Amédée Papineau's (Cat. no. 59) account of the rebellion, which was serialized under the title "La tragique épopée des Patriotes de 1837-38," *La Presse* (Montreal), 5 January to 24 May 1924 (Saturday editions). Other portraits were reprinted from *L'Opinion publique*. It was not until 1973 that the complete collection was published, albeit in a limited edition, by Clément Laurin, *Jean-Joseph Girouard et les Patriotes de 1837-38, Portraits* (Montreal: Bibliophile du Canadiana/Osiris, 1973). The NA purchased the original drawings in 1984: see Diane Tardif-Côté, "Portraits of the *patriotes* of 1837-1838...," *The Archivist*, vol. 12, no. 1 (January-February 1985), 12-13.

2. *Dictionary of Canadian Biography* (Toronto: University of Toronto Press, 1985), 8:330-334, entry for Jean-Joseph Girouard.

3. "Les journaux d'Emélie Berthelot-Girouard," *Rapport des Archives nationales du Québec, 1975* (Québec: Archives nationales du Québec, 1976), 22. Emélie Berthelot was the notary's second wife. For information about the Baillairgé family, see David Karel et al, *François Baillairgé et son oeuvre (1759-1830)* (Québec: Musée du Québec, 1975).

4. *Revue d'histoire de l'Amérique française* (RHAF) 21 (September 1967): 281-311; these documents are at the Institut d'histoire de l'Amérique française, in Outremont, Quebec. A number of Girouard's letters from prison have been published (see Laurin, bibliography).

5. *Nos Racines* 68 (1981): 1341. Previously attributed to Jobin, this plan was probably drawn by Girouard, Jobin contributing only the caption; see J.-J. Girouard to his wife (Marie-Louise Félix), 21 May 1838: *RHAF* 19 (December 1965): 463.

6. *RHAF* 21: 309.

7. The sitter is identified as "W. Hayward Publisher and Importer of English Engravings 74 Chamber St. New York," and the drawing is dated 15 February 1838. Hayward's inclusion among the patriote portraits is difficult to explain. It is possible that he was related to George Hayward, the New York lithographer, and may have come to Montreal to get portraits of the rebels for publication; perhaps he was considering Girouard's drawings.

8. The incarceration and release dates were taken from Laurin.

9. Girouard visited Quebec City in August 1838: NA, Papineau family papers, MG 24 B2, vol. 2, p. 3101, Louis Delagrave to Louis-Joseph Papineau, 28 August 1838.

10. See note 1.

11. J.-J. Girouard to his wife, 16 January 1838 (see *RHAF* 7 [June 1953]: 110). Unfortunately, all of his art materials for pastels as well as for miniature were lost when his house burned down; see Girouard's inventory of losses drawn up in 1846 (*RHAF* 21 [December 1967]: 478-479).

12. Ten portraits, including that of LaFontaine (Cat. no. 58), show evidence of sealing wax, either on the back or on the front; we believe it was already on the paper before Girouard used it.

13. *Dictionary of Canadian Biography* (Toronto: University of Toronto Press, 1972), 10:77-78, entry for R.-S.-M. Bouchette.

14. R.-S.-M. Bouchette, *Mémoires de Robert-S.-M. Bouchette, 1805-1840...* (Montreal: La Cie de publication de la Revue Canadienne, 1903), 56 ff.

15. *Dictionary of Canadian Biography* (Toronto: University of Toronto Press, 1976), 9:440-451, entry for L.-H. LaFontaine.

Me voilà, avec mes longs cheveux & ma casaque, ma canne de jonc & mon chapeau
de paille, car nous
sommes en été. Selon la
coutume de tous les
grands auteurs modernes,
il est très convenable,
j'allais dire indispensable,
que mon portrait & ma
signature autographe
figurent à la tête de mes
Oeuvres. Hum! Hum!!
Augte Edouart fecit 1840
Saratoga

AUGUSTE EDOUART (1788-1861)

59. *Louis-Joseph-Amédée Papineau*, 15 July 1840

Cut paper silhouettes with pencil

23.6 x 19.3 cm

Inscribed in the artist's hand, in pen and blue ink, recto, l.c.: *Augt Edouart fecit 1840 / Saratoga-;* in Papineau's hand, in pen and black ink, recto, l.r.: *LJA Papineau dit Montigny*; t. and u.r.: *Me voilà, avec mes longs cheveux & ma casaque, ma canne de jonc & mon chapeau / de paille, car nous / sommes en été. Selon la / coutume de tous les / grands auteurs modernes, / il est très convenable / j'allais dire indispensable, / que mon portrait & ma / signature autographe / figurent à la tête de mes / Œuvres. Hum! Hum!!*

Donated in 1980

Accession no.: 1982-110-1

Negative no.: C-136454

The dapper young man shown in this silhouette was the eldest son of the patriote Louis-Joseph Papineau. Like his father, Amédée (fully, Louis-Joseph-Amédée) was a fervent supporter of the French-Canadian cause in Lower Canada (Quebec), and in 1837, at only eighteen years of age, he was a founding member of the Fils de la Liberté, an association of young patriote reformists. By November of that year, the growing militancy of the patriotes provoked the colonial authorities, who began arresting its leaders in an attempt to curtail further insurrection. Under the threat of arrest for high treason, Louis-Joseph Papineau took refuge in the officially neutral United States. Amédée was also at risk of arrest, and on family orders followed his father into self-imposed exile. Posing as Joseph Parent, a student going to the States to learn English, he crossed into Vermont on 9 December 1837. Although Amédée was anxious to be involved in the efforts of the patriotes, his father arranged for him to study law with a Mr. Ellsworth at Saratoga Springs, New York. Upon his arrival there, he was welcomed by the first ranks of society, and found sympathetic company among those of republican conviction.

By March 1838 Amédée had started a diary which he titled "Journal d'un Fils de la Liberté réfugié aux Etats-Unis par suite de L'Insurrection Canadienne en 1837" (Diary of a Son of Liberty, taken refuge in the United States following the Canadian insurrection in 1837), which is one of the most vivid and lively accounts of the events of the rebellion, and, in particular, of the activities of the patriotes in the United States. His diary entries also reveal the intensity of his commitment to the patriote cause and the great sense of adventure he experienced during those turbulent years. He continued his diary until 1855, by which time it consisted of seven volumes. These are now in the collection of the National Archives of Canada.

Apart from his law studies and his diary, the young Amédée spent his self-imposed exile reading, visiting, hunting, fishing, and attending lectures and various church services, including those of the Shakers and the Baptists, whose rituals were a great curiosity to the young Catholic. Ingenious in his pursuit of worthwhile activities, he also became a teacher of French at a school for young ladies.

While Amédée's diaries reveal that he sometimes found himself at loose ends during the long winter months, the summer season at Saratoga Springs was anything but dull. It was, and is still, a favourite summer watering hole for those seeking health, amusement and society. The town's grand hotels and mineral springs attracted the great, the near-great, the well-heeled and the fashionable, as well as those who sought the advantage of their company and commerce. Apart from taking the healing waters, visitors amused themselves gambling, sightseeing, attending entertainments and otherwise enjoying the languorous and convivial atmosphere. Among those whose talents were put at their disposal was Auguste Edouart, a French-born silhouette artist, who would cut a portrait silhouette in black paper for a very reasonable fee.

Amédée's diary records that on 15 July 1840 he made a visit to Edouart, who cut his profile, which Amédée autographed, signing it "LJA Papineau dit Montigny," Montigny being an archaic sobriquet that his family had once used and Amédée had recently revived.[1] Edouart gave Amédée this copy of the silhouette (Cat. no. 59), which he mounted into the appendix to his "Journal d'un Fils de la Liberté" as a sort of frontispiece. He acknowledges this conceit in the note he wrote beside it: "Like all great modern authors, it is appropriate, indeed obligatory, that my portrait and signature should appear at the beginning of this work." The silhouette of the dog is one of several such given to Amédée by Edouart a few weeks later on 3 August; this he mounted beside his own silhouette to good effect.[2]

Edouart also cut a silhouette of Jules Lamothe, a friend of Amédée's and fellow Fils de la Liberté, who was visiting Saratoga (Fig. 59.1). The silhouette was cut on 16 July 1840, and is noted in Amédée's diary entry for that date. Their common language and interests appear to have drawn the artist and the young patriote together. Amédée mentions Edouart several times in his diary during the summer of 1840; on 19 July he and Lamothe accompany Edouart on an afternoon walk; on 25 July Edouart introduces Amédée to Mr. Bihin, the Belgian giant (one of the attractions at the Springs); and on 2 August he goes hunting with Edouart and his son Alexandre, who is accidentally shot in the hand, thus prompting several days of visits to the patient.

In the same year Edouart also cut the silhouettes of the James R. Westcott family of Saratoga Springs, which he mounted together on the same sheet (Fig. 59.2). It shows James R. Westcott, his second wife Mary Wayland seated at her needle work, her step-daughter Mary Westcott stands behind her holding a bouquet of flowers; James Westcott Jr. stands beside his father holding a bow and arrow (he was to die eight months later at the age of twelve). Mary Westcott was one of Amédée's pupils at the school for young ladies, and he soon became a frequent visitor to the Westcott home. Only after Amédée returned home to Canada in 1843 did he propose marriage to Mary, who swore to him that as a true Yankee she would ever be a "disloyal subject of her serene Highness [Queen Victoria]," and would so make a fitting wife for the young French-Canadian nationalist.[3] Amédée and Mary (or Marie, as she signed her letters to him) were married in 1846 (Fig. 59.3).

While at Saratoga, Edouart also cut the silhouettes of other visitors from Canada, including the merchants Jean-Baptiste Beaudry of Montreal and Frederick Wyse of Quebec City; a priest, Louis-Misaël Archambault; the banker and politician, Peter McGill; the Sheriff of Montreal, John Boston; and three government officials: Dominick Daly, Edward Dowling and Thomas C. Murdochs (Fig. 59.4). Ironically, several of these were government officials in Lower Canada and opponents of the rebellion. Dominick Daly, for instance, was the provincial secretary whose name appears on the 1837 reward poster offering $4,000 for the apprehension of Amédée's father. While Edouart is not known to have taken their silhouettes, Amédée's diary recounts his meetings with William Lyon Mackenzie, the rebel leader from Upper Canada (Ontario), as well as the patriote leaders Dr. O'Callaghan, Robert Nelson and Dr. Davignon, among others. He also notes from a distance the arrival at Saratoga of Edward Ellice, secretary to Lord Durham, who had been held captive by the patriotes at Beauharnois (Cat. no. 52), and Andrew Stuart, solicitor-general of Lower Canada. It is a curious fact that this genial summer spa played host to rebel, government official and British soldier, who took refuge and respite from the natural, as well as the political climate of Lower Canada.

Edouart's silhouette of Amédée, cut in the holiday atmosphere of Saratoga, makes an interesting contrast to the portrait drawings made by Jean-Joseph Girouard in the Montreal jail in 1838 (Cat. nos. 57-58). Girouard produced some ninety bust-length profiles of patriotes imprisoned during the rebellion in Lower Canada. They are more intimate in nature and appear to be a conscious effort to record the personalities involved in this important event. By comparison, Edouart's silhouettes seek to distinguish the public persona of the sitter. Edouart individualized each portrait and displayed his virtuosity in cutting and clipping the carriage, coiffure and accoutrements of the sitters. Through gesture and the addition of props such as a book, flowers, eyeglasses, or – in the case of Amédée – a hat and cane, Edouart added variety and charm to his portraits. The silhouette of Amédée has a certain grace and daintiness, which characterized Edouart's work. His particular "signature" is the skewed and somewhat levitated placement of the delicate pointed feet of the gentlemen subjects.

It is these details of costume and profile that make silhouettes valuable early sources of information for fashion, especially as worn by the rising businessman and prosperous middle class. The young Amédée, preparing himself for a career in law and a place in the ascending professional class, was no less interested in fashion. Amédée's inscription on the silhouette reads in part, "Here I am, with my long hair, my jacket, my bamboo cane and my straw hat, because it is summer." Amédée wears his hair in a fashionable and almost daring length usually favoured by young men. In 1838, he recorded in his diary his unsuccessful attempt to style his own hair in the latest fashion; undaunted two years later, he designed and had made a summer coat which he calls his "casaque de chasseur" (hunting jacket).[4] It is possibly this very jacket that he wears in the silhouette. It is a fashionable frock coat with full-cut front, narrow waist, generous skirt and tightly gathered sleeves. His trousers are narrow and probably fastened with a strap under the instep, creating a very trim appearance. The feet appear long and narrow, giving the effect of being neat and small, as dictated by the fashion of the day. He holds a broad-brimmed, low-crowned straw hat, suitable headgear for a country setting or the casual holiday milieu of Saratoga Springs. His sporty Malacca, or bamboo walking-stick, was also very much the fashion.[5]

In all, Amédée cuts a fine figure and strikes a very jaunty pose, though he certainly is not as dandified as some of the denizens of Saratoga Springs described by Capt. Henry James Warre (Cat. no. 40) in his diary. Warre, a British Army Officer posted to Canada, visited Saratoga Springs in August of 1842 and observed that many of the gentlemen "dressed in the outré French style, beards and moustaches predominate.... they do not act the character so well as they dress it." He called them "overdressed fops."[6] Whatever the cut of their clothes, Edouart created thousands of silhouettes of the clergy, soldiers, doctors, lawyers, politicians, scientists, journalists and entertainers, and their various wives, sisters and children, among others, who called upon him to immortalize their profiles.

Throughout the first half of the nineteenth century, the demand for inexpensive portraits, especially by the rising middle classes, created a market for the silhouette artist. Portrait painters and miniature artists also filled the need, but their rates were considerably more than that paid for a paper silhouette. Silhouette artists were usually itinerants who travelled from town to town and frequented events and natural attractions that drew large crowds. Edouart had practised his craft through Britain and Ireland, and moved on to the United States in 1839 in search of fresher audiences. His travels took him to many of the larger eastern cities, in particular New York, Philadelphia, Boston, Washington and Louisville. However, it was at Saratoga Springs that he spent most summers catering to the assembled holidayers.

Most silhouette artists were lesser talents than Edouart and sometimes employed tracing or copying contraptions to draw or cut the profile of a client. Edouart, without doubt one of the finest silhouette artists of the time, worked free-hand and with astonishing speed. Using delicate scissors, he cut his silhouettes from thin paper coloured in solid black on one side and left white on the other. The sheet was folded in half with the white side outward. He then cut the folded paper, creating two identical silhouettes simultaneously. One was mounted on plain paper, or on a painted or printed background (see Fig. 59.2) for the client. Often Edouart mounted several silhouettes together on a single sheet, creating a charming grouping as in the case of the Westcott family (Fig. 59.2). The second copy of the silhouette was kept for the artist's collection of duplicates. Upon request, he could provide a copy of any silhouette for which he had a duplicate, much in the same way as a photographer makes prints from a stock of negatives.[7] One could, for instance, have additional silhouettes of loved ones cut, or even order a silhouette of a prominent person such as President Martin Van Buren, whose likeness Edouart had in stock. On principle, however, he would not copy a silhouette of a lady without her permission, thus discouraging any admirer from secretly obtaining a portrait of the object of his desire. Edouart kept meticulous records, and in his *Treatise on Silhouette Likenesses* (London and Cork, 1835) he explains that this was necessary to prevent any confusion over the identity of the sitters, and to allow potential customers examining his albums to readily identify the portraits, especially those of the most prominent subjects. He wrote the name of the person, the date, and often the hometown and profession, in four different places – first, on the back of the duplicate silhouette; second, in his day book; third, in the album where the duplicate was subsequently mounted, and fourth, in a general index. Edouart also kept a diary where he recorded his activities, allowing him to keep track of the number of different silhouettes he produced, whether full length, children, duplicates, public character, busts or animals. In his words "all this is done by myself to avoid mistakes," so obsessive was he. In his *Treatise* he notes that his operation entailed the care, inventory control and transport of three tons of frames and duplicate albums; as well, he had to set up his exhibition of silhouettes in order to attract customers, and to place advertisements in local newspapers announcing his arrival and his rates. His regime also required him to abstain from strong teas, coffee, spirits and any other excitements that he felt would make his hand unsteady.

Edouart complained at length in his *Treatise* that he endured much labour and many privations in order to pursue and improve his art, but met with cautious acknowledgement from the more refined members of society. He got no respect and little social status. This apparent reticence on the part of others was real as much as imagined. Capt. Henry James Warre, mentioned earlier, encountered Edouart during his 1842 visit to Saratoga and left the following account in his diary:

> That amusing rascal Monr. Edouard [*sic*] the silhouettist was taking likenesses & clipping away as usual. He did me the honor of recognizing me, but I had certain misgivings about his proceedings in Dublin[8]; & did not take much interest in him. He is wonderfully clever, with his scissors, however; & his collection of portraits is enormous."[9]

Despite his tenacity in pursuing his occupation, the introduction of photography to the United States in 1839, the very year of Edouart's own arrival, made his efforts futile in the end. The daguerreotype photograph, although not as inexpensive as Edouart's silhouettes, had the appeal of a new and important invention that gave startlingly realistic likenesses. While several portrait artists took up the new medium of photography, Edouart persisted with his silhouettes. In the face of this new competition, the demand for Edouart's services declined after 1845, and in 1849 he returned to England, carrying with him approximately 60,000 silhouette portraits mounted in about fifty albums chronicling his career in England, Scotland, Ireland and America. Unfortunately, all but sixteen of his albums were lost at sea when the ship on which he was travelling was wrecked off the Guernsey coast. He recovered from this disaster under the care of the Lukis family of Guernsey and gave them the salvaged albums as a sign of his gratitude. Disheartened, broken and abandoning his profession, Edouart returned to his home country France, where he died in 1861; by this time, ironically, his son Alexandre had established himself as a photographer in San Francisco.

The remnants of Edouart's work remained with the Lukis family until 1911, when it was discovered by the silhouette enthusiast and historian Emily Jackson. She purchased the collection, and in turn gave or sold many of Edouart's duplicate silhouettes to private individuals and to national institutions. In 1912, the National Archives of Canada acquired sixteen silhouettes of Canadians from Mrs. Jackson, including some of those noted earlier. Many Canadian, American and British museums have examples of Edouart's work, but it would be rare to find one like that of the young Amédée Papineau, whose history and import is still intact.

Soon after his silhouette was cut, Amédée was admitted to the Bar of New York State and practised law for two years in New York City before returning to Canada in 1843, thus ending his four-year exile. He pursued his profession for thirty-two years in Montreal, and following his retirement he moved to the family seigneury at Montebello on the Ottawa River. Upon his death in 1903, he was remembered for his interest in literature and his political writing, as well as for his involvement with the rebellion of 1837 during his youth. Edouart's silhouette of Amédée is a unique record of this confident and spirited young patriote, taken during the formative years of his life.

L.F.

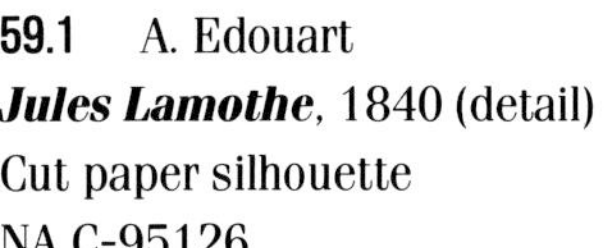
59.1 A. Edouart
Jules Lamothe, 1840 (detail)
Cut paper silhouette
NA C-95126

59.2 A. Edouart
The Westcott Family, 1840
Cut paper silhouettes
Musée du Québec 87.35

59.3 Attributed to O.B. Evans
Amédée Papineau and his wife Mary Westcott, ca. 1851
Daguerreotype
NA C-79115

59.4 A. Edouart
Peter McGill, John Boston and Frederick Wyse, 1843
Cut paper silhouettes
NA C-95131

1. In his diary entry of 7 March 1838, Amédée notes his intention of using the old family name of Montigny, referring to the village in Fance where the family originated. NA, Papineau family papers, MG 24 B2, vol. 32, "Journal d'un Fils de la Liberté," vol. 2, p. 28.

2. For preservation reasons, the NA has removed the page bearing the silhouette from the "Journal."

3. NA, Mary Eleanore Westcott papers, MG 24 K58, letter from Mary Westcott to Amédée Papineau, 12 March 1846.

4. NA, MG 24 B2, vol. 32, "Journal," vol. 2, p. 34, entry for 9 April 1838, and vol. 3, p. 25, entry for 25 May 1840.

5. In 1838, Amédée was given a walking cane cut from Navy Island in the Niagara River, which was briefly the headquarters of rebel leaders in Upper Canada in January of the same year. We can assume that the bamboo cane he sports in the silhouette is not the one from Navy Island, since it is unlikely that it was bamboo. NA, MG 24 B2, vol. 32, "Journal," vol. 2, p. 66, entry for 3 September 1838.

6. NA, Henry James Warre papers, MG 24 F71, vol. 8, "Journal of a trip to Saratoga, August 1842," p. 660, and vol. 11, "Saratoga, August 1842," p. 832.

7. A copy of the silhouette of James Westcott Jr. holding a bow was mounted as a single silhouette (example in the Musée du Québec), while another copy was included as part of the family portrait as shown in Fig. 59.2.

8. The nature of the proceeding in Dublin is not known; however, Edouart is known to have challenged a noted pugilist to a fight while in Ireland.

9. NA, MG 24 F71, "Journal," vol. 8, pp. 674-675.

A PLACE IN HISTORY

Our Times: Art as Record in the 20th Century

The National Archives' acquisition of twentieth-century art has been influenced by the predominance of photography as a medium of record, and by the changing nature of visual exploration in this century. Adjusting to these factors, we have sought out contemporary art that is representational in style, or whose subjects or manner of expression reflects our values and way of life. For instance, our recently acquired portraits of the Dionne Quintuplets and Wayne Gretzky reveal more about their status as cultural icons than they do about their actual appearance, which is often better shown in photographs.

Our on-going acquisitions of posters and other graphic designs reflect the prevalence of commercial art in shaping and responding to fundamental values of modern life. The establishment of the Canadian Museum of Caricature by the National Archives has put a special emphasis on the acquisition of editorial cartoons — the artist's daily response to the changing scene. As a complement to collections of artists' papers held by the National Archives, we have also acquired works that document their activities and careers.

We continue to explore avenues of collecting twentieth-century works of art that will help to document our times and leave a legacy of information and enjoyment for future generations.

TO LET

ERNST NEUMANN (1907-1956)

60. *Victims of the Depression in Canada*, 1933

Pencil with pen and black ink on paper

42.5 x 31.2 cm

Inscribed in pencil, recto, u.r.: *TO LET/* [illegible]; l.r.: *E. Neumann. '33*

Purchased in 1970

Acquisition no.: 1970-96-1

Negative no.: C-43500

Born in Budapest of Austrian parents, Ernst Neumann arrived in Montreal at the age of five. After advanced studies in drawing, including one or two years at Montreal's new École des beaux-arts (opened in September 1923), he worked for a time in a commercial printing firm, where he discovered etching and lithography; at the time, he modelled his work on Rembrandt, Goya and Daumier, three great observers of the human condition and skilled engravers. This short-lived job, of which little is known, occurred before 1932, following which he ran an art school with his friend Goodridge Roberts (1904-1974) between 1936 and 1938.[1] Neumann managed to make a living of sorts from his artistic output, especially prints,[2] and began in the late 1930s to produce portraits and landscapes in oil. A friend remembers that Neumann rode his bicycle past the law offices on St. James Street whistling bits of classical music and offering his prints to members of the bar;[3] he even made gentle fun of them in a series of etchings produced in the 1940s. Using his own press, he printed his engravings on order, and even published an illustrated catalogue of his etchings.[4]

Neumann's talent was very quickly recognized by the public and critics, who frequently had occasion to view his works. In addition to his regular submissions to the spring exhibition of the Art Association of Montreal and the annual exhibition of the Royal Canadian Academy of Arts, he participated in many solo and small group exhibits. In 1939, he applied for a Guggenheim grant, which would have enabled him to study for one year in the United States, but the outcome of this application is unknown.[5] In any event, he did not go to the United States, and it was not until 1955 that he obtained a development grant from the Royal Society of Canada. He settled in Paris, but was struck down by a heart attack and died in March of the following year while vacationing at Vence in the south of France.

Victims of the Depression in Canada (Cat. no. 60) was produced in the darkest year of the Depression, 1933. The source of the title is unknown, since Neumann left it untitled, and no corresponding engraving has been found.[6] However, the title is quite in keeping with the young Neumann's sensibilities. As early as 1931, his friend Leo Kennedy, the poet, noted the artist's deep interest in the human condition, an interest he attributed in particular to members of the Jewish community.[7] That year, at the Royal Canadian Academy, Neumann exhibited a lithograph showing an unemployed man. In 1933, the same date as *Victims of the Depression*, he exhibited two more lithographs of the unemployed, which he titled *Unemployed #4* and *Unemployed #5*.[8] In the interim, arts patron F.N. Southam had made a gift of the first three prints in the series to the National Gallery of Canada. The complete series consists of seven lithographs, all showing one or two men seated, reading a newspaper or pondering their fate (Fig. 60.1). These very topical prints proved quite successful, and some were reproduced in newspapers and on the cover of a Canadian government brochure.[9]

We know from Neumann's titles that the men in these images are unemployed, but during the Depression years such labels were unnecessary. The unemployed were everywhere and represented more than twenty-five percent of the labour force in Canada. The estimated unemployment rate in Montreal, a large industrial city, was even higher.[10] After the October 1929 crash, many companies had to cut back production, and many others simply went bankrupt. The number of unemployed grew rapidly and, for the first time, governments at all levels had to provide assistance to able workers. The initial programs consisted of job creation in public works projects, but local governments, which had difficulty collecting taxes (since so many taxpayers were unemployed), lacked the funds. In addition to paid labour, this work required specialized equipment and tools. Charitable organizations were not up to the task, and the various levels of government had virtually no social policies.

In 1933, Direct Relief was introduced, with the distribution of vouchers that could be exchanged for goods, but this system generated so many administrative costs that it was quickly replaced in Montreal by a single monthly cheque to cover basic needs — heating, food, and later, housing, electricity and clothing. In that same year, an estimated thirty percent of the population of Montreal,[11] the unemployed and their dependents, were on Direct Relief, a difficult and demoralizing situation for many family heads.

The Great Depression was more than just an economic crisis. For many, the very survival of their families was a constant concern. Amusements were rare and, like radio or the movies, too expensive. The situation was a little better for those able to keep their jobs, but all had to accept wage cuts; however, the cost of living did decline.[12]

Neumann's drawing shows a group of people in the front doorway of their Montreal home. We do not know if they were acquaintances of the artist or people he asked to pose at random.[13] However, the strong narrative quality of the drawing invites us to speculate on the scene. We can imagine that it is summer, or at least a warm day, and the relaxation taken on the stoop is their only respite from their tenement. The young father (unemployed?) and mother look with concern on their child and, in turn, their hope for the future. The old gentleman (perhaps the child's grandfather) is similar to Neumann's lithographs of the unemployed (Fig. 60.1).[14] His sad face, asleep or lost in thought, and his dejected posture offer no resistance to the gloomy circumstances. The gaunt faces and ill-fitting clothes are evidence of their dire situation. A sign next to the door advertises a flat for rent; is it theirs? Have they, like so many others of their day, been given an eviction notice by their landlord? Landlords also had to manage as best they could through the Depression. They often tried to rid themselves of tenants who could no longer pay, and they often succeeded, despite the intervention of charities and relief agencies (Fig. 60.2). Many tenants obtained one or two months' grace from their landlord, and if they still could not pay, vanished quickly, usually in the night.

Given this steady turnover in tenants, many landlords no longer bothered to take down "to let" signs. Though they were not particularly interested in tenants on relief, some less scrupulous ones saw an advantage in accommodating them, since the city paid on time. Landlords would even raise the rent on substandard housing up to the amount of the monthly relief allowance.[15]

Yet housing, the theme suggested by *Victims of the Depression*, was only one aspect of the difficult and precarious life endured by many Canadians for ten long years. The situation began to improve very slowly in 1934, but only after Canada entered World War II did the country again achieve full employment, and workers gain better security, thanks in part to introduction of a true system of social security.

Several authors have noted in their works on the Depression the lack of visual records showing its victims.[16] This drawing by Neumann gains importance as direct evidence of a difficult time and its effect on ordinary people. Neumann applied himself diligently in all media, and was very careful to render what he observed with the most meticulous realism. He was sometimes criticized for the "classicism" of his works and their apparent lack of emotion. Although he considered art an exercise in intellect rather than passion, this does not prevent us from responding to his evocative subjects. As a struggling young artist, he had an obvious and deep respect for those who suffered during the Depression.

T.Mc. and L.D.

60.1 E. Neumann
Unemployed No. 7, 1934
Lithograph
NA C-136014

60.2
An eviction in a slum district during the Depression, Montreal, Quebec, c. 1930
Photograph
NA C-30811

1. The Roberts-Neumann School of Art consisted more of informal meetings than traditional courses. Students worked from a live model, and if Neumann lacked the money to pay for a model, he asked one of his students to pose for the class (from information conveyed to the authors by Madeleine Boyer, Alma Duncan and Beatrice Day-Rosseau, February 1989). After this school closed, Neumann kept the premises on Greene Street in Westmount (Montreal) as a studio until his departure for Paris in 1955.

2. Neumann, who lived with his mother, never married. He moved often, but never lived in the Jewish neighbourhood of Montreal, although he was a frequent visitor. Like Louis Muhlstock from the same period, he found several of his unemployed models in Fletcher's Field (now Parc Jeanne-Mance). His practice of never working as a commercial artist is generally attributed to his striving for artistic integrity. During the war, however, he did try to serve his country as an illustrator or camouflage artist, but in vain. National Gallery of Canada, Canadian War Records Applications, 5.41-W, section N-P, Ernst Neumann file, Neumann to H.O. McCurry, director of the National Gallery, 25 March 1941 and 17 November 1942.

3. Harry Mayerovitch, "The Work of the Late Ernst Neumann," *Congress Bulletin* 13 (February 1959): 3.

4. *Etchings by Neumann* (Montreal: Quebec Graphic Arts, n.d.), illustrated.

5. National Gallery of Canada, Correspondence with artists, 7.1-N, Ernst Neumann file, Neumann to H.O. McCurry, 16 October 1939.

6. The fact that Neumann retraced the outline of the drawing in pen and ink suggests that he intended to produce a print, probably an etching, a medium in which he used areas of cross-hatching to render values (similar to that seen in this drawing). His lithographs, on the other hand, were rendered by varying the pressure of a grease pencil on a printing stone. For comparison, see Denis Martin, *L'Estampe au Québec, 1900-1950* (Quebec: Musée du Québec, 1988), 116 (illustration of *The Strong Man*, lithograph, 1931) and 117 (illustration of *Nu féminin vu de dos*, etching, 1946). If Neumann had planned to use *Victims of the Depression* as a model for an etching, he would have had to reverse the lettering on the "To Let" sign on his printing plate in order for it to appear correctly on the finished print.

7. Leo Kennedy, "Portrait of an Artist. Ernest Newman Sits for an Intimate Sketch," *The Jewish Standard* (Toronto), 12 June 1931, p. 589. It was not until 1932 that Neumann returned to the German spelling of his name. At a recent exhibition, Esther Trépanier studied in detail the concerns and works of Montreal's Jewish artists. Although the collective hardship of the Depression provided many artists with an opportunity to divert their attention from nature to their city (which they couldn't afford to leave in any event) and its inhabitants, the experience of the Jewish people made them even more predisposed to "take an interest in the misery and suffering inherent in the human condition": Esther Trépanier, *Jewish Painters and Modernity, Montreal 1930-1945* (Montreal: Centre Saidye-Bronfman, 1987), 44.

8. E. de R. McMann, *Royal Canadian Academy of Arts / Académie royale des arts du Canada: exhibitions and members, 1880-1979* (Toronto: University of Toronto Press, 1981), 302. *Unemployed*, exhibited in 1931, is unnumbered, but *Unemployed #1* and *Unemployed #2* are both dated 1931.

9. Trépanier, 48.

10. P.A. Linteau, R. Durocher et al., *Histoire du Québec contemporain* (Montreal: Boréal, 1986), 2:75.

11. Linteau, 76. Thirty percent represented precisely 44,480 families in a total population of 818,577 (1931 census), but not all ethnic groups suffered equally. While 38 percent of French-speaking Montrealers were affected, only 17 percent of Protestant or Catholic English-speaking Montrealers and 9 percent of the Jewish community fell into this group. Michiel Horn, ed., *The Dirty Thirties. Canadians in the Great Depression* ([Toronto]: Copp Clark Publishing Co., 1972), 255.

12. In 1930, a radio receiver and wooden cabinet cost $99 in Eaton's catalogue. In the 1932-1933 Fall-Winter edition, ladies' day dresses were offered at prices ranging from $5.95 to $10, and three-piece men's suits sold for $15 to $20, a drop from the price of these items in the 1929-1930 catalogue. Between 1926 and 1933, the cost of living declined by an estimated twenty-five percent: L.M. Grayson and M. Bliss, eds., *The Wretched of Canada. Letters to R.B. Bennett 1930-1935* (Toronto: University of Toronto Press, 1971), vi. Relief cheques in Montreal ranged from $3.16 a week for a family of three to $6.43 a week for a family of nine: Linteau, 80. The typical suggested menu for relief recipients totalled $4.58 a week in 1932 for a family of five; a loaf of bread cost 6 cents, a quart of milk 10 cents, and a standard quality roast of beef 13 cents a pound: Paul Mennill, *The Depression Years: Canada in the 1930s* (Scarborough: Prentice-Hall of Canada, 1978), 6.

13. This drawing appears to have had special significance for Neumann or someone else (the provenance of the drawing is unknown), since the corners, especially at the top, are pierced with many thumbtack holes, evidence that it was tacked to a wall for a long time with no protection.

14. Neumann's *Unemployed* are all viewed from a distance and in profile, just as in his engraving *The Park* (1931), an old Jew is seated on a bench, lost in his thoughts. Only a blind man in a 1935 drawing (National Gallery of Canada collection) is shown from a closer vantage point, perhaps because the artist was less fearful of disturbing his model. These works form an interesting comparison to those of Louis Muhlstock, a Montreal Jewish artist who shared Neumann's humanism but was not afraid to work very close to his models, whether they were unemployed or ill, sharing with us his love of humanity and his great compassion.

15. Linteau, 77-78; see also Barry Broadfoot, *Ten Lost Years, 1929-1939. Memories of Canadians Who Survived the Depression* (Don Mills: Paper Jacks, 1975), 178-179 (for information concerning Montreal) and James H. Gray, *The Winter Years. The Depression on the Prairies* (Toronto: Macmillan of Canada, 1966), 58-62 (for information concerning Winnipeg).

16. Gray, xi. For example, the photograph (Fig. 60.2) is used often, apparently because it is one of a few showing such scenes from the Depression.

DAVID BROWN MILNE (1882-1953)

61. *E.B. Eddy Mill, Hull, Quebec*, 1923

Watercolour and drybrush over pencil on paper

37.0 x 54.3 cm

Inscribed in brushpoint and watercolour, recto, u.r.: *DAVID B. MILNE DEC. 1923*; in pen and black ink, verso, u.l.: *# 150.*

Gift of Mrs. J.P. Barwick from the Douglas M. Duncan collection, 1978

Accession no.: 1978-34-1

Negative no.: C-96261

E.B. Eddy Mill, Hull, Quebec is one of only a few works painted by David Milne during his stay in Ottawa in the winter of 1923-1924. Using a drybrush technique, Milne employed a limited range of colours applied directly without mixing or diluting them. The watercolour is applied in a precise, linear manner, leaving large areas of blank paper. The rich, earthy colours capture the atmosphere of the heavy industry and the greyness of a late autumn day.

This watercolour is a fine example of Milne's work during his brief stay in Ottawa. The subject matter of this watercolour is also important, as it documents the architectural and industrial development of Canada's capital city and its neighbour, Hull, Quebec, during the early 1920s. The buildings and smokestacks of the mills are confined to the bottom half of the composition, while the white expanse of the sky carries great billowing clouds of smoke. The Parliament Buildings can be seen across the Ottawa River, rising steeply from the riverbank. Behind, the Château Laurier hotel is silhouetted against the sky.

A Canadian by birth, David Milne had spent the twenty years prior to 1923 in the United States, arriving first in New York in 1903 to study painting. When the commercial art school in which he had enrolled closed down after he had been there only a few weeks, Milne studied at the Art Students' League under Frank Dumond and George Bridgman. Although Milne was dissatisfied with the instruction he received there, the League was situated in the same building as the American Water Color Society and the New York Water Color Club. Here he saw the work of more avant-garde artists, and he began to exhibit with them in 1909.[1]

Finding the city life of New York too hectic, Milne searched for a quieter, scenic residence with his wife, Patsy, in Boston Corners, New York. This was soon interrupted by the advent of World War I. Fulfilling his patriotic duties, Milne enlisted in the Canadian Army in 1918, and to his surprise he was accepted.[2] The next year in Great Britain, Milne sought and was awarded a commission with the Canadian War Records Office. It was in the works executed for this purpose that Milne first employed the drybrush technique.[3]

Milne returned to Boston Corners by the winter of 1919, but he continued his search for a place where he could live cheaply and paint. Over the next four years he and Patsy lived at Dart Lake, Mount Riga and Big Moose Lake, all small towns in the Adirondack Mountains in northern New York State. In the fall of 1923, Milne decided to go to Ottawa, where he hoped to teach art and to submit work to the National Gallery of Canada for inclusion in the British Empire Exhibition at Wembley in 1924.[4] When he first got to Ottawa, he wrote to his good friend James Clarke about his new accommodations:

> Living appears to be very cheap here compared with Big Moose.... I pay $3 a week for a very large room, clean, warm light – with a picture of the Virgin on one side at the head of my bed, and Christ crowned with thorns at the other.[5]

The next month, Milne rented a live-in studio in an office building, the Butterworth Building, at 197 Sparks Street, which he described as "high, light, heated, in which I can both work and sleep (in due order I hope) eat if I like – $16 a month."[6] Two other artists, Ernest Fosbery and Graham Norwell, also lived in the same building.[7]

Milne wrote to Clarke about the progress of his painting:

> [I] have got permission to sketch practically everywhere and everyone in Ottawa .... As to the pictures these days I have made only two – both of the parliament buildings. One is no good and one has some promise. I am anxious to see what the change of subject will do. It hasn't done anything yet but I have some inklings particularly in the direction of night drawings.[8]

Returning to the same letter a few days later, Milne added, "One more picture on the way – from the Eddy Match Works in Hull looking over to Ottawa. Haven't tackled the night ones yet."[9] Milne is describing the present watercolour (Cat. no. 61).

Like earlier works of art, Milne's view follows in the tradition of topographical and scenic views of Ottawa and Hull. With the construction of the Rideau Canal commencing in 1827, Ottawa, then known as Bytown, began to grow. Some of the earliest views of this new settlement were executed by military officers and civilians employed on the canal. John Burrows, overseer of works, executed many watercolours recording the geography of the area and the progress of the canal (Fig 61.1). By the middle of the nineteenth century, scenic views such as William S. Hunter's lithographs, published in *Ottawa Scenery* (Ottawa, 1855), sought not only to depict but also to promote the expanding city. In 1858, Queen Victoria declared Ottawa the national capital, and the ensuing construction of the Parliament Buildings changed the face of the city. Built in the Gothic Revival style, the Parliament Buildings rose from Barrack Hill as a symbol of the new-found importance of Ottawa and of Canada. This famed architecture was frequently drawn by artists; for example

Frederick B. Schell's drawing, *Parliament Buildings, Ottawa* was reproduced as the title page for volume one of *Picturesque Canada*, published in 1882 (Fig. 61.2). The buildings were also popular subject matter for the growing number of photographers.

On the night of 3 February 1916, a great fire burned the Centre Block of the Parliament Buildings to the ground, leaving only the octagonal library standing. John Pearson, an architect from Toronto, designed and rebuilt the central building in a style reminiscent of the original structure. Parliament was officially reopened on "the Hill" in early 1920, although the bell tower was not completed for another seven years. Redesigned as a monument to those Canadians who had fought in World War I, the new Peace Tower rose majestically three hundred feet from its base.

In Milne's watercolour, the Peace Tower has not yet been completed. It can be seen to the right of the library with a temporary flagpole mounted on top. A photograph from the same period indicates the popularity of this vista and also testifies to the accuracy of Milne's depiction (Fig. 61.3). But Milne's view creates its unique drama by contrasting the majestic Gothic Parliament Buildings with the industrial might of the E.B. Eddy Mill in the foreground. The great smoke stacks of the matchworks echo the towers of Parliament, having also become a recognizable beacon above the Ottawa River.

Ezra Butler Eddy, an American from Burlington, Vermont, travelled north to Canada in 1851. He settled across the river from Barrack Hill in Wrightsville (now Hull, Quebec) and established a match factory. Soon it grew to include a pail factory and, in 1866, a great saw-mill. By the 1880s the expansion included several pulp and paper mills. While E.B. Eddy still operates today, the matchworks is now the site of the Canadian Museum of Civilization. The digester tower (the tall square structure at the right in Milne's watercolour) is the only remaining building, and there are plans to restore it as an example of our industrial heritage.

Milne's hopes of teaching art classes in Ottawa came to naught, and as the weather got colder his painting decreased.[10] The only major paintings produced at this time were a series of Dominion Square, Montreal. His wife Patsy had been working in Montreal as a housekeeper, and Milne visited her often during this time. The Art Association of Montreal presented an exhibition of Milne's work that was shown from 1-26 January 1924. The show was then on view at the Arts Club of Montreal until 10 March, but neither showing resulted in any sales. In January 1924, Milne was also exhibiting with the Ottawa Group of Artists at Hart House, University of Toronto, some of the other exhibitors being Graham Norwell, Frank Hennessey, F.H. McGillivray, Yoshida Sekido, Paul Alfred and Harold Beament.[11]

As well, two of Milne's watercolours, *The Village in the Valley* and *The Mountains*, were included in the 1924 Wembley exhibition in London, and the National Gallery had purchased six watercolours, including *Old RCMP Barracks, Ottawa Number 2.*

In spite of all of this, Milne's earnings were sporadic and scarce. He sought work as a commercial artist with the federal government. Ironically, upon arriving in Ottawa, Milne had written to his friend Clarke about the number of artists employed by the government:

> Working for the government is the correct thing here, even artists work for the government.... Ordinarily they seem to have quite a bit of free time. They don't know how lucky they are, it is practically a subsidy to art.[12]

Unfortunately Milne was not so lucky. Discouraged and impoverished, he returned to Big Moose Lake in March 1924. By May of the following year, he had abandoned using watercolours, devoting his time to oil painting and printmaking. The reasons for this are never stated by Milne, but it has been suggested that the medium was not suited to the stylistic changes in his painting at that time.[13]

Milne did return to Canada again, in the spring of 1929, and this time the move was a permanent one. He eventually settled at Six Mile Lake, Ontario, where he met Douglas Duncan, an independently wealthy and somewhat eccentric art patron and founder of the Picture Loan Society. Duncan became Milne's agent, dealer and friend. Through numerous personal purchases and sales at the Picture Loan Society in Toronto, Duncan assured Milne of a steady income that would enable him to continue his painting uninterrupted.

E.B.Eddy Mill, Hull, Quebec was one of the works purchased by Douglas Duncan. After his death in 1968, Duncan's collection was carefully and knowledgeably distributed by his sister Frances Barwick among several public collections throughout the country. It is as a result of this that the Documentary Art and Photography Division acquired this beautiful and informative watercolour by David Milne.

A.T.

61.1 J. Burrows
Bytown Bridges, ca. 1835
Watercolour
NA C-92924

61.2 F.B. Schell
Parliament Buildings, Ottawa, 1881
Brown wash
NA C-40102

61.3
Parliament Hill from Hull
Photograph
NA C-80386

---

1. Rosemarie L. Tovell, *Reflections in a quiet pool: the prints of David Milne* (Ottawa: National Gallery of Canada, 1980), 14.
2. Tovell, 46. Milne apparently did not think he would pass the physical examination. He was pleased when he was accepted, although Patsy was not.
3. Tovell, 47.
4. Tovell, 64.
5. NA, David Milne papers, MG 30 D43, vol. 1, Milne to Clarke, 30 October 1923.
6. NA, MG 30 D43, vol. 1, Milne to Clarke, 30 October 1923.
7. Tovell, 64.
8. NA, MG 30 D43, vol. 1, Milne to Clarke, 30 October 1923.
9. NA, MG 30 D43, vol. 1, Milne to Clarke, 30 October 1923.
10. Tovell, 64.
11. Tovell, 220, note 45.
12. NA, MG 30 D43, vol. 2, Milne to Clarke, November 1923(?).
13. Tovell, 71.

10

YVONNE McKAGUE HOUSSER (1898-)

62. ***Market Scene in Paris*****, 1921-1922**

Brush and black ink with gouache and watercolour over pencil on grey paper
20.7 x 16.7 cm
Gift of the artist, 1983
Accession no.: 1984-165-97
Negative no.: C-96583

In 1983, the National Archives of Canada acquired the Yvonne McKague Housser collection, which included not only works of art but photographs and manuscripts as well. Most of the artwork relates to Yvonne McKague's (later McKague Housser) work as an art student in Paris in the 1920s, as well as to her travels through France, Italy, Spain and England. Comprising sketchbooks, loose drawings, life class studies and illustrated letters, this collection offers a thorough look into the formative years of Yvonne McKague Housser's artistic career.

Market Scene in Paris (Cat. no. 62) is a delightful, colourful work that captures the flavour of the streets of Paris in the early 1920s. These scenes were particularly exciting for Yvonne McKague, a young Canadian art student living and studying abroad for the first time. McKague, born in 1898, had received formal art training in Toronto before coming to Paris. At the age of sixteen she convinced her father to allow her to attend the Ontario College of Art (OCA) for one year. She won scholarships that permitted her to complete her four-year course in 1917, followed by a year of graduate studies.[1]

In her autobiographical writings, McKague comments on her teachers at OCA, expressing her fondness for them, and revealing her frustration with the limited program. William Cruikshank, who taught the antique class, "was a fine and sensitive draftsman... but not a very considerate teacher." Robert Holmes was "a good and conscientious teacher of design, but I found lettering etc. a bit dull when I was longing to be in painting the model." J.W. Beatty was "an excellent teacher except for his prejudice about all painting since Puvis de Chavannes."[2]

In 1920, George Reid, principal of OCA, hired McKague as an assistant teacher. Arthur Lismer had been appointed vice-principal the year before. McKague had great respect for Lismer, who encouraged her to take a leave to travel and study abroad.

By saving all her money, McKague was able to book passage to England in the summer of 1921 with the hopes of studying in Paris. Although it was a great adventure for a young woman, it was not unusual for aspiring Canadian artists to journey to Paris. During the late nineteenth century, Parisian academies and art schools had become the "mecca of every enterprising young Canadian artist."[3] George Reid, William Cruikshank and J.W. Beatty had all studied in Paris. And Lismer, who represented a new movement in Canadian art through the newly formed Group of Seven, offered her continued encouragement to pursue and later to return to her European travels and studies.

McKague's mother decided that her daughter was too young to make the journey alone, and so accompanied her to England. In London they met Elizabeth Muntz (born 1894), a fellow student from OCA. Together they took a short sketching holiday at Rye and Winchester, after which the young women left for Paris.

They found Paris filled with romance and excitement, and they immediately fell in love with the city. They found a small two-bedroom apartment on Rue Soufflot, near the Panthéon. Muntz was to study sculpture with Émile-Antoine Bourdelle at the Académie de la Grande Chaumière in Montparnasse, so McKague enrolled to study painting at the same academy under Lucien Simon.

McKague recounted that she did not find her own classes enlightening, so she would slip into the sculpture classes to listen to Bourdelle, whom she admired immensely.[4] She enjoyed the sketching class, where she could draw from the model, and she also attended some classes next door at the Académie Colarossi.

The two young women did not lead a particularly gay life in Paris, as most of their time was devoted to their studies. McKague seems to have drawn enjoyment from the simpler pleasures of walks through the Parisian streets and visiting the small shops and cafés. She wrote:

> Sunday morning was special. I went out to shop on the Rue St. Jacques. This was fun as the shopkeepers got to know my red hair and all shouted greetings to me.[5]

Market Scene in Paris reveals her fascination with the everyday life in Paris. Robust women select their daily groceries from the colourful carts of fruits and vegetables. This watercolour is based on a chalk drawing (Fig. 62.1) from a sketchbook labelled "1921-22 France and Italy," also in the National Archives. In the watercolour, McKague has added the small girl in the red coat, who huddles close to her mother.[6]

Market Scene in Paris is executed on a sheet of paper torn from the sketchbook (the left edge is perforated), which suggests that it was worked up shortly after the chalk drawing was done. The use of vibrant coloured gouaches and the rich black ink enliven the whole scene, and McKague is able, through her quick yet adept brush-work, to maintain the spontaneity of this scene. In her writings, McKague does not refer to current artists or exhibitions that impressed her while she was in Europe, but it may be remarked that the subject matter and the colourful, direct treatment recall the artists from the Nabis, such as Pierre Bonnard.

Describing her exuberance and wonder at being in Paris, and the people she encountered, McKague wrote:

> When I walked down the Blvd Ste Michel I must have shown my excitement for people smiled at me, and some even said, 'Bonjour.' The flower girl — rather an old girl I'm afraid — would shout at me in her raucous voice and I would wave and call 'Bonjour' and once or twice spent an extravagant franc on a flower or two.[7]

Flower Girl on Corner of St. Michel and My Street (Fig. 62.2) depicts a woman full of character and life. Dressed in a colourful yet tattered dress, she supports her large basket of flowers on her heavy hips. With her hand placed firmly on one hip and her head tilted slightly to one side, she captures and characterizes the noise and gaiety of the Parisian street. One can almost hear her shout "in her raucous voice" through her rounded red lips. The inscription at the top of the page locates the flower seller at the corner of Boulevard Saint-Michel and Rue Soufflot, only a few blocks from the Panthéon and near the apartment shared by McKague and Muntz.

There are two sketches of a woman selling flowers in the France-Italy sketchbook, but neither relates directly to *Flower Girl*. Executed on a piece of irregularly-shaped paper, it was drawn quickly but with great assuredness. This watercolour is not simply a representation of a flower seller; the woman represents the excitement and vivaciousness of the daily life in Paris — for Yvonne McKague, she represents Paris in 1921. This sketch may have been executed in 1922 after McKague had to return to Canada, when the image of the flower seller was still vibrant in her mind.

McKague and Muntz spent their holidays in Italy, principally in Venice and Florence. Muntz had an aunt in Venice who was a watercolourist and, as McKague recalls, had her own gondola. "She was very kind and took us in the gondola to spots outside Venice. How I loved it and sketched continually."[8]

There are several coloured sketches of Venice in the France-Italy sketchbook, including *Venice Canal* (Fig. 62.3). It shows the canal filled with several gondolas, and men gathered on a bridge while colourful building facades rise from the water behind. Again McKague avoids the usual Venetian scenes, preferring instead to depict intimate scenes of common people and daily activities. The bright colours applied in layers evoke the fresh spring air and the clear Venetian light.

McKague returned to Canada in August 1922 for her brother's wedding, and remained in Toronto for the next year to teach at OCA. At the Royal Canadian Academy of Arts the same year, she exhibited a nude study she had done in Paris, and at the Ontario Society of Artists exhibition she showed a work entitled *Boat at Venice*.

During the summer of 1924, she returned to France for a painting holiday with some friends. They travelled and sketched in Paris, the south of France and Spain. After that summer, with the help of Arthur Lismer, McKague was able to obtain a leave of absence from teaching and returned to Paris to study for one more year, this time at the Académie Ranson with Maurice Denis.

McKague returned to OCA in 1925, where she taught for the next two decades. She returned to Paris once again in the summer of 1930, en route to Vienna where she went to study children's art. But it was no doubt her first visit to Paris in 1921-1922 that made the biggest impression on the then young artist.

A.T.

62.1 Y. McKague Housser
Market Scene in Paris, 1921-1922
Coloured chalk
NA C-96590

62.2 Y. McKague Housser
Flower Girl on Corner of St. Michel and My Street, 1921-1922
Watercolour
NA C-96584

62.3 Y. McKague Housser
Venice Canal, ca. 1922
Coloured chalk
NA C-96589

62.4
Betty Muntz (left), Yvonne McKague (centre), Venice, ca. 1921-1922
Photograph
NA C-143759

---

1. Colin S. MacDonald, *A Dictionary of Canadian Artists* (Ottawa: Canadian Paperbacks, 1968), 2:472.
2. NA, MG 30 D305, Yvonne McKague Housser papers, vol. 2, file 9, "Early Years," pp. 2-5.
3. J. Russell Harper, *Painting in Canada: a History*, 2nd ed. (Toronto: University of Toronto Press, 1977), 209.
4. NA, MG 30 D305, vol. 2, file 9, "Early Years," p. 12.
5. NA, MG 30 D305, vol. 2, file 9, "Early Years," p. 14.
6. NA, Accession no. 1984-165-32.9.
7. NA, MG 30 D305, vol. 2, file 9, "Paris," p. 1.
8. NA, MG 30 D305, vol. 2, autobiographical series.

J. Humphrey 1944.

JACK WELDON HUMPHREY (1901-1967)

63. *Men Working in Plate Shop, St. John Dry Dock*, 1944

Gouache over pencil on paper

51.5 x 69.2 cm

Inscribed in brushpoint and beige gouache, recto, l.l.: *J. Humphrey 1944.*; in pencil, verso, t.: *Men Working in Plate Shop, St. John Dry Dock (1944) / (Casein gouache)*

Purchased in 1980

Accession no.: 1980-18-2

Negative no.: C-133332

World War II greatly affected the lives of Canadians, and mobilized all efforts toward the cause of victory. Visual records of this national commitment are especially valuable in documenting the Canadian effort. While countless photographs exist depicting the conditions under which people fought and worked, they cannot be regarded as the sole source of information. Artists, among them Jack Humphrey, also added significantly to Canada's visual legacy of the war. In 1980, the National Archives of Canada acquired a number of Humphrey's works, including the present gouache drawing, *Men Working in Plate Shop, St. John Dry Dock*. Through an examination of this work, we can learn more about the creation of this type of war record, as well as about Jack Humphrey's role as a war artist.

Humphrey was born in Saint John, New Brunswick, in 1901. After several years of artistic training in the United States and Europe, he returned to his home town in 1930, in the midst of the Great Depression. It was an extremely difficult time for any artist, let alone one just starting out, but Humphrey persevered, and by the beginning of World War II he had established a reputation as a fine landscape and portrait painter. With the outbreak of war, many Canadian artists, including Humphrey, sought opportunities to become war artists. Artists felt they could contribute more to the cause by dint of their artistic talents than by joining the armed services or becoming war plant labourers, and pressured the government to develop a war records program.[1] Humphrey's own interest in war art was undoubtedly heightened while attending the historic meeting of the Conference of Canadian Artists held at Kingston, Ontario, in June 1941, where lengthy discussions about the artist's role in the war effort took place.

Following the conference, Humphrey continued to paint in and around Saint John, but he also began seriously to add war subjects to his repertoire. *A Canadian Sailor* (Fig. 63.1) is an example of Humphrey's early attempts to capture the war in his art. It is also the work that focused the attention of H.O. McCurry, director of the National Gallery of Canada and chairman of the Canadian War Artists Committee, on Humphrey as a potential war artist.[2] Interested in doing something more than portraits of Canada's armed forces personnel, Humphrey made an unsuccessful appeal in 1943 to the Wartime Information Board for permission to document "scenes of ship-loading or ship-building or other work where groups of men [were] in action."[3] Later, encouraged by his friend Walter Abell, Humphrey made similar requests to H.O. McCurry for assistance in obtaining authorization to sketch his chosen subjects.[4] The artist had in mind the shipyards of Saint John, which were heavily engaged in wartime activities (Fig. 63.2). At the beginning of the war, artists had often experienced formidable obstacles in simply gaining access to Canada's war plants, often being regarded with great suspicion as possible spies.[5] However, those that did manage to gain access found the work inspiring; among them was Caven Atkins, a Toronto artist, who wrote to Humphrey in August 1942 saying that he was busy sketching, with the government's permission, at one of the local war plants, and found them "really good stuff to do."[6]

By January 1943, the Canadian government recognized the need to authorize a war artists' program. It was not enough to rely on photographs alone, which, for all of their uses, had limitations. "Lucy Van Gogh," a pseudonymous art reviewer, noted that:

> The painter... can do a better job than the photographer..., because of his much greater power of selection. The camera cannot very well leave out...things that are not wanted in the picture.... The artist can concentrate on the essentials, accentuating the vital parts of the machine and the controlling gestures of the operator, shifting the light to suit his purpose, and letting the unimportant background disappear into vagueness.[7]

This understanding eventually penetrated the government's consciousness, and resulted in the Canadian War Records Program, but was understandably reluctant to allow unlimited access to all war plants.

In early February 1944, Humphrey received, through H.O. McCurry's intervention, the long awaited permits giving him government permission to sketch the shipyards at Saint John.[8] By early March he was deeply involved in sketching the dry docks, the workers and the impressive operations taking place in the various shops. *Inside the Plate Shop, St. John Dry Dock* (Fig. 63.3) is one example of his on-the-spot sketches, which were not done "for effect or exhibition so much as an examination and study for future reference and present practice."[9] Based on these preliminary shipyard sketches, the artist produced three gouache drawings, one of which is *Men Working in Plate Shop*.[10] This particular work depicts a corner section of the St. John Dry Dock and Shipbuilding Company's plate shop, which was devoted to manufacturing small ship parts. As identified by James Dixon, a former long-time employee of the Saint John company, Humphrey's gouache accurately documents a variety of operations this area of the shop was involved with, from the formation of smaller curved steel plates, as the two figures in the picture's foregound are shown doing, to the creation of steel ship parts such as rails and stanchions for deck sides.[11] The gouache also provides strong evidence of the working conditions people laboured under in the dry dock's shops during World War II. In an atmosphere of heat, noise and grime, employees worked diligently to build and refit ships for the war effort.

As well as documenting a Canadian war industry and its workers, *Men Working in Plate Shop* was also an experiment in technique for Humphrey.[12] This may be seen in his handling of the gouache pigment he mixed with casein binder (made from fresh curd). By applying the colours as he did to the paper, layering one on top of the other in a very painterly fashion, he created a work, heavy and opague in appearance, which echoes the equally heavy labours depicted. While the experiment suited Humphrey's subject matter, it caused technical problems, and the long-term effects can be seen in the cracking and flaking of the paint layers.[13] Contributing to this problem was the artist's practice of purposely scraping out areas of the paint surface. Humphrey's experiments were probably influenced by ideas and information about painting techniques he had absorbed at the Conference of Canadian Artists in 1941.[14] One of the goals of the conference was to spur Canadian artists to experiment with new techniques, a challenge that several artists took up.[15]

Men Working in Plate Shop also demonstrates Humphrey's desire to study the "character of human activity" and to master the handling of crowd scenes.[16] His goal in this matter was simple; he hoped to be offered the opportunity to do mural work, more particularily a mural series on shipyards.[17] The art of mural painting had been revived in the United States under different federal government programs, including the Works Progress Administration (WPA), which provided much needed work for American artists during the Depression. This revival aroused much interest in Canada. In 1940, the National Gallery arranged to have the exhibition *Mural Designs for Federal Buildings* tour in Canada, and in 1941, the Conference of Canadian Artists, which Humphrey attended, featured Edward Rowan, who gave a lecture-demonstration on the WPA's program. Even H.O. McCurry began to lobby for the establishment of a similar program that would see artists creating murals in various government buildings throughout Canada.[18]

Although the mural program was discussed in some detail, it never materialized; consequently, Humphrey's wish to do a mural series based upon his war records of the Saint John shipyards was not realized. Nor did he have the satisfaction of seeing even one of his dry dock pictures placed in the Canadian War Records collection. This in itself is difficult to explain, because McCurry was quite taken with Humphrey's work, encouraging the artist to do war records and even enquiring whether Humphrey would be interested in becoming an official war artist.[19] Nothing ever came of the offer, or of Humphrey's idea of giving some of his dry dock sketches to the War Records collection.[20] It may be that the sketches were never sent to the National Gallery for McCurry's consideration because Humphrey decided later that as they had been done for study purposes only, they did not warrant being included. In any event, few of Humphrey's war records appear to have left his personal collection during his lifetime. Only since his death have many of them found their way into public and private hands.

The gouache *Men Working in Plate Shop* is just one of a large number of works Humphrey created of the shipbuilding industry in Saint John, New Brunswick. They are unique because during World War II most artists were working in central Canada. By studying Humphrey's work, it is possible to identify specific influences on Canadian artists during the early 1940s, such as the American mural project, to gain insight into the place of artists in Canadian society and to assess their contribution to the war effort.

T. Mc.

63.1 J. Humphrey
A Canadian Sailor, 1942(?)
Oil on canvas
Canadian War Museum

63.2 Smith Studio
Wartime activities of the St. John Dry Dock and Shipbuilding Company, 1945
Photograph
Provincial Archives of New Brunswick

63.3 J. Humphrey
Inside the Plate Shop, St. John Dry Dock, 1944
Charcoal
NA C-133942

1. For instance, the Federation of Canadian Artists petitioned the prime minister. NA, Wartime Information Board records, RG 36/31, vol. 12, file 8-1, Federation of Canadian Artists, Fred Taylor and Dorothy MacPherson of the Federation of Canadian Artists to Prime Minister King, 16 February 1943.

2. In 1942, *A Canadian Sailor* was given to the National Gallery of Canada. At that time, H.O. McCurry, director of the National Gallery of Canada and chairman of the Canadian War Artists Committee of the Canadian War Records program, was uncertain whether the painting would become part of the war art collection or part of the National Gallery's holdings, because according to McCurry, "It would fit quite well into either." National Gallery of Canada, Jack Humphrey papers, file 1, McCurry to Humphrey, 26 December 1942. Quoted with permission of Rose Killam.

3. National Gallery of Canada, 5.42-H, Canadian War Artists, Jack Humphrey file, Humphrey to McCurry, 14 June 1943.

4. National Gallery of Canada, Canadian War Artists, 5.42-H, Jack Humphrey file, Humphrey to McCurry, 14 June 1943; Humphrey to McCurry, 3 January 1944.

5. Lucy Van Gogh, "Canada's Artists Find Inspiration in War Work," *Saturday Night*, 23 January 1943, p. 4.

6. National Gallery of Canada, Jack Humphrey papers, Caven Atkins file, Atkins to Humphrey, 14 August 1942. Quoted with the permission of Rose Killam.

7. Van Gogh.

8. National Gallery of Canada, Jack Humphrey papers, Department of Munitions and Supply file, Gordon Garbutt, director, Publicity Branch, Department of Munitions and Supply, to Humphrey, 5 February 1944, giving permission to work at the St. John Dry Dock and Shipbuilding Company, Saint John; and Gordon Garbutt to the manager of Canadian Comstock Company, Saint John, 5 February 1944, giving permission for Humphrey to work at the Canadian Comstock Company.

9. National Gallery of Canada, Canadian War Artists, 5.42-H, Jack Humphrey file, Humphrey to McCurry, 12 March 1944.

10. The other two gouaches, *Activity in the Pipe Shop, Ship Building Plant* and *Brief Respite*, were exhibited in 1944 at the Canadian Society of Painters in Water Colour. National Gallery of Canada, Correspondence with/re Artists, 7.1-H, Jack Humphrey file 1, letter from Humphrey to McCurry, 21 April 1944.

11. Letter to the author from James Dixon, 3 September 1990.

12. National Gallery of Canada, Correspondence with/re Artists, 7.1-H, Jack Humphrey file 1, Humphrey to McCurry, 21 April 1944.

13. The results of such a painting technique with gouache are examined in Kurt Wehlte, *The Materials and Techniques of Painting*, translated by Ursus Dix (New York: Van Nostrand Reinhold Co., 1967), 232.

14. Several demonstrations and lectures on painting techniques were given at the conference by a trio of representatives of the Painters Workshop from Boston. The information presented at those meetings was later published in December 1941 as part of the conference's proceedings and later republished in 1943 due to public demand.

15. Christine Boyanoski, *The 1940s: A Decade of Painting in Ontario* (Toronto: Art Gallery of Ontario, 1984), 15-17. This catalogue documents some of the experiments that Ontario artists, like Peter Haworth and L.A.C. Panton, conducted involving painting technique following the Conference of Canadian Artists.

16. National Gallery of Canada, Correspondence with/re Artists, 7.1-H, Jack Humphrey file 1, Humphrey to McCurry, 10 December 1943. For example, *Dance at the Seamen's Mission* was done for this very reason.

17. National Gallery of Canada, Correspondence with/re Artists, 7.1-H, Jack Humphrey file 1, Humphrey to McCurry, 10 December 1943.

18. National Gallery of Canada, Vincent Massey correspondence, 9.2, McCurry to Massey, then Canadian High Commissioner in London, 30 January 1940; and National Gallery of Canada, Canadian War Artists Committee, 5.41-C, file 1, McCurry to Leonard Brockington of the Prime Minister's Office, 4 May 1940; and McCurry to H.H. Wrong, Department of External Affairs, 5 September 1942.

19. National Gallery of Canada, Jack Humphrey papers, National Gallery of Canada, file 1, McCurry to Humphrey, 7 March 1945. Quoted with the permission of Rose Killam.

20. National Gallery of Canada, Correspondence with/re Artists, 7.1-H, Jack Humphrey, file 2, Humphrey to McCurry, 29 February 1945 (misdated, 1945 was not a leap year).

HUBERT ROGERS (1898-1982)

64. *Final design for the war poster "Attack On All Fronts,"* 1943

Charcoal, pen and black ink with trace of red chalk, on paper

101.7 x 76.3 cm

Gift of Helen Priest Rogers, 1982

Acquisition no.: 1987-72-216

Negative no.: C-103329

In time of war, the home front is as important as the war front, and all talents are put to use. When Hubert Rogers, who had been pursuing a brilliant career as an artist-illustrator in the United States, came to offer his services in Ottawa in 1942, he was appointed to the Wartime Information Board to design propaganda material.

Originally from Prince Edward Island, Rogers studied commercial art in Toronto.[1] During World War I he served first as a cartographer, then as an artilleryman in Europe; the Soldiers' Civil Re-establishment Program allowed him to finish his studies in Toronto. Not satisfied with working as a designer in a department store in his home province, he emigrated to Boston. He quickly found work and was able to pursue his art studies during the evening. In 1925, he was working for several newspapers and publishers in New York, and began specializing in military and adventure subjects. He designed some fifty covers for the magazine *Adventure*, which are noted for their realism and the prominence given to the human figure.[2] After spending a few years in New Mexico, Rogers returned to New York and became involved in science fiction illustration. His first cover design for *Astounding Science* is dated February 1939.

When World War II broke out, Rogers wanted to serve his country again. He visited Ottawa in 1940, but work for illustrators was scarce. He made a further attempt in 1942 and was hired this time. Among other things, he created the five designs for the popular poster series "Men of Valor." He also painted the portraits of the participants in the 1943 Conference at Quebec, which brought together Churchill and Roosevelt. The portraits were done in preparation for a commemorative painting finished in 1960 and now part of the Canadian War Museum collection.

Hubert Rogers returned to the United States after the war to devote himself to portraiture, while continuing to work for *Astounding Science*. From the mid-sixties on, he divided his time and his clientele between his studio at Battleboro, Vermont, and the one in Manotick near Ottawa, which he acquired from the painter A.Y. Jackson. Following Rogers' death in 1982, his wife made a generous donation to the National Archives of more than two hundred drawings, six oil paintings, and several posters, most relating to his war work.

The present work is the final drawing for the poster *Attack On All Fronts* (Fig. 64.1).[3] The National Archives collection includes several other preliminary drawings for this poster and for another one, *Fight For Tomorrow*, which was never published. For the latter he did a final drawing of the same dimensions as the *Attack* design (Fig. 64.5).[4] Most of the sheets (tracing paper) bear several small sketches, in which Rogers worked out the general layout of the text and the figures.

In his first draft of *Fight*, Rogers placed three soldiers' heads on a diagonal moving downward, the head in the foreground being at the top of the drawing. On the same sheet, which includes more than fifteen sketches, we find the first idea for *Attack*: a group of five or six helmeted soldiers' heads, likewise placed on a diagonal, but moving upwards. Only one other sheet pursues the idea of the three soldiers, without any textual reference to *Fight* or *Attack*. A third sheet (Fig. 64.2) is entirely devoted to *Attack*. Five little sketches work out the placement of the text, and a larger sketch the position of the figures. Rogers relegated the soldiers to the background, placing three workers in the foreground. Shown are a man writing in a notebook, a woman holding an unidentified tool, and an industrial worker (a welder?) wearing a protective helmet. This time the slogan *Attack On All Fronts* refers to civilian efforts as much as to military ones.

The next drawings, which are related only to *Attack*, concentrate on the soldiers in the background and their positioning. In a more precise draft (Fig. 64.3), done after he had decided on the final layout of the text, Rogers gave more importance to the soldiers than to the workers, who are barely sketched in. Perhaps it was after studying this sketch that he decided to keep only three figures: a soldier with a rifle, a miner with a drill and, between them, a woman holding what seems to be a sheaf of wheat (Fig. 64.4). Their arrangement is the same in the final drawing. In the latter, which served as a model for the poster, Rogers has placed the woman in the foreground; she is now holding a hoe.[5] The group of soldiers was not abandoned, however; they can be found in the background of the final draft for *Fight* (Fig. 64.5). In front of them, a man in civilian dress uses a compass and a model globe of the world to calculate the distance from Canada to the European war front.

Attack is not especially original; a number of countries on both sides used similar subjects.[6] In Canada, two posters published at the beginning of the war extolled the same idea. A poster by Eric Aldwinkle depicts a workman holding a hammer and a soldier holding a rifle, both of them in profile; a little later, in a poster by the painter Philip Surrey, a soldier holding a rifle is supported by a workman holding what seems to be a mine, an allusion to the war industry. In both cases, the worker's function is above all symbolic.[7] If Roger's poster also illustrates the military-civilian parallel, the addition of the woman farmer suggests others: man-woman, city-country, eastern-western Canada.... But are we still on a symbolic level? This poster may be distinguished from the earlier ones by the new importance given to women, and by the allusion to specific trades. The final choice of figures is perhaps not arbitrary.

Today it is difficult to determine who was responsible for the contents of the war posters – as no document on this subject seems to have survived – or even which government service was responsible for their production. Beginning on January 1943, the Wartime Information Board and the National Film Board had the same director, John Grierson. According to the inscription at the bottom of the poster, *Attack On All Fronts* was published by the Board under the series number WIB-2, which means it may date to May or June 1943.[8]

From 1940 on, all aspects of information were being regulated by one government agency. Through its propaganda, the information service of the Department of National War Services tried to obtain the support of Canadians for the war effort through slogans and strong images that appealed to their nationalism. But this approach did not take into full account the living and working conditions of Canadians, or their ethnic differences (to which the defeat in Quebec of the plebiscite on conscription in April 1942 is attributed in part), nor could it anticipate Canadians' post-war expectations. In September 1942, with the founding of the Wartime Information Board, an autonomous governmental body under the direction of John Grierson, the term "information" acquired a sociological dimension. After sounding out public opinion, the Board became aware of the hot issues on the home front, and informed the government about them and modified its propaganda accordingly.[9]

In 1943, thousands of Canadians had enlisted and still more had fled the countryside for the cities, attracted by the jobs and high salaries of the war industry. New problems arose: overpopulation in the cities and a reduction of manpower in the essential services, namely agriculture, forestry and mining.[10] The government had to take strong measures. From March 1942 on, the National Selective Services Program decided, among other measures, that it was essential to encourage women to take jobs in industry (which they did with enthusiasm) and to control the migration of agricultural workers, as employing women did not solve all the problems! In the mines, dissatisfied workers went on strike. A decree in May 1943 regulated their mobility as well, forbidding the voluntary enlistment of coal miners, and even recalling miners who had already signed up.[11] In the face of this serious problem, the Wartime Information Board, at the beginning of 1943, set up an Industrial Morale Section. It quickly submitted a detailed program to raise the morale of the coal miners and make their work better understood by the general public.[12]

It was in this context that Rogers produced his poster *Attack On All Fronts*. It is quite probable that the final choice of the three figures, considerably changed from the first drafts, had to conform to government policies on employment. In addition, to encourage Canadian workers, including women, to support the war effort, the poster was more directly aimed at agricultural workers and miners, as if to tell them, "Stay where you are; that is where you will be most useful."

Despite these constraints, Rogers produced a straightforward and strong poster that allows us to examine the practical as well as the psychological aspects of wartime propaganda. Ironically, even as they were being produced, a confidential survey by the Wartime Information Board revealed that posters were the media least affecting Canadians.[13]

L.D.

64.1 H. Rogers
Attack On All Fronts, 1943
Poster
NA C-103527

64.2 H. Rogers
Studies for *Attack On All Fronts*, 1943
Pencil
NA C-103286

64.3 H. Rogers
Studies for *Attack On All Fronts*, 1943
Pencil
NA C-103300

64.4 H. Rogers
Study for *Attack On All Fronts*, 1943
Pencil
NA C-103275

64.5 H. Rogers
Final design for *Fight For Tomorrow*, 1943
Charcoal and pen and ink
NA C-103325

1. Biographical information concerning Rogers is taken from the National Gallery of Canada artist file, which includes two "Information Forms," dated 2 July 1943 and 2 December 1978.

2. Whenever possible, Rogers made use of live models: John Bell, "Against the Modernist Tide: Hubert Rogers and The Art of Illustration and Portraiture," *Arts Atlantic* 18 (Winter 1984): 21.

3. The poster, in colour on a white background, bears a printed signature and date, "Hubert Rogers '43." The Canadian War Museum owns a copy with the text in French.

4. No poster based on this drawing has been located. The author thanks Fred Fagan, Canadian War Museum, for his assistance in this matter.

5. In the drawing, the soldier's American-style helmet has been "Canadianized" with maple leaves. The soldier is given a Canadian helmet in the poster, but we do not know if Rogers himself was responsible for this alteration.

6. An American poster by Jean Carlu, *Give' em Both Barrels*, undated, depicts a soldier and a miner: reproduced in Anthony Rhodes, *Propaganda. The Art of Persuasion: World War II* (New York: Chelsea House Publishers, 1976), 151; an Italian artist simplified the theme, depicting only the upraised arms of a soldier and of a woman in mourning (*Tutto e Tutti per la Vittoria*, reproduced in Rhodes, 93).

7. Eric Aldwinckle, *Whatever Your Job May Be Fight*, 1940 (NA, C-87117); Philip Surrey, *Every Canadian Must Fight*, ca. 1940- 1942 (NA, C-87139); another Aldwinckle poster, *It's Our War*, ca. 1940-1942 (NA, C-87114), is even more symbolic, with its upraised arm holding a hammer. Compare it with a poster from World War I, *Be Yours to Hold it Tight!*, showing a soldier with a flag over his shoulder, and a worker with a hammer on his shoulder. In all these cases, as in *Attack*, if there is more than one figure, attributes are always portrayed in parallel. Another 1918 poster on the same theme, *Keep All Canadians Busy*, used the beaver as a symbol. According to a survey done in Toronto at the beginning of 1942, symbolic posters had the least success: Robert Stacey, *The Canadian Poster Book: 100 Years of the Poster in Canada* (Toronto: Methuen, [1982]), 22, which in Chapter 4 reproduces all the posters mentioned in this note.

8. Rogers mentions it in his Information Form, dated 2 July 1943 (National Gallery of Canada, artist files). His first three posters in the *Men of Valor* series, dated from 1942 to 1943, are part of the "U" series; we know, from newspaper clippings kept by the artist, that they were published at the very beginning of 1943. The Board had no budget for posters after 1 April 1943 (Young, 446, see note 9). It was perhaps on this date that production was entrusted to the National Film Board, and the numbering system was changed to "WIB." It is only, however, at about no. WIB-8 (a poster by Harry "Mayo" Mayerovitch, who was responsible for the poster program at the NFB), published at the end of 1943 or the beginning of 1944, that the posters carry the additional reference "Produced by the National Film Board." Rogers mentions both organizations in his Information Forms.

9. For a detailed study of government information services during the war, see William Robert Young, *Making the Truth Graphic: The Canadian Government's Home Front Information Structure and Programmes During World War II*, Ph.D. thesis (University of British Columbia, 1978), part I; part II, which studies specific themes (Chapter XI: "Workers and Soldiers"), mentions only a few concrete examples. See also Gary Evans, *John Grierson and The National Film Board: The Politics of Wartime Propaganda* (Toronto: University of Toronto Press, 1984), Chapter 3.

10. Robert Bothwell, *Years of Victory 1939-1948* (Toronto: Grolier Ltd., 1987), 35.

11. C.P. Stacey, *Arms, Men and Governments: The War Policies of Canada, 1939-1945* (Ottawa: Queen's Printer, 1970), 405, 411-412.

12. Evans, 287-291, Appendix, detailed report of the Industrial Morale Section, November 1943. The project, submitted in March and carried out during that year, included, among other elements, the NFB's *Coal Face Canada* (October 1943), radio broadcasts, magazine reports and posters illustrating work in the mines. Another NFB film, *Thought for Food* (May 1943), emphasized the importance of agriculture for the present and for the future of the country (Evans, 126).

13. Evans, 109.

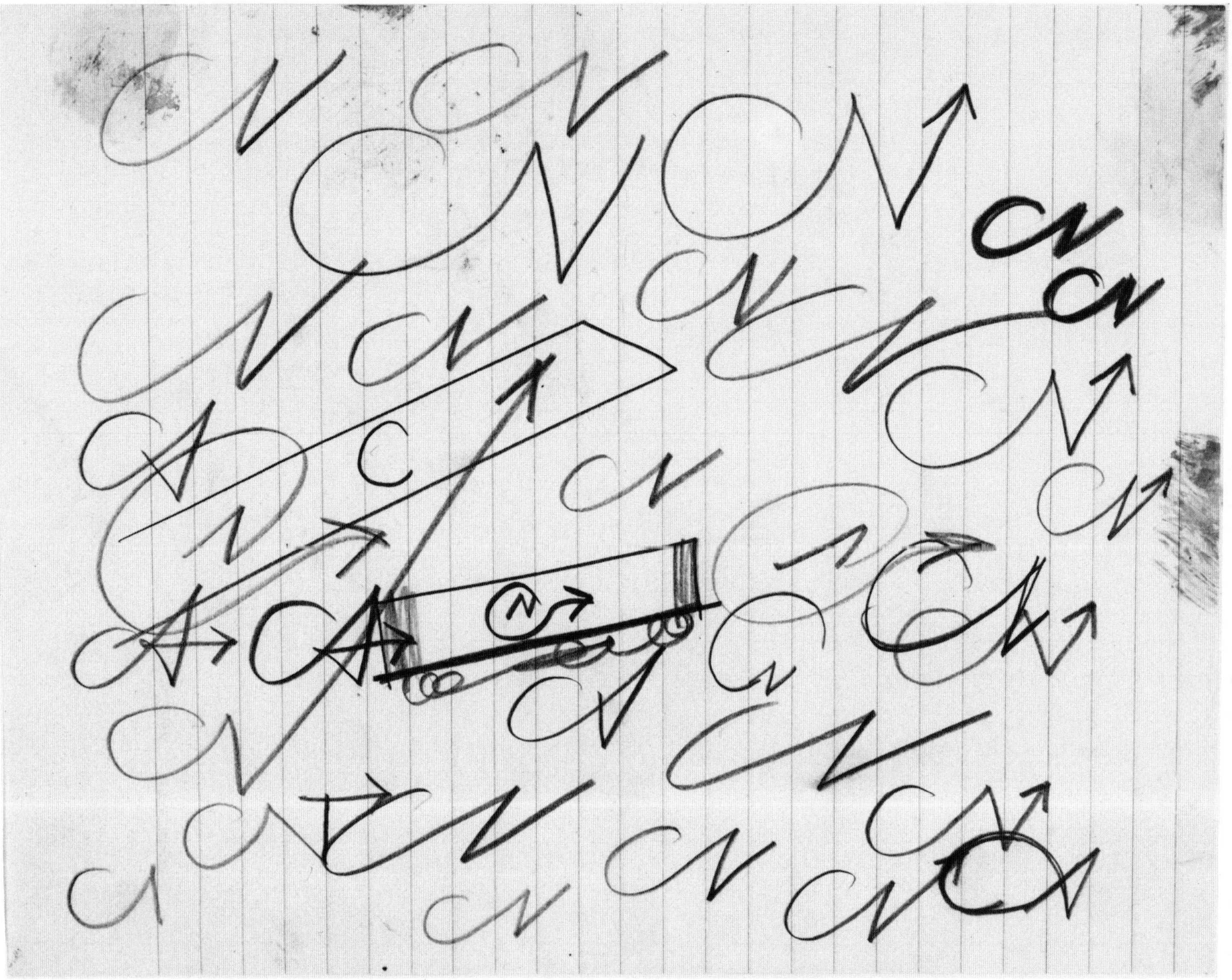

JAMES VALKUS (act. 1950s-1970s), CARL RAMIREZ (act. 1950s-1960s) and ALLAN FLEMING (1929-1977)

JAMES VALKUS

65. ***Preliminary designs for CN logo***, 1959

Pencil and black crayon on paper
21.5 x 27.8 cm
Purchased in 1977
Accession no.: 1977-2-4
Negative no.: C-110429

CARL RAMIREZ

66. ***Proposed design for CN logo***, 1959

Pen and black ink on paper
6.0 x 6.2 cm
Purchased in 1977
Accession no.: 1977-2-70
Negative no.: C-131594

The CN logo, the ubiquitous "wiggly worm," as it is irreverently called, is a national symbol as worthy as the maple leaf itself. The National Archives was able to acquire many of the sketches that document its conception. They describe the processes of design creation and corporate image philosophy and show how the diverging demands of the two were wedded into one powerful image.

The story of this logo's design originates in the early 1950s, when the Canadian National Railways (CN) began an intensive period of renovation, refurbishment and modernization of all its services. Between 1950 and 1960, over $1.7 billion was spent on this campaign under the direction of CN's dynamic and volatile new president, Donald Gordon.[1] Yet a public relations survey conducted in 1959 revealed that, in spite of this enormous effort to modernize, the average Canadian was oblivious to the results. The railway was still considered an old-fashioned, nineteenth-century mode of transportation.[2] To address this problem, W.R. Wright, director of public relations, initiated a program to develop a new trademark for CN. He started by hiring James Valkus, a New York designer, to work on the project. After reviewing the old CN logo and its use on the company's equipment, Valkus realized that more than a new trademark was in order; CN's visual image needed a complete overhaul.

To this end, Valkus set about analyzing everything from sugar packets to tickets, carpeting to diesels, letterhead to boxcars in order to come up with a coherent, unified design plan. He hired a thirty-year-old Canadian designer, Allan Fleming, the typographic director of the design agency Cooper and Beatty, to work on the actual trademark. Trained in Canada and Britain, Fleming's career was just beginning to take off when he started the design that was to make his reputation.

In the series of sketches in the National Archives collection – an assortment of scribbles, doodles, false starts and dead ends – we can follow the process by which the final design was created. They represent the circuitous dialogue of suggestions and ideas between the two designers. Dozens of sketches and proposals passed between them before exactly the right image came to life.

The CN logo design, like any corporate image, was a visual challenge as well as a philosophical one. The former involved the difficulties inherent in combining letters of the alphabet in a coherent design. In this case, "C" and "N" are formally disparate and not easily united in a harmonious image. CN wanted a trademark that, in addition to being visually attractive, would suggest efficiency, modernity and functionality. It had to be a design that could be enlarged, reduced and reproduced on a multitude of different surfaces and articles without losing its visual integrity or identity. It had to unify the vast and varied functions and services of not just a railroad, but a huge transportation enterprise including ferries, trucking companies, hotels and communications.

Fleming examined the visual power and timelessness of such ancient symbols as the Christian cross and the Egyptian symbol for life. He attributed their enduring quality to the fact that they were non-figurative and drawn with a single thick line. By following these principles, he endeavoured to create a strong, lasting image.

In an early page of sketches (Cat. no. 65), we see Valkus' first attempts at combining "C" and "N", trying to imbue them with some sense of dynamism. Based on these ideas, Fleming submitted a design (Fig. 65.1), but he later suggested to Valkus that it too closely resembled a hammer and sickle.[3]

Valkus tried another tack with a group of designs that took a rectangular approach (example, Fig. 65.2). Meanwhile, Fleming returned to the curvilinear form, but combining the large circular "C" and the smaller, angular "N" did not work (Fig. 65.3). We can see how crucial shape and proportion are to a successful visual symbol. The slightest imbalance of the two makes the difference between a good logo and a weak one.

At one point, discouraged by their results so far, Valkus commissioned another designer, Carl Ramirez, to do some designs. What is particularly fascinating about Ramirez's proposal (Cat. no. 66; he did twenty in all) is how closely it resembles the final design, yet the proportion and the elongation of the "C" place it far from the successful design.

Valkus was disappointed in Ramirez's sketches and put them away without showing them to Fleming.[4] Shortly thereafter, Fleming sent a sketch (Cat. no. 67) to Valkus, whose triumphant response "Make thinner and we've got it" clinched it as the final choice. The rectangular shape gave the logo solidity and harmonized the conjunction of the "C" and the "N." The rounded corners suggested fluidity and dynamism. The sleek and futuristic logo resembled a length of track snaking its way across the country.

Satisfied with the new design, Valkus and Fleming had the daunting task of convincing the railway men that such an image was exactly what CN needed. Fortunately, their liaison people, the head of the corporate design program, Robert Ayre, and his assis-

CN
allan
Make thinner
& we've got it.
Jim

ALLAN FLEMING

67. ***Final design proposal for CN logo***, 1959

Pencil and black crayon on paper

21.7 x 27.9 cm

Inscribed in pencil, recto, l.r.: *Allan / Make thinner / & we've got it. / Jim*

Purchased in 1977

Accession no.: 1977-2-73

Negative no.: C-110428

tant, Lorne Perry, knew visual design and knew railways; Fleming's design and Valkus' proposals for its use with a strong colour scheme were presented in such a way that the Board of Directors could not but approve. And the omission of the "R" made the logo bilingual – a fortunate choice at a time when CN was under fire for its lack of bilingual policies.[5]

By December 1960, the new logo was appearing on CN trucks and boxcars, and the company released its story to leading Canadian newspapers. Over the next five years, CN's logo would be incorporated into all equipment and materiel of the many companies under CN's directorship.

The logo's initial success was ensured when the contemporary design journals *Domus* and *Industrial Design* featured articles citing CN's program as an exemplary corporate visual image.[6] As soon as a sizable amount of rolling stock had been painted with the new logo, its true power became evident (Fig. 65.4). It is instantly recognizable and visible for a great distance. In a string of boxcars, the ones with the CN logo stand out. Several other railways soon modified their logos: the Soo Line, Pacific Great Eastern, Chicago and Eastern Illinois, Erie Lackawanna, Ontario Northland, Baltimore and Ohio. All owe an obvious debt to the CN design, but none have surpassed its visual impact. It continued to have an influence on the development of corporate design not only in Canada, but also abroad, for many years.

Both James Valkus and Allan Fleming made their reputations on the success of the CN logo and used the principles of its design to create other corporate logos. Fleming went on to design logos for the Toronto Symphony, Ontario Hydro and the Ontario Science Centre, among others. He also designed covers for *Maclean's* and produced the book *Canada: A Year of the Land* before his premature death in 1977.

The CN logo has become part of the Canadian identity. A long line of CN boxcars threading through the countryside is "a Fleming one man show," to quote one of his colleagues, and a sight that all Canadians recognize.[7] The real proof of the design's success is the fact that today, thirty years later, the CN logo has the same vitality and power it had the day it was unveiled.

S.N.

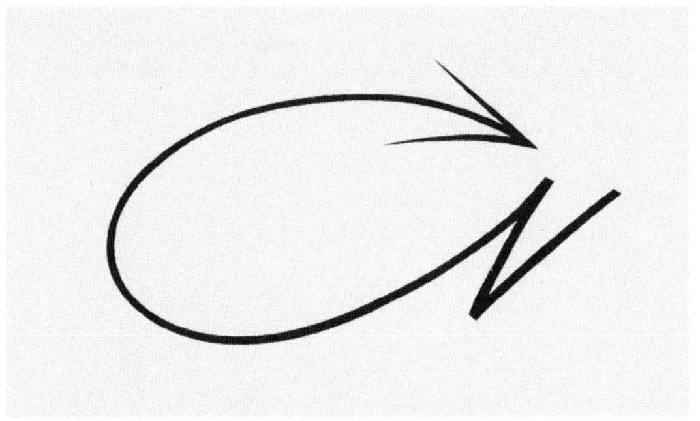

65.1 A. Fleming
Proposed design for CN logo, 1959
Photoreproduction
NA C-136035

65.2 J. Valkus
Proposed design for CN logo, 1959
Blue chalk
NA C-131596

65.3 A. Fleming
Proposed design for CN logo, 1959
Photoreproduction
NA C-136034

65.4
CN logo on a boxcar
Photograph
Courtesy of CN

---

1. Joseph Schull, *The Great Scot* (Montreal: McGill-Queen's University Press, 1979), 191.

2. Ben Rosen, *The Corporate Search for Visual Identity* (New York: Van Nostrand Reinhold Co., 1970), 18.

3. Annotation from Allan Fleming to Jim Valkus on a page of designs on which both had worked, NA, Accession no. 1977-2-26.

4. NA, CN Logo collection, Accession no. 1977-2, Valkus to G.S. Vickers, May 1975(?).

5. Schull, 197.

6. Irma M. Weini, "Face to Match the Figures," *Industrial Design*, no. 8 (July 1961), 52-58; and "L'invenzione di un simbolo," *Domus*, no. 391 (June 1962).

7. John Reeves, as quoted in "Bridging Culture and Commerce," *Applied Arts*, vol. 2, no. 3 (Fall 1987), 76-81.

CANADA STEAMSHIPS Co
ROCHESTER
NIAGARA
MONTREAL
QUEBEC CITY
SAGUEANY
MURRAY BAY
SEE QUEBEC
by LUXURIOUS
STEAMSHIPS

HAROLD ABRAHAM PEARLE (1891-1977)

68. *See Quebec by Luxurious Steamships*, ca. 1935

Gouache over pencil on commercial board

38.5 x 26.1 cm

Inscribed in brushpoint and gouache, recto, u.c.: *CANADA STEAMSHIPS Co*; u.r.: *ROCHESTER / NIAGARA / MONTREAL / QUEBEC CITY / SAGUEANY / MURRAY BAY*; l.c.: *SEE QUEBEC / by LUXURIOUS / STEAMSHIPS*; in pencil, verso, l.r.: *H.A. Pearle / 5 COURT TERRACE*

Purchased in 1987

Accession no.: 1987-60-3

Negative no.: C-131832

Many of Canada's best-known artists, including Tom Thomson, Frederick Varley, Charles Comfort and Franklin Carmichael, worked at one time or another as commercial artists, designing such items as advertisements, posters and greeting cards. Not so well known are the large number of artists who made long-term careers in commercial design. Today their names and careers are largely forgotten, and most of their drawings and artwork are lost or destroyed. The National Archives was fortunate to acquire a collection of some forty designs and illustrations by Harold Abraham Pearle[1] dating from the 1920s and 1930s, among them this design promoting luxury cruises to Quebec. Pearle worked in Toronto from about 1916 until 1939,[2] and like many established and aspiring artists in Canada between the wars, he earned much of his income as a commercial artist and art teacher.

Pearle's art education began in Brockville, Ontario, where he studied under Robert Henry Lindsay (1869-1938), a local artist who ran an art school and also worked as an interior decorator. Between 1913 and 1915, Pearle was working as a salesman for a haberdasher in Brockville and by 1916 had moved to Toronto, joining other members of his family who had established themselves there. He worked as a show card writer during the day,[3] and soon began attending evening classes at the Ontario College of Art (OCA).[4] During the 1916-1917 session, he studied drawing from the antique cast under William Cruikshank, for which he was awarded a certificate of proficiency by the examining board, which consisted of Frederick S. Challener, Frederick Varley and James Ernest Sampson.[5] On 13 June 1917, he enlisted in the army as a private and served in France from June 1918 with the First Canadian Machine Gun Battalion. He was discharged in Toronto in May 1919 and again enrolled in evening courses at OCA. He received a certificate of proficiency in 1920 for drawing the costumed figure, a useful skill for a commercial artist.[6] He was on the student roll in 1921 at the age of thirty, and it is possible that he continued to take evening courses, particularly since in 1921 OCA introduced a commercial art program aimed at providing education in graphic design for those aspiring to or already working in advertising and the printing trades.

During his nearly twenty-five years in Toronto, Pearle spent at least thirteen years – from 1920 to 1932 – in the advertising department of Eaton's department store, where he designed show cards, the attention-getting signs used to promote merchandise in the store. He also produced window displays and possibly illustrations for Eaton's catalogue and newspaper advertisements. He may have been at Eaton's as late as 1936,[7] after which he spent at least two years working for Reliance Engravers, also in Toronto. After a brief period in Montreal and Ottawa, 1939-1940, he returned to his birthplace, Brockville, Ontario, at the age of fifty. There, abandoning his career as a commercial artist, he opened a gift and china shop in 1941, which he operated until 1965 when his business was destroyed by fire.[8] He spent his remaining years in retirement, and continued his avocation of painting, producing several lively canvases. He died in 1977 at the age of eighty-six.

Pearle's commercial work from his Toronto years reveals that his designs were very up-to-date. His typography, layout and smart copy make his work unmistakably a product of 1920s and 30s sensibilities. Progressive design from this period was referred to as "modern," but is now generally known as "art deco" (from *art décoratif*). Its stylistic elements were manifest in architecture and industrial design, the design of furniture, clothing, textiles and interiors, as well as in posters, book and magazine illustration, labelling and packaging. The new look of art deco found its impetus in the avant-garde art movements of the day, particularly cubism and futurism, and in the technological advances that heralded the "machine age." It was the job of the advertising business to find buyers for the new mass-produced consumer goods and more widely accessible services. To do this effectively, the advertisements also had to look and sound modern.

The promise of new technology and a modern lifestyle was nowhere more apparent than in the burgeoning travel industry. While the airplane represented the pinnacle of modern locomotion, the automobile, the train and the cruise ship were redesigned to improve and enhance the experience of travelling by offering comfortable, modern and, above all, fast transportation. Advertisements now proclaimed that getting there would be half the fun. On board a cruise ship every new convenience would be available, and the company of fellow passengers was sure to provide "bright conversation and care-free laughter," the whole effect being "deliciously and shamefully lazy."[9] Such "affordable luxury" is the subject of Pearle's present illustration for the Canada Steamship Lines, done about 1935 as a design for a show card or a brochure cover.

An examination of this illustration demonstrates his adept use of the art deco vocabulary. The unusual perspective, the simplification of details, the varied lettering styles and the strong colour fields are all elements calculated to evoke the spirit of the time and to capture the promise, if not the reality, of luxury travel. The softly swirling smoke and the graceful swoop of the seagulls suggest the elegance and carefree pace such travel afforded. By contrast, the geometrical shapes of the ship's funnel (painted in the company's colours of black, white and red) and the lifeboats stand for the improved quality and safety offered by steamship travel. In 1927, the Canada Steamship Lines, which operated the largest fresh-water transportation company in the world, carried over 1.25 million passengers on its twenty-three passenger steamships plying the Great Lakes and the St. Lawrence River.[10] It was the heyday of the passenger ship, and some of the best-known poster designs from this period advertise travel by luxury liner. Among these is the work of the French-born artist, A.M. Cassandre (1901-1968), whose posters certainly influenced Pearle's work. Pearle's design for the *Queen Mary* (Fig. 68.1) and Cassandre's 1931 poster for the cruise ship *L'Atlantique* (Fig. 68.2) have strikingly similar compositional elements. In imitation of Cassandre's work, Pearle depicts a ship casting a long reflection on the water as it towers above a tugboat nestling at its bow. Smoke from the tug wraps around the side of its larger companion. Other designs by Pearle further indicate that he owed a direct debt to Cassandre's work. However, his work often displayed great originality, as in his brochure cover design for West Indies cruises (Fig. 68.3). It vibrates with yellow, green and three pink flamingoes, and is more typical of the art deco idiom used by North American designers.

In addition to the three gouache illustrations (Cat. no. 68 and Figs. 68.2 and 68.3), the National Archives also has a portfolio of twenty-five advertising designs by Pearle for various Canadian businesses, all executed in pencil on tissue paper and carefully mounted in a folder. The advertisements represent several companies, including Molson's, Greyhound Coach Lines, Canada Steamship Lines, Johns-Manville, Canadian National Railway (Fig. 68.4, compare with Cassandre's "Nord Express" poster of 1927), Canada Cement, Canadian Pacific, Winchester Cigarettes and Canadian National Exhibition. It is likely that these drawings, along with the three gouache illustrations, formed a portfolio that Pearle showed to potential clients as samples of his work, demonstrating his versatility in both black and white and colour work. No evidence has yet been found to suggest that any of these drawings were actually commissioned and used by the companies they advertise.[11]

Pearle was also engaged in book illustration. In 1934, he contributed forty line drawings to *Saints for School and Home* by T.S. Melady (Toronto: J.M. Dent, 1934). He is also known to have produced some thirty five large pencil drawings depicting industry and commerce in Canada, five of which are in the collection of the National Archives (Fig. 68.5). They are thought to have been done in the late 1930s for a government publication, as yet unidentified. Also part of the National Archives collection are eight colour presentation drawings depicting elaborate installations for an automotive trade show (Fig. 68.6), and a watercolour showing the front elevation of a chic dress shop. These were done about 1938 and demonstrate Pearle's talents as an interior designer and a committed practitioner of the art deco style.

While his commercial work provided his living, Pearle's artistic pursuits also included printmaking. His etchings appeared in various exhibitions in Toronto — including those of the Ontario Society of Artists (1923, 1925, 1926), the Canadian Society of Graphic Artists (1924, 1925, 1928), the Society of Canadian Painter-Etchers (1930), and the Canadian National Exhibition (1922, 1923, 1925, 1926) — as well as at the Art Association of Montreal (1939). Known prints and the existence of over thirty etched plates indicate that Pearle produced more than fifty different prints during his career. He apparently studied printmaking at the Ontario College of Art and went to Europe around 1921-1922, where he studied etching. While it is uncertain who his teachers were, he apparently received some instruction from S.S. Finlay, and may have studied under Fred Haines at OCA. Pearle himself is reported to have taught an evening class in etching at the Northern Vocational School (Toronto) in the late 1930s.[12] Among his etchings are several European subjects, as well as urban scenes in Toronto and Montreal and a few landscapes (Fig. 68.7). They show another side to Pearle's talents, quite different from his commercial work. The spontaneous, nervous quality of his etched lines demonstrates the freedom with which he explored the medium, and the volume of his production speaks of his enthusiasm for it.

During the period in which Pearle worked, designers turned their hand to anything from package and logo design to interior and theatre design. Their dedication and talent helped to legitimize commercial art and make it a profession worthy of aspiration. With the establishment of college programs in graphic design and the advent of advertising as an important new industry, the work of the commercial artist became more specialized. The next generation of graphic artists would reap greater benefits and wider recognition, as in the case of the designers of the Canadian National Railways logo whose work for this project also appears in this catalogue (Cat. nos. 65-67).

L.F.

68.1 H.A. Pearle
Queen Mary, ca. 1935
Gouache
NA C-134468

68.2 A.M. Cassandre
L'Atlantique, 1931
Poster
Collection of Merrill C. Berman

68.3 H.A. Pearle
Cruise the West Indies, ca. 1935
Gouache
NA C-134469

68.4 H.A. Pearle
Travel by Canadian National Railway,
ca. 1935
Pencil
NA C-128203

68.5 H.A. Pearle
A Railroad Terminal, Montreal, ca. 1935
Pencil
NA C-135447

68.6 H.A. Pearle
Design for Automobile Display, ca. 1938
Gouache
NA C-128181

68.7 H.A. Pearle
Down on the St. Lawrence, ca. 1925
Etching
NA C-128198

1. Pearle often spelled his name "Pearl" (without the final "e"), but in later life he restored the "e" permanently. His middle name, Abraham, appears in the 1891 census records for Brockville (NA, RG 31), where Pearle was enumerated at the age of two months. The census also reveals that the Pearle family immigrated from England ca. 1885 and that his father, Henry, worked as a house painter.

2. Pearle's career in Brockville and Toronto has been traced largely through listings in the respective city directories. Unfortunately, Brockville directories for the years 1901-1912 were not available for consultation. Pearle's obituary in the *Brockville Recorder and Times*, 12 December 1977, has also been a useful source of information, as has been information communicated to the author by individuals who knew Pearle.

3. When Pearle enlisted in the army in 1917, he gave his occupation as a show card writer. He also spelled his name "Pearl."

4. Information regarding Pearle's attendance at OCA is derived from information in the Minutes of the Council in the archives of OCA.

5. Cruikshank was a noted illustrator and teacher at OCA; Challener, an established painter, muralist and commercial artist; Varley, a member of the Group of Seven; and Sampson, an accomplished illustrator and poster designer.

6. The certificate is in the NA, Accession no. 1989-352-6.

7. It was not possible to trace Pearle's employment record through the Eaton's archives (now in the Archives of Ontario), since early personnel records were apparently lost. The Eaton's advertising department often contracted out the services of their artists, so Pearle may well have done work for other companies in addition to Eaton's.

8. While Pearle did not work as a graphic artist after opening his china shop, he did design several newspaper advertisements for his business, and in 1950 he redesigned the interior of his store.

9. Excerpts from the 1926 Canadian Pacific brochure *Cabin class Steamships between Montreal-Quebec and Southamton-Liverpool...*, copy in NA, pamphlet collection, no. 1926 (174).

10. Michael M. Gutwullig, "Growth of a Giant," part 2, *Canadian Shipping and Marine Engineering News*, November 1951, p. 24.

11. Evidence of this is the fact that Pearle has wrongly called the Canada Steamship Lines the Canada Steamships Co. and mis-spelled Saguenay in the list of destinations appearing on Cat. no. 68. If this work was meant for presentation to a client, these oversights would certainly have been corrected.

12. Andrew J. Oko, *The Society of Canadian Painter-Etchers and Engravers in Retrospect* (Hamilton: Art Gallery of Hamilton, 1981), 76, reference to Pearle in the entry for Wilbur K. Peacock.

Philias Bédard

CHARLES COMFORT (1900-   )

69. *Philéas Bédard*, 26 May 1928

Pencil on paper

30.4 x 23.0 cm

Inscribed in pencil, recto, c.l., on angle: *Comfort 1928*; in Bédard's hand, l.c.: *Philias Bédard*

Purchased in 1981

Accession no.: 1981-69-17

Negative no.: C-104574

70. *Joseph Rousselle*, 26 May 1928

Pencil on paper

28.5 x 23.1 cm

Inscribed in pencil, recto, r.c. on angle: *Comfort 1928*; in Rousselle's hand, l.c.: *Jos Roussel*

Purchased in 1981

Accession no.: 1981-69-16

Negative no.: C-104573

These two portrait sketches by the Canadian artist Charles Fraser Comfort were acquired in 1981 as part of a larger group of drawings. At the time of their purchase, little was known about them except that they were portraits of two French-Canadian folk singers, Philéas Bédard and Joseph Rousselle, but considerable research concerning the two drawings and the circumstances surrounding their creation has subsequently uncovered much more information about them.

Comfort has had a long and distinguished career, from his work in oil to his work as a mural painter and as a war artist. During the late 1920s, though, Comfort was just beginning to make a name for himself in the world of Canadian art. In 1928, he was employed full time as a "creative designer and figure draftsman" for the commercial art firm of Brigden's in Toronto.[1] He had started working for the company in its Winnipeg studio when he was fourteen, after his family had immigrated to that city from Scotland two years earlier, in 1912. Comfort remained in Winnipeg until 1919, during which time he received some formal artistic training at the Winnipeg Art School, and then transferred to Brigden's Toronto studio for a period of two years. At the end of that time, Comfort returned to the Winnipeg branch. In the fall of 1922, he went to study art in New York at the Art Students' League, where he stayed for two years before returning to Winnipeg and to Brigden's once more. In 1924, he married Louise Chase. The following year, Comfort and his wife moved to Toronto, leaving Winnipeg for good.

Comfort sketched Bédard and Rousselle while he was attending the 1928 Canadian Folk Song and Handicraft Festival in Quebec City. Comfort and two fellow Brigden artists, André Lapine and Harold Ayres,[2] drove to Quebec City "expressly to witness and enjoy" the festival.[3] It was Comfort's second visit to the province of Quebec. His first had occurred in August 1926 when he, Harold Ayres and their wives had gone there on a sketching trip. Comfort and Ayres were therefore well aware of Quebec's natural beauties. The trio's interest in the festival had probably been sparked in 1927, when glowing reviews about the first Canadian Folk Song and Handicraft Festival had appeared in the press. Both Augustus Bridle and Lawrence Mason, writers for the Toronto *Daily Mail* and the Toronto *Globe* respectively, had covered the 1927 festival in some detail, highly praising the entire event.[4] If the previous year's newspaper accounts did not provide enough incentive for the three artists to make the journey to Quebec City, Arthur Lismer's comments may have convinced them. Lismer had been at the first Folk Song Festival, and he designed some of the set designs for the 1928 event. It is therefore quite possible that he regaled Comfort with stories about it at the Arts and Letters Club in Toronto, where they were both members.

The festival began on 24 May 1928, and ran for four days. However, Comfort and his colleagues did not arrive at the Château Frontenac hotel, where the festival was being held, until Saturday, 26 May. Once there, Comfort throughly enjoyed himself. In his unpublished autobiography, "Sketches from Memory," the artist described the event and his impressions of it. He wrote:

> Quebec was in a colourful festive mood for the occasion, with dancing and music in the streets, many of the participants in 18th century costume. Others appeared as habitants and couriers des bois [*sic*]. The planned programme took place in the various banquetting [*sic*] halls and ballrooms of the hotel, and at the Auditorium Theatre... I shall never forget the sight and sound of six costumed fiddlers, playing rollicking folk music as they approached in a single line abreast down one of the hotel corridors, bowing and fingering in unison with great vitality and spirit.
>
> I love good choral music and in the afternoon that is just what we had. The Canadian Singers rivalled their Welsh counterparts in a splendid programme. Sir Ernst conducted with youthful zeal and the Singers responded likewise. I cannot itemize the programme but voices like Jeanne Dusseau and the great French Canadian tenor, Rodolphe Plamondon from the Paris Opera, were superb, as was J. Campbell McInnes.
>
> ...The one-act Folk Comedy Opera produced that evening lives on in memory like other great operatic firsts in my experience. It was entitled *Le jeu de Robin et Marion....*[5]

Although Comfort enjoyed taking in everything that this historic cultural affair had to offer, he made only a few sketches. The only time that he appears to have taken out his pencil and paper during the entire trip was when he made his informal sketches of a pair of the festival's senior "chanteurs," Philéas Bédard and Joseph Rousselle. This was done on the evening of Comfort's arrival and just prior to his going into the Auditorium Theatre to attend the production *Le jeu de Robin et Marion.*[6]

In each of his drawings (Cat. nos. 69-70), Comfort skilfully captured the characters of his subjects with a few quick strokes of the pencil. Rousselle's portrait shows him as a weathered man of some years, looking very steadfastly out at the world. There are no extraneous details to take one's attention away from Rousselle's face. Comfort manages this by rendering Rouselle's broad-brimmed hat with a single continuous line that effectively frames Rousselle's face. Comfort created a most direct and honest depiction of Rousselle.

A similar observation may be made about the sketch of Philéas Bédard. Judging from photographs of Bédard taken by Marius Barbeau and Édouard-Zotique Massicotte, Comfort's portrait is a good physical likeness of the man. He did not attempt to romanticise Bédard, but chose rather to create a simple and true record of one of French Canada's best known and respected folk singers. With his "Norman face and twinkling blue eyes," Bédard was a favourite subject amongst artists.[7] Arthur Lismer and Edmond J. Massicotte also sketched Bédard during the 1920s, with several of Lismer's drawings being reproduced in Marius Barbeau's publications about French-Canadian folksongs and in the annotated program of the 1928 Canadian Folk Song and Handicraft Festival.

Both of Comfort's 1928 drawings are similar in style to his earlier pen and ink portraits reproduced in W.J. Healy's 1923 book, *Women of Red River* (Winnipeg: Russel, Laing & Co. Ltd.) (Figs. 69.1 and 69.2). The portrait illustrations in Healy's publication were based upon pencil sketches Comfort had done while accompanying the author during his interviews with the different pioneer women. Years later, Comfort recalled in "Sketches from Memory" that the women did not pose for him during those meetings.[8] About one particular woman, Harriette Cowan (Fig 69.1), he remembered how he had made his pencil sketches of her while she "talked endlessly and interestingly to Healy." He also noted, "For me it was an unforgettable experience to be privileged to hear these fascinating interviews, and to have this pleasant contact with this charming old lady." Like his portraits of Bédard and Rousselle, the portraits in *Women of Red River* show that he was most interested in making a direct and informal study of the characters of these men and women who spoke and sang of an earlier time in Canadian history. According to H.M. Jackson:

> A face to [Comfort] is a reflection of character and he feels that since it takes so many years to impinge character on a man's face, a portrait must take into consideration the imprint which experience has left there. In the same way which he endeavors to delineate what time and nature have done to a rock, so he tries to depict the result of an individual's life on his countenance. He searches for the meaning there is in people.[9]

Another common trait shared by the portraits in Healy's book and Comfort's later sketches is that they all bear the signatures of their subjects.[10] Such a practice was not unique to Comfort's work. In one known instance, Philéas Bédard signed a sketch of himself drawn by Arthur Lismer now in the Canadian Museum of Civilization. A possible explanation with regards to the folk singer sketches might be that the signatures were added at the request of Marius Barbeau. Apparently Comfort gave his sketches of Bédard and Rousselle to Barbeau sometime during the Folk Song Festival.[11] Therefore, it is possible that Barbeau was present at the time that they were created and suggested they be signed.

The 1928 Canadian Folk Song and Handicraft Festival was a result of the growth in the study of folklore traditions that occurred at that time, especially in Quebec. The interest was generated partly because intellectuals perceived that French Canada's culture was suffering as a result of social changes. The population shift from the country to the city saw the loss of rural values and traditions, and, as a means of preserving the old Québécois way of life, an interest developed in the study of French Canada's folksong traditions. Folk music apparently reflected all the traditions that the intellectuals wanted to ensure would continue in Quebec life – "religion, patriotism, attachment to the land, nobility of heart, and courage."[12] Marius Barbeau was certainly the most active individual in studying this material. However, the interest was not just in recording and studying folksongs; there was an attempt to educate Canadians about the role of folksongs in society and to promote them as part of contemporary life through publications, soirées, talks and festivals. Beginning in 1927, a series of festivals was organized at Quebec City under the auspices of the National Museum of Canada, with the co-operation of the Canadian Pacific Railroad. They were dedicated, as Lawrence Mason noted in 1927, to "the promotion of a better knowledge and appreciation of Canada's great wealth of folk music, dances, arts, textiles, and many handicrafts of the fireside or the workshop."[13] Native singers as well as professional performers were featured. The festivals were very well attended and were even viewed as making "a splendid contribution to Canada's national development."[14]

Bédard and Rousselle were typical examples of folk singers in Quebec at that time. Both men were informants of the folklorist Édouard-Zotique Massicotte. Joseph Rousselle was born in 1872 at Saint-Denis (Kamouraska), and as a young man had worked as a lumberjack. By 1928, he was living in Montreal. Amongst Rousselle's repertoire of ballads, "complaintes" and narrative songs, Marius Barbeau singled out his work and dance songs as being best adapted to his voice and temperament. He was also a violinist and an accomplished raconteur with a "highly dramatic style."[15]

Philéas Bédard was born in 1864, his ancestors having originally come to Canada around 1640 from Normandy, France. He was a native of Saint-Rémi de Napierville, where he earned his living as a farmer, but he often left his plough to give musical performances. For instance, in 1919, he and Rousselle participated in the "Veillées du bon vieux temps." The first folk soirées were organized by Marius Barbeau and Édouard-Zotique Massicotte, held at the Bibliothèque Saint-Sulpice (now the Bibliothèque nationale du Québec) in Montreal. Bédard also performed at the Quebec City festivals of 1927, 1928 and 1930.

Bédard's performances were not restricted to the province of Quebec. Dressed in his costume of homespun and ceinture fléchée, he often accompanied Marius Barbeau when the latter gave talks on French-Canadian folksongs. For example, on 25 April 1920, he performed for the Canadian Club in New York. Five years later, he and Barbeau entertained the Empire Club and the Canadian Authors' Association in Toronto. Based on sketches by Arthur Lismer, it seems that Bédard also gave an impromptu performance on 10 April 1925 to the members of the Arts and Letters Club (Fig.69.3). Bédard made a second appearance before the Empire Club on 7 March 1929, when Barbeau gave an address entitled "Folk Songs of French Canada." Events such as these helped to make Bédard's reputation as one of Quebec's favourite folksingers. They also helped to focus people's attention upon the wealth of folk music in that province.

The acquisition of Comfort's drawings by Marius Barbeau is noteworthy. Certainly the subject matter of the sketches would have interested Barbeau; yet he probably did not collect them solely for that reason. Barbeau was concerned about the development of Canadian art, and actively supported it in various ways. One way was through the organization of exhibitions of Canadian work. For example, during both the 1927 and 1928 Folk Song Festivals, he arranged to have historic and contemporary Canadian art lent from the National Archives of Canada and the National Gallery of Canada. He also invited artists to join him on his field trips. One such trip included Charles Comfort in 1935, when Comfort and his wife Louise went to the Tadoussac area of Quebec with a group of artist friends and joined Barbeau. Louise Comfort recalls how Barbeau took them with him one at a time when "he was calling on elderly people in the area recording the songs which had been in their families for generations, but never recorded."[16] Through trips such as this, artists were able to gather images for later use.

Barbeau also supported the cause by having Canadian artists illustrate his many publications. Arthur Lismer's work frequently appeared in Barbeau's books, as did that of Marjorie Borden, George Pepper and others. Even Comfort's sketch of Rousselle was eventually used as an illustration in Barbeau's 1962 publication *Le rossignol y chante*.[17] It was obviously not specifically commissioned for that book. Rather, like the book itself, which was a collection of folk-songs Barbeau had gathered over the years, the illustrations and photographs are an odd assortment drawn from Barbeau's collection.

Comfort's pencil sketches of Philéas Bédard and Joseph Rousselle document two interesting French-Canadian folk singers as well as an important but little-documented Canadian cultural event. By studying Comfort's drawings, one is also made aware of the importance of the work of people like Marius Barbeau and Édouard-Zotique Massicotte, without whom much of Canada's folklore heritage would have been lost forever.

T.Mc.

69.1 C. Comfort
Harriette Cowan, 1923(?)
Pen and ink
Reproduced from *Women of Red River*

69.2 C. Comfort
Sœur Laurent, 1923(?)
Pen and ink
Reproduced from *Women of Red River*

69.3 A. Lismer
Philéas Bédard singing at the Arts and Letters Club, 10 April 1925
Charcoal
NA C-119897

1. NA, Charles Comfort papers, MG 30 D81, vol. 9, "Sketches from Memory," file 5, p. 215. He worked in this position at Brigden's throughout the 1920s.

2. Letter to the author from Louise Comfort, 16 November 1988. Louise Comfort remained at home during this trip to care for their first daughter, Ruth.

3. NA, MG 30 D81, vol. 9, "Sketches from Memory," file 5, p. 225.

4. Augustus Bridle, "Folk Singers Capture the Ancient Capital," *Daily Mail* (Toronto), 21 May 1927, p. 24; Augustus Bridle, "People from Hinterland of Old Quebec Province Mingle with Grand Artists," *Daily Mail*, 23 May 1927, p. 20.; Lawrence Mason, "Festival of Folk-Song and Age-Old Handicraft Opens in Ancient Capital," *Globe* (Toronto), 21 May 1927, p. 6; Lawrence Mason, "Festival Proves Revelation of Riches of Canadian Music," *Globe*, 23 May 1927, p. 4.

5. NA, MG 30 D81, vol. 9, "Sketches from Memory," file 5, pp. 225-225a.

6. NA, MG 30 D81, vol. 9, "Sketches from Memory," file 5, p. 225.

7. *Canadian Folk Song and Handicraft Festival* (n.p., 1928), brochure, 22.

8. NA, MG 30 D81, vol. 8, "Sketches from Memory," file 1, p. 183.

9. H.M. Jackson, *Charles Comfort the Man and the Artist* (n.p., 1935-1936), 5.

10. The authenticity of the signature on the Bédard portrait was recently confirmed by comparing it to Bédard's signatures on letters to Marius Barbeau held by the Canadian Centre for Folk Culture Studies in the Canadian Museum of Civilization. See Cat. nos. 57-58 for similarly autographed portraits.

11. NA, MG 30 D81, vol. 8, "Sketches from Memory," file 2, p. 224.

12. Charlotte Cormier and Donald Deschênes, "1850-1940: The Pioneering Age of Folksong in Québec," in Janice Seline, *The Illustration of the Folksong in Québec* (Montreal: Montreal Museum of Fine Arts, 1980), 16.

13. Mason, "Festival of Folk-Song."

14. Lawrence Mason, "Folksong Festival opens with Program of Rarest Quality," *Globe*, 25 May 1928, p. 2.

15. Marius Barbeau, in *Canadian Folk Song and Handicraft Festival* (n.p., 1928) general program, 3.

16. Letter to the author from Louise Comfort, 31 October 1988.

17. Marius Barbeau, *Le rossignol y chante* (Ottawa: Musée national du Canada, 1962), 243.

DOROTHY STEVENS (1888-1966)

71. *Nicholas Hornyansky*, 1943-1944

Oil on canvas

91.6 x 76.5 cm

Inscribed in brushpoint and red paint, recto, l.r.: *Dorothy / Stevens*

Purchased in 1987

Accession no.: 1987-63-1

Negative no.: C-131136

This portrait of the printmaker Nicholas Hornyansky was painted by Dorothy Stevens for the 72nd Annual Exhibition of the Ontario Society of Artists, held in the spring of 1944. It was part of a special section of thirty-five portraits of artists painted by fellow artists that was displayed in the Octagonal Room of the Art Gallery of Toronto (now the Art Gallery of Ontario).[1] According to one review of the show, the portraits showed that:

> ...artists, on the whole, do not see one another as the unregenerate bohemians, misanthropes or saints that the unenlightened layman sometimes does. In fact, artists – in the eyes of fellow artists – appear to be quite tangible and presentable persons.... [They are] but little removed from "solid citizens."[2]

The exhibition was very popular. After closing in Toronto, it travelled to the Williams Memorial Art Museum in London, Ontario, where it was opened by Hornyansky himself.[3] Subsequently, at the invitation of the provincial government of Quebec, the exhibition opened in October at the Musée de la province de Québec (now Musée du Québec), in Quebec City, accompanied by a bilingual catalogue.[4] Stevens' portrait of Hornyansky was frequently singled out by the critics. In one instance it was cited as a representation of the "old world culture" artist as opposed to the "frontier painters," such as the Group of Seven and its followers.[5]

Having received extensive art training in several European centres, Hornyansky was, in fact, an excellent model of the European trained artist. He was born in Budapest, Hungary, in 1896, where he also began his art studies.[6] Although he at first studied painting and did some portraiture in Europe, he was converted to printmaking through his encounter with master printmakers in Antwerp and Paris. Upon settling in Toronto in 1929, he established himself as one of Canada's most innovative printmakers of the first half of this century, perfecting a one-pull colour aquatint method. He taught printmaking at the Ontario College of Art from 1945 to 1958, and he shared his ideas and innovations through the numerous lecture-demonstrations he gave in public galleries and to art societies throughout the country.[7] He also campaigned to enhance the artistic status of the intaglio (metal engraving) print.[8] An active member of the Society of Canadian Painter-Etchers and Engravers, he was remembered "as a continual stimulus to the membership both for his technical expertise and innovative spirit."[9]

Hornyansky was slightly eccentric in his ideas. In campaigning for government help for artists in 1941, he stated "the nobility of the artist's Art is shrouded into the eternal protection of its uselessness."[10] However, he then proposed new uses for art, claiming it should be developed into "cultural consumption so wide spread [*sic*] that it becomes part of every day life and a civilized necessity."[11] He crusaded for establishing a New Saturday, "the day made free by progress for the enjoyment of life and culture" when people get away from "the passive receptiveness of modern mass entertainment".[12] However, he also had a very practical side; as chairman of the Society's exhibition committee from 1939 to the 1960s, he was responsible for the considerable growth in the touring exhibitions program and for the Society's participation in international exhibitions.[13] At the time this portrait was done, Hornyansky was president of the CPE, a post he held until 1946. He died in Toronto in 1965.

One critic described the portrait as being "very very formal."[14] This description, however, refers more to the attire of the sitter than to the painting itself. In a traditional portrait, the model usually poses either full or three-quarter face, whereas Hornyansky is represented in profile, reminiscent of Thomas Gainsborough's well-known portrait of Mrs. Siddons (National Gallery, London). The relaxed posture allowed the painter to make a careful study of the artist's hand, surely a very deliberate choice, since manual labour is such a major part of an artist's occupation. In fact, the hand dominates the left side of the canvas, placed in sharp contrast to the intense green of the furniture. Showing Hornyansky in formal attire disconnects him completely from his printmaking, a rather messy trade, and shows him as a man "bred in old world subtlety."[15] Hornyansky may very well have appreciated being cast in such a role. A photograph published in 1951 shows him wearing a wing collar, popular in the 1890s, indicating that he may have been an eccentric in dress as well as ideas.[16] The informal setting, with furniture cut at odd angles, sets up another dichotomy between the formally attired artist and the homeliness of his surroundings, a point noted by a contemporary critic, who called the background "incongruous."[17] The portrait is successful because it simultaneously captures Hornyansky's likeness and poses questions about him.

The execution of the portrait is quite typical of Stevens' method of working. It is painted in lean, thin oils that enabled her to work very quickly, for she was capable of painting a portrait in one evening's sitting.[18] She usually began with a charcoal underdrawing that she would fix with a spray, and would then use "plenty of yellow for the skin tones and transparent sienna for the shadows."[19]

Dorothy Stevens was best known for her portraits of children and of beautiful and elegant Toronto society women, as for example her portrait of Mrs. Laidlaw (Fig.71.1). Hornyansky's foreign elegance likely appealed to her. During an exhibition of her work at Simpson's department store gallery in 1949, where she made on-the-spot sketches of children, she was reputed to have asked the management to find her some "colored kids... negro or Chinese kids... kids with character and eloquence in their eyes" to replace the "dough-faced Aryan kids" who had been modelling for her.[20]

Stevens was born in Toronto and, like Hornyansky, received extensive art training abroad, at the Slade School in London in portrait and figure painting, and at the Colarossi and Grande Chaumière Academies in Paris.[21] She began her artistic career in Canada as an etcher, showing her work at the Canadian National Exhibition in Toronto in 1912 and winning a silver medal in 1915 in San Francisco at the Panama Pacific Exposition.[22] In the same year, she won a $1,000 scholarship from the Royal Canadian Academy and travelled to Spain to paint.[23] When Stevens returned to Toronto, she made portraiture and the human figure her specialty at a time when many Canadian artists were exploring landscape painting, culminating in the work of the Group of Seven. She was elected a member of the Ontario Society of Artists in 1914 and a full academician of the Royal Canadian Academy in 1949. In the 1930s she took up subjects such as portraits of black women, and in the late 1940s and early 1950s she travelled to Mexico, Haiti and the British Virgin Islands in search of new subjects. Her paintings, however, are purely decorative and lack the social commentary of her contemporaries such as Prudence Heward and Isobelle Reid. During World War I, Stevens was a commissioned war artist and produced six etchings for the Canadian War Memorials collection.[24] She was active in women's associations all her life, and was president of the Lyceum Club, the Women's Art Association and the Heliconian Club among others. One of her paintings was included in the 1947 exhibition *Canadian Women Artists*, held in New York. She conducted art classes for both adults and children, and may have worked briefly as a commercial artist for Eaton's department store.[25] She was also known as a colourful and outspoken hostess who threw lively parties in her pink stuccoed house in Rosedale, a posh area of Toronto.[26]

The portrait collection of the National Archives contains numerous portraits of artists, many of them self-portraits. Dorothy Stevens' portrait of Nicholas Hornyansky is a fine addition to these unique documents.

E.M.-M.

71.1 Dorothy Stevens
Mrs. John Baird Laidlaw, 1929-1930
Oil on canvas
National Archives of Canada
NA C-132994

1. "Artists Paint each other to Liven up Art Show," *Telegram* (Toronto), 18 March 1944.
2. Paul Duval, "Artists Portray Fellow-Artists in O.S.A. Show," *Saturday Night*, 8 April 1944, p. 4.
3. Archives of Ontario, Ontario Society of Artists papers, MU 2257, President's Report for the year ending 28 February 1945, p. 7.
4. Archives of Ontario, MU 2257, President's Report... 1945, p. 8.
5. Pearl McCarthy, "Artists Portray Fellow-Artists," *Globe and Mail* (Toronto), 17 March 1944.
6. Andrew J. Oko, *The Society of Canadian Painter-Etchers and Engravers in Retrospect* (Hamilton: Art Gallery of Hamilton, 1981), 75.
7. *Nicholas Hornyansky Retrospective* (Owen Sound, Ontario: Tom Thomson Memorial Art Gallery, 1978), 4.
8. *Maritime Art* 3 (December-January 1942-1943): 64, letter to the editor from Hornyansky.
9. Oko, 75.
10. Nicholas Hornyansky, "Memorandum: "The Spade" A.E.A." (Artists' Economic Assembly), typewritten script, 1941, National Gallery of Canada, artist file.
11. Hornyansky, "Memorandum...."
12. David Mawr, "Better Use of New Leisure Eminent Artist's Subject," *Daily Star* (Windsor), 13 January 1951.
13. Oko, 75.
14. Duval.
15. McCarthy.
16. Mawr.
17. *Telegram*.

18. "Canadian Portrait Painter Surprises Lindsay Art Guild," *Thursday Post* (Lindsay, Ontario), 22 January 1958.

19. *Thursday Post.*

20. Lisa Ramsay, "You Splash Plenty of Color Around," *Maclean's Magazine*, 1 July 1950, p. 48.

21. National Gallery of Canada, artist file, Information Form 5, completed by Stevens in 1925 and 1944.

22. Chris Petteys, *Dictionary of Women Artists* (Boston: G.K. Hall, 1985).

23. NA, Royal Canadian Academy of Arts papers, MG 28 I126, vol. 17, Minute Books 1906-1927, p. 227, 19 November 1915 and vol. 15, Scrapbook 1915-1933, newspaper clipping from *Le Devoir* (Ottawa), ca. 1916.

24. R.F. Wodehouse, *A Check List of the War Collections of World War I, 1914-1918 and World War II, 1939-1945* (Ottawa: National Gallery of Canada, 1968), 56.

25. *1941 Toronto City Directory* (Toronto: Might Directories Ltd., 1941).

26. Letter to the author from Carolyn Neal, architectural historian with a special interest in the Rosedale area of Toronto.

ANDREW LOOMIS (1892-1959)

72. *School Days (The Dionne Quintuplets)*, ca. 1938

Oil on canvas

76.4 x 96.3 cm

Inscribed in brushpoint and white paint, recto, l.l.: © *1938 NEA SERVICE INC.*; l.r.: *ANDREW / LOOMIS / © / B & B*

Purchased in 1986

© 1938 Newspaper Enterprise Association, Inc., and Brown & Bigelow, a division of Atwater Group, Inc.

Accession no.: 1986-37

Negative no.: C-128266

In the mid-1930s, Callander, located southeast of North Bay, Ontario, was, like many small communities, suffering through the Depression. On 28 May 1934 an event occurred there that not only changed its economic outlook, but also put it on the international map. Five identical girls were born to Elzire and Oliva Dionne, doubling the number of offspring to be raised on their farm homestead. The Dionne Quintuplets began their struggle to fame by miraculously surviving their premature birth, the smallest weighing less than two pounds. Yvonne, Annette, Cécile, Émilie and Marie spent their first days of life wrapped in sheeting and huddled together in a basket covered with heated blankets, which was set in front of the open oven door.[1] Two midwives safely delivered the first two children, with the country doctor, Roy Allan Dafoe, who was to become as famous as the quintuplets,[2] arriving for the birth of the last three (Fig. 72.1).

Being quintuplets was exceptional enough, but being the only recorded identical ones to survive infancy made the Dionnes the focus of world-wide attention. From the day of their birth, the world beat a path to their door. First came the media, then the entrepreneurs with schemes to exhibit them at expositions, with the manufacturing companies following suit, hoping to get the girls to endorse everything from toothpaste and Quintuplet dolls to automobiles. In the whirlwind of activity that followed, the world was to witness the growth of a multi-million dollar industry built around them.[3]

The Dionnes were a boon to the northern Ontario tourist industry of the 1930s and 1940s. The road from Callander led to a wonderland of sorts, dubbed "Quintland," built around the site of their birthplace. It featured the Dionne farmhouse; Oliva Dionne's two souvenir shops; the Dafoe Hospital, where the Quintuplets were cared for by a team of surrogate doctors and nurses; a private playground; a public playground where the children were on display twice a day, which was surrounded by a large horseshoe-shaped observation gallery through which the "invisible" crowds shuffled;[4] and the Midwives' Souvenir Pavilion. A seven-foot wire security fence encompassed the complex.

No history of the Dionne Quintuplets is complete without mention of their nine-year separation from their parents,[5] and the guardianship struggle that turned into a tug-of-war between the doctor and the parents, with the Ontario government caught in the middle.[6] The numerous lawsuits and court battles that occurred in those years filled the newspapers.

Although Dr. Dafoe attended to the Quints' physical well-being, there emerged a growing concern for their social and intellectual development in such an artificial confinement[7] (Fig. 72.2). In the spring of 1935, Dr. William Blatz, Director of the Institute of Child Study at the University of Toronto, who had pioneered then revolutionary ideas in the study of child guidance, moved into the nursery. By their second birthday, the girls were well past their first precarious moments. The five little girls were charismatic, healthy and attractive, and possessed charming personalities that they revealed to a captivated audience during their playground performances:

> Few could resist a gasp on first seeing the Quints. By 1936, when the new playground was first opened, the two-year-olds were glowing with health, cheeks pink, enormous eyes framed by long lashes, hair in soft curls. The contrast between that spectacle and the memory of the early photographs, which had shown them as tiny inhuman creatures...was one reason why the sight of them was almost magical. To add to the fantasy, each was a carbon copy of the others.[8]

The three-year presence of Blatz at such a crucial period of the youngsters' development was likely beneficial for them. Within a strictly scheduled daily routine, they were given ample opportunity to learn through various structured and non-structured play activities. At this point, the nursery was redesigned to include two playrooms, a children's dining room, and an isolation room for bad behaviour. The Dionnes retained fond memories of their home:

> The happiest, least complicated years of our lives were spent in the nursery...We had everything we wanted.... We had dolls, tricycles, building blocks, paints, soft toys, hard toys, blackboards, easels, playthings of every description.... We dabbled with watercolors and we squeezed Plasticine. We learned, with much chewing of tongues, how to write our names and how to produce a tremendously satisfying din from the drums, tambourines, bells and xylophone....[9]

In the Andrew Loomis painting *School Days* (Cat. no. 72), the artist has attempted to record a glimpse of life at the nursery, likely sometime near the end of Blatz's stay. Yvonne, dressed in sunny yellow and matching hair bow, sitting in centre front, waves her right arm in the air, beckoning the viewer into the painting with her beaming face. Her four sisters surround her in a semi-circle, all turned in toward her. Cécile is shown in pink with head resting on her left arm. Émilie, dressed in blue-green and sitting in the middle ground, is given prominence by smiling directly at the viewer and holding up her drawing. In the right middle ground, Marie, in lilac and with her head bent over her book, sits in a quarter turn toward Yvonne. Annette, dressed in peach, turns us back to the starting point, with her profile gaze and the lines of her body and left arm.

Each of the girls had a distinctive colour and unique picture symbol assigned to them to help identify belongings and places. According to Blatz, Yvonne's preferred colour was purple and her symbol a bluebird; Annette's green, her symbol a maple leaf; Cécile's turquoise blue, her symbol a turkey; Émilie's pink, her symbol a tulip; and Marie's yellow, her symbol a teddy bear. Although the girls' recollections of symbols match Blatz's, the colours do not; they recall that Annette's assigned colour was red, Cécile's green, Émilie's white, Marie's blue and Yvonne's pink.[10] Loomis' choice of colour does not correspond exactly to the formula, perhaps owing to his distance from his subjects, but likely also because the coding was not strictly adhered to, even in official photographs.

In the painting each of the girls has her own child-sized table, topped with paper, pencils and seemingly unsuitably large textbooks. A child-sized chair is shown in the background under the chalkboard. Shelves in the right background corner hold indistinguishable blocks of colour, and a sunny window at the right floods potted flowers and children with light. Photographs suggest that the artist has faithfully rendered the faces and dress of the children, even placing the ever-present hair bows on the correct side (Fig. 72.2). It is known that a series of photographs was taken of the Quints and sent to Loomis, from which he assembled a final image, a practice which he advocated.[11] He creates a feeling of atmosphere of the room, and seems not to have laboured over the accuracy of physical details of the surroundings.

The painting was made specifically for reproduction as part of a large calendar advertising the firm Brown & Bigelow, a company producing graphic products and advertising specialties, which today still operates out of St. Paul, Minnesota. The calendar included at the top an impressive 48.5 x 61.0 cm lithographic reproduction of the painting framed in a "trompe-l'œil" wooden school slate frame, with the identification of the painting, the company name and their product lines printed below. The version of the calendar now at the National Archives has unfortunately had the bottom part removed, where the calendar pad used to be (Fig. 72.3).[12] An advertisement appeared on the back of the calendar, printed beside five small reproductions of the babies' faces, crediting Loomis for his realistic portrayal, and appealing to prospective clients who, it was hoped, would identify with the parental emotion of sending children to school for the first time. The National Archives owns a second calendar, *First Dates – The Dionne Quintuplets*, ca. 1948, also based on a painting by Loomis. For several years an annual calendar portraying the Quints was distributed throughout North America by the firm, the series of sixteen beginning with *School Days* in 1940, and ending with *Grown Up* (Fig. 72.4) in 1955. One painting, *Four Quints Visiting Fifth Quint in Convent*, was never used for a calendar, because of Émilie's sudden death in 1954.[13] Just two years earlier, the five girls had been honoured when they appeared at the winter carnival in St. Paul, Minnesota, "as guests of the calendar manufacturers, who had been spreading Quintuplet pictures around by the millions for the past eighteen years."[14]

The *School Days* painting bears the copyright symbol of NEA Service Inc., which stood for Newspaper Enterprises of America,[15] an American syndicate, which obtained exclusive world rights to take pictures of the Quintuplets. After 1935, the girls did not appear in photographs with their parents and siblings, because that year the *New York Daily News* had obtained the photographic rights for the rest of the family.[16] This meant that no unauthorized photographs were allowed, and not even Oliva Dionne could steal a snapshot of his own famous daughters.[17]

Andrew Loomis was born in Syracuse, New York, and studied in New York with the Art Students' League. Service in the army interrupted his work in Chicago, where, upon his return, he was employed at two firms, Charles Everett Johnson Advertising Art Studio, and Bertch and Cooper, eventually opening his own studio and working freelance. His successful career included a position as teacher at the American Academy of Art in Chicago, and the publication of several art books dealing with the basics of drawing and painting, as well as the techniques of successful commercial illustration.[18] Another of his accomplishments was that he was the only artist commissioned by the British Crown to paint the Dionne Quintuplets.[19] In addition to the calendar illustrations, his paintings of the Dionne Quintuplets were reproduced in magazine advertisements, such as those for Palmolive soap that appeared in magazines such as *Chatelaine*.[20] In his book *Creative Illustration*, published in 1947, Loomis stated that the subjects chosen for calendar illustration should promote goodwill and friendliness and elicit feelings of tranquility and contentment, the idea being to sell the firm itself rather than a specific product.[21] The image worked best if it could offer an escape into fantasy. In the case of portraits, the sitters had to convey a story or meaning. Since one of the broad categories Loomis considered successful material was the "maternal instinct," the Dionne Quintuplets intrinsically met many of the basic appeal criteria. They were beautiful children, magically unique, and they were equated with success. The design of the image was simple in order to maintain an attention value across a large room. Because calendar reproduction involved lithographic printing, a wide range of colour was used. Since the printing of large flat planes and patches of colour was easier, the broad economical brushstrokes, which were part of Loomis' personal modelling style, were ideal and are evident in *School Days*.

Although the painting creates a general impression of health and happiness in "Quintland," the absence of other family members underlines their existence as an isolated unit during their formative years, an estrangement that in later years could not be reversed.[22] The happy little room of the nursery is a testament to the efforts of well-intentioned people who provided the best that money could buy but could not foresee the future. The girls at four years of age formed such a tight-knit group that coping alone with events in the outside world was to be a tremendous strain on each of them. When the government finally built the long-promised, new seven-bedroom brick home, to become known as the "Big House," where the family was reunited in 1943, this painting was hung above the mantle-piece of the living room (Fig. 72.5). Yet the fleeting childhood years were over. The painting is emblematic of the Quintuplets as everyone wished to remember them.

Three later married and had children of their own. Two are now deceased. Apparently the three remaining women live as virtual recluses in a Montreal suburb. Their father Oliva passed away in 1979,[23] and Elzire died in November 1986. Even though time has passed, it seems impossible that the world will ever forget the five smiling Canadian children of the 1930s, the Dionne Quintuplets, as they were painted by Andrew Loomis.

M.M.

72.1 NEA Service Inc., Photogelative Engraving Co. Ltd.
The Dionne Quintuplets at Callander, Ontario, Canada, ca. 1938
Photoreproduction
NA PA-26034

72.2 NEA Service Inc.
The Dionne Quintuplets in their train car, on the trip to Toronto, 1939
Photograph
NA PA-122615

72.3 A. Loomis
School Days, Brown & Bigelow Calendar, ca. 1939
Offset lithograph
NA C-128092

72.4 A. Loomis
Grown Up, ca. 1955
Oil on canvas
Private collection
© 1953 Brown & Bigelow, a division of Atwater Group, Inc.

72.5
***The Dionne Family at the Big House*,**
ca. 1943
Photograph
NA C-128091

1. Pierre Berton, *The Dionne Years* (Toronto: McClelland and Stewart, 1977), 37-40.

2. Berton, 30, 81-94, 192-194. Dr. Dafoe, whose country doctor practicality saved the life of the Quintuplets and Mrs. Dionne, became as well known as they. He was constantly photographed with the children and was one of the official guardians.

3. Berton, 12.

4. James Brough with Annette, Cécile, Marie and Yvonne Dionne, *We were Five* (New York: Simon and Schuster, 1965), 62. "In theory, the onlookers were invisible to anyone in the playground. The idea was that since the passageway was dark, the wire screening would disperse the light so that we would see nothing of the crowds who streamed in to gaze at the show. But of course we knew very well that we were watched every minute.... We could plainly hear our guests chuckle...."

5. Berton, 64, 75, 79. They were first separated from the rest of the family members, who were cordoned off to the second floor of the farmhouse, out of the necessity to provide the delicate infants with a controlled environment, free from germs and temperature fluctuations, where they could be monitored without interference. Eventually the babies were moved across the road into the newly built log nursery, to become known as the "Dafoe Hospital"; the parents had visiting privileges. The arrangement was to be temporary, but the separate lodging was to continue for the better part of the next nine years.

6. Berton, 72, 104, 194. The Quintuplets became wards of the Crown in 1934. They were removed from their parents' control and placed under a board of four guardians, including Dr. Dafoe and the grandfather of the children, Olivier Dionne. After two years a second guardianship was established, with a view to protecting their finances; Dafoe was again on the board and this time one parent, Oliva Dionne, was included. Although this last guardianship arrangement was to last until their eighteenth birthday, the parents regained physical custody of their children in 1943, when all were reunited in their new house.

7. Berton, 181; Brough, 84-86, 133. The first time the Quintuplets would be allowed to escape from their "goldfish-bowl existence" was just before their fifth birthday, when they travelled to Toronto to meet King George VI and Queen Elizabeth. Quints, parents, doctor, nurses and teacher met the sovereigns, while brothers and sisters were denied the privilege, being made to wait outside the room. The girls met royalty a second time in 1952, when Princess Elizabeth and the Duke of Edinburgh made a brief stop at the North Bay airport.

8. Berton, 15.

9. William E. Blatz, *The Five Sisters* (Toronto: McClelland and Stewart Ltd., 1938), 11-14.

10. Blatz, 111, n.1, and 122; and Brough, 57.

11. Letter to the author from Stan Guignard, former owner of the painting, 13 August 1986. Mr. Guignard spoke to Mrs. Dionne, who explained that Loomis was sent photographs from which he worked. Mr. Guignard took over the farmhouse and moved it to the outskirts of North Bay, opening it to the public as a museum, complete with artifacts and pictures of the Quintuplets. The site is now run by the City of North Bay.

12. *The Dionne Quintuplets – School Days* calendar has a printed text on the back: "School Days – for the five most famous little girls in the world, the Quintuplets of Callander, Ontario! School days – for the five Dionne babies who are babies no more! They will be six years old this year – growing up."

13. Berton, 199-200. Emilie, who had suffered epileptic seizures since the age of twelve, died 5 August 1954, while left alone at the convent in Ste. Agathe, where she was preparing to become a nun. Her death followed a series of seizures she had experienced that week.

14. Brough, 133-134.

15. Berton, 76. The American firm Newspaper Enterprises Association, Inc., part of United Media, appears to be the present-day equivalent of NEA Services Inc., and was contacted by the author during the course of the research for this entry. NEA Service Inc. published a picture book, *The Dionne Quintuplets Growing Up* (London: Putman & Company Ltd., 1935), showing the girls in photographs with captions that are often more cute than informative.

16. Berton, 76.

17. Brough, 63.

18. Walt Reed, *The Illustrator in America 1900-1960's* (New York: Reinhold Publishing Corporation, 1966), 98.

19. Letter from Brown & Bigelow to Stan Guignard, 8 January 1975. Copy made available to the author.

20. See *Chatelaine Magazine*, October, November 1936; February, July 1937.

21. Andrew Loomis, *Creative Illustration* (New York: The Viking Press, 1947), 259-263.

22. Brough, 102. "Reunion must have shattered so many dreams on both sides of our divided family. We had no wish for it. The last thing we wanted to have to do was leave the nursery....We were uneasy about the unknown years ahead with the family, who we sensed had mixed feelings about us....We were transferred into the Big House as a conquered army might be, one group of five clinging together as if for protection against the inquisitive looks of the other six brothers and sisters."

23. John Nihmey and Stuart Foxman, *Time of Their Lives* (Ottawa: Niva Publishing, 1986), 222.

3 Cols
[Cartwright and Corruption.]
¶ When the $52,000,000 estimates were brought down to the House this week, a peaceful expression rested upon the features of Sir Richard Cartwright.
¶ But.]
¶ On May 7, 1895, he thundered forth in this wise:

OCTAVE HENRI JULIEN (ca. 1852-1908)

73. *Cartwright and Corruption*, ca. 21 July, 1899

Brush, pen and black ink over pencil on paper

44.8 x 33.7 cm

Inscribed in pen and brown ink, recto, l.l.: *3 cols*; b.: *Cartwright and Corruption. / When the $52,000,000 estimates were brought down to the / House this week, a peaceful expression rested upon the / features of Sir Richard Cartwright. / But / On May 7, 1895, he thundered forth in this wise;* l.r.: *48*; verso, u.l.: *3 col / Thursday today* [crossed out] *sure* [?] / ... [illegible]

Donated in 1984

Acccession no.: 1984-206-1

Negative no.: C-97660

In this drawing, Sir Richard John Cartwright (1835-1912), minister of Industry and Commerce in the first Laurier government, is settled comfortably in his seat in the House of Commons, and is apparently unimpressed by what he hears.

Cartwright was born in Kingston in 1835 of Empire Loyalist stock, and was a businessman and entrepreneur.[1] Sir Richard was first elected to Parliament in 1863 as an independent Conservative and was re-elected in 1867 (the year of Confederation) to Sir John A. Macdonald's government. He anticipated being given the Finance portfolio, but Macdonald passed him over, perhaps because Cartwright was an ardent promoter of reciprocity (free trade) and the prime minister was not. Shortly thereafter, Cartwright switched allegiances and joined the Liberal Party. The Liberals came to power in 1873 under Alexander Mackenzie, and Cartwright was finally made minister of Finance. He was then thirty-eight years old.

When the Conservatives returned to power in 1878, Cartwright became finance opposition critic, a position he held until 1896. It was in this role, one for which he seemed ideally suited, that he made his mark; he was a man of principle rather than action, and more defensive than constructive by temperament. However, his relentless defence of unlimited reciprocity may well have contributed to the Liberal defeat under Wilfrid Laurier in the 1891 election.

Thanks to a less aggressive policy on reciprocity and numerous Conservative scandals, which were strongly attacked in the newspaper *Grip* by the cartoonist Bengough, Laurier finally came to power in 1896. Cartwright, who once again had his sights set on the Finance position, was instead given the Department of Industry and Commerce, which he retained until the Liberal defeat in 1911. In the meantime he was appointed to the Senate in 1904, and became Senate leader in 1909.

A brilliant and refined orator, Cartwright used words with a caustic irony that earned him Laurier's friendship and the respect of his colleagues, but not the love of the people. On the other hand, his unusual face was always a favourite subject of cartoonists, among them Henri Julien, the celebrated cartoonist of the *Canadian Illustrated News* and later of the *Montreal Daily Star*. The present drawing (Cat. no. 73), one of Julien's best-known political portraits, was published on Friday, 21 July 1899, in the *Star*. It was part of a series on the topic of "Cartwright and Corruption," published over a three-day period. The two other drawings show him on his feet, thundering away (published on 20 July), and patiently explaining his point of view (published on 22 July).[2]

"Cartwright and Corruption" refers to an incident that happened on 18 July 1899. The minister of Finance, W.S. Fielding, had asked that an extra five million dollars be added to the budget, making a total of close to fifty-two million dollars. Outraged by the enormity of the amount, a Conservative member invited Fielding to ask fellow Liberal Cartwright, who in the past had been quick to denounce Conservative budgets, if the latter had ever before asked for such large amounts; but Sir Richard remained silent.[3] His attitude was denounced the following day by the editor of the *Montreal Star*, who was a supporter of the Conservatives. Leafing quickly through the *Debates*, the editor found three occasions on which Cartwright had vehemently denounced, in the name of the overtaxed Canadian people, Conservative budgets that were far less exorbitant.[4]

Henri Julien initially had not been very inspired by the 1899 session of Parliament.[5] On 19 July, he decided that he too would go after Cartwright instead of the minister of Finance, and rushed to his sketchbook. The drawing, planned for Thursday 20 July (according to the inscription on the back of the drawing), did not appear until the next day. In the captions for these three cartoons, the artist repeated the three previous protestations by Cartwright, which had been cited by the editorial writer.[6] But Julien was careful to refer to the original texts of the debates in order to quote the minister correctly.[7]

This perfectionism is characteristic of the artist's work. In the *Album*, published in 1916, Henri Julien's friends described his work methods at length. He would observe members from the reporters' gallery in the House of Commons, sketching their most typical poses in the pages of his notebook.[8] Then he would choose one or more sketches to illustrate the *Star*'s daily report on the parliamentary session. When starting to rework the drawing in ink, Julien often referred to photographs of his subjects.[9] This is probably the case for the drawing of Cartwright, judging from a comparison with one of Cartwright's official photographs (Fig. 73.2).[10] It may have been this concern for authenticity that delayed publication of the drawing.

Each year Julien would choose a different theme to illustrate the newspaper's parliamentary reports. In 1894 and 1895, the series "Scenes in Parliament" showed members of Parliament debating in the House, or, conversely, choosing not to debate.[11] In another series, "Light and Shadows," the subjects were paired with the silhouettes of their usual opponents in the House.[12] The most famous series is the "By-Town Coons" (Cartwright is shown playing the banjo), which dates from the end of the 1890s, and which was later published by the *Star* in book form.

Julien's portraits are not caricatures in the normal sense, as they do not exaggerate the physical characteristics of the subjects.[13] Rather, it is his gift for subtle irony that gives a very personal tone to his graphic reporting. He focused on the personality rather than the event, and showed no political bias when analysing his subjects.

It was not always so, however. At the beginning of his career, Henri Julien's satirical commentary frequently adorned the cover of the *Canadian Illustrated News*, and more often than not the subjects were inspired by the current session of Parliament. Thus, in the 6 March 1875 issue, we see the then young minister of Finance, a certain Richard Cartwright, performing an extraordinary magician's trick (Fig. 73.3). Previously, on 16 February, during his second budget speech, Cartwright had explained how the new customs tariffs had made it possible to transform (miraculously!) an undeniable deficit (1873 was a year of economic crisis) into a certain surplus for the fiscal year 1873-1874.[14] He advocated the same procedure for the 1875-1876 fiscal year. Owing to new taxes, there would be no deficit, and there would even be hope for an appreciable surplus![15] A simple cooking of the books![16]

A comparison of these two portraits of Cartwright, done twenty-four years apart, and both relating to the budget, clearly illustrates the evolution of Henri Julien's satirical art. On the conceptual level he moved from allegorical references to more straightforward representations of the personalities involved in an event, which enabled him to concentrate on the subject's demeanor and attitude. On the artistic level, Julien progressed from a drawing that is full of detail and densely cross-hatched, and in which the size of the head is slightly exaggerated, to a simplified style, respectful of the subject, in which the black of the ink and the white of the paper are skilfully balanced.

If the 1875 drawing is an editorial caricature, then the 1899 drawing is more of a political portrait, albeit a portrait tinged with irony: If we compare Cartwright's eyes and mouth in the drawing with those of the photograph that served as the model, we can see how Julien has imbued Cartwright with an air of smugness.

L.D.

73.1 H. Julien
Study of a Man (Sir Richard Cartwright), ca. 1890-1896
Pencil
NA C-105026

73.2 W.J. Topley
Sir Richard Cartwright, 1906
Photograph
Copy of a c. 1899 photograph by George Lancefield
NA PA-12278

73.3 H. Julien
Good Cooking, 1875
Wood engraving
Reproduced from the *Canadian Illustrated News*, 6 March 1875
NA C-62582

1. His grandfather was Sir Richard Cartwright (1759-1815), an influential Kingston merchant and a member of the Legislative Council. His father, who died when Cartwright was still a child, was an Anglican clergyman. The NA owns four watercolours by his mother, Harriet Dobbs Cartwright (1808-1887), showing views of Kingston around 1832-1834 (Accession nos. 1945-29 to 1945-32).

2. Cat. no. 73 and the drawing of 20 July are reproduced in the *Album Henri Julien* (Montreal: Librairie Beauchemin, 1916), 88 and 91, "Political Portraits."

3. House of Commons, *Debates*. 8th Parl., 4th Session, 18 July 1899, col. 7696 .

4. "Machine Oil!," *Montreal Daily Star*, 19 July 1899. The author (probably Hugh Graham) sees in Cartwright's non-intervention an open invitation to a "carnival of corruption."

5. These three drawings of Cartwright are Julien's only illustrations for the 1899 session, because the following week the newspaper would assign him to the Seawanhaka regattas, west of Montreal. At this time, the *Star*, which was not yet using photographs, also hired the artists R.G. Mathews and P.F. Copland.

6. The dates of Cartwright's earlier interventions, quoted in the editorial of 19 July, and referred to again by Julien during the next three days, are 28 March 1894 (20 July); 7 May 1895 (21 July); and 27 March 1890 (22 July).

7. House of Commons, *Debates*, 6th Parl., 4th Session, 27 March 1890, col. 2581-2582; 7th Parl., 4th Session, 28 March 1894, col. 313; 7th Parl., 5th Session, 7 May 1895, col. 654.

8. The NA has two of Julien's sketchbooks (Accession no. 1979-51), one of which contains a sketch of Cartwright (Fig. 73.1). This sketch was the model for one of the drawings reproduced in the *Album* on p. 58, but Julien has eliminated the profile of the bearded man (G.E. Foster, Conservative minister of Finance, 1888-1896).

9. *Album*, 115, recollections of Brenton A. Macnab.

10. The negative from the Topley collection was made in 1906 from a positive image in a mat. The original photograph was attributed to George Lancefield. *City of Ottawa, Capital of the Dominion of Canada* (Ottawa: The Ottawa Free Press, 1899), 68.

11. For example, a delightful portrait of Cartwright reading a book while the Conservative minister of Finance, G.E. Foster, reads his Budget. *Montreal Daily Star*, 19 March 1894.

12. In Cartwright's case, it is Charles Tupper, finance critic for the Conservative Party: *Album*, 49.

13. In 1899, the illustrator for the Toronto *Globe*, F. Lake, also illustrated the reports of the session with numerous portraits of members of Parliament, but he always exaggerated their heads, a technique popular in the nineteenth century and the first half of the twentieth.

14. "The Budget Speech," *Globe* (Toronto), 17 February 1875.

15. "The Revenue and Expenditure," *Globe*, 4 March 1875.

16. A number of Julien's caricatures for the *Canadian Illustrated News* were also published by *L'Opinion publique*, but not this one. The theme of Richard the Magician would be taken up again by James G. MacKay (ca. 1846-1885) also in the *Canadian Illustrated News*, 11 March 1876, "The Black Crow back again" (with the same culinary theme and the same magician's costume as Julien, but Surplus, a goose, has flown away, and Deficit, a crow, has come back to perch on the edge of the cooking pot), and on 22 April 1876, "A Gay Deceiver"; in both cases, MacKay exaggerates the shape of the head.

Lismer's drawing of
Andrée Bieler, at
opening meeting of
Fed. of Can. Artists,
March 6, 1942
A.R.S.

ARTHUR LISMER (1885-1969)

74. *André Biéler at the First Montreal Meeting of the Federation of Canadian Artists*, 6 March 1942

Pencil on paper

27.9 x 21.6 cm

Inscribed in F.R. Scott's hand, in pencil, recto, l.l.: *Lismer's drawing of / Andrée Biéler, at / opening meeting of / Fed. of Can. Artists, / March 6, 1942. / F.R.S.*

Donated in 1986

Accession no.: 1987-2-9

Negative no.: C-130252

In the evolution of artists' groups in Canada, the formation of the Federation of Canadian Artists represents a milestone. It was an organization that evolved out of the 1941 Conference of Canadian Artists held at Queen's University (Kingston, Ontario). The resulting group was very active, particularly during the war years, in trying to address artists' interests and concerns. Unfortunately, too few records of the group's participants and activities seem to have survived; therefore any visual records are quite valuable. Charles Comfort took some photographic slides during the first national meeting of the Federation of Canadian Artists in May 1942, and Arthur Lismer did a few informal drawings of the Quebec division of the Federation, including one of André Biéler at the Federation's first meeting of the Quebec regional branch. The National Archives is fortunate to own many of such records, including Lismer's drawing of Biéler, donated as part of the Frank Scott manuscript collection.

Lismer's sketch of Biéler is a typical example of his work in pencil. Lismer is principally remembered for his oil paintings, especially those done while he was a member of the Group of Seven. However, in the last dozen years, two different studies have focused specifically upon Lismer's graphic oeuvre. In 1977, the artist's daughter, Marjorie Lismer Bridges, published *A Border of Beauty*, which dealt with the development of Lismer's pen and pencil work. More recently, in 1985, Ian Thom organized an exhibition at the McMichael Canadian Collection (Kleinburg, Ontario), which was devoted to Arthur Lismer's "cartoons." The attention that his drawings have been receiving demonstrates that they were in fact an important component of his art.

Arthur Lismer was born on 27 June 1885 in Sheffield, England. When just thirteen years old, he won a seven-year scholarship to attend evening classes at the Sheffield School of Art. During those seven years, he was also apprenticed to the photo-engraving firm of Willis Eadon and Company. As part of his apprenticeship, Lismer was called upon to work as an illustrative reporter for the Sheffield *Independent*. Even as a young child, Lismer exhibited an aptitude and love for drawing. John McLeish, in his biography on the artist, comments that for Lismer "Sketching was as natural as breathing...."[1] From his experience as a newspaper illustrator, Lismer received ample opportunity to develop his skills as a draughtsman and as an observer of life. These skills stood him in good stead in his later artistic endeavours. As an illustrator, he also learned how to capture quickly the essence of a subject in his sketches. He was later to recall, "All those years of sketching were the most important to my training."[2]

Following the completion of his apprenticeship and scholarship training in 1907, Lismer went to Antwerp, where he received additional schooling at the École des beaux-arts. After a year and a half of study, he returned to Sheffield and went into business as a graphic designer. The business did not fare well and, in an effort to build a better life for himself and his future wife, Esther, Lismer emigrated to Canada. Once here he began a very long and productive career as an artist and educator, while continuing to exhibit a strong interest in the graphic arts. This is demonstrated by the untold number of drawings Lismer did during his lifetime. Sometimes his drawings were finished works of art, while at other times, they were simply preliminary thoughts for his paintings. More frequently, Lismer's sketches were done for his own and others' entertainment. Having developed the habit of never going anywhere without drawing material in his pocket, Lismer would set about doing cartoons or informal portraits of a subject no matter where he was.

Despite Lismer's flair for creating cartoons and caricatures, he was constantly giving them away, never really considering them to be an important part of his artistic work. The 1942 sketch of André Biéler (Cat. no. 74), for example, was given to Frank Scott. Although Lismer himself may not have placed much lasting value on his quick sketches, they were an aspect of his art that received some acknowledgement through publication in newspapers and periodicals of the day. For instance, his caricature sketch of J.E.H. MacDonald, reportedly done on the occasion when MacDonald was made president of the Arts and Letters Club (Toronto), in 1928,[3] was later published in the February 1929 issue of *Canadian Forum* (Fig. 74.1). It was accompanied by a piece of verse J.E.H. MacDonald had written, entitled "Hark the Herald Angels Sing." MacDonald has been described by John McLeish as a dreamer, very intense and introspective – as much a poet as a painter. McLeish also noted how MacDonald "always appeared to Lismer's eyes as a secular monk."[4] One wonders if McLeish did not have Lismer's image of MacDonald in mind whenever he was making his observations about the painter. Certainly the portrait displays many, if not all, of the characteristics McLeish attributed to MacDonald.

In 1942, Lismer was equally successful in capturing the essence of André Biéler upon paper (Cat. no. 74). An artist in his own right, Biéler was also the head of Queen's University's fine art program. To his credit as well, he was the impetus behind the Conference of Canadian Artists, held at Queen's University in June 1941. Biéler's first reason for organizing the Conference of Canadian Artists was to give artists the opportunity "to get acquainted, to meet each other and thereby to appreciate each other."[5] Such an opportunity was deemed important by Biéler, because on a trip he had taken during the previous summer to Banff and Vancouver, he had become very concerned about the complete lack of communication between western and eastern Canadian artists regarding one another's problems and accomplishments. Other important reasons for the conference were to study the function of art in society, to educate artists about technical aspects of their art, and to discuss the contribution of artists to the war effort (for example, see Cat. no. 63).

More than one hundred and fifty artists, museum workers, art historians and interested laymen attended the four-day event, and during that period discussed, amongst other things, the need to create a national organization that would focus upon issues concerning the visual arts.[6] However, during the conference the delegates were unable to come to a consensus about how that organization should be arranged. They asked:

> Should it be a Federation of existing bodies, or should it be a new association of individual artists? Should it be limited to artists and their problems, or should it be thrown open to laymen who – as some feared – might overrun it?[7]

These concerns were referred to a Continuation Committee, headed by André Biéler, for further attention.[8] To determine what type of permanent national organization Canada's artistic community wanted, the committee did a wide mail survey in July 1941. As a result, it was decided that a federation of Canadian artists would work best, rather than one of existing artists' societies. This decision was taken after evaluating the replies the committee had received and after considering the ideas expressed in Kingston.

Named the Federation of Canadian Artists, the organization was created in the fall of 1941. It was headed by a National Executive Council, of which André Biéler served as president until 1944 when he resigned because of poor health. From the national level, the Federation was divided into five regions – West Coast, Western, Ontario, Quebec and Maritimes, each of the five divisions being looked after by its own regional committee.

In 1942, efforts were made to attract members into the Federation. As part of that effort, Arthur Lismer, as the first chairman of the Quebec region, arranged for his region's inaugural meeting to take place on 6 March at the Montreal Museum of Fine Arts. Two hundred painters, sculptors, architects, designers, teachers, craftsmen and laymen attended the event and heard the McGill professor and lawyer, Frank Scott, speak on the Federation's organization and constitution.[9] Scott was one of the group's lay members and a frequent contributor to Federation affairs.[10] For example, in addition to participating in Quebec's regional meetings, he was the keynote speaker at the Federation's May 1942 national conference in Toronto. He was also a valuable asset to the organization's special National Petition Committee, a committee which was established to petition the government for more artist involvement in the war effort.

As the organization's president, Biéler also attended the historic 6 March meeting in Montreal. He was in fact the principal speaker of the night, and addressed the aims of the Federation. It was during this meeting that Lismer, employing only a few quick pencil strokes, sketched the portrait of Biéler now held by the National Archives (Cat. no. 74). According to Frances Smith, an authority on Biéler and his art, the sketch documents the "controlled dynamism" of the painter at that time.[11] Other Lismer drawings that focus upon the Federation of Canadian Artists, like *Fred Taylor at a National War Effort Petition Meeting* (Fig. 74.2), also demonstrate the artist's ability to document significant figures and events relating to the organization's history, particularly in connection with its Quebec region. These visual records, especially when combined with the surviving textual records of the Federation, form a very clear picture of the importance and uniqueness of this Canadian cultural group.[12]

T.Mc.

74.1 A. Lismer
J.E.H. MacDonald, 1928
Pencil
Reproduced from *Canadian Forum*, February 1929, p. 171

74.2 A. Lismer

Fred Taylor at a National War Effort Petition Committee Meeting, February 1943

Pencil

NA C-135508

---

1. John A.B. McLeish, *September Gale* (Toronto: J.M. Dent & Sons (Canada) Ltd., 1955), 3-4.

2. Gail Scott, "Famed Group Formed an Infamous Quorum," *Daily News and Sentinel* (Amherst, Nova Scotia), 26 April 1968, p. 6.

3. Letter to the author from Raymond Peringer, archivist, Arts and Letters Club, Toronto, 2 March 1989.

4. McLeish, 3.

5. André Biéler and Elizabeth Harrison, eds., *Conference of Canadian Artists: Proceedings* (n.p.: 1941), 4-5.

6. The final day of the conference, 29 June, was spent in Ottawa.

7. Robert Ayre, "Canadian Artists Urge War Records as Works of Art," *Standard* (Montreal), 5 July 1941, p. 9.

8. Members of the Continuation Committee were André Biéler, Frances Loring, Walter Abell, A.Y. Jackson, Jean-Paul Lemieux and Arthur Lismer.

9. Robert Ayre, "Art News and Reviews: Montreal Division of Federation of Artists Will Hold Symposium," *Standard*, 21 March 1942, p. 25.

10. Lay members of the Federation of Canadian Artists were allowed to speak, but they were not allowed to vote in the organization.

11. Letter to the author from Frances K. Smith, 22 February 1989. Smith is the author of *André Biéler an Artist's Life and Times* (Toronto: Merritt Publishing Company Ltd., 1980).

12. Many of the records of the Federation of Canadian Artists are in the archives of Queen's University, Kingston, Ontario.

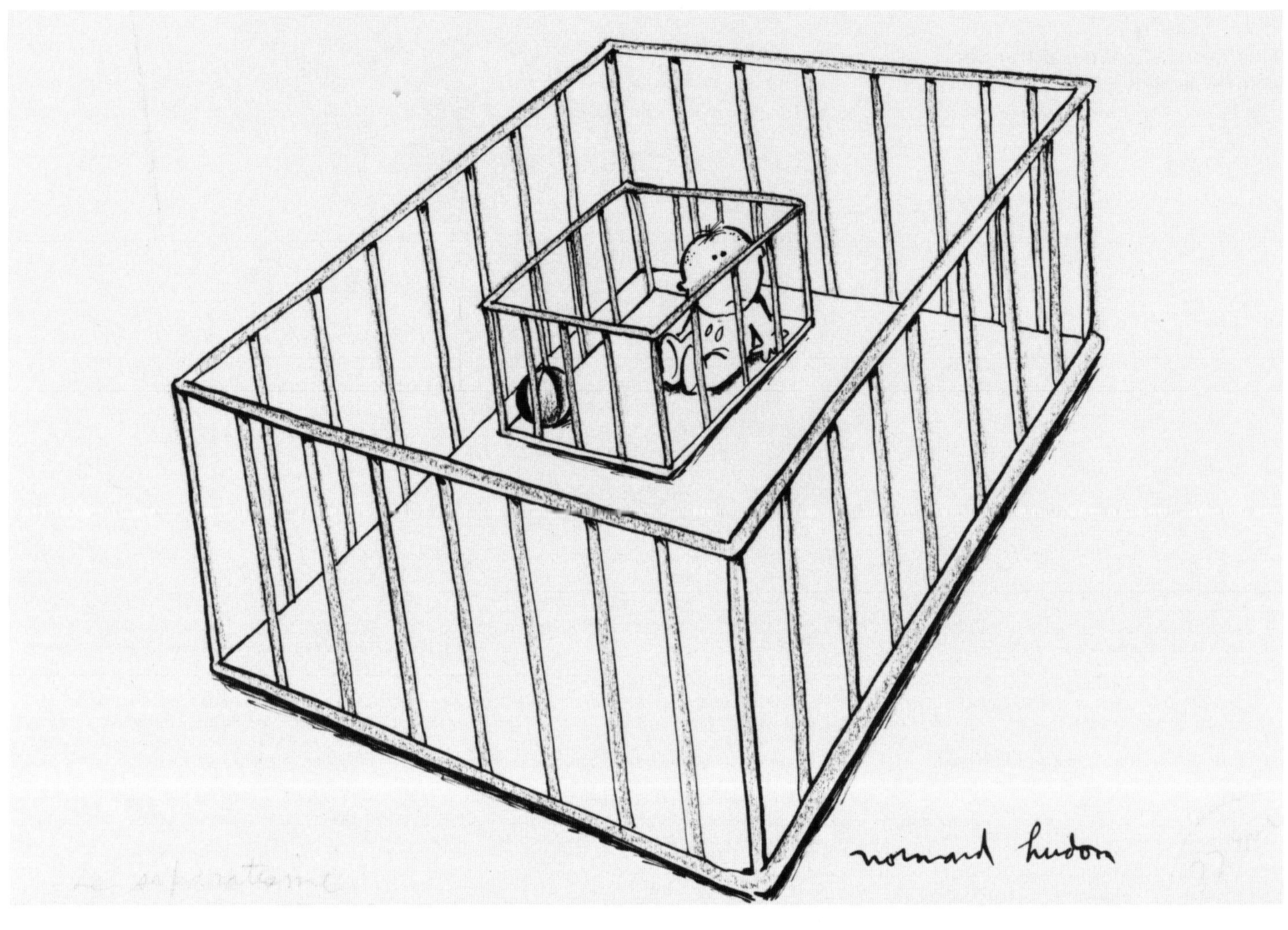
normand hudon

NORMAND HUDON (1929-)

75. *Separatism*, ca. 4 July 1961

Pen and black ink, with black crayon, on cardboard

18.3 x 27.1 cm

Inscribed in pencil, recto, l.l.: *Le séparatisme*; in pen and black ink, recto, l.r.: *normand hudon*; in pencil, l.r.: *32 ems*

Purchased in 1985

Acquisition no.: 1985-189-27

Negative no.: C-127596

Normand Hudon studied at the École des beaux-arts in Montreal and in Paris. His first cartoons were published in *Le Quartier Latin*, and his first comic strips in *Le Petit Journal*. During the fifties, while working freelance for a number of Montreal weeklies, he produced caricatures for nightclub patrons and for television. Starting on 2 February 1959, he replaced Robert La Palme as editorial cartoonist at *Le Devoir*. His favourite targets were the ministers in Maurice Duplessis' Quebec government. Although "le Chef" died in September 1959, Hudon continued to refer to him in cartoons for a long time to come.[1]

After a short stint at *Le Devoir*, Hudon again replaced La Palme starting on 2 September 1961, this time at *La Presse*, where he was to remain for four years. Then came Expo 67. Hudon painted a mural for the Pavilion of Humour, as well as ceiling decorations for part of the Canada Pavilion. He continues to have a busy career and is currently devoting himself as much to painting and illustration as to cartooning.[2]

Separatism (Cat. no. 75) was published less than two years after the death of Duplessis.[3] An editorial cartoon on this theme would have been unthinkable during the time of the "grande noirceur" or "great darkness" (as Duplessis' time as Quebec premier is known), but, at the beginning of the summer of 1961, a year after the election of "l'équipe du tonnerre," or "thundering team" of Jean Lesage (Liberal), separatism was already the subject of passionate debates. The "indépendantistes" banded together,[4] and a survey organized in January and February 1961 by the Montreal daily *La Presse* indicated that forty-five per cent of the respondents favoured independence.[5] *Le Devoir*, where Hudon was then working, organized its own referendum at the end of May, and preceded it with a long series of articles on different aspects of the issue.[6] The results were even more surprising: 75.2% of the respondents thought that Quebec's independence was desirable, and almost the same proportion (74.7%) thought that it was achievable.[7]

This debate was of little interest to Hudon, who continued to be more interested in the Union Nationale, whose activities were the subject of a royal commission of inquiry. He found in Daniel Johnson, whom he nicknamed "Danny Boy," a better subject than Premier Lesage, and he did not hesitate to bring back to life his favourite victims, Duplessis and Antoine "Ti-Toine" Rivard, Duplessis' solicitor-general and minister of Transportion and Communications (Fig. 75.1).[8] It was the height of the Cold War and numerous international conflicts (war in Algeria and the Congo, an abortive American invasion of Cuba, and a confrontation between the two Germanys), though these barely caught Hudon's attention, except for a few caricatures he did on the Kennedy-Khruschev summit in Vienna at the beginning of June. His attention was more on the home front in Quebec.

Separatism does not caricature an individual, but rather an idea. The artist poses a question about one of the possible consequences of independence: Would a young Quebec be isolated within a vaster and equally isolated entity? To represent this idea, the artist has put Quebec in a playpen, which is in turn in a larger playpen. The drawing has a certain, perhaps intentional, ambiguity. Does it represent Quebec in Canada, and/or the French-Canadian community isolated in an Anglo-Saxon sea?

Another caricature by Hudon (Fig. 75.2) on the same subject – and the only one published alongside the series of articles on independence – anticipates *Separatism*. If the idea of isolation is less clear in this earlier one, its subtitle, "The Box of Myths," reveals more about the artist's thinking. Two years later, Hudon would go farther by suggesting that the "indépendantistes" did not seem to be getting anywhere (Fig. 75.3). His point of view can be compared with that of André Laurendeau, his editor-in-chief at *Le Devoir*, who, while he understood that the demand for independence stemmed from injustices suffered, was worried about the letdown that the separatists were setting themselves up for.[9]

L.D.

75.1 N. Hudon
Danny Boy Goes for a Dime?..., ca. 15 May 1961
Pen and ink
NA C-127582

75.2 N. Hudon
Separatism — The Box of Myths, 1961
Reproduced from *Le Devoir*, 9 May 1961, p. 4
Photoreproduction courtesy of the Archives nationales du Québec

75.3 N. Hudon
A True Centrifugal Force, ca. 24 January 1963
Pen and ink
NA C-127591

1. "Why the Cruelest Cartoonist in Canada Misses the Good, Old Days of Duplessis," *Maclean's Magazine* 7 (22 February 1964): 47.

2. Information from research conducted by Guylaine Desrosiers, NA summer student in 1985.

3. *Le Devoir* (Montreal), 4 July 1961, p. 4.

4. Michel Roy, "Trois mouvements, un seul but: l'indépendance du Québec," *Le Devoir*, 13 May 1961, p. 1. The Alliance Laurentienne (right wing) was founded in 1957, the Rassemblement pour l'indépendance nationale (R.I.N., centre-left) and Action socialiste pour l'indépendance du Québec (left wing), in 1960. From the beginning of the debate on independence, many rejected the term "separatism," because "one can only separate what is united": Raymond Barbeau, as quoted by Michel Roy in "Trois mouvements." They preferred the term "souverainisme" (sovereignty) or, better yet, "indépendantisme" (independence). But for most people, who have no interest in semantic quarrels, the words "separatism" and "separatist" are clearer.

5. *La Presse* (Montreal), 21 January 1961, p. 8, and 1 February 1961, p. 18 (voting form); 18 March 1961, p. 5 (results). The primary aim of the survey was to evaluate the attitude of French-Canadians towards English-Canadians.

6. Fourteen articles, written for the most part by Jean-Marc Léger, André Laurendeau and Michel Roy, appeared from 5 to 20 May 1961. The voting form was published on the front page of the 20 May edition.

7. *Le Devoir*, 10 June 1961, p. 9.

8. Daniel Johnson was still just a member of Parliament for Bagot; he would be elected leader of the Union Nationale on the following 23 September. This caricature was published in *Le Devoir*, 15 May 1961, p. 4.

9. André Laurendeau, "Blocs-Notes," *Le Devoir*, 20 February 1961, p. 4.

MODERNIZED ROMAN SCULPTURE
CLOSURE
PIPELINE ISSUE
THE LAOCOÖN GROUP
CHAMBERS/56

ROBERT WILLIAM (BOB) CHAMBERS (1905-)

76. *Pipeline Issue — The Laocoön Group*, ca. 23 May 1956

Brushpoint and black ink with black crayon on paper

36.7 x 28.9 cm

Inscribed in black crayon, recto, u.c.: *MODERNIZED ROMAN SCULPTURE*; l.c.: *3 cols. Wed. ChronHer*; l.r.: *R425*; in brushpoint and black ink, recto, l.c.: *CLOSURE*; c.: *PIPELINE ISSUE*; l.l.: *THE LAOCOÖN GROUP*; l.r.: *CHAMBERS / 56*

Donated in 1968

Acquisition no.: 1982-166-22

Negative no.: C-102317

By the time he retired in 1976, Bob Chambers had become a veritable Halifax institution. Since 1933, his cartoons had adorned the editorial page of *The Chronicle*, then its rival, *The Herald*, and finally, after their merger in 1949, *The Chronicle-Herald*. Appreciated by his peers as much as by his readers, he has received numerous honours.

The present editorial cartoon (Cat. no. 76) comments upon the famous TransCanada Pipeline debates that rocked the federal government in the spring of 1956 and contributed in part to the defeat of the Liberal Party the following year, after twenty-two years in power.[1] The pipeline, destined to carry Alberta natural gas to the vast markets of southern Ontario and Quebec, was the last mega-project of Liberal Trade and Commerce minister Clarence Decatur Howe (1886-1960). He decided that the pipeline would be constructed entirely within Canada, a more expensive route than one going partly through the United States. With this aim in mind, he had facilitated the merger of two companies into a single one, the TransCanada Pipe Lines Limited, made up of Canadian and American businessmen, to whom he promised a substantial government loan by 7 June 1956, so that work could begin at the beginning of July.

The Conservative and CCF oppositions sharply criticized the presence of American interests, which were temporarily necessary in order to enable the company to purchase steel in the United States. The opposition revealed, moreover, the existence of another project, entirely Canadian, which Howe had not taken into account. The Opposition was also against Howe granting a loan to a private company, even though the project stipulated that the stretch north of the Great Lakes would be built by a Crown corporation, which would then lease it to TransCanada Pipe Lines Ltd. When the bill was finally submitted to Parliament on 8 May, the opposition acted quickly to block it, and the rest of the week was spent debating procedures.

Howe made a fresh attempt on 14 May with a slightly altered project. He got around obstruction by immediately enforcing closure, a rule that for all practical purposes ended rational debate on the project. The bill passed its first reading in the early hours of 16 May. The debate then concentrated on parliamentary rights, the government denouncing the systematic obstructionism, and the Opposition denouncing the dictatorial behaviour of the Liberal majority. The quarrels over procedural technicalities would follow one after another until Friday, 1 June, nicknamed "Black Friday" because for many it marked the lowest level ever reached by the Canadian parliamentary system. The rule of closure was invoked at all stages of the bill, which received royal assent just in time on 7 June.

It was not until 9 May that the Halifax *Chronicle-Herald* published, on the front page, a news story on the debate.[2] On 11 May, Chambers published his first commentary on the parliamentary wrangles that, like a pipeline valve, were blocking free discussion of the project (Fig. 76.1). His second caricature, published the day after closure was enforced, showed C.D. Howe having succeeded in closing the valve, interrupting the delivery of gas to the furnace of the leader of the opposition, "Chief Cook" George Drew (Fig. 76.2).

A week later, the day after the bill was approved in second reading, the two protagonists found themselves completely entangled in the procedural knots represented by pipes (Cat. no. 76). C.D. Howe, on the left, raises higher and higher his threat of closure, while Drew tries to get away, under the contrite but helpless eye of Parliament, symbolized by the Peace Tower. The position of the hands of the clock emphasizes this feeling, while perhaps evoking the long nights spent in the House of Commons.

Perhaps it was the association of "entanglement-serpents-pipes" that gave Chambers the idea of using as a model the Laocoön (Fig. 76.3), a Greek sculpture from the Hellenistic period (and not Roman, as Chambers believed). It was discovered in Rome in 1506, and "restored" shortly after to a state still unchanged in 1956.[3] Laocoön, a priest of Poseidon, had warned the Trojans in vain about the huge wooden horse offered by the Greeks and consecrated to Athena; in revenge, the goddess sent two serpents to slay him and his sons.[4]

A comparison of the caricature and the sculptured group shows that Chambers followed his model closely: his three figures, including Parliament, to which he gave arms and legs, faithfully assume the positions of the three Trojan figures. On the other hand, the position of the Parliament-Laocoön's head is different, because the sentiment expressed is also different: the priest expresses agony, the anthropoid Parliament, exasperation. As well, Howe's head is seen from the front, while the young son's face is turned towards that of his father.

Chambers was not the only cartoonist to think of using the Laocoön to comment upon the initial debates on the pipeline project. On 7 May 1956, just before the bill was to be tabled, John Collins published an interpretation of the celebrated sculpture in the Montreal *Gazette* (Fig. 76.4).[5] The pugnacious Howe-Laocoön (his boxer shorts replacing the figleaf of the original) is trying to disentangle himself from the pipeline-serpent's coils, which are also wrapped around Ontario Premier Leslie M. Frost (1895-1973), and Uno Who, the Mister Everyman of Collins' cartoons.

The presence of Frost in Collins' caricature is hard to explain, because he was not an important participant in the debate of May-June 1956, but Howe had his support because, although he was a Conservative, Frost wanted to bestow the benefits of Alberta gas on his province. As in the Chambers cartoon, the figure on the right is trying to escape, which corresponds to the pose of the scultpured model; however, whereas Laocoön's elder son shares the fate of his father and his brother, Chambers' Drew and Collins' Uno Who do not wish to suffer Howe's fate – much to the contrary! The question of whether Chambers was aware of his colleague's caricature remains unanswered, as the two caricaturists could quite easily have associated the same ideas in choosing their themes.[6]

Chambers devoted two other editorial cartoons to the pipeline debate.[7] On 6 June, commenting on the fact that the project had passed the committee stage after two weeks of futile procedural quarrels, he entitled his drawing *Hit and Run*. The government automobile is pictured speeding toward the pipeline construction site, upsetting the opposition's apple cart along the way.[8] On 28 June, this same opposition, symbolized by a boxer spinning into space, continues the "pipeline fight," while the caretaker cleans the premises after the departure of the MPs (and the final passage of the bill).[9]

L.D.

76.1 R.W. Chambers
Valve Trouble, ca. 11 May 1956
Black crayon
NA C-102349

76.2 R.W. Chambers
Somebody turned off the gas!, ca. 16 May 1956
Black crayon
NA C-102316

76.3
The Laocoön, ca. 50 B.C. (before latest restoration)
Vatican Museums

76.4 J. Collins
Uno Who's National Gallery, ca. 7 May 1956
Photoreproduction
Reproduced from *Cartoons 1955-1959 by John Collins* (Montreal: *The Gazette*, [1959]).

1. For a detailed account of the debate, see William Kilbourn, *Pipeline: TransCanada and the Great Debate, a History of Business and Politics* (Toronto: Clarke, Irwin, 1970). Cat. no. 76 and Figs. 76.1 and 76. 2 were donated to the NA by the Liberal Party of Canada.

2. "Rough Reception Is Given Government's Pipeline Loan Plan," *The Chronicle-Herald* (Halifax), 9 May 1956, p. 1.

3. The *Laocoön* was again restored in 1957-1960, after in-depth study; Laocoön's right forearm (bent towards his head) had been found in 1905. Filippo Magi, *Il Ripristino del Laocoonte*, Rome: Pontificia accademia romana di archeologia, *Memorie*, vol. 9 (1960).

4. Virgil, who wrote after the date given for the Laocoön, popularized this legend: *Aeneid*, II, 40-56 and 199-233. He based his account on Greek post-Homerian authors. Pierre Grimal, *Dictionnaire de la mythologie grecque et romaine* (Paris: Presses universitaires de France, 1976), 250-251.

5. While *The Chronicle-Herald* did not speak of the pipeline before 9 May, *The Gazette* (Montreal) correspondent, Arthur Blakely, had been holding his readers spellbound since 2 May, almost a week before the tabling of the bill before the House.

6. Collins made use of another theme taken up at a later date by Chambers, that of a cooking pot on a gas stove, but in a different spirit: Collins shows C.D. Howe attempting to cover the pot of "pipeline stew," but ends by falling into the boiling water himself (see *Cooking with Gas*, *The Gazette*, 9 May 1956, p. 8, compare with Fig 76.2).

7. Although the NA has a large collection of original cartoon drawings by Chambers, these two works are not among them.

8. *Hit and Run*, *The Chronicle-Herald*, 6 June 1956, p. 4.

9. *Still in There Slugging*, *The Chronicle-Herald*, 28 June 1956, p. 4.

THEY LOVE ME...
THEY LOVE ME...
THEY LOVE ME...
THEY LOVE ME...
THEY LOVE ME...
AISLIN 78
MTL. GAZETTE

AISLIN (TERRY MOSHER) (1942-)

77. *They love me... they love me...*, ca. 19 September 1978

Pen and black ink on paper

36.0 x 28.2 cm

Inscribed in pen and black ink, recto, u.r.: *THEY LOVE ME...* [repeated five times]; l.r.: *AISLIN 78 / MTL. GAZETTE*; b.: *33 EMS – TUESDAY*

Purchased in 1978

Acquisition no.: 1978-47-3

Negative no.: C-128816

While the cartoonist comments on news from the point of view of the ordinary man, the caricaturist attempts to bring a public figure down to the level of the man on the street. This at least is the way Aislin defines his work, not to say his mission;[1] and if you take him to task for being mean from time to time, he replies that his job is to diagnose the illness, not to suggest treatment.[2] His favourite patients are public figures, politicians and sports heroes, not necessarily because the public knows them better, but because they have chosen the pretention of public life, which opens them to criticism. For Aislin, they are basically like you and me: They all have dandruff![3]

Moreover, when a caricaturist takes a shot at a particular figure, he is aiming at the public image, not the private person. Jean Drapeau was mayor of Montreal for more than twenty-five years (1954-1957, 1960-1986). It is therefore understandable that he became a favourite subject of Aislin's, whose wit was particularly busy during the entire "Olympic period," from the time the Games were announced in 1970 to the tabling of the Malouf report in 1979, and even afterwards. After the Metro subway and Expo 67, the 1976 Olympic Games marked the height of Drapeau's megaprojects, but also the height of criticism of his enterprises. At the request of the Quebec government, a commission headed by Judge Albert Malouf was given a mandate to investigate the excessive cost of the Games, which burgeoned from a projected $310 million to the real figure of over a billion dollars.

Our caricature was published in the Montreal *Gazette* on Tuesday 19 September 1978, the day on which Drapeau was questioned for the first time by the Malouf Commission. The drawing was probably done some days earlier, since it was on display in a Montreal gallery at the beginning of September.[4] Aislin, or his editor-in-chief, must have waited for the most opportune moment to publish it.

The public hearings of the Malouf Commission began on 8 September, meeting three days per week. When Drapeau appeared on 19 September, the investigators – and the general public, by way of the newspapers – had already learned a number of troublesome facts regarding the incompetence of a particular company that held a service contract; on the relationship between the mayor and the architect Roger Taillibert; and also on the "underhandedness" of Drapeau in regard to the true cost of the Games. But the ineffable mayor stated that he was a victim of the federal government, which had been slow in granting approval for the self-financing methods that he had advocated. And the facilities were so expensive because the people of Montreal had a right to the best, since in the final analysis it was they who would pay the bill![5]

During the course of the hearing, Drapeau appeared to be very sure of himself and of the affection of the people of Montreal ("They love me... they love me...") – in short, exactly the image that Aislin presented to his readers that morning. And the mayor got the best proof of this affection on the following 12 November, when he was re-elected with a strong majority (sixty per cent); the members of his party, the Parti civique, obtained fifty-two of the fifty-four aldermanic seats.[6] The opposition was virtually eliminated – this in spite of the disclosures made before the Malouf Commission for the past two and a half months.

Aislin published two other caricatures of Drapeau during the election campaign.[7] However, neither of them sums up the man as much as *They love me...*, which is a generalized representation and could have been used to portray any number of public figures, from Louis XIV to... to whomever you like. For Aislin, it is exactly this ability to generalize that makes the difference between a true caricature and a humorous drawing, which is more closely tied to its time and place.[8]

In terms of technique, one notices the fine penwork, particularly in the way the artist renders shadows and textures. Meticulous in his drawing, Aislin is the same in his research: The Montreal coat of arms, "Concordia Salus," is faithfully depicted, and the mayor's chair is in the same style as the furniture in his office at City Hall.[9] As for the cleats and the checkered socks, they allude, of course, to the subject's Olympic spirit.

The proportions of the mayor's head reflect Aislin's opinion. For him, it is necessary to give the head more emphasis than the rest of the body; it is the most "personal," and therefore the most easily identifiable, element of an individual.[10] He sees in this the influence of television, which has taught us to see public personages close up.[11] But even if portrayed smaller, the entire body, including the clothes and the bearing, may also be used by the caricaturist to express his views. The caricature of Claude Ryan (Fig. no. 77.1), produced at the time when the latter resigned his position as editor-in-chief of the Montreal daily *Le Devoir* to stand as a candidate for the leadership of the Quebec Liberal Party, is an excellent example of just this.[12]

L.D.

77.1 Aislin

How Could I Refuse My People in their Time of Need?, ca. January 1978

Pen and ink

NA C-108976

---

1. Leon Harris, "Cartoonist Aislin goes for 'the jugular'," *The Gazette* (Montreal), 8 April 1972, p. 7. Aislin studied fine arts in Toronto and Quebec City; he then worked for the *Montreal Star* and, since 1972 (alternating with John Collins until 1982) for *The Gazette*, all the while contributing to many other publications. Numerous collections of his caricatures have already been published. Twice the recipient of the National Newspaper Award (1977 and 1978), he also carried out research, and collaborated with Peter Desbarats on the book *The Hecklers* (Toronto: McClelland and Stewart, 1979). His research files are now at the NA.

2. Hubert de Santana, "A Tiger Stalking Sacred Cows," *Maclean's*, 27 August 1979, p. 9.

3. This explains the little dots scattered around Drapeau's head, as well as around those of Aislin's other victims. Aislin calls dandruff the "great equalizer." De Santana, 10.

4. The exhibition was held at the Darwin Restaurant, Montreal, in September 1978. It was a display of limited edition reproductions of forty caricatures chosen by Aislin from among his best from the previous two years; *Jean Drapeau As Man of the Year* was no. 26 in the exhibition.

5. Hubert Bauch and Don Stevenson, "Why Did Olympic Costs Soar? Ottawa Blew it, Drapeau Says," *The Gazette*, 20 September 1978, p. 1.

6. René Laurent, "MAG, MCM virtually shut out on council, Drapeau Breezes Back," *The Gazette*, 13 November 1978, p. 1.

7. Both cartoons appeared in *The Gazette*, untitled. One showed Drapeau with MAG candidate Serge Joyal as a bodybuilder, 14 October 1978, p. 8; the other, Drapeau with an unplugged vacuum cleaner, 7 November 1978, p. 8.

8. A. Bardo, "Scorpio Rising," *Montreal Star*, 11 April 1970, p. 36.

9. See a photograph of Drapeau (and his chair) in Guy Roy, *La véritable histoire de Jean Drapeau* (Montreal: Éditions Québécor, 1982), 44. The emblem of Montreal, in addition to the beaver and the maple leaves, is composed of the symbol of the four founding peoples of the city: the French fleur de lys, the English rose, the Scottish thistle and the Irish shamrock.

10. As for the bump on the mayor's head, one may find it in all of the caricatures Aislin has done of Drapeau; we can only speculate on its significance.

11. De Santana, 10.

12. This caricature was prepared for the television broadcast *The Editors* on CTV, either for the 7 January 1978 broadcast, on which Aislin had been invited to appear (a retrospective on political caricature during 1977) or, more likely, the 21 January broadcast to which Ryan himself was invited. In fact, it was only on 9 January that Ryan announced his resignation, and the caricature is dated 1978. Claude Ryan is definitely not a member of the clergy, as his cassock would lead one to believe, but Aislin makes use of it to emphasize a certain aspect of his personality. The caricaturist has dressed him in the same way in another caricature concerning the same event. *The Gazette*, 12 January 1978, p. 8.

ANDY WARHOL (1928-1987)

78. *Wayne Gretzky, No. 99*, 1983

Serigraph on paper

101.6 x 81.2 cm

Inscribed in pencil, recto, l.l.: *95 / 100 Andy Warhol*; l.r., in Gretzky's hand: *Wayne Gretzky / 99*

Donated in 1987

Accession no.: 1988-8-1

Negative no.: C-131833

During the opening of the 1978 exhibition "Athletes by Andy Warhol," a series depicting ten of the world's top professional athletes, Warhol made one of his sweeping statements: "Athletes are the true superstars of today, much more exciting and intelligent than movie stars."[1]

Ironically, Warhol had achieved his own artistic superstardom with the depiction of stars such as Marilyn Monroe, Elizabeth Taylor and Elvis Presley, along with Campbell Soup cans and Brillo cartons. His techniques, which included the photo-silkscreen process and the use of highly coloured, overblown, repeated images, were borrowed from contemporary commercial art. Warhol turned to portraiture in the early 1970s, realizing that his painting method had business potential.

> Rich collectors would pay many times more for Warhol portraits of their wives than for conventional ones, even though the portrait would often be no more than a blow-up photograph screenprinted by a member of [Warhol's] Factory.[2]

He produced portraits of friends, prominent public figures, art dealers and collectors, the rich and the famous. The portrait *Wayne Gretzky, No. 99* (Cat. no. 78) belongs to this final period of Warhol's career.[3]

The year after Warhol's 1978 "Athletes" series of sports stars was produced, Wayne Gretzky burst onto the sports scene and into the hearts of sports fans. *Wayne Gretzky, No. 99*, produced in 1983, immortalizes the hockey superstar at the pinnacle of his career, and like the "Athletes" series, this print represented investment potential to both the artist and the purchasers. "Athletes" was conceived as a business venture by art collector, investment banker, and sports enthusiast Richard Weisman, who, in his own words, contrived for "the world of art and the world of sport – the two most popular leisure time activities... – [to] have a real meeting of the minds at the highest level."[4] The idea for *Wayne Gretzky, No. 99* was similarly conceived by a Vancouver art dealer, Frans Wynans, who engaged a brokerage firm to sell the proposal of a limited-edition series to several Canadian investors.[5] Upon completion, the portrait was unveiled at a star-studded gala at New York's Metropolitan Club, where members of the jet set and prospective buyers were invited to party and, presumably, to purchase.[6]

Warhol's technique was to make multiple images of his models, varying the poses or the colouring of the portraits or both. These images could be displayed together, as in his first commissioned portrait, *Portrait of Ethel Scull*, 1963, where thirty-five images of the sitter were made into a kaleidoscopic portrait. Or, as in the case of the Gretzky portrait, the same image was made into an edition of three hundred on paper, in addition to six "painted" images, from a slightly different photograph, which were silkscreened onto canvas using acrylic paint.[7] The photo-silkscreen process Warhol used for his portraits placed no size limitations on his images. He could make the format of his multiple images the size of the traditional painted portrait, with over-life-size faces.

Warhol's technique differs from the reproductive printmaking tradition that flourished between the sixteenth and early nineteenth centuries. Large printmaking studios were in the lucrative business of producing prints after painted portraits of famous men and women. However, these prints served to create the iconography of royalty, aristocracy and prominent men and women. In the case of a Warhol image, the iconography of a member of the jet set or of a sports hero such as Gretzky was already in existence, created by the media. Therefore Warhol's images are not so much portraits of the individuals, but represent instead the constellation of famous artist/society celebrity.

> [A portrait by Warhol] is not a matter of flattery in the usual sense, but of a flattering inclusion in a timeless, privileged realm of art – art here practically identical with social prominence, which in turn is practically identical with money and celebrity (usually both).[8]

The production method used for *Wayne Gretzky, No. 99* was similar to all of Warhol's portraits. The hockey player, accompanied by his business manager Michael Barnett and his friend Charles Henry, visited Warhol in his studio in New York during the summer of 1983. Gretzky posed for Warhol's Polaroid camera wearing his well-known Edmonton Oilers 99 shirt. After some one-hundred snap-shots were taken, Warhol and Gretzky proceeded to select the best image. The choice, not surprisingly, showed Gretzky holding a hockey stick. Next Warhol took a whole new series of photos, all with the hockey stick. A second image was selected from this session. This was followed by a final photo session when Gretzky struck poses close to the just-selected photograph. The choice of the final image was once again a joint decision by model and artist.[9] Because Warhol wanted patrons to be pleased with their commissioned "vanity portraits," he always involved them in the selection of both the final image and the colours to be used for the portrait.[10]

The first step in turning the selected Polaroid image into a print was to rephotograph it in 35mm format.[11] It was then sent out to be enlarged and made into half-tone positives on acetate sheets of the same size as the final print. The most suitable half-tone was then made into a silkscreen. Warhol used the acetate sheet to work out the composition, using the Oilers' colours, blue for the background with a rectangle of reddish-orange cut-out paper. The white rectangle, which is used to focus on Gretzky's face, gives the portrait a hockey card look. Warhol also drew on the acetate to reinforce the features of the model, which had been lost through the high-contrast printing and the enlargement of the Polaroid snap-shot. These modifications were then rephotographed to make other screens. The printing sequence likely began with the blue background, followed by the addition of the lower-left red rectangle, establishing the Oilers' colours. The photograph would have been printed next, followed by the drawn and painted overlay printed in "rainbow rolls."[12]

Warhol's portrait output includes only two other Canadians. The first was Karen Kain, prima ballerina of the National Ballet of Canada, whom Warhol portrayed in 1980. Part of her two hundred silkscreened portrait edition was used to raise money for the National Ballet.[13] The other Canadian was prominent businessman Conrad Black, of whom three screenprint acrylic portraits on canvas were made in 1982.[14]

As a portrait of one of hockey's most sensational players, and one of Canada's best-known celebrities, *Wayne Gretzky, No. 99* has an important place in the National Archives national portrait collection. This portrait, showing Gretzky in his Edmonton Oilers uniform, has an additional significance because in 1988 he was traded to the Los Angeles Kings hockey club, a business move that outraged many Canadians. As one journalist wrote at the time of the trade: "Edmonton [Oilers] owner Peter Pocklington... had treated this symbol [Gretzky] as grist for the capitalist mill."[15] It is a reminder to Canadians that the business under-pinnings of the game do not take national pride into account. In a similar way, the marketing of Warhol's portrait of Gretzky demonstrates that art could be as much about investment as about art appreciation. Gretzky's image alone was considered a good investment, not just for selling Nike running shoes in advertisements, but as a product in itself.

E.M.-M.

---

1. Roy Proctor, "Warhol Mobbed at "Athletes' Show," *Richmond News Leader* (Richmond, Virginia), 24 January 1978. The sports figures represented were: Muhammad Ali, Rod Gilbert, Chris Evert, Pelé, Tom Seaver, Willie Shoemaker, Kareem Abdul-Jabbar, Dorothy Hamill, Jack Nicklaus and O.J. Simpson. The exhibition "Athletes by Andy Warhol" was conceived and produced by Richard L. Weisman and was held at the Virginia Museum (Richmond, Virginia), 23 January to 26 February 1978.

2. Alastair Mackintosh, "Andy Warhol," in Colin Naylor, ed., *Contemporary Artists*, 3rd ed. (Chicago and London: St. James Press, 1989), 1013.

3. This edition of one hundred (NA has copy no. 95) was printed by Rupert Jasen Smith (New York) and published by Frans Wynans (Vancouver). It was printed on Lenox Museum Board. There are fifty artist's proofs and six printer's proofs. Frayda Feldman and Jorg Schellmann, *Andy Warhol Prints* (New York: Ronald Feldman Fine-Arts, 1985), 96.

4. "Museum to Exhibit 'Athletes' by Warhol," *Richmond News Leader* (Richmond, Virginia), 31 December 1977.

5. Arthur Perry, "The great Gretzky deal," *Canadian Art* 1 (Fall 1984): 103.

6. Perry, 103.

7. The painting is reproduced in Perry, 103.

8. Peter Schjedahl, "Warhol & Class Content," *Art in America* 68 (May 1980): 118.

9. Information provided to the author in conversation with Charles Henry, 28 October 1989.

10. Marco Livingstone, "Do It Yourself: Notes on Warhol's Techniques," in Kynaston McShine, ed., *Andy Warhol: A Retrospective* (New York: The Museum of Modern Art, 1989), 75.

11. This discussion of Warhol's printmaking technique is based on Livingstone, "Do It Yourself," and on Hans Gerd Tuchel, "Andy Warhol as Graphic Artist," in Hermann Wünsche, *Andy Warhol: Das Graphische Werk 1962-1980* (Cologne: Bonner Universität Buchdruckerei, 1980).

12. "A process in which different colored inks appear on the paper in a rainbow-like progression." Livingstone, 75.

13. "Kain dances into Warhol's pop art world," *Toronto Star*, 20 June 1980.

14. Information provided to the author in conversation with Frans Wynans, January 1988.

15. Brian Fawcett as quoted in Kenneth Whyte, "Nobody's Fifteen Feet Tall," *Saturday Night* (January-February 1990), 29.

A PLACE IN HISTORY

PLATES

Peter Rindisbacher. 1824

Inside of an Indian Tent

Deputation of Indians from the Missisipi Tribes
to the Governor General of Brittish North America - Sir George Prevost, Bar.t Lieut. General &c. in 1814.

20.

29.

31.

37.

A Fancy Ball at the Victoria Rink

39.

44.

48.

56.

61.

CANADA STEAMSHIPS Co

ROCHESTER
NIAGARA
MONTREAL
QUEBEC CITY
SAGUEANY
MURRAY BAY

SEE QUEBEC
by LUXURIOUS
STEAMSHIPS

72.

NOMINAL INDEX

E

F

G

H

I

J

K

L

M

T

V

W

Y

GEOGRAPHICAL INDEX OF ILLUSTRATIONS